TAIWAN'S DEVELOPMENT

Recent Titles in
Contributions in Economics and Economic History

TAIWAN'S DEVELOPMENT

Implications for Contending
Political Economy Paradigms

Cal Clark

Contributions in Economics
and Economic History, Number 100

GREENWOOD PRESS
New York • Westport, Connecticut • London

TO JANET
For all her love and support

Library of Congress Cataloging-in-Publication Data

Clark, Cal.
  Taiwan's development : implications for contending political
economy paradigms / Cal Clark.
    p.   cm.—(Contributions in economics and economic history,
ISSN 0084–9235 ; no. 100)
  Includes bibliographies and index.
  ISBN 0–313–25448–6 (lib. bdg. : alk. paper)
    1. Taiwan—Economic policy—1945–   2. Taiwan—Economic
conditions—1945–   3. Taiwan—Politics and government—1945–
I. Title.   II. Series.
HC430.5.C67   1989
338.95124'9—dc20   89–7494

British Library Cataloguing in Publication Data is available.

Library of Congress Catalog Card Number: 89–7494
ISBN: 0–313–25448–6
ISSN: 0084–9235

First published in 1989

Greenwood Press, Inc.
88 Post Road West, Westport, Connecticut   06881

Printed in the United States of America

The paper used in this book complies with the
Permanent Paper Standard issued by the National
Information Standards Organization (Z39.48–1984).

10 9 8 7 6 5 4 3 2 1

Copyright Acknowledgment

The author gratefully acknowledges permission to quote from the following:

Source: Teng-hui Lee: *Intersectional Capital Flows in the Economic Development of Taiwan, 1895–1960*. Copyright © 1971 by Cornell University. Used by permission of the publisher, Cornell University Press.

From William P. Avery and David Rapkin, eds. *Markets, Politics, and Change in the Global Political Economy*. © 1989 Lynne Rienner publishers. Reprinted by permission of the Publisher.

Extracts from: Samuel P. S. Ho, *Economic Development in Taiwan, 1860–1970*. Copyright © 1978. Reprinted by permission of Yale University Press.

Extracts from: Shirley W. Y. Kuo, Gustav Ranis, and John C. H. Fei, *The Taiwan Success Story*. © 1981 Westview Press. Reprinted by permission of Shirley W. Y. Kuo.

Extracts from: Martin L. Lasater, *The Taiwan Issue in Sino-American Strategic Relations*. © 1984 Westview Press. Reprinted by permission of the publisher.

From: *International Studies Quarterly* 31:3 (September 1987) pp. 327–356. Reprinted by permission of International Studies Association.

From: *Journal of Asian and African Studies* 12:1–2 (January–April 1987) pp. 1–16. Reprinted by permission of the publisher.

Contents

Illustrations

Acronyms

BAIR	Bureaucratic authoritarian industrializing regime
CCP	Chinese Communist Party
CSC	Central Standing Committee (of Kuomintang)
DPP	Democratic Progressive Party
ECLA	Economic Commission for Latin America (of United Nations)
EPZ	Export processing zone
F-5E	Fighter plane sold to Taiwan by United States
FX	Advanced fighter that United States refused to sell to Taiwan
GDCF	Gross domestic capital formation
GDP	Gross domestic product
GNP	Gross national product
JCRR	Joint Commission on Rural Reconstruction (between United States and R.O.C.)
KMT	Kuomintang Party
MNC	Multinational corporation
MT	Million tons
NDP	Net domestic product
NICs	Newly industrializing countries
NT$	New Taiwan dollar
OPEC	Organization of Petroleum Exporting Countries
P.R.C.	People's Republic of China

REER   Real effective exchange rate
R.O.C.   Republic of China on Taiwan
TIM   Taiwan Independence Movement
TRA   Taiwan Relations Act
U.N.   United Nations
U.S.   United States of America
USSR   Union of Soviet Socialist Republics

Preface

The central theme of this book is that the major theoretical frameworks for analyzing international political economy are too simplistic in that their various contending visions either omit key factors or overly generalize from relations that are found in limited situations. This argument is advanced by recourse to a detailed case study of the Republic of China on Taiwan, whose history of extremely rapid growth over the past four decades suggests that development and dependency in the contemporary world are more complex and indeterminate than most scholars and policymakers are willing to admit. What stands out in Taiwan's economic success story is a development strategy based on economic flexibility and periodic regime change that has made this flexibility possible.

Given this thesis, it is quite fitting that my own interest in Taiwan arose from relatively random events. A former student arranged a visiting professorship for me; during my visit I became increasingly intrigued in applying my general theoretical interest in political economy to Taiwan's developmental pattern. My previous research had focused on the political economy of Eastern Europe, which perhaps was ironically appropriate in view of the Leninist organization of Taiwan's ruling Kuomintang party. A first, superficial comparative impression was the tremendous mass consumption on Taiwan compared with that of Eastern Europe, whose nations average approximately the same gross national product per capita. Longer reflection, though, brought economic flexibility and ongoing political evolution to the fore as the hallmarks of the "Taiwan miracle." These characteristics, moreover, appear important to understanding the growing economic problems of America and other advanced industrial economies where past success has created economic and political barriers for future adaptation. Taiwan's story, I hope, will be of more general interest than might normally be warranted for a small, out-of-the-way island.

I am extremely grateful for a grant from the Pacific Cultural Foundation in the Republic of China, which helped to support the research underlying this book. The University of Wyoming also provided a most welcome sabbatical that allowed me to complete the manuscript. My work, of course, has been influenced by a multitude of other scholars. Three in particular have read earlier drafts of significant portions of this volume; their comments have had considerable influence on the final analysis, although, alas, I cannot in any conscience ask that they share the blame for the book's shortcomings. Thus I extend especial thanks to Winberg Chai of the University of Wyoming, Steve Chan of the University of Colorado, and Patrick McGowan of Arizona State University. I am also grateful to a number of scholars and political officials in Taiwan who have shared their insights and friendship. Because all of them would find much to quarrel with in my interpretations (and among themselves as well), I hope that they are not insulted by my leaving them anonymous. I am also extremely grateful for the editorial assistance and patience of Cynthia Harris of Greenwood Press. In addition, Linda Marston did an excellent job of preparing the map used in chapter 3.

A few parts of the book are taken fairly directly from previous publications. The section on Taiwan's response to the oil crisis of the mid–1970s in chapter 6 comes from "External Shocks and Instability in Taiwan: The Dog That Didn't Bark," in William Avery and David Rapkin, eds., *Markets, Politics, and Change in the Global Political Economy* (Boulder, Colo.: Lynne Rienner, 1989), pp. 173–197; the first section in the conclusion comes with some revision from "Economic Development in Taiwan: A Model of a Political Economy," *Journal of Asian and African Studies* 12:1–2 (January–April 1987), pp. 1–16; and the last two sections of the conclusion are considerably revised and expanded forms of the arguments in "The Taiwan Exception: Implications for Contending Political Paradigms," *International Studies Quarterly* 31:3 (September 1987), pp. 327–356. I am grateful for the various publishers' permission to reprint these materials.

I am also grateful for permission by the publishers and by Shirley W. Y. Kuo to reprint materials from the following scholarly books: Samuel P. S. Ho, *Economic Development in Taiwan, 1860–1970* (New Haven, Conn.: Yale University Press, 1978); Shirley W. Y. Kuo, Gustav Ranis, and John C. H. Fei, *The Taiwan Success Story: Rapid Growth with Improved Distribution in the Republic of China, 1952–1979* (Boulder, Colo.: Westview Press, 1981); Martin L. Lasater, *The Taiwan Issue in Sino-American Strategic Relations* (Boulder, Colo.: Westview Press, 1984); and Teng-hui Lee, *Intersectoral Capital Flows in the Economic Development of Taiwan, 1895–1960* (Ithaca, N.Y.: Cornell University Press, 1971).

Finally, my wife, Janet, and daughters, Emily, Ellen, and Evelyn, deserve my most heartfelt thanks, both for their support during the long process of research and writing and for providing a refuge from the strains of professional responsibilities.

TAIWAN'S DEVELOPMENT

CHAPTER 1

The Puzzle of Rapid Growth in Taiwan

Economic development is one of the rare socioeconomic phenomena that is almost universally perceived as desirable and good. Development, by definition, brings new resources into a society that allow for a higher standard of living[1]; empirical studies demonstrate that, in the long run at least, development is associated with increased equality.[2] Greater resources also allow a country to augment its power capabilities and military strength, thus giving it a more favored position in international relations.[3] Moreover, economically developed nations are more likely to have democratic polities than poorer ones.[4] Although there has been some concern with the socioeconomic dislocations and degradation of the physical environment that accompany rapid industrialization,[5] these are generally viewed as inevitable and acceptable costs of progress. Because development appears to be such a highly valued "commodity," arguments about what promotes or retards development have advanced far beyond the cottage industry stage both in academic circles and among political officials whose decisions affect the developmental possibilities for their own and other nations.

The first general approach to analyzing development was based on what appeared to be the reasonable premise that a theory of development should seek to abstract the key elements in the experience of the Western nations that had led the industrial revolution. Thus the "developmentalist" perspective emphasized the economic system, change in social values, and political institutions that marked Western Europe and North America in the late nineteenth and twentieth centuries. There were certainly many ongoing debates within this tradition, such as whether governments should promote laissez-faire economics or try to smooth out business cycles with Keynesian macro management techniques. Still, there was a broad consensus that economic development depended on a combination of capitalism, a culture that emphasized individualism and entrepreneurship, and democracy. Furthermore, there was the assumption that the key to development lay within a society, since development would flow from the requisite economic, political, and social transformations. The prescription for less developed countries, therefore, was to emulate these political and economic institutions and sociocultural values.

This theory of development has come under increasing challenge over the past three decades from scholars and politicians concerned with the Third World, where hopes for development have been largely frustrated. Many countries, especially in Africa and South Asia, have fallen further and further behind the Western industrial states; impressive spurts of industrial growth that have occurred, such as in Brazil in the 1960s, only benefited small sectors of the population, unlike the Western experience; the oil wealth that accrued to the Middle East, Nigeria, Venezuela, and Mexico vanished by the mid–1980s, leaving most of these economies tottering; and the international debt crisis threatened to wipe out whatever gains had been made in many, if not most, developing nations.

As a result, a ''dependency'' perspective on development emerged that argued that the Western capitalist pattern of development, rather than offering a model for developing countries, was actually based on the continuing subordination and exploitation of the Third World. According to dependency theory, advanced industrial states and the multinational corporations headquartered in them used their political and economic power to perpetuate a global division of labor between producers of advanced and primary products that was weighted heavily in the favor of the former and prevented the latter from replicating the West's industrialization. Moreover, the few elites in Third World countries who benefited from this system used support from the advanced nations to hold in check the very social, political, and economic changes advocated by developmentalists. In short, development in a core of industrialized societies could only occur because of the underdevelopment of the vast periphery of the global economy that was dependent on the core both economically and politically. Thus only the revolutionary overthrow of capitalism could free the developmental potential of dependent societies.

These two perspectives on development are so opposed that perhaps only a dialogue of the deaf could occur between them. The experience of a new region of the world, however, suggests that there may be another pattern besides the development of Western Europe and North America and the underdevelopment of Africa and Latin America. This is East Asia, which has seen the most explosive economic growth of the post–World War II era. Japan, despite the devastation of World War II, took off on a rapid growth trajectory and is now challenging the United States for the most powerful economy in the world. The four ''little dragons'' of Hong Kong, Korea, Singapore, and Taiwan have had even more spectacular growth and transformed themselves from less developed countries to industrial societies. To show that ideology is not the determining factor, furthermore, the People's Republic of China (P.R.C.), despite the horrendous social and economic costs of the Great Leap Forward and the Cultural Revolution, has also manifested an impressive economic growth record in many regards over the past decade.

This success has certainly not gone unnoticed; there is a growing number of attempts to decipher an East Asian development model, many with such catchy titles as *The Pacific Century*,[6] *The Eastasia Edge*,[7] *Japan as Number One*,[8] *Asia's "Miracle" Economies*,[9] *Trading Places*,[10] and *The Reckoning*.[11] These analyses stress such factors as the strong role of the state in guiding development strategy; the efficacy of industrial policy; the impact of Confucian culture on government officials, business, and labor; the ability of objectively "weak" states to negotiate with and even manipulate the core; and the consequent pronounced upward mobility of the East Asian nations in the world's international economic and political systems. These preliminary conclusions about rapid growth in East Asia constitute a challenge to most of the basic premises of both the developmentalist and the dependency approaches. Thus a consideration of East Asia may help to move the study of development beyond the increasingly sterile debates between the advocates of these two dominant theoretical traditions. In fact, the East Asian experience has provided key material for a nascent alternative framework for explaining development in terms of the activities of strong developmentalist states.[12]

This book presents a case study of the Republic of China (R.O.C.) on Taiwan as a means for elaborating an East Asian development model. Taiwan certainly qualifies as a successful example of development. Although there is really no complete normative theory of development, general agreement probably exists that development entails sustained growth and industrialization in the economic realm; an improved standard of living, decreased income inequality, and the emergence of a middle-class society in the social sphere; and democratization and effective policymaking in the polity.[13] The R.O.C. scores well on all these dimensions. Sustained economic growth since the early 1950s has produced an increasingly sophisticated industrial economy; Taiwan is widely cited as a case of "growth and equity" in terms of decreasing inequality and a rising popular standard of living[14]; a significant and growing proportion of the population had attained middle-class status by the late 1980s[15]; the state was generally credited with implementing a highly effective development strategy[16]; and substantial political liberalization and democratization occurred over the 1980s.[17]

In terms of the standard economic indicators, for instance, the R.O.C. has experienced extremely rapid development. In 1950 it was still recovering from the ravages of World War II. Gross national product (GNP) per capita was about $100; agriculture dominated economic activity; the natural resource endowment was poor; the country had been severed from its traditional export market in Japan; the government was in chaos after suffering a humiliating defeat in the Chinese civil war; and the threat of a communist invasion was high. Thus Taiwan was certainly an underdeveloped nation by any standard with a developmental outlook far worse than many Third World countries whose economic stagnation in the coming years would form the staple of dependency theory.

The next thirty-five years witnessed an economic miracle by any definition. Real GNP growth averaged over 9 percent a year, one of the highest in the world, as income per capita rose to about $6,000 by the end of 1988. The domestic economy was transformed from agricultural to industrial, and Taiwan became strongly competitive in world markets in a wide variety of manufactured products. The export-led nature of Taiwan's development is clear as well. Exports as a proportion of GNP almost quadrupled from 11 percent to 42 percent between 1962 and 1973, and became overwhelmingly industrial. This export surge also transformed a chronic negative trade balance into a ballooning surplus (which now, for U.S. trade, is a political embarrassment); in 1988 Taiwan had the highest per capita foreign reserves in the world. Rapid growth and economic transformation in the R.O.C., in addition, differed from those of many other developing societies, in that they were not accompanied by growing inequality but instead brought improvement in the quality of life for most of the population.

The sustained rapid economic growth that has occurred on Taiwan over the past three and a half decades can be viewed as a puzzle in several respects. First, at the simplest level, it would seem almost astounding that such economic success could be recorded by a poor country with few natural resources and with a government that had failed miserably in promoting development in China during the 1930s. Second, because rapid growth occurred simultaneously in various other East Asian countries, the R.O.C. is clearly not an accidental or idiosyncratic blip in terms of its development experience. Rather, one is forced to look for factors common to the "exotic East."

At a more abstract level, Taiwan constitutes a puzzle because its developmental history challenges the fundamental assumptions of both the developmentalist and dependency approaches. This challenge is perhaps more obvious for dependency theory. Taiwan's rapid growth and industrial transformation occurred despite strong economic and political dependency on the capitalist core. The island's incorporation into the international capitalist economy as an exporter of agricultural goods did not prevent it from rapidly upgrading its "comparative advantage." The benefits of industrialization were widely dispersed throughout the population. The primary determinants of most policies seem to have been internal rather than external; in particular, multinational corporations have been subjected to strong regulation by the indigenous government.[18]

The Taiwan case is also inconsistent with the basic tenets of developmentalism as well, though. The strong role that the state played in guiding economic strategy is at considerable variance with assumptions of laissez-faire capitalism. Confucian, much more than "modern" Western, values appear to have mediated the nation's developmental drive. Finally, the relation between political and economic change in Taiwan has been far more complex than the usual postulates of the developmentalist model.

In addition, although Taiwan is often cited as the epitome of a strong developmentalist state, its history suggests some caveats about the emerging statist perspective as well. The question of how a failed military regime turned into a promoter of economic development is certainly a "puzzlement." In addition, the strength of the R.O.C. regime vis-a-vis its own society has contrasted greatly with its weakness and dependency in the international sphere.[19] The nature of the relation between the regime and society has also changed significantly over time without producing a major disruption in the economic realm.

Because Taiwan appears representative of a broader East Asian pattern of development, dismissing it as just an "odd duck" is hard. Thus, while the developmental history of the R.O.C. is certainly interesting in itself, the major premise of this book is that Taiwan's development can also illuminate broader perspectives on development and dependency in the contemporary world. Consequently the R.O.C.'s experience will be used to compare and evaluate the competing scholarly perspectives on Third World development in what has been called the "comparative case study" methodology.

Although many case studies of individual countries tend to be primarily descriptive, the case study approach can be designed to build and test general theories and hypotheses if the case being considered is treated in terms of theoretical concepts and relations. In such instances the results from case studies can be applied in several ways: (1) providing detailed descriptive support for abstract or statistical relations, (2) inductively generating new hypotheses, and (3) using individual deviations from theoretical predictions to suggest important additional explanatory factors and relations. For such an approach to be fruitful the case or cases to be studied must be carefully selected in terms of their importance for the key variables in the theoretical formulation.[20]

Taiwan would seem to constitute an excellent case study for evaluating the competing perspectives on development. First, simply its success in promoting rapid growth and socioeconomic transformation argues for paying analytic attention to its policies and record. Second, the R.O.C.'s East Asian location should provide an important contrast to the generalizations drawn from Western Europe and North America by the developmentalists or from Latin America and Africa by the *dependencistas*. Finally, as suggested above, Taiwan's experience apparently challenges many key assumptions in each of the three frameworks for analyzing development.

A consideration of the rapid economic growth in the R.O.C. over the past thirty-five years, therefore, should perform all of the functions of a theoretically informed case study. It should provide a richer description from one country of the abstract hypotheses and formulations used by each approach. Inevitably such descriptions show social reality to be more complex (or perhaps "messy") than the depictions of grand theories. There are two ways to respond to such complexities or exceptions to a theory. First, the theory can be elaborated or expanded. For example, Peter Evans argues that although the East Asian pattern of development disproves overly simplistic or "vulgar" versions of the dependency approach, it should stimulate a more sophisticated version of this theory (and one could make a similar argument about developmentalism).[21] Second, and more fundamentally, Taiwan's divergence from theoretical predictions could stimulate scholars to question the overall theoretical frameworks or lenses through which they view the world.

This book, then, is conceived as an essay on development sparked by an East Asian success story. Unfortunately the experience of one small island cannot generate a full-blown new theory of development. It does, however, suggest that we should draw on both the insights and drawbacks of all the competing theories to try to make sense of a world that is far more complex than either scholars or national policymakers would desire.

Chapters 2 and 3 in part I provide two very different kinds of background materials about the "environment" of this study. Chapter 2 presents the intellectual environment by sketching the different approaches to studying development that provide the basic concepts used in the analysis. Chapter 3 gives a historical setting for Taiwan's postwar development by briefly describing the development of the island before World War II and the rise and fall of the Kuomintang government that came to rule it on the Chinese mainland during the interwar period.

The second part considers political and economic development on Taiwan over the past three and a half decades. The analysis of Taiwan's "performance" begins with a discussion of the international and domestic political context within which rapid development took place and then moves on to a description of Taiwan's "economic miracle." The first chapter in this descriptive section evaluates Taiwan's international political linkages, including its client-state relationship with the United States, the continuing rivalry with the P.R.C., and the special diplomatic problems caused by its lack of official relations with most other countries. Chapter 5 then argues that substantial reform and development have occurred in the political realm as well as in the economic in terms of the expanding nature of political and economic elites, the growth of democratic political institutions, and the ability of the regime to formulate and implement an effective development strategy. Chapter 6 describes economic growth and change, breaking the island's economic history down into several subperiods according to changes in economic strategy: agricultural reform, import substitution, the export surge, responding to external instability, and the movement to capital-intensive and high-technology industry.

The conclusion in part III then tries to draw implications from the Taiwan success story. It begins by constructing an analytical model of the political economy of the R.O.C. that posits the key economic and political factors and sketches the dynamic relations among them. This pattern of development is also briefly compared and contrasted with several other types of political economies. It then analyzes the implications of the Taiwan case for the developmentalist, dependency, and statist paradigms in seven general areas: (1) the results of Taiwan's incorporation into the global division of labor for the development and distortion of its economy; (2) the operation of "free markets" in Taiwan's rapid growth; (3) the role of the R.O.C. state in promoting development; (4) the social determinants of state activity in Taiwan; (5) the impact of the country's Confucian culture; (6) the nature and effects of the R.O.C.'s external dependency; and (7) the nature of Taiwan's political development. These implications then form the basis for a brief discussion of what insights can be drawn from each explanatory framework for understanding development and dependency in the contemporary world.

Notes

1. Simon Kuznets, *Modern Economic Growth: Rate, Structure, and Spread* (New Haven, Conn.: Yale University Press, 1966); and Hollis Chenery and M. Syrquin, *Patterns of Development 1950–1970* (New York: Oxford University Press, 1975).

2. As first stated by Simon Kuznets, "Economic Growth and Income Inequality," *American Economic Review* 45:1 (March 1955), pp. 1–28, the relation between development and inequality is not entirely direct. Initially, development usually produces greater inequality in a society that declines as development proceeds; so that the most developed nations in the world have the lowest rates of inequality. Thus inequality displays an "inverted U–shaped" relation with development level. See also Irma Adelman and Cynthia Taft Morris, *Economic Growth and Social Equity in Developing Countries* (Stanford, Calif.: Stanford University Press, 1973); Robert W. Jackman, *Politics and Social Equality: A Comparative Analysis* (New York: John Wiley, 1975); and Kuznets, *Modern Economic Growth*.

3. Lloyd Jensen, *Explaining Foreign Policy* (Englewood Cliffs, N.J.: Prentice-Hall, 1982), chs. 6 and 7.

4. Phillips Cutright, "National Political Development: Measurement and Analysis," *American Sociological Review* 28:2 (April 1963), pp. 253–264; Karl W. Deutsch, "Social Mobilization and Political Development," *American Political Science Review* 55:3 (September 1961), pp. 493–514; Seymour Martin Lipset, "Some Social Requisites of Democracy: Economic Development and Political Legitimacy," *American Political Science Review* 53:1 (March 1959), pp. 69–105; Jackman, *Politics and Social Equality*, pp. 66–73; and Jack Sawyer, "Dimensions of Nations: Size, Wealth, and Politics," *American Journal of Sociology* 73:2 (September 1967), pp. 145–172.

5. The conclusion that rapid growth may stimulate social dislocations and political instability has been reached from a variety of perspectives. For example, see S. N. Eisenstadt, *Modernization, Protest, and Change* (Englewood Cliffs, N.J.: Prentice-Hall, 1966); Ted R. Gurr, *Why Men Rebel* (Princeton, N.J.: Princeton University Press, 1970); Samuel P. Huntington, *Political Order in Changing Societies* (New Haven, Conn.: Yale University Press, 1968); and Mancur Olson, "Rapid Growth as a Destabilizing Force," *Journal of Economic History* 23:4 (December 1963), pp. 529–552. Donella Meadows et al., *The Limits to Growth: A Report for the Club of Rome's Project on the Predicament of Mankind* (New York: Universe Books, 1972), represents the burgeoning arguments about the environmental costs of the traditional paths to industrialization.

6. Staffan Burenstam Linder, *The Pacific Century: Economic and Political Consequences of Asian-Pacific Dynamism* (Stanford, Calif.: Stanford University Press, 1986).

7. Roy Hofheinz, Jr., and Kent E. Calder, *The Eastasia Edge* (New York: Basic Books, 1982).

8. Ezra F. Vogel, *Japan as Number One* (Cambridge, Mass.: Harvard University Press, 1979).

9. Jon Woronoff, *Asia's "Miracle" Economies* (Armonk, N.Y.: M. E. Sharpe, 1986).

10. Clyde V. Prestowitz, *Trading Places: How We Allowed Japan to Take the Lead* (New York: Basic Books, 1988).

11. David Halberstam, *The Reckoning* (New York: Avon, 1986).

12. This statist approach is best represented by Peter B. Evans, Dietrich Rueschemeyer, and Theda Skocpol, eds., *Bringing the State Back In* (Cambridge: Cambridge University Press, 1985). For theoretical treatments emphasizing the East Asian experience, see Bruce Cumings, "The Origin and Development of the Northeast Asian Political Economy: Industrial Sectors and Political Consequences," *International Organization* 38:1 (Winter 1984), pp. 1–40; and Stephan Haggard, "The Newly Industrializing Countries in the International System," *World Politics* 38:2 (January 1986), pp. 343–370.

13. Thomas A. Metzger, "Developmental Criteria and Indigenously Conceptualized Options: A Normative Approach to China's Modernization in Recent Times," *Issues and Studies* 23:2 (February 1987), pp. 19–81, provides an excellent analysis of Western and Chinese normative views on development.

14. Shirley W. Y. Kuo, Gustav Ranis, and John C. H. Fei, *The Taiwan Success Story: Rapid Growth with Improved Distribution in the Republic of China, 1952–1979* (Boulder, Colo.: Westview Press, 1981).

15. Wen Lang Li, "Social Development in the Republic of China, 1949–1981," in Hungdah Chiu and Shao-Chuan Leng, eds., *China: Seventy Years After the Hsin Hai Revolution* (Charlottesville: University of Virginia Press, 1984), pp. 478–499.

16. Thomas B. Gold, *State and Society in the Taiwan Miracle* (Armonk, N.Y.: M. E. Sharpe, 1986).

17. John F. Cooper, *A Quiet Revolution: Political Development in the Republic of China* (Washington, D.C.: Ethics and Public Policy Center, 1988); and Ramon H. Myers, "Political Theory and the Recent Political Developments in the Republic of China," *Asian Survey* 27:9 (September 1987), pp. 1003–1022.

18. Richard E. Barrett and Soomi Chin, "Export-oriented Industrializing States in the Capitalist World System: Similarities and Differences," in Frederic C. Deyo, ed., *The Political Economy of the New Asian Industrialism* (Ithaca, N.Y.: Cornell University Press, 1987), pp. 23–43; and Richard E. Barrett and Martin King Whyte, "Dependency Theory and Taiwan: Analysis of a Deviant Case," *American Journal of Sociology* 87:5 (March 1982), pp. 1064–1089, present such a critique from a "conventional" perspective. Alice H. Amsden, "Taiwan's Economic History: A Case of Etatism and a Challenge to Dependency Theory," *Modern China* 5:3 (July 1979), pp. 341–379; and Gold, *State and Society*, use a statist approach that is much more sympathetic to the basic dependency concepts.

19. Steve Chan, "Developing Strength from Weakness: The State in Taiwan," *Journal of Developing Societies* 4:1 (Spring 1988), pp. 38–51.

20. Harry Eckstein, "Case Study and Theory in Political Science," in Fred I. Greenstein and Nelson W. Polsby, eds., *Handbook of Political Science*, Vol. VIII (Reading, Mass.: Addison-Wesley, 1975), pp. 79–138; and Alexander L. George, "Case Studies and Theory Development: The Method of Structured, Focused Comparison," in Paul G.

Lauren, ed., *Diplomacy: New Approaches in History, Theory, and Policy* (New York: Free Press, 1979), pp. 43–68.

21. Peter Evans, "Class, State, and Dependence in East Asia: Lessons for Latin Americanists," in Frederic C. Deyo, ed., *The Political Economy of the New Asian Industrialism* (Ithaca, N.Y.: Cornell University Press, 1987), pp. 203–226.

PART I

ENVIRONMENT

CHAPTER 2

Alternative Paradigms of Development

This chapter outlines the three basic theoretical frameworks that have been developed for conceptualizing and analyzing economic and political development—the developmentalist, dependency, and statist perspectives. All these theoretical traditions are rich and complex, and contain competing schools centered on more or less arcane arguments and issues. This overview chapter, then, is limited to a discussion of the central premises in each approach and to a broad-brush comparison of their basic assumptions and world views.[1] The objectives here are to present the basic ideas that are used in the analysis of Taiwan's development and to contrast the central insights of each approach.

These alternative approaches for viewing development can be interpreted within a broader framework of Thomas Kuhn's argument that the key factor in the history of science has been the successive development of broad "paradigms" that define the principal problems for and methods of scientific inquiry.[2] The first section of this chapter describes this theory and discusses its relevance for comparing the three types of theories about development. The next three sections summarize each of these perspectives in the order that they evolved: developmentalism, *dependencia*, and statism. The chapter concludes with a brief comparison of their basic scholarly orientations.

Scientific Paradigms and Theories about Development

To the uninitiated—which includes most of the people who study economic development—"science" is an impressive if not imposing endeavor conducted by physicists, mathematicians, biologists, and others of their ilk. Universal laws applicable to all phenomena can be stated in precise (if generally incomprehensible) mathematical formulations and verified or disconfirmed by replicable experiments whose results can be easily evaluated by the initiates of the discipline in question. This certainly contrasts with the social sciences, in which, as the discussion of the contending approaches to development theory well illustrates, fundamental disagreement about theoretical frameworks or even basic facts is ongoing and seemingly not amenable to rational resolution.

There is also the view that science is essentially a cumulative process. That is, the facts and experimental results are added to each other over time in a "building-block" approach as knowledge expands in a linear manner. Thomas Kuhn presents a much different picture of the history of science in *The Structure of Scientific Revolutions*, however. He contends that science has advanced through a series of revolutions in which one way of viewing the world, which he calls a "paradigm," is replaced by an alternative formulation. A paradigm, according to Kuhn, is an accepted model of scientific practice that dominates a particular field of inquiry. It provides the general theoretical framework within which research and discussion are carried out, sets the research agenda by posing questions that are considered worthy of analysis, and delineates the methodology considered appropriate for scientific inquiry. In contrast to the construction of paradigms, most research constitutes "normal science," which accepts the basic assumptions of the overarching paradigm and seeks to find new facts or supply more detailed proofs within its framework.[3]

A good example of two radically contrasting paradigms comes from the field of astronomy. The traditional, or Ptolemaic, astronomy assumed that the earth was at the center of the universe with the moon, planets, and stars revolving around it. Geometrical and mathematical systems were then derived to fit astronomic observations within this paradigm. The Copernican revolution in astronomy assumed that the earth and planets rotated on their axes and revolved around the sun. Surprisingly, its ability to supplant the Ptolemaic paradigm did not come, however, from any great superiority in its predictions. Rather, it was a growing crisis of confidence in the traditional system that led to the acceptance of a successor paradigm with a radically different view of the world.

With respect both to planetary position and to precession of the equinoxes, predictions made with Ptolemy's system never quite conformed with the best available observations. Further reduction of these minor discrepancies constituted many of the principal problems of normal astronomical research for many of Ptolemy's successors. . . . For some time astronomers had every reason to suppose that these attempts would be as successful as the ones that had led to Ptolemy's system. Given a particular discrepancy, astronomers were invariably able to eliminate it by making some particular adjustment in Ptolemy's system of compounded circles. But as time went on, a man looking at the net result of the normal research effort of many astronomers could observe that astronomy's complexity was increasing far more rapidly than its accuracy and that a discrepancy corrected in one place was likely to show up in another. . . . In the sixteenth century, Copernicus' co-worker, Domenico da Novara, held that no system so cumbersome and inaccurate as the Ptolemaic had become could possibly be true of nature.[4]

In sum, Kuhn concluded that paradigms are not really subject to "scientific" evaluation and comparison, but are accepted and rejected because of their ability to solve "acute problems" of interest to a specific scholarly community. Paradigms fall into question when "anomalies" within them become perceived as serious enough to constitute an "acute" crisis. A new paradigm can do one of several things. It can incorporate important new phenomena into the subject matter of a discipline, such as new classification schemes in botany or geology; it can correct false assumptions, such as the Copernican revolution; or it can subsume existing scientific theory into a more encompassing framework, such as Einstein's theory of relativity did to Newtonian physics.[5]

This interpretation of the history of science clearly applies to the history of theories of development. Each of the three theories or paradigms was constructed to explain a particular "acute" problem related to the general subject of development of interest to a considerable scholarly community—why Western Europe and North America supported the industrial revolution for the developmentalists, why much of the Third World remained underdeveloped for the *dependencistas*, and why rapid development was possible in one peripheral region for the statists. As we will see, the second and third paradigms evolved when their adherents realized that previous frameworks did not provide adequate explanations for their central analytic concerns. That is, anomaly stimulated new paradigms.

In history and the social sciences paradigm construction and change are much more common than in the physical sciences. Because universal laws applicable to all phenomena or relations akin to $E = MC^2$ cannot be developed, it is always easy to find instances or cases that do not fit a particular theoretical framework. The challenge for theory development, then, is to winnow inconsequential "deviant cases" from fundamental "anomalies" that create an "acute problem" for a paradigm. This book tries to establish that the "Taiwan exception" is such an anomaly by matching the Republic of China's (R.O.C.'s) experience to the central postulates of each tradition and by arguing that Taiwan's experience suggests alternative hypotheses that are reasonable and generalizable.

The Developmentalist Approach

The developmentalist approach constituted the initial attempt to explain why development had occurred in some countries and to draw lessons and prescriptions for promoting development in the poorer parts of the world. It was based on the reasonable assumption that the experience of the nations in Western Europe and North America that had led the industrial revolution provided a fertile ground for deciphering the economic, social, and political components of development. It then assumed, perhaps less reasonably, that the pattern of development in the West forms a universal model of development that must be replicated by any developing nation that wanted to achieve economic success.

The research agenda of developmentalism, therefore, was to isolate the key factors that promoted and accompanied the industrial revolution in the West. In essence, this entailed case studies of the developmental leaders (e.g., England) whose results led to the positing of broad generalizations about the processes of development. The comparative aspects of such studies were generally limited to contrasting the economic history of rapid developers with that of the European laggards (e.g., Spain and Portugal). In particular, the developmentalist perspective is based on four sets of assumptions about the processes of change in different sectors of society: (1) neoclassic economics, (2) modernization theories of cultural change, (3) definitions of political development in terms of democratization and institutionalization, and (4) the argument that complex interdependence forms the central feature of contemporary international relations and political economy.

Unlike some dimensions of development, there is a consensus about what constitutes the core of economic development—a sustained growth in national product:

We identify the economic growth of nations as a sustained increase in per capita or per worker product, most often accompanied by an increase in population and usually by sweeping structural changes.[6]

The economic strand of the developmentalist school sought to chart the key economic changes that occur during such sustained growth, to measure the relations that exist among these economic processes and factors, to identify the major causes or stimulants for growth, and to find whether growth produced regular socioeconomic consequences.

In a strictly economic sense, sustained growth was seen to depend on a confluence of two factors. First were technological innovations or breakthroughs that would increase production, and second was the growth of savings and investment that would permit the application and spread of this technology. Thus economic growth normally entailed rising productivity that was tied to increases in the capital-labor ratio. This was associated with "sweeping" structural changes in the economy—first from agricultural to industrial and service pursuits and then, within the industrial sector, from labor-intensive light industry (e.g., food and textiles) to heavy industry (e.g., steel and machinery) to high-tech industry (e.g., computers and advanced electronics).

This economic transformation, moreover, did not just rest on changes on the "supply side," but was fueled by changes in demand without which the structural development of production could not occur. Rising income produces major changes in societal demand, in particular a substantial decrease in the share of agricultural products in total demand. Thus the changing production structure from light to heavy industry reflects both an increasing demand for producers' goods and an upgrading of the consumers' goods that are used. Foreign trade can also contribute considerably to effective demand by providing much broader markets, as well as cheaper sources for a variety of products. Consequently economic development usually brings increases in the ratios of foreign trade to gross national product and of manufactured to primary products among exports. Finally, the inflow of foreign resources through investment and aid programs can augment domestic savings and investment to help finance economic growth in late-developing nations.[7]

Economic analysis of rapid growth in the nineteenth- and twentieth-century West found several important regularities. First, the growth pattern of many of these economic variables follows an S curve in which stagnation is followed by a prolonged growth spurt that levels off when the stage of an advanced industrial economy is attained. Second, despite the emphasis on industrialization, increased productivity was needed in agriculture because agricultural development provided cheap food and export goods, built up a surplus that could be used to finance industrialization, released workers for the industrial sector, and created a demand for manufactured products—all of which were viewed as supporting the economic takeoff. Third, accumulation in terms of savings and investment, the creation of human capital through mass education programs, and the stockpiling of financial resources in government occurs early in the developmental processes, since sustained growth rests on adequate financing. Once a sustained rise in income begins, though, an increasing percentage of national income is channeled into the sectors that have the highest propensity to save, such as entrepreneurs and governments, thereby reinforcing the growth trend. Finally, pronounced changes in production structure begin fairly early in the growth spurt, but the transformation of foreign trade usually occurs much later.[8]

Growth is also viewed as having a direct impact on a society's population and income structure. The concentration of production in the industrial revolution obviously brought about the increasing urban concentration of populations. Urbanization, in turn, was associated with growing national populations but also with a distinctive demographic shift toward smaller families and a reorganization from extended to nuclear family organization. Initially economic growth in most societies was associated with increased inequality among individuals, classes, and regions as development is concentrated in a few industrial and regional nodes. Over time, however, participation in and benefits from industrialization begin to be spread more widely throughout society, creating an inverted U–shaped relation between economic growth and inequality. Moreover, a strong empirical relation exists between a nation's development level and the average standard of living and "physical quality of life."[9] Thus developmentalists believe that economic growth produces a variety of desirable socioeconomic spin-offs.

Developmentalism moves from these economic relations to the assumption that capitalism provided the primordial force driving the industrial revolution. That is, the emergence of the economy as a sphere that operated relatively autonomously from governmental control or the constraints of a rigid social hierarchy explains "how the West got rich."[10] This does not mean that all developmentalists are extreme devotees of laissez-faire economics a la James Buchanan, Milton Friedman, or Ludwig von Mises.[11] For example, Keynesian macroeconomic management to smooth out business cycles is generally accepted;

and there is widespread recognition that government can make a vital contribution by supplying such "social overhead capital" as transportation infrastructure and public education programs. In fact, there is at least partial agreement among most developmentalists with Alexander Gerschenkron's "statist" argument that the state must play an enhanced role in late-developing societies.[12] Still, neoclassic economics clearly forms the core of developmentalist thought.

The neoclassic assumption of the developmentalists that the operation of the economic free market leads to the optimum allocation of resources and production specialization also produces a stress on the contribution that foreign trade can make to development if nations trade according to their international "comparative advantage" (i.e., export goods whose domestic prices are lowest relative to world markets and import goods whose relative prices are highest).[13] This theoretical assumption has received empirical support, moreover, in the work of economists like Bela Balassa and Hollis Chenery, who have found that industrializing countries in the Third World fare much better in terms of both growth and income equality if they pursue strategies that emphasize labor-intensive production for export as opposed to those that use protection to promote "import substitution" for capital-intensive heavy industries.[14]

Economic specialization based on international comparative advantage raises one potential problem, though. If economic growth is primarily associated with industrialization (as it is in developmentalist theory), what happens to a country whose comparative advantage is in growing bananas or mining tin? It is here that Raymond Vernon's theory of the product cycle offers hope to developing countries for upgrading their production structures within the global capitalist economy. Vernon argues that new products and technological innovation are most likely to occur in the most advanced economies that are marked by high incomes and capital-intensive production. Once a new product proves itself in such a market, though, its production becomes more standardized, leading to lower costs and marketability in less wealthy economies. As a result, as the product moves from "new" to "maturing" to "standardized," its center of production is diffused from the innovative country to other developed states to developing nations, which even begin exporting back to the "center" as the product cycle comes to an end.[15] The operation of the product cycle, therefore, provides Third World nations an opportunity to begin industrialization; economic development occurs as countries upgrade their productive processes and gradually shift their comparative advantage forward along the product cycle.[16]

The developmentalist view of economic development, to sum, is that it moves through fairly well defined stages and becomes self-reinforcing once the initial stages are under way. This perspective is perhaps best summarized by Walter Rostow's theory of "the stages of economic growth," although ironically most developmentalist economists believe that Rostow's model is far too simplistic and deterministic.[17] Rostow posits five stages of growth: (1) the traditional economy before development; (2) the establishment of such "preconditions for takeoff" as rising savings, the creation of social overhead capital, and the growth of entrepreneurial norms; (3) the "takeoff" in which growth becomes self-sustaining owing to strong investment and the establishment of at least one dynamic industrial sector; (4) the drive to maturity as sustained growth is transformed to a broad range of industrial sectors; and (5) the age of high mass consumption in which the bulk of the population draws material benefits from industrialization and supplies the demand to keep the economy strong.[18]

Whatever the assumptions of microeconomic theory, it is clear that economic markets do not function in social or political vacuums. Thus other dimensions of the developmentalist approach are concerned with conditions or changes in additional spheres that either promote or retard economic growth. One prominent theory is that social "modernization" is necessary for the successful operation of a capitalist economy. Modernization thought takes its lineage from Max Weber's influential theory that the norms involved in the "Protestant ethic" promoted economic accumulation and growth, whereas other value systems, such as traditional Confucianism, inhibited the large-scale pursuit of economic objectives in a society.[19]

This approach was gradually systematized by sociological theorists, such as Talcott Parsons, into a fundamental dichotomy between "traditional" and "modern" societies according to the dominant societal values and norms. Several important "modern" values have thus been identified that are seen as actively promoting capitalist economic growth. A central value here is secularism in terms of a focus on the material world and the belief that it can be manipulated for one's betterment (the Protestant ethic has been dubbed a secular religion). This is supplemented by a belief in the equality among people, as opposed to placing them in a rigid social hierarchy, and by a high psychological achievement need within a population. Such values create an individualistic society. The material needs of people are stressed, as well as the fact that there are no inherent social barriers to attempting to fulfill individual goals. This, in turn, creates a "spirit of enterprise." People are encouraged to pursue their material interests through competition in the economic marketplace. Norms of equality and equal access to the marketplace, furthermore, ensure that the most capable make the largest contribution to economic activity and draw the largest rewards from the marketplace.[20]

Social modernization is viewed as a prerequisite for economic development, since it appears essential to overcoming two important blockages to capitalist growth. First, developmentalists believe that the peasantry that dominates traditional societies holds values at sharp variance with the individualism and entrepreneurship necessary for economic dynamism,[21] although such stereotypes of traditional agricultural societies have been vigorously challenged by many anthropologists.[22] Second, the dominant landholding and merchant classes in preindustrial economies have strong material interests to use their political and economic power to prevent economic change from occurring.[23] Thus according to developmentalists, the "passing of traditional society,"[24] at both the elite and mass levels, forms an almost necessary concomitant of the economic "takeoff."

Modernization theory broadens the schema of a self-reinforcing set of developmental processes. Once development starts, it produces more savings and expanded demand to fuel further growth. The resulting urbanization, shifts in employment, changing family patterns, and the ultimate emergence of a middle class create the "modern" values that permit economic change and development to continue. Despite this optimistic view that the developmental processes constitute a "virtuous cycle," there is still the "chicken-or-the-egg" question of what sparked development in the first place. Why, for example, was the timing of the industrial revolution so different even among the European nations? This suggests a return to Weber's emphasis on cultural norms at the beginning of development rather than cultural change stemming from development.

Modernization theory does differ in one important respect from developmentalist theories of economic growth, in that rapid social change is viewed as potentially destabilizing. Urbanization and industrialization break down the traditional way of life and mechanisms for social solidarity and control, producing the strong potential for psychological stress, social alienation, and political discontent and upheavals.[25] If economic development continues, adjustments to the modern (and assumedly superior) lifestyle should occur. However, the modernization strand of developmentalism does imply that the rapid change associated with economic takeoff can produce sufficient social anomie and disruption to abort the developmental processes (witness the recent revolution in Iran).

Development, according to the developmentalists, therefore, requires both a conducive environment for laissez-faire economics *and* a means for ameliorating or controlling the side effects of the social dislocations produced by rapid change. Varying concerns with these two tasks explain why definitions of political development have been much more variegated than those for economic or social development and modernization. Different conceptualizations of political development abound in the literature, but almost all can be fit within two broad dimensions. One is "democratization," or increasing popular participation in and influence over government; the other is "institutionalization," or the ability of a government to formulate and implement effective policies.[26] As will be seen, although these two dimensions were initially seen as being compatible, an important strand of developmentalism now views them as antithetical for many developing nations.

Democracy has been linked with a developmentalist syndrome in several important ways. First, the rise of democracy is historically associated with capitalism and the industrial revolution in a reciprocal relation. On the one hand, economic and social modernization stimulated participatory demands. On the other, the transition from authoritarian or absolutist rule to limited government provided much more autonomy for the economy, as opposed to the previous mercantilist era. Additionally, the rise of popular government undermined the power of traditional elite classes with a vested interest in preventing socioeconomic change. Second, democratic practice and philosophy helped to spur the individualism and entrepreneurship seen as central to social modernization. Third, democratic government promoted much greater responsiveness to the needs of the middle and working classes. This was reflected, for example, in the rise of public education, which created the skilled labor forces necessary for industrialization. More important perhaps, democratic governments over time regulated labor relations and provided welfare policies so as to lessen inequality and develop mass demand—which is viewed as a key ingredient in the Western development pattern.[27]

Initially democratic government was also viewed as effective government. Its presumed responsiveness to popular desires should help to alleviate social discontent and alienation; the limitations on governmental power provided by constitutionalism should provide a supportive environment for laissez-faire economics; and a rational division between policymaking by elected leaders and implementation by a professional bureaucracy should create effective policies. In Weber's terms, democratization was part of a movement toward establishing a political order on the basis of "rational legal" authority.[28] That is, democratization and institutionalization were seen as being high compatible, if not part of the same overall process.

This view that democratization and institutionalization were self-reinforcing components of political development came under strong questioning by developmentalists. One reason was pervasive Third World failures during the 1950s and 1960s in both the political and the economic realms. Developmentalism certainly has some highly optimistic implications about the possibilities for development. Thus decolonialization was seen as opening the way for rapid economic, social, and political development. Unfortunately the history of the Third World after World War II was at goodly variance from such optimism. The gap between the rich and the poor countries generally widened; most "new nations" came to be ruled by dictatorial regimes; and the primary results of social change appeared to be massive unemployment and squalid urban squatters' slums.[29]

The developmentalist response to these conditions was to stress the dislocations produced by change and development, in particular the conclusion that the increased popular participation brought on by democratization could overload weak political institutions with demands for results and services that far exceeded a fledgling government's capabilities, resulting in chaos, corruption, and "political decay," which make economic development impossible. As a result, as best exemplified by Samuel Huntington's *Political Order in Changing Societies*,[30] developmentalist theory began to stress institutionalization as something of an antithetical process to democratization and to argue that authoritarian governments in the Third World might be necessary to provide political and social stability. Thus democratization was seen as increasing rather than reducing social discontent. This also represented a significant shift in what was assumed to be government's major role in development from nonintervention in the economic marketplace and the provision of social overhead capital to preventing the social and political instability that make long-term economic calculations impossible. There was also obviously a changing emphasis from ameliorating social discontent through democratization to controlling it through institutionalization.

The growth of the welfare state in Western Europe and North America created another reason for more conservative developmentalists to question the necessary compatibility of democracy and economic vitality, since expanding government powers and regulations over the economy were viewed as distorting and inhibiting the optimum functioning of the market. This strand of thought took perhaps its most sophisticated form in Mancur Olson's stimulating theory about "the rise and decline of nations." Olson argued that dislocations in the economy result from the use of monopoly economic or political power to distort economic outcomes in the favor of particular groups or classes, which he calls "distributional coalitions." According to this conceptualization, political intervention in the economy primarily occurs because distributional coalitions or interest groups successfully pressure government to aid them. Over time in a stable polity, moreover, the number and strength of distributional coalitions should increase, thereby putting increasing pressure on economic performance.[31] Thus Olson's theory presents a paradox for developmentalist thought. Political stability seems to be a necessary (although far from sufficient) condition for a vibrant economy. However, long-term political stability stimulates political conditions (i.e., the formation of distributional coalitions) that undercut economic performance. This also raises the questions, which Olson did not address, of whether "institutionalization" in the form of strong authoritarian governments might be used to curb the disruptive effects of distributional coalitions, as has evidently happened in several East Asian countries,[32] and whether authoritarian governments themselves might become potent "distributional coalitions."

Although not normally associated with the developmentalist approach, several theories about the nature of the international political and economic system provide a vital context necessary for the functioning of these presumed developmental processes. As Olson's theory of distributional coalitions makes clear, economic and political power can be applied to extract "monopoly rents" and distort economic development. The question then follows of why strong countries and economic actors, such as multinational corporations, will not use their power in the generally anarchic international system to monopolize economic benefits for themselves. Certainly the history of colonialism shows that the strong are not loath to assert the "right" to exploit the weak.

The answer that developmentalists can give to this question is that the very processes of economic transformation have created a new international system. Richard Rosecrance begins this line of argument with his theory that the industrial revolution set in motion the "rise of the trading state" (i.e., a nation primarily concerned with economic matters) and the decline of the "territorial state" (i.e., a nation primarily oriented toward traditional politico-military goals).[33] The movement toward the "trading state" was augmented by several other major changes in the post–World War II international order. The communications and transportation revolutions greatly expanded trade and capital flows and created a "global village"; nonstate bodies, such as multinational corporations (MNCs) and international organizations, became increasingly important in international politics and economics; and international norms gave more respect to national sovereignty. The result, according to Robert Keohane and Joseph Nye, was a world of growing "complex interdependence" among the different countries and areas of the world and between political and economic issues.[34]

This system of complex interdependence has several implications for the maintenance of a liberal or laissez-faire international economy and the relative bargaining power of the weak and the strong within it. The theory of "hegemonic stability" argues that when the global economy is dominated by one strong nation or hegemon, such as Great Britain during most of the nineteenth century or America after World War II, the dominant power has a vested interest in a free trade system and, thus, will use its power to maintain a liberal economic order, although declining economic performance may create a more "predatory hegemon."[35] Complex interdependence also helps the bargaining power of the weak. Political superpowers may subsidize, rather than exploit, their client states[36]; the weak can somewhat neutralize the power of the strong by concentrating on a few issues of prime importance to themselves that are lost in their negotiating partners' "crowded agendas."[37] In the important economic area of foreign investment, for example, MNCs have the advantage before an investment is made, but once substantial resources have been committed, the advantage begins to swing toward the host country, creating an "obsolescing bargain."[38] Moreover, dominance within the system appears to be cyclical, allowing both upward and downward mobility. For example, George Modelski has delineated a pattern of "long cycles" of international politics of approximately a century that begin with a single hegemonic power dominating the world and are composed of its gradual loss of power owing to the increasing capabilities of its rivals and to its own military and economic overextension.[39]

To sum, this perspective generally views development as fairly mechanistic and linear once the initial processes have commenced. The presumed spark for economic growth that sets off the processes depicted in this model comes from a combination of economic opportunity and a supportive social and political context. Thus four "necessary" conditions appear to be required: (1) a technological breakthrough to increase production, (2) sufficient investment funds from either internal or external sources, (3) a significant social segment that possesses entrepreneurial abilities, and (4) a permissive or supportive set of political policies.

Figure 2.1 summarizes the central assumptions of the developmentalist approach. The arrows indicate which factors are assumed to affect others. A plus by an arrow indicates that an increase in the effected item is expected; a minus predicts that the impact will result in a decline; and a question mark denotes some controversy over a relation. The self-reinforcing nature of the developmentalist model is depicted by the positive feedback loop from *industrial ex-*

Figure 2.1
The Developmentalist Model

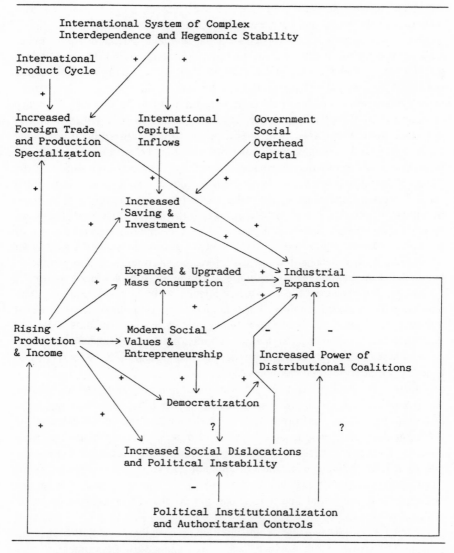

+ Positive Relationship
- Negative Relationship
? Direction of Impact Controversial

pansion (i.e., the ultimate "effect" in this model) to *rising production and income* (i.e., the initial cause). Once sustained development begins, it is largely self-reinforcing as the various economic, social, and political components work together to produce more investment, economic expansion, modern social values, and a conducive domestic and international political context for laissez-faire economics. Two contradictory tendencies are posited, though, in the social dislocations and political instability that can result from rapid change and in the effects of distributional coalitions. Sustained development, therefore, depends on the positive forces outweighing the negative ones.

The Dependency Approach

Dependency theory emerged as an explicit reaction against and challenge to the developmentalist approach. While developmentalism tried to abstract the reasons for rapid development in Western Europe, *dependencia* focused on the reasons for continuing underdevelopment in Latin America and Africa. There were two potential paths for pursuing this second research question. The tack taken by developmentalists was to contrast the European experience with Latin American or African history and draw up a checklist of what the former did right and the latter did wrong. The other taken by dependency theorists was to reject the Western model as nonapplicable to the developing world and search for an alternative paradigm of development. Consequently developmentalists searched for factors internal to a nation and society that determined whether an economy would take advantage of the potentialities of capitalism. *Dependencistas*, on the other hand, concluded that the workings of the global capitalist system provided the explanation for absence of development in the Third World periphery.

This overview of the dependency paradigm begins with a discussion of its intellectual precursors; two principal emphases within the general approach are sketched. The central tenets of *dependencia* are then presented with the focus on its view of capitalism and how capitalist economic relations limit the developmental possibilities of Third World countries and on the effects of these economic linkages on class structure and political relations within dependent societies. Finally, the theory of "dependent development," which was formulated to explain the industrialization that has occurred in the Third World, is considered.

Dependency theory united two rather different scholarly traditions. One was the analysis of "unequal" economic relations between advanced industrial powers and weaker less developed nations. Although this approach contradicted the developmentalist optimism about the benign functioning of international economics, it was compatible with conventional assumptions about the global political economy. The second, which was based on theories of imperialism, on the other hand, constituted a direct challenge to the developmentalist paradigm. To use a phrase often applied to Marx's application of the Hegelian dialectic, these theories stood developmentalism's assumptions about the nature and consequences of capitalism "on their heads."

As suggested in the previous section, the assumption that the international capitalist economy will operate in a neutral manner beneficial to both rich and poor, powerful and weak is open to strong questioning based on the obvious tremendous differences in economic and political power that exist among nations. Not surprisingly, several analyses suggest that this potential is far from inconsequential. Based on the experience of Nazi Germany's interwar relations with Eastern Europe, Hirschman found that ties between a large, advanced industrial economy and small economies based on primary products are quite asymmetrical in the sense that they are much more important to the smaller partners than to the larger one. This creates a dependency that can then be manipulated by the dominant partner in the pursuit of its own economic and political objectives.[40] Such blatant examples are harder to find in the political economy of the 1970s and 1980s. Still, David Baldwin contends that "economic statecraft" can be an integral component of foreign policy.[41] Moreover, the decline of America's economic hegemony is now associated with a growing movement to channel international economic ties through interstate agreements[42]—which can only increase the impact of disparities in bargaining power.

Such general theories about the possible dependency that could be established between strong and weak economies were extended to an explicit critique of how the liberal economic world order perpetuated underdevelopment in the Third World by Raul Prebisch and the United Nations' Economic Commission for Latin America (ECLA). Prebisch and the ECLA school argued that the international economic system operated to perpetuate a division of labor between producers of primary products in the Third World and producers of manufactured goods in Europe and North America. Industrial technology was concentrated in Western firms; the tariff policies of the First World closed their markets to the industrial products of the developing nations; domestic markets in the Third World were too small and poor to support industrialization; and world market prices for exports tended to be quite unstable and to decline in the long term.[43]

Several things are noteworthy about this line of analysis. First, it goes well beyond the concern with bilateral dependency links in Hirschman's theory to posit a "structuralist" explanation for the absence of development in the Third World. That is, it argues that there are certain long-term institutional features of the international political economy that explain the continuing gap between the rich and the poor. Second, it is also assumed that a frozen international division of labor that prevents many nations from industrializing also denies them the putative benefits of "modernization," such as rising income and standard of living and expanded educational opportunities. Third, despite this structuralist perspective, this theory was not so much a rejection of capitalism, but a call to reform it to operate more in line with the vision of the developmentalists through ending discrimination against Third World industrial exports, increasing resource flows from the developed to the developing worlds, promoting industrialization through import-substitution policies (i.e., erecting protectionist walls to stimulate domestic industries to replace previously imported items), and giving less developed countries a more equitable voice in setting the rules under which the international economy operated.[44]

Theories of imperialism, especially those associated with Marxists, in contrast, believed that reformism was impossible and that the structures of world capitalism would have to be eradicated before development in the periphery would be possible. Lenin's theory of imperialism provided the starting point for this approach. Lenin argued that the ever intensifying crises in developed European capitalist states forced them to grab colonies and spheres of interest in the less developed world in order to secure cheap raw materials, markets for their industrial goods, and more surplus with which to momentarily buy off their own working classes. Thus imperialism was "the highest stage of capitalism" that provided a respite before the contradictions inherent in capitalism would destroy the system (e.g., the idea that capitalism had become a world system that would break at its "weakest link" provided a handy explanation for the first socialist revolution's occurrence in Russia). In terms of developmental outcomes, though, Lenin's orthodox Marxist views of the stages of historical development led him to conclude that bringing capitalism and industrialization to the Third World represented a progressive step for the imperialized colonies and countries.[45]

Later theorists about imperialism, though, challenged the view that imperialism might promote development. Rather, they argued, Third World countries were coerced into a dependent position within the global economy as producers and exporters of primary products and importers of Western manufactures. This prevented them from industrializing, kept their national incomes at poverty levels, and stifled the development of entrepreneurial and labor skills among their population. Consequently the capitalist development of the "core" depended on the imperialist exploitation of the "periphery." Andre Gundar Frank states this theory directly and forcefully:

My thesis is that these capitalist contradictions and the historical development of the capitalist system have generated underdevelopment in the peripherial satellites whose economic surplus was expropriated, while generating economic development in the metropolitan centers which appropriate that surplus.[46]

Dependency theory, then, developed these themes about the structural consequences of imperialism and the dominance of inequalitarian relations in the international economy to produce a broad model of underdevelopment in the Third World. Two primary emphases in the *dependencia* perspective may be distinguished. One is a "top-down" approach that assumes that the creation of the world capitalist economy provides the major explanation for developmental outcomes. Thus it traces the implications of this global system for economic relations among nations and for economic and social conditions within societies occupying different positions in what Immanuel Wallerstein calls "the modern world system.''[47] The other has more of a ''bottom-up'' focus and is perhaps best represented by the work of Fernando Henrique Cardoso. It describes the results of incorporation into the international system for particular dependent societies in rich historical detail, tracing out the evolution of economic structures, class relations, social change, and links with the industrial core.[48]

These two approaches can obviously be complementary—the first providing a broad theoretical framework and the second giving detailed historical analysis of how these processes operate in specific contexts and perhaps suggesting further elaborations of the general paradigm. Thus, although significant differences do exist among schools of dependency theorists, several central postulates can be discerned. Six of these are briefly sketched below: (1) the importance of incorporation into the global capitalist system, (2) the forces that make the world division of labor fairly permanent, (3) the exploitation that is inherent in the relation between the capitalist core and the imperialized periphery, (4) the economic distortions and underdevelopment that result from these linkages, (5) the effect of incorporation into the global economy on class relations in the periphery, and (6) the social and political consequences of this system.

A fundamental assumption of the dependency paradigm is that a country's or colony's future is essentially determined by its initial incorporation into the global economic order as either a producer and exporter of manufactured products or a producer and exporter of primary products (e.g., foodstuffs and raw materials). The former form the dynamic ''core'' of the world economy, while the latter become a stagnant and dependent ''periphery,'' with a few countries moving into an intermediate position of a ''semiperiphery'' that has some of the characteristics of both the two extreme positions.

The creation of the ''modern world system'' around a fundamental division of labor between core and periphery proceeded in three principal stages. The first in the ''long'' sixteenth century was based on the rise of a pluralistic system of nation-states in Europe whose competition allowed their economies to escape from stringent political controls. Once economic market forces were allowed to follow their own logic, the world began to move toward national and regional specialization based on the dominant form of production and labor control. In this division of labor some areas (e.g., Eastern Europe) became the providers of primary goods, while others specialized in manufactured goods and positioned themselves to be the leaders of the industrial revolution.[49]

This initial structuring of the world economy evolved through the two subsequent stages. The several waves of colonialism that the ''core'' European powers periodically engaged from the sixteenth through the early twentieth centuries brought much of the rest of the world into the global system and subjected the colonies to the direct manipulation of the metropoles. For example, Frances Moulder explains Japan's developmental success and China's failure by the latter's much stronger incorporation into the capitalist system and by the activities of a developmental state that the former's autonomy permitted.[50] Second, especially after World War II, leading corporations from the core began to establish subsidiaries throughout the developing world. These MNCs came to dominate many Third World economies, and their activities became a major influence on the economic performance of much of the developing world. Thus the MNCs came to be viewed by dependency theorists as assuming the central role in the global capitalist economy.[51]

The initial insertion of a country or colony into the world system was viewed as largely determining its long-term developmental potential because the division of labor between the industrial core and the agricultural and mining periphery was perpetuated by a series of economic and political processes. If industrialization and development are seen as being highly desirable, as they are by both developmentalists and *dependencistas*, then countries with power resources would certainly be expected to use them to try to monopolize the benefits of industrialization. The core, almost by definition, could use its industry and technology to expand its military power; the subjugation and manipulation of colonial economies for the benefit of the imperialist power was just an extreme example of this logic of political power.

The emphasis of dependency theory, however, is much less on the vagaries of power politics than on the inexorable logic of capitalist markets, implying that the perpetuation of core or periphery status should result primarily from economic forces. First, the very fact that the core nations specialized in industrial goods meant that capital and new technology were concentrated in them; so that these countries possessed an ever increasing advantage for further development. The industrial revolution then produced a tremendous concentration of production and population both within and among societies. For example, even conventional economic historians date the industrial revolution as the beginning of vastly increasing international differentiation among countries in terms of income levels, production structures, and living standards.[52]

This tendency toward a concentration of industrial production and technological innovation in the core was greatly exacerbated, according to dependency theory, by the variety of inequalitarian mechanisms that link the periphery to the core. The very fact of economic dependency made the periphery vulnerable to the pressures of economic and political actors in the core and ensured that economic outcomes in the Third World were primarily the result of decisions made in the advanced industrial nations. The spread of multinational corporations denied potential peripheral economic elites the chance to develop entrepreneurial talents and meant that decisions about the worldwide location of production facilities remained in the core. Thus the end of colonial domination did not lead to economic nationalism and industrial development in the Third World, as predicted by the developmentalists. Rather, the fundamental division between core and periphery was perpetuated by ''neocolonial'' relations.[53]

Dependency theorists further argue that this division of labor is highly exploitative of the periphery in a manner that goes far beyond the generally acknowledged ''extraction of surplus'' by colonial powers and that it involves the essential functioning of international markets. First, the dependent position of the periphery means that it is a "taker" of world market prices whose terms of trade are forced downward by simple bargaining power. Second, *dependencistas* (as well as the ECLA school) believe that primary products suffer special disadvantages on the world market in terms of cyclical price instability and of declining real value in relation to manufactured goods. The price volatility of many primary products is undeniable (as American farmers can sadly attest), although long-term historical studies indicate that the trend of relative prices for primary and industrial goods has reversed itself several times.[54] More broadly, there is also Arrighi Emmanuel's argument that trade between the high-wage core and low-wage periphery constitutes "unequal exchange" in itself because surplus is extracted from the exploitatively low wages.[55]

Much of the emphasis on the "pillage of the Third World,"[56] at least in recent decades, falls on the activities of MNCs in the developing areas. Dependency theorists challenge the developmentalist assumption that foreign investment brings in capital and resources to developing societies. Rather, they argue that much of the MNCs' "risk capital" is raised locally. Consequently the activities of foreign firms can actually lead to a net outflow of capital, or exploitation, through such practices as the remittance of profits abroad, weighting the "transfer pricing" of their products and particularly technology against the periphery (e.g., charging Third World subsidiaries exorbitant prices for "new" technology), and monopolizing profitable economic sectors, thereby preventing the local accumulation of capital.[57]

The ill effects of this system of dependency go far beyond a specialization in primary production or exploitative economic relations with the core. In addition, the condition of dependency on the core brings substantial "distortions" and "disarticulation" in peripheral economies. First, production for international markets (whether tin mines, sugar plantations, or low-wage "processing" assembly) generally forms "enclaves" that are linked to foreign markets or supplies but are almost totally cut off from linkages to the domestic market. Thus expansion in these foreign-linked "enclaves" does not produce the "multiplier effect" normally associated with economic activities. Any benefits that might accrue from development, such as capital accumulation or increased wages, are limited to the enclave, while the bulk of the society remains impoverished and unaffected.[58]

A second major distortion is that there is either little technology transfer to the developing country, which inhibits its further development, or MNCs introduce "inappropriate technology." That is, MNCs replicate their production processes in the First World by importing capital-intensive technology into the periphery, where there is abundant labor, thereby creating a small "labor aristocracy," exacerbating unemployment problems, and increasing socioeconomic inequality. The penetration of MNCs into dependent economies, moreover, retards the development of local business and entrepreneurial talents in several ways. The MNCs preempt the most dynamic industries; they tend to use external suppliers; and their activities create capital outflows. Thus foreign capital prevents the development of an indigenous business class and gravely hinders local capital formation.[59]

Another important distortion occurs in the agricultural sector, where production for export creates pressures for concentrated and repressive land tenure systems based on the exploitation of a landless peasantry (e.g., the imposition of the "second serfdom" in Poland at the end of the sixteenth century or the expansion of cash-crop agriculture in contemporary Brazil).[60] Thus international market forces reinforce, instead of overcome, feudal patterns of land tenure and agricultural production. Finally, because of the absence of industrialization that results from all these distortions, there is little development of human capital through either educational programs or participation in skilled labor.[61]

Dependency theory also argues that the economy cannot simply be viewed as an isolated and autonomous subsystem of social action. Rather, economic forces create a specific class structure within a society, and the dominant classes use their power to control the polity and to ensure that their economic position is safeguarded. Traditional Marxist analysis views the development of class structure as deriving from control over the domestic means of production in any society. The dynamic of the historical dialectic comes from the growing contradiction between the technological potential for expanding production and social welfare inherent in the "means of production" and the political and social "relations of production" that act to prevent further development that would undermine the vested interests of contemporary economic elites. Revolution results when this contradiction becomes too great.[62]

Dependency analysis builds on this orthodox Marxist perspective by arguing that class relations and alliances have become international in character. In particular, the capitalist class in the core forms an alliance with elites in the periphery, such as compradors and large agricultural landowners, who act as "bridgeheads" in furthering the economic interests of the core. In turn, the economic and military support of the core allows these elites to maintain power and prevent the industrialization of their countries, which would send them to the "dustbin of history" by creating new modes of production and emergent classes (e.g., the bourgeoisie, workers, and the intelligentsia) who would challenge their hegemony. The purely economic mechanisms of exploitation and distortion, therefore, are strongly supplemented by the class effects of dependency, since change to the system is opposed by a dominant internal class whose external support from the core negates the normal revolutionary potential of dialectical contradictions.[63]

This class dominance results in a society in which there are a very few indigenous beneficiaries of the economic system coupled with the impoverishment of the huge mass of the population. Thus, unlike the Western model of development, in which growing mass demand was a driving factor, expansion of demand in dependent societies is generally limited to the demand of elites for luxury products that must be imported from the core.[64] The resultant growing inequality and social upheaval also creates a strong push toward authoritarian

Figure 2.2
The Classic Dependency Model*

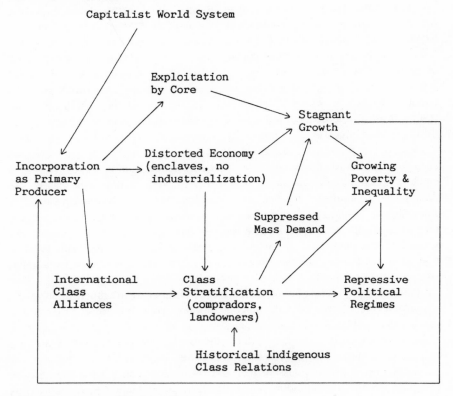

*All relations are assumed to be positive.

forms of government to control the incipient political instability and preserve the "distorted and disarticulated" social order, especially at times when economic change (e.g., industrial deepening or export expansion) threatens social interests or requires large capital stocks.[65]

This model of "classic dependency," therefore, portrays dependent societies and their economies as supine and stagnant. The development of the core is predicted on the underdevelopment of the periphery. Figure 2.2 sketches these relations. Note that they are all assumed to be positive, so that the signs are omitted by the arrows. Thus this model is more deterministic than developmental. Part of this determinism comes from the *dependencia* assumption that the nature of the international system is the principal driving force that determines developmental outcomes around the world (in contrast to the developmentalists, who see the international system as playing a secondary facilitative role). Once a country assumes a place in the global division of labor, its long-term developmental potential is essentially established. For the peripheral nations, their initial place as producers of raw materials leads directly to exploitation by the core, distorted economic structures, and class stratification. These, in turn, combine to produce stagnant growth, growing inequality, and political repression, which prevent any change of status within the global capitalist economy, as indicated by the feedback loop from stagnant growth to international production role.

Despite the permanency that might be implied by the operations of the world system and of these internal feedback loops, substantial growth and industrial transformation did occur in a number of developing countries such as Brazil, Mexico, South Korea, and Taiwan, in the 1960s and 1970s. This "anomaly" led several *dependencia* theorists, such as Fernando Henrique Cardoso and Peter Evans, to construct a theory of "dependent development." In essence, they argued that this development was explicable in terms of the workings of the global capitalist system, and moreover, it still represented dependent and distorted economic and social structures within the periphery.

Industrialization in the Third World was seen as dependent for several reasons. First, MNCs dominated the leading industrial and export sectors; the local business sector was much weaker economically and politically than had been the case in the more autonomous Western pattern of growth. Second, an "internationalization" of the domestic market occurred, in the sense that many capital goods, intermediate products, and even industrial raw materials had to be imported. Thus industrialization in the periphery brought a deepened dependency on foreign capital and trade.

The industrialization that did occur, moreover, continued the distorted peripheral economy, albeit in a somewhat different form. The dual economy continued, in that only a relatively small part of the society and economy was incorporated into the "modern" industrial and urban sector. The manufacturing production that was transferred to the periphery, in addition, was at the bottom of the product cycle (i.e., the most standardized and least technologically advanced production). Industrialization also spawned a growing "informal sector" of small businessmen and temporary workers whose livelihoods depended on whether the business cycle was up or down. Consequently dependent development had little effect on the extreme poverty and inequality in these societies; no linkage was established between industrialization and a growing domestic mass market.

The causes of dependent development, in turn, were attributed to the evolution of the capitalist world economy. Expanding organizational capabilities within MNCs allowed them to move production overseas and take advantage of the logic of the product cycle. The periphery also benefited from two types of competition within the core in the post–World War II era. First, growing competition among the MNCs themselves increased the pressures to produce in the periphery; in addition, a growing divergence of interest between the MNCs and their home governments meant that the Great Powers in the core became less wont to use their politico-military power to support MNC interests in the periphery (e.g., American's greatly declining recourse to the Hickenlooper amend-

Figure 2.3
Dependent Development Model: Changes from Classic Dependency

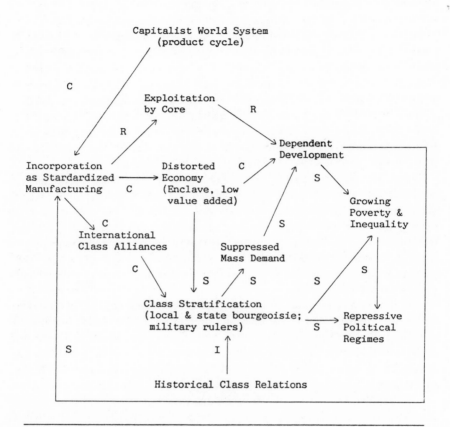

S, similar impact to classic dependence; C, changed nature of impact from classic dependence; R, reduced impact compared with classic dependence; I, increased impact compared with classic dependence.

ment). Finally, dependent development was conditioned by the expanding power of the state in the periphery, which was seen as playing an essential role in bargaining with foreign capital, in creating an interlocking "triple alliance" between foreign, local, and state enterprise, and in applying coercion to control the large segments of the populations excluded from the modern sector.[66]

Figure 2.3 summarizes the central assumptions in the theory of dependent development by indicating how they differ from the processes assumed by the model of "classic development." The operations of the capitalist world system are still viewed as the primary driving force, but now the operation of the product cycle is viewed as permitting standardized production in parts of the periphery. This manufacturing is associated with a reduction of direct exploitation by the core, but it still produces economic distortions and a skewed class stratification (albeit in changed forms), which contribute to impoverishment, inequality, and repression. Thus dependent development constitutes a new historical form of dependency, rather than being a negation of the basic processes posited by dependency theory. However, this strand of dependency theory is not as deterministic as classic dependency, since the question is raised of why dependent development occurs in some societies but not others.

Dependency theory, therefore, constitutes a direct challenge to the basic premises of developmentalism. *Dependencistas* assume that a permanent world capitalist economy determines developmental outcomes throughout the world. The Third World is viewed as being dependent on and exploited by the industrialized European and North American core. The emphasis of developmentalism on neoclassic economics and modern values, such as the spirit of enterprise, for explaining development in the West is viewed as spurious. Rather, the West developed by "extracting surplus" from the periphery. The stress of dependency theory, then, is on how capitalist economics and the class relations that derive from them serve to "disarticulate" and "underdevelop" Third World societies and economies. Quite a few of the more specific conclusions of the developmental perspective are questioned as well. For example, the dependency approach argues that MNCs *de*capitalize the Third World, that the international product cycle perpetuates "unequal exchange," and that social and political unrest in rapidly industrializing societies is caused by economic class conflict, not the breakdown of the traditional social order.

The Statist Approach

In contrast to the developmentalist and dependency paradigms, the statist approach is much more of an enumeration of factors that affect developmental outcomes than an integrated set of theoretical formulations about causal relations among economic, social, and political factors. The series of spectacular growth records that were recorded in East Asia provided a major impetus for "bringing the state back in."[67] All the successful East Asian countries (Japan, the four "little dragons," and the P.R.C.) were marked by strong states committed to developmentalist policies, and all shared a Confucian culture that, among other things, included respect and veneration for political authorities.[68]

The keystone of the statist approach, though, is probably Alexander Gerschenkron's earlier economic history comparing "early" and "late" developers, primarily in Europe (e.g., Great Britain versus Germany and, more extremely, Russia). Gerschenkron argued that the state generally had to play a much stronger role in late-developing (e.g., the East Asian nations), as opposed to early-developing, countries. The "catch-up" nature of industrialization in the late

developers required rapid massive accumulations of capital for infrastructure and
"new" industries (i.e., steel) that were simply beyond the capabilities of private
entrepreneurs in poorer economies. More broadly, state ideological commitment
and industrial strategy appeared necessary to push backward economies toward
industrialization.[69]

This perspective can also be traced to a broader intellectual tradition of giving
the state an independent role in historical theories about social change. The work
of Charles Tilly furnishes perhaps the best example of this approach. Tilly
conceptualizes the state in modern history as being strongly affected by the
evolution of capitalism and social class relations. However, he also views the
rise of the centralized nation-state as having its own dynamics associated with
war-making and the concomitant necessity of extracting resources from subject
populations. Thus "state-making" is an important phenomenon in itself that is
grounded in the political, social, and economic realities of individual nations;
differences among states should lead to significant differences in policies and
socioeconomic outcomes. In addition, the mobilization of the population for
military purposes ultimately sets off pressures for political participation.[70]

This approach is also reflected in several other historical and sociological
theories that conceive the state as being both linked with the social structure and
constituting a national institution with significant autonomy and variability. Barrington Moore, for instance, traces differences in current political regimes to the
historical development of class structure in their societies in what he calls the
"social origins of dictatorship and democracy."[71] Theda Skocpol argues that
the nature, especially the strength, of the state is a central determinant of the
success of "social revolutions" that produce a dramatic transformation in social
and political structures.[72]

More directly connected to the subject of development, Ellen Trimberger
analyzed "revolutions from above" in which states dominated by military leaders
and bureaucrats implemented broad-based industrialization programs. She attributed these industrialization projects to a combination of nationalism in specific
peripheral societies and weaknesses in the global capitalist system, but she also
reached the pessimistic conclusion that the results of these revolutions from
above produced the limitations and distortions of what had been termed "dependent development" here.[73] Thus these broader historical and sociological
theories assume that domestic and, in some cases, international class relations
provide a central explanation for social and economic change. However, they
also view the state as an autonomous structure that can have a strong independent
effect on economic and social outcomes.

This emphasis on the state as a key promoter of economic development,
therefore, reversed the general neglect of the state by both the developmentalist
and dependency perspectives. The former's reliance on neoclassic economics
led it to view the state as a potential source of interference in and disruption of
the developmental processes. *Dependencistas*, for their part, assumed that the
state was simply the handyman of the dominant economic classes in a society

and, thus, had little independent impact on economic or social policies.[74] The statist perspective, then, represents an attempt to bring "politics" into a more central place in the study of political economy, which has been dominated by the two very different types of economic determinism associated with its competing principal paradigms.

The new attention devoted to the state's role in the developmental processes, however, does not totally reverse developmentalism and *dependencia*. In fact, precursors of the statist perspective can be discerned within each tradition. Thus many developmentalists now believe that the state should aggressively promote development through providing basic infrastructure, manipulating taxes and subsidies to give incentives for industrialization, and both enticing and regulating foreign capital.[75] Even significant public involvement in direct production through state entrepreneurship is now viewed as normal in the developing world.[76] More broadly, a variety of scholars interested in both development and international relations have concluded that differences in state strength and policy among less developed countries are important for bargaining with stronger countries and for influencing economic growth and success.[77]

Studies of the foreign economic policies of industrialized nations have also placed more emphasis on the ability of states to promote the national interest through their policy initiatives and bargaining strategies. The international economy over the 1970s and 1980s was marked by America's declining ability and willingness to enforce global free trade policies as its economic hegemony eroded and by the burgeoning technological and transportation revolutions that made comparative advantage increasingly "arbitrary," in the sense that many countries could potentially produce a wide range of manufactured products profitably. Consequently nations' domestic macroeconomic and industrial policies began to affect their economic structures to a considerable extent, and international trade became increasingly "managed," in the sense that what a country produced and traded was determined by bilateral bargaining among nations.[78] In such conditions "strong states" in the industrial world were able to achieve more favorable economic outcomes.[79] For example, John Zysman has argued that national "adjustment" strategies in the face of the economic upheavals of the past two decades have been largely conditioned by the financial systems in various countries because they structure the state's capacity to affect economic policy and corporate strategies.[80]

The theory of dependent development, with its conclusion that the state assumes a central role in the "triple alliance," also pointed the way toward the conceptualization of a more activist and autonomous state within the dependency framework. This is consistent, furthermore, with Wallerstein's conclusion that the core is marked by strong states and the periphery by weak ones.[81] Peter Evans, in particular, has extended his theory of dependent development to credit the state and its economic managers with more independence in creating and implementing developmental strategies as a result of historical changes in the global economy and polity that have promoted economic nationalism in the periphery, increased the bargaining power of at least some parts of the periphery vis-a-vis the core, and granted the state some autonomy in relation to dominant economic classes within developing societies.[82] Thus, as exemplified by the theoretical work of Raymond Duvall and John Freeman, dependency theory has been expanded to see the state's "technobureaucracy" as forming an independent class who uses its governmental power to promote industrialization and capital accumulation in the periphery, albeit in a form responsive to its own material interests.[83]

This line of argument is taken further in David Becker's neo-Marxist critique of dependency theory based on a case study of Peru. Becker concludes that the neocolonialism described by dependency theory was a transitory stage of capitalism that has been replaced by a new system in which a global division of accumulation operates to move production into the periphery. Within the developing world domestic sources of class relations and political structures have become much more important. In particular, the dominant class in industrializing Third World countries has become a "corporate national bourgeoisie" that combines nationalist and developmentalist beliefs with a commitment to international capitalism and internationalist norms of technology and management. Despite the rise of the corporate national bourgeoisie, the state still exercises "relative autonomy" both in mediating corporatist compromises between capital and labor and in bargaining with foreign capital to ensure that it contributes to national development.[84]

Some scholars within both the dependency and developmentalist paradigms do believe that the state can assume an important role in promoting economic development. As might be expected, though, these perspectives differ considerably about what the state does or should do. Developmentalists believe that the state should essentially act to reinforce capitalism by providing investment in infrastructure and industry that is generally not forthcoming from the private sector (but that stimulates private business) and by using its powers to aid the rise of business classes as opposed to more traditional elites. Dependencia, in contrast, sees the state's role as a nationalist response to the inequities of global capitalism but also argues that even state-led capitalist development is inherently dependent and distorted.

The statist perspective goes beyond this to combine creatively strands of both paradigms in terms of their views about the role of the state in development. Bruce Cumings' theory of the "bureaucratic-authoritarian industrializing regime" (BAIR) is a major example of such an approach. BAIRs can play a key role in development by using their autonomy from domestic interests to implement optimum industrialization strategies that are made possible by the operation of the international product cycle, such as the case of Japan and the Asian newly industrializing countries, which absorb the declining industries for which the more advanced Japan is losing its comparative advantage.[85] Extending Cumings' work, one might also explain the appearance of BAIRs in the North Asian political economy, rather than elsewhere in the Third World, by the nature of the dominant Confucian culture there, with its special values that affect regime-society relations.[86]

Stephen Haggard provides another excellent example of this perspective in his essay on the positive role that the state in developing nations can assume in stimulating economic growth and transformations. He argues that state-guided developmental policies can (and have) been used to promote economic changes consistent with international comparative advantage, rather than to distort market forces in some politically desired direction, as is normally assumed to be the case by most developmentalists. This requires that the state be able to control and suppress interest groups from both "dominant" and "subordinant" classes that are seen as distorting development by, respectively, *dependencistas* and advocates of "political institutionalization." Also of interest is Haggard's provocative argument that domestically determined development strategies structure the nature of external dependency rather than vice versa—which stands a central dimension of dependency theory "on its head." This approach, therefore, turns analytic attention to the internal and external factors that help to create a developmentalist state, in particular the nature of the governing coalition that controls a specific state and how its participants' interests and abilities promote or retard development.[87]

Still, the statist perspective is more an argument to incorporate the role of the state into developmental models than a full-fledged paradigm presenting an integrated set of causal propositions. Thus the criticism of Greenberg and Page appears well taken:

Perhaps what is most distressing about it is the failure to go beyond the admonition to "bring the state back in" and to take state institutions and actors seriously. Left there, such an admonition is merely trivial, being both obvious and without theoretical direction. Such an admonition gives us no guidance about how much weight to give the state—or to what components of it—under various circumstances.[88]

This suggests that the statist perspective must do far more than simply link industrialization in some peripheral societies to the existence of a strong developmentalist state. After all, not all strong states pursue industrialization projects, and not all developmental policies prove effective. As John Ruggie has aptly noted, there is equal danger in assuming that development is solely a function of "the magic of the marketplace, the immutable international hierarchy, or the omnipotent state."[89]

Thus a recent edited volume on "state and development" found a series of caveats about the nascent statist approach. First, the reasons why strong states have developed in some peripheral societies but not in others remain murky, so that a key factor in the statist model remains inexplicable. Moreover, states that are highly autonomous domestically may be quite dependent internationally (for example, Taiwan). Second, there is certainly no guarantee that a strong state will have a developmentalist orientation (e.g., the Philippines under Marcos).

Figure 2.4
An Implied Statist Model

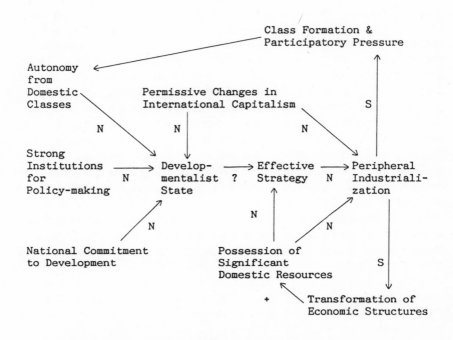

N, necessary condition; S, sufficient condition; ?, effect problematic; -, negative relation; +, positive relation.

Third, the efficacy of developmental strategies is by no means predetermined. For example, pursuit of heavy industrialization through import substitution in Latin America and Algeria was much less successful than the East Asian strategy of export-led growth; even in such East Asian countries as Malaysia and Korea several economic programs were clearly ill chosen. Finally, there is a paradox in regime-society relations in that the socioeconomic changes initiated by state-led development may ultimately undercut the strength and autonomy of these states. Thus state autonomy, administrative capacity, and policy effectiveness do not necessarily form a cohesive or stable syndrome.[90]

These caveats suggest the very preliminary or "implied" model presented in Figure 2.4. Unlike the more fully developed paradigms described in the previous two sections, it does not seem possible yet to specify a complex causal model for the statist perspective. Thus Figure 2.4 lists sets of conditions that appear to be necessary prerequisites for the emergence of a developmental state and successful peripheral industrialization, and two presumed major consequences of such an industrialization program.

The central driving force behind state-led development is, by definition, the existence of a capable developmentalist state. The various theoretical traditions summarized above imply that there are four necessary conditions for its emergence, all of which must be present. First, state structures must be "strong," in the sense that they are capable of formulating and implementing policy. Such strength in the periphery is usually associated with either a long history of bureaucratic institutions, such as in Confucian societies, or a colonial empire that had the grace to leave a trained indigenous bureaucracy and military establishment. This prerequisite of a strong state is not necessarily compatible with the second condition, that the state be fairly autonomous from domestic pressures. For example, strong states in countries with long histories of high civilization and bureaucratic rule will probably be constrained by a well-entrenched class structure, and the autonomy of rulers will probably be the greatest in amorphous postcolonial regimes and societies in which state capabilities are quite weak. The third precondition is change in the political and economic nature of the international capitalist system, which allows peripheral nations to become more assertive. Finally, even if these three necessary conditions exist, the state and its leaders must also have a strong commitment to promoting development and industrial transformation.

The next link is between the developmentalist state and a successful industrialization project. The creation of an effective economic strategy is viewed as a central intervening variable between the developmental state and peripheral industrialization. The question mark denoting the influence of the developmental state on strategy shows that, as noted above, not all strategies are necessarily well conceived. As Steve Chan has argued, "statecraft" or the application of effective policy is still a neglected dimension of the statist perspective.[91] The ability of a developmental state to even formulate an effective strategy, though, depends on the possession of significant domestic resources that can be used to stimulate industrialization, such as a skilled but low-cost labor force, natural resource wealth, and a large domestic market. Domestic resources, effective strategy, and changed international conditions, then, are all seen as necessary prerequisites for industrialization in the Third World context.

Another key component of policy effectiveness is that the state's economic strategy must actually affect economic outcomes—which is by no means assured. For example, Japan is generally viewed as one of the most successful illustrations of state-led development. Yet David Friedman convincingly contends that state policies to centralize production in a number of key sectors (e.g., machine tools and automobiles) largely failed, and that Japan's rapid growth resulted, to a goodly extent, from the alternative industrial structures that evolved and that allowed Japan to establish a competitive advantage in "flexible production" rather than "mass production."[92]

Finally, industrialization in the periphery has consequences that feed back into earlier stages in the model. On the one hand, industrialization increases productive capabilities and usually helps to increase human capital, thus augmenting the available domestic resources. On the other hand, it promotes new class formation (i.e., the national corporate bourgeoisie) and spurs participatory norms as part of "modernization." These processes, in turn, almost inevitably undermine state autonomy. Thus this preliminary statist model suggests that the continuation of peripheral industrialization is determined by the balance between antithetical processes.

Implications

The intellectual history of development studies seems to fit Thomas Kuhn's theory of "the structure of scientific revolutions" quite well. Paradigms were constructed to provide answers to "acute" research problems. Anomalies arose when a previous paradigm did not work when applied to a situation that a community of scholars believed to constitute a significant research question. When such a "scientific crisis" occurred, the assumptions of the old paradigm were first questioned and then, ultimately, a new way of looking at developmental phenomena emerged that provided acceptable answers to the fundamental and acute research problems.

The developmentalist paradigm was based on the research problem of explaining economic growth and transformation in the West and assumed that the experience of the leaders of the industrial revolution provided a universal model of development. After examining Western history its advocates concluded that laissez-faire economics form the primary stimulus for economic growth conditioned by a proper social and political context. When the Western model did not seemingly apply to the postcolonial world, a new paradigm rose to challenge the conventional conclusions. Dependency theory encompassed all three changes associated with a paradigmatic revolution. First, it flatly contradicted several important developmentalist assumptions, such as MNC contribution to net capital flows going into and out of dependent economies and the link between rapid growth and social unrest. Second, it argued that a new factor, class structure and relations, is essential to the analysis of development. Third, and most broadly, it provided a more generalized framework for analyzing developmental phenomena. The factors basic to developmentalism were trivial, according to the *dependencistas*, because what happened within the core could only be understood in terms of the total world capitalist system. That is, the development of the core was a function of the underdevelopment of the periphery.

At a broader theoretical level, developmentalism is concerned with micro behavioral phenomena within societies, whereas *dependencistas* argue that macro structural factors linking societies together are the key determinants of developmental potential. The statist approach began at an intermediate level of structural analysis with the argument that the role of the state was an important structural feature that varied among developing societies and explained differences in developmental success. The various caveats raised about the statist perspective, though, suggest a need to look at both micro behavioral and macro structural factors for explaining the composition, orientations, and statecraft of particular Third World states.

The East Asian economic miracles of the past few decades present challenges to both original paradigms, although many of their adherents are rather loath to admit so. Developmentalists point to East Asia as successful market-based growth, while overlooking the role of the state and the effects of Confucian culture, which depart markedly from the Western model.[93] Dependency theorists argue that East Asia is simply an example of dependent development and upward mobility from the periphery to the semiperiphery, while generally ignoring the substantial social and economic differences between industrialization in Asia and Latin America.[94] East Asia, hence, would seem to constitute an anomaly that cannot be comfortably explained by either paradigm. A new factor, the role of the state, seems quite important, and several important "universal" conclusions by both dependency and developmentalist analysis appear limited in time or geographic space.

Moreover, Taiwan's good performance on all the dimensions of development noted in chapter 1 is anomalous in itself, since all three paradigms imply that at least some of these dimensions are unattainable or incompatible. This is clearest for dependency theory, which is skeptical about the possibility for either political or economic development in the Third World. Yet many developmentalists implicitly assume that social development in the form of income inequality and the popular standard of living should be suppressed to promote economic efficiency by way of laissez-faire economics, and that institutionalization and democratization are incompatible forms of political development. The latter view is also shared by the statist assumption that an autonomous state, not the free market, provides the basic dynamic of economic growth. Unfortunately there is no paradigm as yet that satisfactorily explains the East Asian miracle. Still, applying the East Asian experience to extant theories might well be valuable in a field where none of the major frameworks appears totally satisfactory.

Notes

1. Vicky Randall and Robin Theobald, *Political Change and Underdevelopment: A Critical Introduction to Third World Politics* (Durham, N.C.: Duke University Press, 1985), provides a good overview of the dependency and developmentalist approaches.

2. Thomas S. Kuhn, *The Structure of Scientific Revolutions*, 2nd ed. (Chicago: University of Chicago Press, 1970).

3. Ibid.

4. Ibid., pp. 68–69.

5. Ibid., chs. 5–10.

6. Simon Kuznets, *Modern Economic Growth: Rate, Structure, and Spread* (New Haven, Conn.: Yale University Press, 1966), p. 1.

7. Hollis Chenery, *Structural Change and Development Policy* (New York: Oxford University Press, 1979); Everett E. Hagen, *The Economics of Development*, rev. ed. (Homewood, Ill.: Richard D. Irwin, 1975); Kuznets, *Modern Economic Growth*; and W. Arthur Lewis, *The Theory of Economic Growth* (Homewood, Ill.: Richard D. Irwin, 1955).

8. Hollis Chenery and Moises Syrquin, *Patterns of Development, 1950–1970* (New York: Oxford University Press, 1975). For a discussion of agricultural development see Bruce Johnston and Peter Kilby, *Agricultural and Structural Transformation* (New York: Oxford University Press, 1975); and John W. Mellor, *The Economics of Agricultural Development* (Ithaca, N.Y.: Cornell University Press, 1966).

9. Irma Adelman and Cynthia Taft Morris, *Economic Growth and Social Equity in Developing Countries* (Stanford, Calif.: Stanford University Press, 1973); Robert W. Jackman, *Politics and Social Equality: A Comparative Analysis* (New York: John Wiley, 1975).

10. Nathan Rosenberg and L. E. Birdzell, Jr., *How the West Grew Rich: The Economic Transformation of the Industrial World* (New York: Basic Books, 1986).

11. James M. Buchanan, *Liberty, Market, and the State: Political Economy in the 1980s* (New York: New York University Press, 1986); Milton Friedman, *Bright Promises, Dismal Performance: An Economist's Protest* (San Diego: Harcourt Brace Jovanovich,1983); Milton Friedman and Rose Friedman, *Free to Choose: A Personal Statement* (New York: Avon Books, 1981); and Ludwig von Mises, *Nation, State, and Economy: Contributions to the Politics and History of Our Time* (New York: New York University Press, 1983).

12. Alexander Gerschenkron, *Economic Backwardness in Historical Perspective: A Book of Essays* (Cambridge, Mass.: Harvard University Press, 1962).

13. Michael P. Todaro, *Economic Development in the Third World*, 3rd ed. (New York: Longman, 1985), ch. 12, provides a good discussion and critique of the theory of international comparative advantage.

14. Bela Balassa, *Change and Challenge in the World Economy* (New York: St. Martin's Press, 1985); Bela Balassa, *The Newly Industrializing Countries in the World Economy* (New York: Pergamon, 1981); and Hollis Chenery, *Structural Change*, pt. I.

15. Raymond Vernon, "International Investment and International Trade in the Product Cycle," *Quarterly Journal of Economics* 80:2 (May 1966), pp. 190–207.

16. Bruce Cumings, "The Origins and Development of the Northeast Asian Political Economy: Industrial Sectors, Product Cycles, and Political Consequences," *International Organization* 38:1 (Winter 1984), pp. 1–40.

17. Hagen, *Economics of Development*, pp. 213–215.

18. W. W. Rostow, *The Stages of Economic Growth: A Non-Communist Manifesto* (Cambridge: Cambridge University Press, 1960).

19. Max Weber, *The Protestant Ethic and the Spirit of Capitalism* (New York: Charles Scribner's Sons, 1958); and Max Weber, *The Religion of China: Confucianism and Taoism* (Glencoe, Ill.: Free Press, 1951).

20. Talcott Parsons, *The Social System* (New York: Free Press, 1964). See also George Gilder, *The Spirit of Enterprise* (New York: Simon & Schuster, 1984); Alex Inkeles, *Exploring Individual Modernity* (New York: Columbia University Press, 1983); and David McClelland, *The Achieving Society* (New York: Van Nostrand, 1961).

21. S. N. Eisenstadt, *Tradition, Change, and Modernity* (New York: John Wiley, 1973); George M. Foster, *Tzintzuntzan: Mexican Peasants in a Changing World* (Boston:

Little, Brown, 1967); and Oscar Lewis, *Five Families: Mexican Case Studies in the Culture of Poverty* (New York: Basic Books, 1975).

22. Polly Hill, *Development Economics on Trial: The Anthropological Case for a Prosecution* (Cambridge: Cambridge University Press, 1986).

23. Cyril E. Black, *The Dynamics of Modernization: Essays in Comparative History* (New York: Harper & Row, 1966); and Eisenstadt, *Tradition, Change, and Modernity.*

24. Daniel Lerner, *The Passing of Traditional Society: Modernizing the Middle East* (New York: Free Press, 1958).

25. S. N. Eisenstadt, *Modernization, Protest, and Change* (Englewood Cliffs, N.J.: Prentice-Hall, 1966).

26. Lucian W. Pye, *Aspects of Political Development* (Boston: Little, Brown, 1966), provides an excellent overview of the various definitions of this concept.

27. Gabriel Almond and G. Bingham Powell, Jr., *Comparative Politics: A Developmental Approach* (Boston: Little, Brown, 1966); Reinhard Bendix, *Nation-Building and Citizenship: Studies of Our Changing Social Order* (Berkeley: University of California Press, 1964); and Pye, *Aspects of Political Development*. Theodore J. Lowi, *The End of Liberalism: Ideology, Policy, and the Crisis of Public Authority* (New York: W. W. Norton, 1969), chs. 1 and 2, provides an excellent theoretical analysis of how democracy has served to "reform" capitalism.

28. Max Weber, *Theory of Social and Economic Organization* (New York: Oxford University Press, 1947).

29. Eisenstadt, *Modernization, Protest, and Change*. Charles Tilly, *Big Structures, Large Processes, Huge Comparisons* (New York: Russell Sage Foundation, 1984), chs. 1–3, provides an intellectual history and critique of this line of thinking.

30. Samuel P. Huntington, *Political Order in Changing Societies* (New Haven, Conn.: Yale University Press, 1968).

31. Mancur Olson, *The Rise and Decline of Nations: Economic Growth, Stagflation, and Social Rigidities* (New Haven, Conn.: Yale University Press, 1982).

32. Cumings, "Northeast Asian Political Economy"; Stephan Haggard, "The Newly Industrializing Countries in the International System," *World Politics* 38:2 (January 1986), pp. 343–370; Thomas B. Gold, *State and Society in the Taiwan Miracle* (Armonk, N.Y.: M. E. Sharpe, 1986); Clive Hamilton, "Capitalist Industrialization in East Asia's Four Little Tigers," *Journal of Contemporary Asia* 13:1 (No. 1, 1983), pp. 35–73; Roy Hofheinz, Jr., and Kent E. Calder, *The Eastasia Edge* (New York: Basic Books, 1982); and Chalmers A. Johnson, *MITI and the Japanese Miracle* (Stanford, Calif.: Stanford University Press, 1982).

33. Richard Rosecrance, *The Rise of the Trading State: Commerce and Conquest in the Modern World* (New York: Basic Books, 1986).

34. Robert O. Keohane and Joseph S. Nye, *Power and Interdependence: World Politics in Transition* (Boston: Little, Brown, 1977).

35. Robert Gilpin, *The Political Economy of International Relations* (Princeton, N.J.: Princeton University Press, 1987), pp. 72–92; Robert O. Keohane, "The Theory of Hegemonic Stability and Changes in International Economic Regimes, 1967–1977," in Ole R. Holsti, Randolph M. Siverson, and Alexander M. George, eds., *Change in the International System* (Boulder, Colo.: Westview Press, 1980), pp. 131—162; and Charles P. Kindleberger, "Dominance and Leadership in the International Economy: Exploitation, Public Goods, and Free Rides," *International Studies Quarterly* 25:2 (June 1981), pp. 242–254.

36. Cal Clark and Donna Bahry, "Dependent Development: A Socialist Variant," *International Studies Quarterly* 27:3 (September 1983), pp. 271–293; and Neil R. Richardson, *Foreign Policy and Economic Development* (Austin: University of Texas Press, 1978).

37. Steve Chan, "The Mouse That Roared: Taiwan's Management of Trade Relations with the U.S.," *Comparative Political Studies* 20:2 (July 1987), pp. 251–292; Richard L. Rothstein, *The Weak in the World of the Strong: The Developing Countries in the International System* (New York: Columbia University Press, 1977); and David B. Yoffie, *Power and Protectionism: Strategies of the Newly Industrializing Countries* (New York: Columbia University Press, 1983).

38. Thomas H. Moran, *Multinational Corporations and the Politics of Dependence: Copper in Chile* (Princeton, N.J.: Princeton University Press, 1974); and Raymond Vernon, *Storm Over the Multinationals: The Real Issues* (Cambridge, Mass.: Harvard University Press, 1977).

39. George Modelski, *Long Cycles in World Politics* (Seattle: University of Washington Press, 1986). This approach also seems quite compatible with the arguments about the decline of leading powers advanced by Paul Kennedy, *The Rise and Fall of the Great Powers: Economic Change and Military Conflict from 1500 to 2000* (New York: Random House, 1987).

40. Albert O. Hirschman, *National Power and the Structure of Foreign Trade* (Berkeley: University of California Press, 1945).

41. David A. Baldwin, *Economic Statecraft* (Princeton, N.J.: Princeton University Press, 1985).

42. Vinod Aggarwal, *Liberal Protectionism: The International Politics of Organized Textile Trade* (Berkeley: University of California Press, 1985); I. M. Destler, *American Trade Politics: System Under Stress* (New York: Twentieth Century Fund, 1986); and Yoffie, *Power and Protectionism*.

43. Raul Prebisch, *The Economic Development of Latin America and Its Principle Problems* (New York: Free Press, 1950). For other major expositions of this school of thought see Gunnar Myrdal, *Economic Theory and Underdeveloped Regions* (New York: Harper & Row, 1971); and Ragnar Nurkse, *Problems of Capital Formation in Underdeveloped Countries* (New York: Blackwell, 1953).

44. Stephen D. Krasner, *Structural Conflict: The Third World Against Global Liberalism* (Berkeley: University of California Press, 1985), gives a broader theoretical perspective of Third World resistance to a liberal international economic order.

45. V. I. Lenin, "Imperialism: The Highest Stage of Capitalism," in Henry M. Christman, ed., *Essential Works of Lenin* (New York: Bantam Books, 1966), pp. 178–270.

46. Andre Gundar Frank, *Capitalism and Underdevelopment in Latin America* (New York: Monthly Review Press, 1969), p. 3. See also Samir Amin, *Accumulation on a World Scale: A Critique of the Theory of Underdevelopment* (New York: Monthly Review Press, 1974); and Paul Baran, *The Political Economy of Growth* (New York: Monthly Review Press, 1968).

47. Immanuel Wallerstein, *The Modern World System I: Capitalist Agriculture and the Origins of the European World-Economy in the Sixteenth Century* (New York: Academic Press, 1974); Immanuel Wallerstein, *The Modern World System II: Mercantilism and the Consolidation of the European World Economy, 1600–1750* (New York: Academic Press, 1980); and Immanuel Wallerstein, *The Capitalist World Economy* (Cambridge: Cambridge University Press, 1979).

48. Fernando Hernique Cardoso and Enzo Faletto, *Dependency and Development in Latin America* (Berkeley: University of California Press, 1979).

49. Wallerstein, *Modern World System I*.

50. Frances V. Moulder, *Japan, China, and the Modern World Economy: Toward a Reinterpretation of East Asian Development ca. 1600 to ca. 1918* (Cambridge: Cambridge University Press, 1977). More broadly, see Benjamin J. Cohen, *The Question of Imperialism: The Political Economy of Dominance and Dependence* (New York: Basic Books, 1973).

51. Thomas J. Biersteker, *Distortion or Development? Contending Perspectives on the Multinational Corporation* (Cambridge, Mass.: MIT Press, 1978); and Volker Bornschier and Christopher Chase-Dunn, *Transnational Corporations and Underdevelopment* (New York: Praeger, 1985).

52. Paul Bairoch, *The Economic Development of the Third World Since 1900* (Berkeley: University of California Press, 1977); Paul Bairoch and Maurice Levy-Leboyer, eds., *Disparities in Economic Development Since the Industrial Revolution* (New York: Macmillan, 1981); and E. L. Jones, *The European Miracle: Environments, Economies, and Geopolitics in the History of Europe and Asia* (Cambridge: Cambridge University Press, 1981).

53. Amin, *Accumulation on a World Scale*; Frank, *Capitalism and Underdevelopment in Latin America*; Johan Galtung, "A Structural Theory of Imperialism," *Journal of Peace Research* 13:2 (No. 2, 1971), pp. 81–118; and Kwame Nkrumah, *Neo-Colonialism: The Last Stage of Imperialism* (New York: International Publishing Company, 1965).

54. Bairoch, *Economic Development of the Third World*, pp. 111–134.

55. Arrighi Emmanuel, *Unequal Exchange: A Study of the Imperialism of Trade* (New York: Monthly Review Press, 1972).

56. Pierre Jalle, *The Pillage of the Third World* (New York: Monthly Review Press, 1968).

57. Biersteker, *Distortion or Development?* ch. 1, provides an excellent overview of hypotheses concerning the deleterious effects of MNCs in developing societies.

58. Amin, *Accumulation on a World Scale*; Bornschier and Chase-Dunn, *Transnational Corporations and Underdevelopment*; Frank, *Capitalism and Underdevelopment in Latin America*; Galtung, "Structural Theory of Imperialism"; and Vincent Mahler, *Dependency Approaches to International Political Economy: A Cross-National Study* (New York: Columbia University Press, 1980).

59. Biersteker, *Distortion or Development?* ch. 1.

60. Alain de Janvry, *The Agrarian Question and Reformism in Latin America* (Baltimore: Johns Hopkins University Press, 1981); and Wallerstein, *The Modern World System I*.

61. Galtung, "Structural Theory of Imperialism."

62. For introductory summaries of Marxist theory see Karl Marx and Friedrich Engels, "The Manifesto of the Communist Party," in Robert C. Tucker, ed., *The Marx-Engels Reader*, 2nd ed. (New York: W. W. Norton, 1978), pp. 469–500; and Friedrich Engels, "Socialism: Utopian and Scientific," in Robert C. Tucker, ed., *The Marx-Engels Reader* (New York: W. W. Norton, 1978), pp. 681–717.

63. Frank, *Capitalism and Underdevelopment in Latin America*; Galtung, "Structural Theory of Imperialism"; James Petras, *Class Perspectives on Imperialism and Social Class in the Third World* (New York: Monthly Review Press, 1979); and Wallerstein, *The Capitalist World Economy*.

64. Mahler, *Dependency Approaches*, chs. 1–4, discusses dependency relations in terms of elite manipulation of dependent societies.

65. David Collier, ed., *The New Authoritarianism in Latin America* (Princeton, N.J.: Princeton University Press, 1979); and Guillermo O'Donnell, *Modernization and Bureaucratic Authoritarianism: Studies in South American Politics* (Berkeley: Institute of International Studies, University of California, 1973).

66. Bornschier and Chase-Dunn, *Transnational Corporations and Underdevelopment*; Fernando Henrique Cardoso, "Associated Dependent Development: Theoretical and Practical Implications," in Alfred Stepan, ed., *Authoritarian Brazil: Origins, Policy, and Future* (New Haven, Conn.: Yale University Press, 1973), pp. 149–172; and Peter Evans, *Dependent Development: The Alliance of Multinational, State, and Local Capital in Brazil* (Princeton, N.J.: Princeton University Press, 1979). Alejandro Portes and John Walton, *Labor, Class, and the International System* (New York: Academic Press, 1981), discuss the "informal sector" and its problems in some detail.

67. Peter B. Evans, Dietrich Rueschemeyer, and Theda Skocpol, eds., *Bringing the State Back In* (Cambridge: Cambridge University Press, 1985), represent the most comprehensive treatment of this subject, although their theoretical innovations do not appear directly stimulated by the East Asian experience.

68. Hofheinz and Calder, *The Eastasia Edge*; Johnson, *MITI and the Japanese Miracle*; and Jon Woronoff, *Asia's "Miracle" Economies* (Armonk, N.Y.: M. E. Sharpe, 1986).

69. Gerschenkron, *Economic Backwardness*, especially ch. 1.

70. Tilly, *Big Structures*; Charles Tilly, *From Mobilization to Revolution* (New York: Random House, 1978); and Charles Tilly, ed., *The Formation of National States in Western Europe* (Princeton, N.J.: Princeton University Press, 1975).

71. Barrington Moore, Jr., *Social Origins of Dictatorship and Democracy: Lord and Peasant in the Making of the Modern World* (Boston: Beacon Press, 1966).

72. Theda Skocpol, *States and Social Revolutions* (Cambridge: Cambridge University Press, 1979).

73. Ellen Kay Trimberger, *Revolution from Above: Military Bureaucrats and Development in Japan, Turkey, Egypt, and Peru* (New Brunswick, N.J.: Transaction Books, 1978).

74. Tony Smith, "Requium or a New Agenda for Third World Studies?" *World Politics* 37:4 (July 1985), pp. 532–561.

75. For a current representative treatment of the state's role in economic development see Edward G. Stockwell and Karen Laidlaw, *Third World Development: Problems and Prospects* (Chicago: Nelson-Hall, 1981).

76. Malcolm Gillis, "The Role of State Enterprises in Economic Development," *Social Research* 47:2 (Summer 1980), pp. 248–289; Leroy P. Jones, ed., *Public Enterprise in Less-Developed Countries* (New York: Cambridge University Press, 1982); and William G. Shepherd, ed., *Public Enterprise: Economic Analysis of Theory and Practice* (Lexington, Mass.: D. C. Heath, 1976).

77. Haggard, "Newly Industrializing Countries"; Rothstein, *The Weak in the World of the Strong*; John Gerard Ruggie, "Introduction: International Interdependence and the National Welfare," in John Gerard Ruggie, ed., *Antinomies of Interdependence: National Welfare and the International Division of Labor* (New York: Columbia University Press, 1983) pp. 1–39; Tony Smith, *Patterns of Imperialism: The United States, Great Britain, and the Late-Industrializing World Since 1815* (Cambridge: Cambridge University Press,

1981); and Tony Smith, "The Underdevelopment of Development Literature: The Case of Dependency Theory," *World Politics* 31:2 (January 1979), pp. 247–288.

78. Gilpin, *Political Economy*, especially chs. 1, 3, and 5; and John Zysman, *Governments, Markets, and Growth: Financial Systems and the Politics of Industrial Change* (Ithaca, N.Y.: Cornell University Press, 1983), ch. 1.

79. Peter J. Katzenstein, ed., *Between Power and Plenty: Foreign Economic Policies of Advanced Industrial States* (Madison: University of Wisconsin Press, 1978); and Stephen D. Krasner, *Defending the National Interest: Raw Materials Investments and U.S. Foreign Policy* (Princeton, N.J.: Princeton University Press, 1978).

80. Zysman, *Governments, Markets, and Growth*.

81. Wallerstein, *The Capitalist World Economy*, ch. 5.

82. Peter Evans, "Transnational Linkages and the Economic Role of the State: An Analysis of Developing and Industrialized Nations in the Post-World War II Period," in Peter B. Evans, Dietrich Rueschemeyer, and Theda Skocpol, eds., *Bringing the State Back In* (Cambridge: Cambridge University Press, 1985), pp. 192–226; and Dietrich Rueschemeyer and Peter Evans, "The State and Economic Transformation: Toward an Analysis of the Conditions Underlying Effective Intervention," in Peter B. Evans, Dietrich Rueschemeyer, and Theda Skocpol, eds., *Bringing the State Back In* (Cambridge: Cambridge University Press, 1985), pp. 44–77.

83. Raymond D. Duvall and John R. Freeman, "The State and Dependent Capitalism," *International Studies Quarterly* 25:1 (March 1981), pp. 99–118; and Raymond D. Duvall and John R. Freeman, "The Techno-Bureaucratic Elite and the Entrepreneurial State in Dependent Industrialization," *American Political Science Review* 77:3 (September 1983), pp. 569–587.

84. David G. Becker, *The New Bourgeoisie and the Limits of Dependency: Mining, Class, and Power in "Revolutionary" Peru* (Princeton, N.J.: Princeton University Press, 1983).

85. Cumings, "Northeast Asian Political Economy."

86. John C. H. Fei, "Economic Development and Traditional Chinese Cultural Values," *Journal of Chinese Studies* 3:1 (April 1986), pp. 109–124; Hofheinz and Calder, *The Eastasia Edge*; and Lucian W. Pye, *Asian Power and Politics: The Cultural Dimensions of Authority* (Cambridge, Mass.: Harvard University Press, 1985).

87. Haggard, "Newly Industrializing Countries."

88. Edward S. Greenberg and Benjamin I. Page, "Why the State Does What It Does: A Nested Conceptual Model." Paper presented at the Conference on State Change, University of Colorado, May 25–27, 1988, p. 25.

89. Ruggie, "International Interdependence and National Welfare," p. 3.

90. Cal Clark and Jonathan Lemco, eds., *State and Development* (Leiden: Brill, 1988). The individual articles include Cal Clark and Jonathan Lemco, "The Strong State and Development: A Growing List of Caveats"; Jonathan Lemco, "Economic and Political Development in Modernizing States"; Philip Akre, "Industrialization in Algeria: The State and the Role of U.S. Capital, 1970–1980"; Steve Chan, "Developing Strength from Weakness: The State in Taiwan"; Alasdair Bowie, "Redistribution with Growth? The Dilemmas of State-sponsored Economic Development in Malaysia"; Chung-in Moon, "The Demise of a Developmentalist State? Neoconservative Reforms and Political Consequences in South Korea"; Jennifer McCoy, "The State and the Democratic Compromise in Venezuela"; and Cal Clark, "Dependency, Development, and Constituency Appeals as Determinants of State Entrepreneurship in Industrializing Nations: The Taiwan Case."

91. Steve Chan, "Developing Strength from Weakness: The State in Taiwan," in Cal Clark and Jonathan Lemco, eds., *State and Development* (Leiden: Brill, 1988), pp. 38–51. See also Davis B. Bobrow and Steve Chan, "Assets, Liabilities, and Strategic Conduct: Status Management by Japan, Taiwan, and South Korea," *Pacific Focus* 1:1 (Spring 1986), pp. 23–56; and Davis B. Bobrow and Steve Chan, "Understanding Anomalous Successes: Japan, Taiwan, and South Korea," in Charles F. Hermann, Charles W. Kegley, Jr., and James N. Rosenau, eds., *New Directions in the Comparative Study of Foreign Policy* (Boston: Allen & Unwin, 1987), pp. 111–130.

92. David Friedman, *The Misunderstood Miracle: Industrial Development and Political Change in Japan* (Ithaca, N.Y.: Cornell University Press, 1988).

93. See especially the interpretations of the East Asian model by Cumings, "Northeast Asian Political Economy"; and Haggard, "Newly Industrializing Countries."

94. This point is well made by Alice Amsden in regard to the state's role in economic development in Taiwan, although she is fairly sympathetic to several dimensions of dependency theory. Alice H. Amsden, "The State and Taiwan's Economic Development," in Peter B. Evans, Dietrich Rueschemeyer, and Theda Skocpol, eds., *Bringing the State Back In* (Cambridge: Cambridge University Press, 1985), pp. 78–104; and Alice H. Amsden, "Taiwan's Economic History: A Case of Etatism and a Challenge to Dependency Theory," *Modern China* 5:3 (July 1979), pp. 341–379. Richard E. Barrett and Martyn King Whyte, "Dependency Theory and Taiwan: Analysis of a Deviant Case," *American Journal of Sociology* 87:5 (March 1982), pp. 1064–1089, present a conventional interpretation.

CHAPTER 3

Historical Legacies

The Republic of China's (R.O.C.'s) transformation from a poor rural society to a dynamic industrial economy on Taiwan did not arise in a historical vacuum. This chapter provides a brief historical background of the primary factors that conditioned the economic and political development of the R.O.C. In particular, the "Taiwan miracle" resulted from a merging of two historical stories—one the social and economic development of Taiwan and the other the rollercoaster history of the Kuomintang party (KMT) that evacuated to Taiwan in 1949 after losing the civil war on the Chinese mainland. Both had positive and negative aspects. Although their short-term consequences did not look promising—which makes Taiwan's subsequent growth all the more remarkable—the traditions of the Kuomintang and the economic structures bequeathed by Chinese modernization in the late nineteenth century and by fifty years of Japanese colonialism ultimately created a political economy that was conducive to rapid growth and to continuing political and economic change.

More specifically, both the obvious advantages of prewar development on Taiwan and disadvantages of KMT failure on the mainland were intertwined with countervailing factors. While economic change before World War II laid a base for future growth and industrialization, much of the physical capital was destroyed during the war and regime-citizen relations were poisoned by repressive and rapacious administration during the late 1940s. Moreover, the realization after the war of the potential for development was far more automatic, and depended on the activities of both the population and the government. Conversely, although the abysmal defeat of the Republic on the mainland certainly did not auger well for the regime's setting off an "economic miracle," there were some potentially positive aspects as well. The government legitimized itself by a nationalistic modernizing ideology, and the economic and political chaos of the 1930s and 1940s provided a valuable learning experience if the regime were willing to reform. Thus the historical background contained both positive and negative portents; the key appeared to be whether the regime that evacuated to Taipei in 1949 was willing to apply the positive and avoid the negative.

The Historical Development of Taiwan

Taiwan itself is a large island located on the Tropic of Cancer. It is approximately 100 miles from the coast of Fukien (Fujian in Pin-yin)[1] Province in China, about halfway between Shanghai and Hong Kong, and about 700 miles south of Japan and 200 miles north of the Philippines. The R.O.C., in addition to the main island of Taiwan, currently encompasses several islands and groups of islands in the vicinity of Taiwan, most notably the Pescadores, and a few islands close to the Chinese mainland. None of these other territories has figured prominently in Taiwan's developmental history, although Quemoy and Matsu (two islands near the mainland) certainly rate more than a footnote in the postwar competition between the R.O.C. and the People's Republic of China (P.R.C.).

Figure 3.1 presents a relief map of Taiwan, including the major topographical features and largest cities. The island is oval-shaped, approximately 250 miles long and 100 miles wide at its broadest point. Most of the island is covered by mountains with peaks in the 10,000-to–13,000-foot range. Consequently only about a quarter of the land, mostly on the western plain, is arable. As a tropical island, it has a hot and humid climate with rainfall in many places averaging 100 inches per year. Thus it provides an excellent agricultural environment for the land that can be cultivated, although intensive farming over the centuries has generally depleted the land and necessitated increasing applications of fertilizers. Except for some significant deposits of coal, the island is generally poor in natural resource endowment. Because of the topography, the bulk of Taiwan's current population of 19.5 million is concentrated in cities on the western plain. The largest cities are the capital, Taipei, in the north at 2.5 million; the major southern port of Kaohsiung, which is approximately half that size; and Taichung and Tainan, with populations approaching 700,000.[2]

Although the first people in Taiwan were aborigines of Malay-Polynesian descent, the island has been primarily settled by Han Chinese, overwhelmingly from Fukien Province. Taiwanese of Fukien descent now constitute about two-thirds of the population (they were over 80 percent at the beginning of the century[3]) with about another 15 percent each being Hakka from Kwangtung (Guangdong) Province and ''mainlanders'' who came in the aftermath of 1949.[4]

The initial major Chinese settlement in the late sixteenth century was the result of growing commerce along China's Pacific coast. Unfortunately for the Chinese this commerce also brought more powerful outsiders to their shores. Portuguese merchants named Taiwan ''Ilha Formosa'' or ''Beautiful Island.'' More important, the Dutch East India Company established a permanent colony near what

Figure 3.1
Landforms of Taiwan

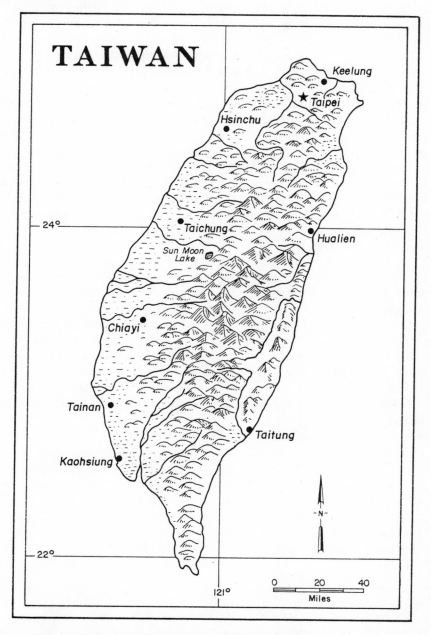

Source: Chaio-min Hsieh, ''The Physical Setting of Taiwan,'' in Paul K. T. Sih, ed., *Taiwan in Modern Times* (New York: St. John's University Press, 1973), p. 5.

is now Tainan in 1624; there were some shorter-lived Spanish settlements in the north as well. The Dutch used their new colony as a trading center and encouraged the immigration of Chinese to provide labor and expand the island's agricultural capabilities; the population approximately quadrupled from 25,000 to 100,000 between 1624 and 1650. Their treatment of the Chinese, though, was fairly harsh and exploitative; they provoked several uprisings among the Chinese.[5]

Events in China led to a change in Taiwan's status. The crumbling Ming dynasty had been ousted from Beijing in 1644 by Manchurians, who founded the Manchu, or Ch'ing dynasty. Resistance to the somewhat alien Manchus continued in southern China for several decades. One of the major Ming loyalists, Cheng Ch'eng-kung or Koxinga, decided to retake Taiwan from the Dutch to use as a Ming redoubt. He attacked the Dutch colonies in the summer of 1661 and after a long siege forced their surrender early in 1662. He died soon thereafter and is now regarded as a Chinese nationalist hero. He was succeeded by his son, who continued Ming control of Taiwan for another two decades. A traditional Chinese administration was established; immigration was encouraged for both agricultural expansion and military security; and total population tripled to between 250,000 and 300,000.[6]

The Ch'ing finally reconquered Taiwan in 1683 and incorporated it into their empire as a prefecture of Fukien Province. Beijing paid little attention to the island for the next two centuries and generally did not send highly qualified officials to this periphery. For most of this time a loosely enforced prohibition against emigration from the mainland to Taiwan existed, but this did not prevent the population from growing to an estimated two million at the beginning of the nineteenth century. The island was seen as a frontier where there were opportunities for personal advancement. Not coincidentally, Taiwan was the scene of considerable social turmoil, lawlessness, and political unrest. The economy remained overwhelmingly agricultural, based on fairly traditional and primitive methods.[7]

In the second half of the nineteenth century the winds of change came to Taiwan, again emanating from external sources. The growing pressure of Western powers to penetrate Chinese markets finally resulted in the opening of four ports in Taiwan in the early 1860s. This led to a growing commercialization and increased agricultural production to meet export opportunities for sugar and tea.[8] However, the constraints of the traditional economy that had long been ignored by China are well illustrated in Samuel Ho's description of the rise and fall of Taiwan's tea trade:

In 1866 John Dodd, a British trader, by importing plant slips from Fukien and providing working capital to the farmers, was successful in producing oolong tea in Taiwan that was acceptable on the world market. . . . The demand for Taiwan's oolong tea in the United States spurred export of tea from 82 MT in 1866 to 8,188 MT in 1888. . . . The preference of the Chinese merchants and growers for quick profit and their lack of interest in quality control . . . resulted in a rapid deterioration of the Taiwan tea. The fraudulent practice of adulterating high quality tea with poor leaves from the mainland became widespread . . . While the Taiwan tea industry was floundering, Ceylon, Japan, and India were carefully fostering their tea industry, and soon Taiwan found itself unable to compete on the world market.[9]

Imperialist pressures beginning with a Japanese threat in 1874 and culminating in French attacks a decade later finally forced Beijing to take Taiwan more seriously. As a result, the Ch'ing dynasty belatedly extended its "self-strengthening movement" to Taiwan after 1874 in an effort to ward off foreign encroachment. A strong and innovative leader, General Liu Ming-ch'uan, served as governor of Taiwan from 1884 to 1891; Taiwan was upgraded to a province in 1887. The primary goal of Liu and his immediate predecessors was to enhance the island's defense capabilities, but these programs had a strong developmentalist thrust as well. Rail and telegraph lines were started; harbor construction was expedited; Chinese immigration was strongly encouraged; an extensive land survey was conducted; the tax system was expanded; more attempts were made to control the aborigines and open mountain areas for agriculture; some support was given to education; and Taipei even received electric lighting. Thus, in about a quarter of a century, parts of Taiwan were transformed from the most backward places in the empire to some of its most advanced and commercialized areas. This significant development had some effects on Taiwan's social structure as well. The land-owning elites diversified their financial interests into commercial and small-scale industrial ventures and became significantly more educated and sophisticated, thus creating a good basis for what dependency theorists view as a "comprador" class. However, Liu's dynamism departed with him in 1891, indicating the dependence of Taiwan on the whims of Beijing and ironically leaving many of Liu's projects to be completed by the Japanese.[10]

Thus, as the nineteenth century came to a close, Taiwan appeared condemned to remain a rural backwater in decaying Manchu China. However, the island's fortunes came in for another externally administered shock in 1895 when Japan forced China to cede Taiwan to it at the end of the Sino-Japanese War. The Taiwanese welcomed their new overlords by declaring a republic and militarily resisting for five months. Thus the initial Japanese goal in its first colony was to promote security and prove to the Western powers that Japan had joined the imperialist club; until 1919 the Japanese governors-general were all active military officers. Japan soon developed a second goal in regard to Taiwan. Rapid population growth had raised fears in Japan about its self-sufficiency in food, so that a large tropical island that already had a positive agricultural trade balance appeared a welcome acquisition.

These two goals were combined somewhat in Japanese policies, especially under the strong and pragmatic administration of Governor-General Kodama Gentaro and his chief civilian administrator, Goto Shimpei. A Japanese administration and police force were established down to the village level. In rural

Table 3.1

Indicators of Agricultural Development (in constant Taiwan dollars at 1935–1937 value)

	Ag Production Per Worker		Ag Investment Per Worker		Farm Household Income p.c.	
	T$	Index	T$	Index	T$	Index
1911	156	100	8	100	49	100
1915	148	95	6	73	46	95
1920	172	110	10	135	50	103
1925	238	153	24	315	72	148
1930	258	165	23	308	72	148
1935	289	185	12	155	82	170
1940	290	186	31	408	81	168

Source: Teng-hui Lee, *Intersectoral Capital Flows in the Economic Development of Taiwan, 1895–1960* (Ithaca, N.Y.: Cornell University Press, 1971), p. 13.

areas farmers' associations were created that supplemented the control functions of the administrative structure but also served as an agricultural extension service to further the Japanese goal of increasing agricultural production. The Japanese did not radically change the basic institutions of rural life in Taiwan,[11] but tried to make the existing peasantry much more productive. Better strains of seeds were developed or imported; fertilizer use was greatly expanded; large-scale irrigation projects were begun; and infrastructure development, such as railroads, benefited the farm economy as well. The farmers' associations were given a central role in introducing this new technology into the countryside.

As the data in Table 3.1 clearly demonstrate, the Japanese program was extremely successful in the long run. This table presents per capita production, investment, and consumption figures for agriculture made comparable by expressing them in "constant" 1935–1937 dollars (i.e., adjusting them for inflation). An index where 100 equals the 1911 value for each indicator is also included to show the growth percentages. Agricultural production grew slowly until about 1920 (e.g., agricultural production per worker only increased 10 percent between 1910 and 1920) but then rose quite rapidly until the ill effects of the Great Depression were felt in the mid–1930s (e.g., agricultural production per worker jumped almost 50 percent between 1920 and 1925). The reason for this pattern of growth was that the new technologies were not widely implemented until after World War I, as indicated by the data series on investment (note also the precipitous fall in investment in the mid–1930s because of the Depression). Finally, farm incomes rose but not quite as steeply as production.[12]

Agricultural development, moreover, made a major contribution to Taiwan's

Table 3.2
Indicators of Agriculture's Contribution to Taiwan's Development

	1911-15	1916-20	1921-25	1926-30	1931-35	1936-40
Product (Mil T$ in 1935-37 prices)						
Net Dom Prod	$294	$337	$399	$560	$706	$797
Total Ag Prod	$156	$168	$209	$291	$334	$382
Real Capital Outflow from Ag	$50	$62	$60	$59	$89	$90
Ag Terms of Trade* (1935-37=100)						
Terms of Trade	121	130	112	100	107	102
Ag Role (%)						
Ag Prod/NDP	53%	50%	52%	52%	47%	48%
Outflow/Ag Prod	32%	37%	29%	20%	27%	24%
Outflow/NDP	17%	18%	15%	11%	13%	11%
Ag Invst/Total Invst	3%	5%	14%	15%	6%	5%
Rice Sold/Total Output	48%	50%	59%	66%	74%	74%
Food Exports/Tot Food Supply	16%	20%	23%	29%	38%	42%
Govt % Farm Inc	7%	6%	8%	7%	8%	8%

*The lower this index, the more favorable the terms of trade are for agriculture.

Source: Teng-hui Lee, *Intersectoral Capital Flows in the Economic Development of Taiwan, 1895–1960* (Ithaca, N.Y.: Cornell University Press, 1971), pp. 19–20, 29, 64, 72, 75, 174.

development by supplying a large outflow of capital, according to the estimations summarized in Table 3.2 of Teng-hui Lee, which include commodity and capital exchanges between the agricultural and nonagricultural sectors, government taxes, and relative price relations. The first three rows in this table present Taiwan's net domestic product, total agricultural output, and Lee's estimate of net capital outflow from the agricultural sector for the six five-year periods between 1911 and 1940 expressed in constant 1935–1937 Taiwan dollars. These data indicate that the major spurt in agriculture of 1921–1930 slightly preceded the largest increase in the island's total production from 1925 to 1935. This growth of agricultural production during the 1920s was stimulated by a boost in agricultural investment that averaged 15 percent of total investment for that period, as opposed to 5 percent for the preceding and succeeding decades. Moreover, the terms of trade for agriculture (i.e., the relative prices of goods bought and sold by the farm sector) improved sharply by 30 percent over the 1920s.

Lee's analysis shows that there was a substantial capital outflow of about $60 million for the first four periods and $90 million for the last two, although direct government extraction through taxes remained fairly low at about 7 percent of farm income. This constituted over a third of agricultural production and almost a fifth of net domestic product (NDP) before 1920 and a quarter of agricultural production and about 13 percent of NDP during the 1920s and 1930s. In addition, the percentage of rice that was sold, rather than consumed by the cultivators, rose steadily from 50 percent in 1911–1920 to over 60 percent during the 1920s to almost 75 percent in the 1930s; the proportion of the island's food supply that was exported (primarily to Japan) doubled from 18 percent in the 1910s to 40 percent in the 1930s. Thus agriculture certainly made a major contribution to Taiwan's colonial economy. It accounted for approximately half of total production and two-thirds of employment, created a major source of capital to finance the development of other sectors, and produced a growing food surplus for sale and export.[13]

The extraction of these agricultural surpluses was associated with expanding industrialization, as conventional modernization theory would prescribe. The food-processing industry had been stimulated by the commercialization of the 1880s; the Japanese expanded it as part of their policies of agricultural development, with the most rapid growth occurring in the 1910–1920 period. The Japanese-controlled sugar industry was the centerpiece of this expansion, and in 1921 it accounted for 61 percent of the total value of factory production.

Sugar production, with government encouragement and under Japanese management, increased dramatically, rising from an annual average output of 82,000 MT in the 1900s to 251,000 MT in the 1910s, 498,000 MT in the 1920s, and 948,000 MT in the 1930s.[14]

Agricultural demand for fertilizer helped to stimulate the chemical industry as well, and in the 1930s, with World War II looming, the Japanese began moving some heavier industries to Taiwan. Still, as Table 3.3 indicates, food processing remained by far the dominant industry throughout the colonial period, reflecting Japanese treatment of Taiwan as an agricultural periphery. In addition, the figures that show industry having generated about 40 percent of Taiwan's gross national product (GNP) during the colonial period present a somewhat misleading picture. For example, manufacturing's share of total employment only increased from 6.2 percent in 1905 to 8.5 percent in 1930.[15]

The fifty-year period of Japanese colonialism produced substantial growth on Taiwan. Table 3.4 summarizes the overall economic effects by presenting growth indices (i.e., the value of an economic indicator in relation to a value of 100 for the base year of 1910). Over the colonial period Taiwan averaged 4 percent

Table 3.3
Industrialization in Taiwan

	1915-19	1920-24	1925-29	1930-34	1935-39
Ind Product/ Total Prod	38.8%	41.2%	38.8%	43.3%	43.0%
Share of Ind Production					
Food Processing	--	74.6%	70.3%	73.3%	69.4%
Chemicals	--	7.9%	9.3%	7.8%	9.9%
Machinery & Metals	--	4.0%	4.2%	4.8%	7.6%
Textiles	--	1.7%	1.5%	1.1%	1.5%

Source: George W. Barclay, *Colonial Development and Population in Taiwan* (Princeton, N.J.: Princeton University Press, 1954), p. 38.

Table 3.4
Growth Indices for Colonial Taiwan (in constant 1937 prices)

	1910	1920	1930	1935
Population	100	111	140	158
Net Domestic Product	100	108	214	276
Agricultural Production	100	114	188	233
Industrial Production	100	125	291	367
Export Volume	100	113	313	462
Ave Ag Wages*	100	137	138	117
Ave Manufacturing Wages*	100	138	161	152

*Computed for five-year averages.

Source: Samuel P. S. Ho, *Economic Development in Taiwan, 1860–1970* (New Haven, Conn.: Yale University Press, 1978), pp. 27, 92.

growth in real GNP and 2 percent growth in GNP per capita annually, which were quite high for that period. Industrial production grew much faster than GNP, but because of its low value in the base year, the high growth percentages are somewhat artificial. The export-led nature of the island's growth can be clearly seen in Table 3.4 as well, since export volume increased almost twice as fast as domestic product. Japan dominated its colony's trade, as would be expected, taking 80 percent to 90 percent of Taiwan's exports after 1910 and accounting for an increasing share of imports, from 60 percent in 1910 to 80 percent during the 1930s. Food products dominated the island's foreign sales, as they actually rose from 76 percent to 85 percent of total exports between

1900–1909 and 1930–1939, making the island a rice and sugar "basket" for the metropole. For example, between 1903 and 1935 Taiwan exports jumped from 1 percent to 6 percent of Japan's rice consumption and from 7 percent to 83 percent of its sugar consumption.[16]

The question of how much Taiwan benefited from this growth is open to more ambiguous conclusions, however. On the positive side, Taiwan's agriculture was transformed to become much more innovative and productive. Moreover, the substantial development of infrastructure and transportation and the nature of much of the industry that was developed (e.g., food processing and fertilizer) meant that the agricultural and industrial sectors on the island were much more integrally linked, both functionally and geographically, than the "enclave segmentation" typical of many developing countries. The standard of living in terms of diet quality and the possession of consumers goods rose significantly too. Finally, the Japanese helped to promote human capital to a significant extent as well. Lower-elementary schooling was provided on a fairly widespread basis, although higher schooling was much harder to obtain for Chinese; public health programs resulted in substantial decreases in infant mortality and the crude death rate.[17]

On the other hand, there were many unfavorable aspects of colonialism. The Japanese primarily viewed Taiwan in terms of what it could contribute to the empire; Japan clearly exploited its colony for its own benefit. The fortuitous nature of Taiwan's colonial experience is indicated, for example, by the much harsher imposition of Japanese rule on Korea and Manchuria.[18] For example, Tables 3.1 and 3.4 show that income and consumption in Taiwan increased much less rapidly than total production, indicating that the Chinese standard of living was suppressed to benefit the Japanese overlords. Also, although there was an inflow of Japanese capital before World War I, Taiwan's economic expansion after the war was largely financed by internal resources. Finally, the island's huge positive trade balances with the metropole imply a considerable outflow of resources. Thus several estimates indicate that Japan's rate of extraction of resources (or surplus) from Taiwan was quite high compared with many other colonial situations.[19]

More broadly, Taiwan's role as an agricultural periphery produced several of the constraints and distortions posited by dependency theory. The Japanese clearly did not have much interest in broadening Taiwan's industry beyond agriculturally related sectors (e.g., the lack of development of textiles indicated in Table 3.3) because this would compete with the importation of Japanese manufactures. Local Taiwanese were also largely excluded from larger industrial ventures (e.g., the dominant sugar industry) and limited to small-scale commercial and industrial ventures (e.g., rice milling and noodle-making). The Japanese also monopolized governmental and administrative positions at all but the lowest levels. Some political liberalization occurred after civilians began to occupy the position of governor-general in 1919. However, a movement to increase "home rule" in the 1920s proved totally unsuccessful; the colonial

Table 3.5
Ratio of 1945 Production to Peak Colonial Output

	1946 Output	Ratio to Colonial Peak
Cotton yarn	410,182 Kg	75.9%
Salt	217,128 MT	46.7%
Electric Power	472,002 KWH	39.5%
Coal	450,324 MT	38.0%
Cement	97,269 MT	32.1%
Tobacco	537,499 Kg	28.9%
Fertilizer	3,204 MT	27.8%
Camphor	472,893 MT	24.1%
Sugar	86,074 MT	6.3%

Source: Anthony Y. C. Koo, "Economic Development of Taiwan," in Paul K. T. Sih, ed., *Taiwan in Modern Times* (New York: St. John's University Press, 1973), p. 402.

administration became more conservative and repressive after the late 1920s in conjunction with the growing militarism in the metropole. As a result, there was little or no development of a "bourgeois" elite with entrepreneurial or administrative talents; the leading Taiwan families were forced into a comprador role.[20]

This mixed colonial heritage was eroded, furthermore, by the way in which the Japanese left Taiwan. The island was subjected to heavy American bombing during the war that destroyed "three-quarters of industrial capacity, two-thirds of power, and one-half of the transport network."[21] The mass evacuation of the Japanese at the end of the war also deprived the island of most of its skilled administrative and business leaders. In addition, the dependent periphery was sundered from its major markets and attached to the Chinese mainland, which was undergoing an extreme economic and political crisis of its own. Although Taiwan was not itself actively involved in the Chinese civil war, the retrocession to China had several significant economic costs. The KMT, or Nationalist, regime viewed Taiwan as simply a source of resources for its desperate battle against the Communists. Thus they dismantled factories and grabbed raw materials for shipment to the mainland, compounding the economic crisis. Moreover, the rampant inflation on the mainland was quickly transmitted to Taiwan as well.

The result for Taiwan was economic devastation and chaos whose magnitude is only hinted at by the cold economic data in Tables 3.5 and 3.6. Table 3.5 contains the ratio of physical production in 1946 to peak output at the end of the colonial period; Table 3.6 shows the ratio of production in the major economic sectors to a 1937 index of 100 for the 1946–1950 period to indicate the pace of the postwar reconstruction. NDP in 1946 was only 55 percent of the prewar level and took until 1950 to reattain its 1937 value. The relative decline of agriculture was not as great, but the bottom dropped out of manufacturing, which had not reached even a third of prewar production by 1947 and was at only 70

Table 3.6
Indices of Economic Production, 1945–1950 (1937 = 100)

	1946	1947	1948	1949	1950
Net Domestic Product	55	62	76	91	105
Ag, Forest, Fish	64	75	88	104	110
Manf, Mine, Constr	25	29	46	61	70
Services	66	73	84	99	127
Transport, Pub Utilities	62	73	90	103	111
Trade	48	56	71	86	94
Pub Adm, Defense	84	84	77	107	240

Source: Simon Kuznets, "Growth and Structural Shifts," in Walter Galenson, ed., *Economic Growth and Structural Change in Taiwan: The Postwar Experience of the Republic of China* (Ithaca, N.Y.: Cornell University Press, 1979), p. 34.

percent of prewar levels in 1950. The data in Table 3.5 show that the previously dominant sugar industry was particularly hard hit and that this industrial decline was nearly universal, with the exception of cotton manufactures. Trade was also slightly slower than normal to recover. Finally, the evacuation of the R.O.C. government to Taiwan in 1949 was reflected in the huge jump in spending for public administration and defense in 1950.

These economic problems were exacerbated by political tensions as well. Despite the fact that the Taiwanese welcomed Republican troops as liberators when the island reverted to China at the end of World War II, the KMT tended to view the Taiwanese as collaborators with the hated Japanese and, thus, justified the corrupt, brutal, and exploitative policies of the military commander, Ch'en Yi, who administered Taiwan. Ch'en's repression finally sparked a spontaneous uprising on February 28, 1947. A compromise between Ch'en and Taiwanese leaders seemed to settle the crisis. However, KMT troops invaded the island in mid-March, killing between 10,000 and 20,000 Taiwanese and singling out the intelligentsia and leadership class for slaughter. Although Ch'en was quickly replaced afterward by a more conciliatory administrator and later publicly executed, the trauma and hatred remained; a longstanding legacy of distrust had been created. When the KMT government of Chiang Kai-shek moved to Taiwan in 1949, hence, political officials were primarily "mainlanders" who were viewed with some suspicion by much of the "islander" population.[22]

This conflict also raises the question of whether the Taiwanese had become a separate society and ethnic group or whether they remained essentially Chinese, no more distinctive from mainland residents than were different provincial communities from one another. Significant arguments can be adduced for either position. On the one hand, in terms of distinctiveness, Taiwan had been largely isolated from the rest of China until the late nineteenth century, had much more of an open "frontier" society, had been considerably affected by Japanese culture and education, and had moved much further in the direction of agricultural "modernization," thereby stimulating different values and nationalism on the part of the Taiwanese.[23] Such factors as these led John Copper and George Chen to conclude that the island was more commercialized and open to foreign economic models than the rest of China—conditions that should obviously promote development.[24]

Conversely, the animosity between the ruling KMT and subject Taiwanese population could only hinder broad-scale participation in economic development. Therefore, the factors that suggest commonality between Taiwan and China were also highly relevant for the island's developmental potential. For example, the Taiwanese, except for the small aborigine minority, are ethnically Han Chinese with roots and language dialects coming from Fukien and Kwangtung provinces; their initial response to the island's reversion to China at the end of World War II appeared enthusiastic. More theoretically, Ramon Myers has argued that dramatic Sinicization did occur in Taiwan during the nineteenth century, so that the provincial elite on the island differed little from other parts of China by the coming of Japanese colonialism, although the economy was more commercialized and less subject to state control.[25] Thus a basis for rapprochement between the KMT and the population certainly existed.

Historically, Taiwan can be viewed as a "periphery" for several reasons. It was always on the far edge of a state or empire; changes in its political and economic status generally occurred because of events and decisions taken elsewhere in the world that were little concerned with the well-being of the island per se; and Taiwan's economy was centered on primary production. Yet certain aspects of Taiwan's peripheral nature helped to create a positive environment for economic development and transformation after World War II. The economic changes that occurred under Liu's self-strengthening program and Japanese colonialism were quite positive in several respects. Agriculture became much more productive and innovative, reflecting technological upgrading, change in peasant attitudes, and the development of an agricultural extension system; infrastructure investment created a good transportation system; and industrial development, especially in food processing, was geographically dispersed and integrally linked with the dominant rural sector, unlike the enclave development of many less developed countries. Additionally, Taiwan had several historical experiences distinctive from the rest of China that should have fostered development, while retaining enough similarity to preserve the potential for commonality with the new KMT regime.

These positive factors, however, were far from unequivocal. The island's developmental potential had been circumscribed by the facts that the Japanese had not pursued a broadening of Taiwan's nascent industrialization into such "natural" fields as textiles and especially that the Taiwanese had generally been prevented from obtaining the entrepreneurial and administrative skills that play a crucial role in the developmental processes. Moreover, the destruction of so much of the island's infrastructure and capital during the closing stages of World War II and the rupturing of ties between the society and regime during Ch'en Yi's murderous and exploitative administration created horrendous physical and psychological barriers to utilizing the previously existing potentials for development. On balance, therefore, the end of Japanese and the beginning of Chinese rule had created a rather bleak picture in the late 1940s.

The Rise and Fall of the Kuomintang in China

The fortunes of the KMT, or Nationalist party, in China followed a rapid parabola, rising from a small and impotent revolutionary group to the rulers of all China and then falling to a total loss in the civil war with the Chinese Communist party (CCP) in approximately half a century. The reasons for this "shooting star" quality of the KMT are somewhat obscure and remain highly controversial among detached historians, not to mention partisans of one or another of China's various political movements. The brief review of the Nationalists in this section describes the major historical events during their rise and fall and offers a middle-of-the-road interpretation that both their successes and their failures derived from a combination of their own actions, and factors and conditions well beyond their control.

The Nationalist movement was spawned by the political and economic crises that engulfed China during the nineteenth century. The Ch'ing, or Manchu, dynasty was clearly in decline, becoming progressively weaker, more corrupt, and more brutal, and unable to respond to deteriorating economic conditions throughout the country, such as periodic massive famines. The domestic decay was greatly exacerbated by the increasing penetration of China by imperialist powers, first European countries and then Japan. Economically, the opium trade and forced concessions and reparations drained Chinese resources, while the provisions for "extraterritorial" areas in which Chinese laws did not apply were viewed as a national humiliation by a country that considered itself the "Middle Kingdom" and that had had its foreign relations conducted by the Board of Rites, which was charged with teaching "barbarians" how to act in civilized company.[26]

The decay of the Ch'ing dynasty produced a number of highly negative reactions. One was an almost incessant series of peasant uprisings caused by woeful economic conditions in many rural regions. The most famous was the Taiping Rebellion of 1851–1864, which caused more casualties than World War I. At their high point the Taipings controlled most of China south of the Yangtze River except for the large ports. The Ch'ings were finally able to defeat the Taipings only with the aid of several foreign mercenary armies and privately raised and led Chinese armies. The latter were not disbanded after the rebellion and set the precedent for the development of "warlordism."[27]

A second reaction was growing nationalism that was directed against both foreigners, who were blamed for China's problems, and the alien Manchu rulers.

Nationalism took several distinct forms. First, there was deep-seated popular resentment expressed most spectacularly in the Boxer Rebellion of 1899–1900 about which the court's position was rather ambiguous, to say the least.[28] At quite another level, nationalism was also reflected in the official policy of "self-strengthening" in the latter part of the nineteenth century that aimed at applying Western technology to promoting defense capabilities and economic development and, thus, saving Chinese culture and society (and the Ch'ing dynasty) from obliteration at the hands of the imperialist powers.[29] A concern with "self-strengthening," however, raised the question of whether a technological fix would be sufficient without more far-reaching political and economic reforms. Thus there was an anti-regime movement to reform the traditional Confucian governmental organization and practices within a continued dynastic system. There was a brief reformist administration led by K'ang Yu-wei in 1898, but it was deposed in a coup by the empress dowager.[30]

As the twentieth century began, therefore, neither peasant insurrections nor moderate reform appeared likely to succeed, although the Ch'ing dynasty was certainly tottering from internal rot. Another possibility was the overthrow of the dynasty by a revolutionary movement aimed at destroying the traditional Chinese polity and inaugurating a new system. Beginning in the late nineteenth century there was growing support for such a movement, especially among the intelligentsia, who were alienated by Western-imposed humiliations and the corruption and ineffectiveness of the traditional ruling order. The dominant figure in what was still a minuscule movement became Dr. Sun Yat-sen. Sun's attempts to foment revolution proved largely ineffectual, but he provided a philosophy and ideology that helped to transform China.[31]

Sun's revolutionary doctrine was expressed in "The Three Principles of the People" (or *San Min Chu I*), which he saw as the major goals for the revolutionary order. The first was nationalism. Sun argued that China needed to be strong and united in order to overcome its internal difficulties and exploitation by foreign powers. He believed that an emphasis on the ancient learning and values of Confucianism (as opposed to its perverted form practiced by the Ch'ing dynasty) coupled with modern science would produce a strong and independent China. Thus there was some echo of the self-strengthening and reformist movements but also a firm (and probably justifiable) rejection of any possibility of attaining these nationalist goals under a dynastic system.

Sun's second principle focused on tutelary democracy. He believed that the new government must be responsive to the needs of the people, and proposed a democratic system based on a division of power among the three traditional branches of Western governments (the executive, legislative, and judiciary) plus two others derived from traditional Chinese practice (one to oversee the examinations for government officials and one to act as an ombudsman by reviewing government actions). However, he also believed that a "tutelary period" would be needed when a modernizing and revolutionary party would educate the Chinese people in the ways of democracy and develop a progressive bureaucracy. This tutelary period was initially seen as quite short—three to six years—but repeated political failures made Sun more pessimistic as time passed about the Chinese people's ability to adapt to democracy.

The last of the People's Principles focused on "people's livelihood." Sun believed that a government could be justified or legitimatized only if it promoted and protected the well-being of its citizens. A concern for economic justice was reflected in proposals for massive land transfers to end exploitative relations in the countryside, tax reform, and educational programs. He also proposed the nationalization of industries deemed vital to national development and governmental regulation of businesses. Thus Sun advocated a leading role for the government in directing economic development and ensuring a minimum standard of living for the Chinese people. His theses looked both backward to traditional Confucian paternalism and forward to the central ideas of democratic socialism.[32]

When the Ch'ing dynasty was finally forced to abdicate by the Revolution of 1911–1912, the cause was much more its weakness than the strength of revolutionary forces. A revolutionary outbreak in Wuhan in October 1911 set off a spark of takeovers throughout southern China by groups committed to Sun Yat-sen's ideal of creating a republic. The Ch'ing unretired a leading general, Yuan Shih-k'ai, to suppress the revolution. Yuan captured Wuhan and then began negotiating with both the royal court in Beijing and the Republican forces of Sun Yat-sen in Shanghai. As a result of his intrigues, the child emperor abdicated; Yuan himself became president of the R.O.C., although the KMT, which Sun founded in 1912, won a strong victory in elections for a constituent assembly; after a disagreement with Yuan, Sun and his followers were again forced into exile. Yuan seemed well on his way to establishing himself as a new emperor. However, his willingness to accept Japan's humiliating "Twenty-one Demands" that would have made China something of a Japanese protectorate (which were ultimately withdrawn because of American pressure) created a nationalistic outburst of popular revulsion that led to his resignation in March 1916; he died suddenly soon thereafter.

Yuan's resignation and death were followed by a degeneration into what came to be called "warlordism." Political leaders, generally with their own private armies and territorial fiefdoms, made and broke alliances in attempts to take over the increasingly chaotic and corrupt formal government in Beijing and to set policies that were regarded as irrelevant in most of the fiefdoms. No dominant faction of warlords emerged, so that changes in the central government were common, contributing to the breakdown of government and public order. Sun and the KMT participated in the central government after Yuan's death but were chased out of Beijing once more when they opposed the dominant general's move to declare war on Germany in 1917. They then took refuge in Canton under the protection of the dominant warlord in Kwangtung Province, Ch'en Chiung-ming, who appeared committed to the Republican cause.[33]

This unsalubrious situation continued until 1919 and the outburst of the May

Fourth Movement, which began with massive student demonstrations in Beijing against the Versailles Peace Conference's decision to give Japan territorial concessions in China. Demonstrations spread to other parts of China and were strongly anti-Japanese, involving violence against the Japanese and a boycott of Japanese goods. It was also clear that it was directed against the current government for being too weak and ineffectual to protect China's interests.[34]

The May Fourth Movement (besides stimulating the founding of the CCP by intellectuals in Beijing and Shanghai) inspired General Ch'en with the vision that warlordism was doomed and that the nationalist ideology of the KMT could serve as the rallying point for a new regime. The new Bolshevik government in the Soviet Union was also beginning to take interest in the revolutionary nature of China and concluded that the KMT was a much more viable force than the still embryonic CCP. The early 1920s then witnessed Sun and the KMT's involvement in a complex set of negotiations and intrigues with General Ch'en and other sympathetic military leaders in south China and with the Soviet Union, several Russian advisors, and Chinese Communists. These various endeavors moved along three lines that came together in the mid–1920s to change the face of China. First, there was general agreement among all concerned that a campaign should be launched from southern China against Beijing to topple the warlords and establish a republic. Second, the infighting among General Ch'en, allegedly sympathetic military leaders, and the KMT brought home the fact to Sun that the KMT needed its own independent military organization in such an uncertain and threatening political environment. As a result, the KMT opened the Whampoa Military Academy in 1924 to train officers for its army. The academy provided the backbone for what would become a strong and independent military force and gave its commandant, Chiang Kai-shek, a major boost in his career within the party. The Nationalist Army grew rapidly after 1924 from about 1,000 to over 100,000 in 1926 and controlled most of Kwangtung Province by early 1926. Third, under the Sun-Joffe agreement in early 1923, the KMT and CCP agreed to form a "united front," although ideological and factional tensions quickly began to escalate. After Sun Yat-sen's death in 1925 Chiang Kai-shek gained control of the KMT through something of a coup, although the Communists and leftist KMT remained fairly strong and rather suspicious of him.[35]

The Northern Expedition to conquer and unify China was finally launched in the summer of 1926. In the first stage the Republic forces (consisting of the KMT, the Communists, and a variety of allied warlords) successfully took control of most of south China as much by political dealings as by military conflict, culminating with Chiang Kai-shek's occupation of Shanghai in March 1927. Initial success exacerbated the political cleavages within the alliance; the second stage was constituted by open conflict over who would control the new regime. This stage began when the army, controlled by the Communists and leftist KMT faction, captured Wuhan, declared it the new capital, and rejected Chiang's leadership. Chiang then attacked the leftist trade unions in Shanghai, whose uprising had allowed him to move into Shanghai unopposed in a brutal suppression and massacre. This led to an open break between the KMT and CCP and to a futile Communist uprising. The final stage after the Communists had been defeated, then, was the conquest of north China, again with warlord alliances playing a central role, and the founding of the Nationalist government with its capital in Nanking (Nanjing) in 1928.

The new government of the R.O.C. was established by the Organic Law of October 4, 1928. The government consisted of a president and five formal branches, called 'yuans,'' each with its own president, in correspondence with Sun Yat-sen's outline—the Executive Yuan, Legislative Yuan, Judicial Yuan, Control Yuan, and Examination Yuan. Applying the "tutelary" approach of the new regime, all these officials (including the members of the Legislative Yuan) were appointed by the dominant Nationalist party. Chiang Kai-shek became president of both the Republic and the Executive Yuan, much to the consternation of his opponents both within the KMT and among ostensibly allied warlords. KMT offices were opened in all of China's provinces, although they exercised effective power only in areas controlled by the party's own armed forces; party membership doubled from about 200,000 in 1926 to over 400,000 in 1929.[36]

The decade of Nationalist rule until full-scale war with Japan broke out in 1937 is generally considered a failure even (or perhaps especially) in terms of the KMT's putative ideological goals set out in "The Three Principles of the People." The nation was not unified and continued to suffer open humiliations at the hands of foreign imperialists, culminating in the conquest of large parts of northern and eastern China by the hated Japanese. There was little reform or improvement in government over the previous regimes, as the bureaucracy remained almost as inefficient, imperious, and corrupt as ever. Finally, the gains in "people's livelihood" were rather limited; the Nationalists turned their backs on the peasants, workers, and small merchants to whom their ideology had initially appealed.

The nationalist objectives of unifying China and forcing foreign powers to treat China with respect and equality clearly eluded the KMT. At the founding of the Republic in 1928, the Nationalists controlled less than a quarter of the Chinese population. Although much of the rest of the country was formally integrated into the Republic, it was essentially ruled by a variety of warlords who continued to view their areas as private fiefdoms and to scheme about coalitions for improving their power positions and taking over the central government. Thus most of the decade of the Republican era witnessed an almost continuous series of wars between the Nationalists and one or more warlords. The warlords, though, clearly represented the old and discredited China and had little popular support. Thus they appeared to be a declining force in Chinese politics.[37]

The Communists, in contrast, theoretically represented a major rival in the competition for the new China in that their ideology promised national revival, rule by the people, and an upgraded livelihood for all (except feudalists, capitalists, and compradors). In actuality, the Republican decade was not a good one for the CCP. The Communists suffered from sharp internal cleavages between more orthodox Marxists backed by Stalin and Moscow and Mao Tse-tung (Mao Zedong), who argued that the Communist revolution in China should be based on the increasingly radicalized peasantry. The Communists were also rather unsuccessful in either attracting popular support or battling the forces of Chiang Kai-shek. In the early 1930s they were driven from the major cities and joined Mao's headquarters in rural Kiangsi (Jiangxi) Province. This position did not turn out to be impregnable; in 1934 the Communists broke out of encirclement by KMT forces and began their dramatic Long March to Yenan (Yanan) in north central China, beyond the reach of the KMT but also far out of the political limelight.[38]

These debilitating internal conflicts with the warlords and Communists undermined the Nationalists' ability to stand up to foreign powers that intervened in Chinese affairs. The Northern Expedition had been stimulated and accompanied by widespread demonstrations against foreign merchants, settlements, and nations. The Nationalist victory, therefore, was greeted with hope by the Chinese people and some trepidation by foreign interests that turned out to be quite ill-founded. The Nationalists demanded that extraterritorial privileges for foreigners be ended and tried to open negotiations on this subject with the major powers. When these demands were ignored, however, nothing happened; the government clearly "lost face" with an increasingly nationalistic people. In the economic realm the government made a substantial and at least partially successful effort to decrease foreign debt and the external dependence that accompanied it; increased tariff rates both brought in much needed revenues and asserted national sovereignty against foreign economic pressures. On the other hand, China's economic weakness resulted in continued issuing of bonds to foreigners at favorable rates and a lack of any concerted move to curb the privileges of foreign capital.[39]

The Nationalists' greatest humiliations were sustained at the hands of Japan. The growing Japanese presence in and pressure on China well illustrates the fundamental problems that faced the Republic. After World War I the Japanese presence in China, both economic and military, grew considerably, eliciting growing popular revulsion and cyclical bursts of anti-Japanese violence. At times the KMT and Japanese seemed willing to work out a mutual accommodation. The Nationalists, however, were unable to control the anti-Japanese sentiments of the Chinese, especially in areas under warlord domination, and were afraid that agreements with Japan might lead to an uprising against them (witness the fall of Yuan Shih-k'ai). The Japanese, for their part, became increasingly aggressive and uncompromising with the rise of militarism in Tokyo.

This growing conflict led to two major Japanese military conquests. First, after growing strains with the local warlord, the Japanese used the fabricated Mukden Incident as an excuse to overrun Manchuria and establish the satellite state of Manchukuo in September 1931 (with a subsequent brief occupation of China's largest port, Shanghai). This was certainly a major loss for the Chinese (even though the KMT had been generally excluded from the area) because Manchuria was the nation's industrial heartland (e.g., it contained 20 percent of the people, 50 percent of the railroads, and 80 percent of the iron industry) and provided a considerable revenue source from the customs duties at Dairen (Dalien) and Port Arthur. Second, with war seeming inevitable to both sides, a small-scale and evidently accidental clash at the Marco Polo Bridge near Beijing on July 7, 1937, provoked the Japanese invasion of China, which effectively ended the normal government of the Republic.[40]

Sun Yat-sen's second goal of democracy, enlightened tutelage, and effective administration fared only a little better. The KMT itself was riven with factionalism. Chiang Kai-shek was the titular leader and strongest figure, but his power was challenged and clearly limited. For example, a major rival served as chairman of the party, and most of the original presidents of the other Yuans were either enemies or neutrals. Bitter and ongoing factional conflicts were exacerbated by the fact that there was hardly any improvement in the administrative bureaucracy. Most of the government officials from the warlord period kept their jobs, and many of the new ones were chosen by political criteria (cronyism and bribery). Consequently embarrassing parallels could easily be discerned between "court politics" in Nanking and the Forbidden City of the empress dowager—vicious political infighting and intrigues and escalating corruption that gravely undermined any attempt to promote the national interest or to respond to interests outside the "court."

This degeneration of politics brought with it growing political repression, including a considerable number of political murders. In addition to Communists and military opponents, these activities were directed against factions within the KMT, intellectuals who criticized the regime, and workers and peasants. Several groups, as well as the official military and police, deserve blame for gross human rights violations. KMT factions had their own spies and bullies. Especially provocative in this regard were the "Blue Shirts," a youth group founded by Chiang Kai-shek in 1932 along fascist lines that harassed Chiang's critics among students and intellectuals and became deeply involved in factional politics. In addition, the "Green Gang," probably the most important criminal organization in China that dominated the Shanghai underworld, took a significant role in political feuds.

The political situation was not entirely bleak, however. The KMT had attracted many nationalists, intellectuals, and businessmen before the revolution, and they endeavored, with at least a little success, to reform the regime and keep Sun Yat-sen's ideals alive. Although they were later accused of massive corruption, financiers T. V. Soong and H. H. K'ung, the brothers-in-law of Chiang Kai-shek, who assumed leading governmental positions, made significant contributions to the Republic during the 1930s in terms of economic policy planning and financial reform and stabilization. Such KMT leaders as Hu Han-min and Sun Yat-sen's son and wife, Sun Fo and Soong Ch'ing-ling, were highly critical of the regime; Chiang Kai-shek himself echoed many of their criticisms about corruption, bureaucratic inefficiency, and terrorism, although his enemies certainly questioned his sincerity.[41]

This mixed picture carries over into the area of promoting the "people's livelihood." When the Nationalists took over after years of draining civil war and mismanagement, government finances were in a mess and the economy was rather shaky. China had a typical "dependent economy." It exported raw materials and imported manufactures and was developing processing industry, most particularly cotton textiles, in the coastal cities based on the exploitation of cheap labor and on the fairly extensive domination of foreign capital. The land tenure system was highly concentrated and exploitative, which created considerable rural misery. The Northern Expedition, thus, raised hopes that the KMT would live up to Sun Yat-sen's legacy of bringing economic justice for workers and peasants by controlling landlords, businessmen, and foreign capitalists.

Given the chaos of the late 1920s and the impact of the Great Depression in the early 1930s, the Nationalists certainly deserve some credit for stimulating development. Although fairly grandiose plans to diversify and upgrade China's industry did not come to fruition, industry grew steadily during this period; government sectoral targeting through control of credit had some effect (although this was also seen as an attack on private banks); and the country's financial condition improved considerably. The price for this, however, was that the KMT abjured its populist commitment to helping those at the bottom of society. Unions were harassed, perhaps because they were seen as having ties to the Communists; there was almost no effort to effect land reform even in areas controlled by the KMT; and the regime generally ignored the small capitalists who had originally supported it.[42]

This is not to say that the Nationalists became lackeys of landlords and capitalists. Rather, the rulers either looked after their own interests in splendid isolation or concluded that "production" should come before "redistribution." In the urban realm the new regime first helped large capitalists exclude the small merchants from the leadership of business organizations but then proved fairly unresponsive to them. For example, much of the regime's economic strategy was based on "bureaucratic capitalism" or the leading role of private and quasi-state monopolies controlled by top officials, such as T. V. Soong, and H. H. K'ung; the government engaged in nearly open extortion to extract revenues from the business sector.[43] In rural areas the extension of the Republic's "state-building" activities to the villages destroyed the traditional fabric of society, including the ability of the rural gentry to provide leadership and mediating roles; village leadership was assumed by "entrepreneurs" and "village bullies," whose primary goal was to gain personal profits from the rapidly escalating revenues that were being extracted from the countryside. Thus the growing rural alienation that figured so strongly in the Communists' ultimate victory evidently derived much more from the regime's intrusive new activities than from government support of the traditional landlord class.[44]

In fact, by 1936 the situation in China had improved significantly, and some glimmers of hope were beginning to emerge that the Republic might succeed in bringing a better government and an improved economy to a long-ravaged China. The Nationalists had finally beaten most of the warlords and their private armies into submission; national unification was finally more a fact than an empty slogan. A constitutional movement had been initiated that resulted in the election of a National Assembly that was seen as a harbinger of more democratic politics. The economy was in better shape than probably anyone could remember, owing to industrial growth, financial reform, and a bumper harvest. Moreover, with the glaring exception of Japan, foreign relations were fairly good with the major powers. Consequently Chiang Kai-shek was emerging in both domestic and foreign views as a successful nationalist and the most popular leader in China.[45]

The Republic's day in the sun, unfortunately, was to be extremely brief. In December 1936 the "Sian Incident" provoked a brief political crisis of the first order. Chiang was kidnapped while trying to coerce a recalcitrant general and his army (the refugees from the Japanese attack on Manchuria who were receptive to the Communist argument that Chinese should not fight among themselves when war with Japan was imminent) to attack the Communists. Under threat of execution he was forced to sign a "united front agreement" with the Communists, which turned out to be most appropriate, given the Japanese invasion six months later.[46]

Initially the Japanese hoped to cut off and destroy the Nationalist armies. The Nationalists retreated from north China, held out much longer in defending Shanghai than anticipated, but then quickly lost the capital of Nanking. What followed was the infamous "Rape of Nanking" that the Japanese hoped would intimidate their future enemies. After the battle of Nanking the Japanese chased the KMT up the Yangtze valley but lost the chance to surround them and end the war. The Nationalists finally reestablished their capital in Chungking (Chongqing) in Szechwan (Sichuan) Province; the military front at least partially stabilized, with Japan occupying major portions of the country but unable to complete its conquest.[47]

The war years of 1937 to 1945 brought decisive changes in the KMT's relations with the Communists, the Chinese people, and the United States that were to set the stage for the Chinese civil war of the late 1940s. The United Front between the KMT and CCP, fueled by the fact that the Soviet Union was by far Chungking's largest aid supplier, was maintained for several years, with the Communists centered in the North and the Nationalists in the South. There was little direct coordination between them, though; by the early 1940s their ideological and political rivalry and different military missions led to almost complete estrangement and, at times, open battles between their military forces (both of which traded and reached "understandings" with the Japanese in more than a few instances).

The KMT had a formal government and capital and pursued a primarily conventional battle on several fronts against the Japanese. In contrast, the Communists pursued irregular and guerrilla warfare and more informally organized political control over the countryside within their areas of operation. Initially these differences benefited the KMT, but by the end of the war they were working in the Communists' favor. The KMT, as the formal government and as the army engaged in the central conflict with the invaders, benefited from the nationalist outpouring of the Chinese people and received most of the foreign aid. As the war wore on, however, things changed considerably. The Nationalist armies became increasingly defensive. In contrast, the Communists, whose strategy could be more flexible, were more aggressive and spectacular, thus improving their image both within China and among the Western allies. The CCP was also able to promote rural redistribution policies, thus winning support among the peasantry in their areas. On the other hand, the Chiang Kai-shek government became increasingly tied to landlord interests and was held responsible by many for the grossly deteriorating political and economic situation.[48]

Clearly, the war brought economic disaster even to the areas beyond Japan's reach. The government had been successful in bringing skilled artisans and even hundreds of disassembled factories (including a major steel mill) up the Yangtze to Chungking to the benefit of both the economy and the war effort, but this stimulus was short-lived, as the war threatened to lead to the economic disintegration of the regime by the early 1940s. There was general impoverishment within the Nationalist areas; the 1940–41 famine is viewed, for instance, as one of the severest in Chinese history. Moreover, rising government debt fueled escalating inflation. The regime's political response only exacerbated matters, as it became more distant, authoritarian, intolerant of criticism, and blatantly corrupt.[49]

The United States' growing conflict with Japan that culminated in Pearl Harbor and America's entrance into World War II had both positive and negative consequences for the Nationalists. Roosevelt's strategic embargo against Japan in September 1940 helped to relieve the military pressure on China; once America entered the war, it began to supply extremely valuable military and economic aid. Moreover, the war effort increased China's popularity in the United States. For example, Roosevelt pushed China's status as a great power, and the R.O.C., under American sponsorship, became one of the five permanent members of the U.N. Security Council after World War II. More important perhaps, General Claire Chennault, commander of the Flying Tigers, which began as a group of American volunteers fighting in China, became a staunch friend of Chiang Kai-shek and a leader of what came to be called the "China Lobby" in the United States after the war.

Relations between the United States and the R.O.C. were far from entirely smooth, however; this undoubtedly contributed to America's somewhat hands-off policy toward China in the late 1940s. General Joseph Stilwell, chief U.S. military representative in Chungking, soon developed a strong mutual antipathy with Chiang and the Nationalists. Stilwell complained that the Chinese were too timid and passive militarily. Chiang, for his part, argued with some justification that his forces were exhausted after years of fighting while America sat on the sidelines, and that they should be saved for major Japanese attacks (as well as for anticipated postwar conflicts with the Communists). Most American observers also felt that the inefficiency and corruption of the regime were a major cause of the growing economic disintegration. Consequently the United States became more hesitant to supply aid, which added another irritant to Sino-American relations. Finally, several State Department representatives, later dubbed the "old China hands," sent in reports that were extremely critical of the Nationalists and partisan toward the Communists (although these were probably far more important in domestic U.S. politics during the McCarthy era than they were for setting American policy toward China in the 1940s).[50]

These varying American perceptions of China led to the perhaps contradictory policies of trying to revive the United Front and of providing assistance to the KMT in reoccupying the major cities in eastern and northern China and (against U.S. advice because of their strategic vulnerability) in Manchuria. The result suggests the adage "cursed be the peacemakers," since both sides became somewhat suspicious of and alienated from the Americans. U.S. mediation attempts, culminating in the mission of General George C. Marshall in the winter of 1945–46, failed miserably. Given the contradictory political goals of and past implacable hatred between the KMT and CCP, though, the possibility of creating a viable coalition government was probably closer to nonexistent than to slim. As Marshall wearily concluded:

On the one hand, the leaders of the Government are strongly opposed to a communist form of government. On the other, the communists frankly state that they are Marxists and intend to work toward establishing a communistic form of government, though first advancing through the medium of a democratic form of government of the American or British type.[51]

China and the Nationalist government were also beset by continuing economic disintegration. The end of the war brought many factory closings; the civil war that erupted in 1946 devastated much of the countryside. Perhaps most important, the wartime hyperinflation continued unabated, undermining both the living standard and faith in the government among most groups and classes of Chinese. The government responded with increased repression; the wholesale corruption and profiteering of many KMT leaders undercut the regime's legitimacy both at home and abroad. Thus, in the late 1940s, the Republic certainly appeared to be losing the "mandate of heaven."[52]

Full-scale civil war broke out in the spring of 1946 with each side blaming the other. Initially the Nationalists scored several victories, but the tide soon turned. A major Communist victory was signaled by the surrender of the KMT garrisons in Manchuria in 1948; after a crushing Communist victory in an ill-chosen last stand north of the Yangtze in the winter of 1948–1949, Nationalist resistance collapsed. America's response had been to suspend military aid, first in the hope of drying up the conflict and then because a Communist victory appeared inevitable. As CCP troops overran the mainland, the United States pledged noninterference in the civil war; it appeared only a matter of time before the KMT's last redoubt in Taiwan would fall.[53]

The KMT, in sum, were transformed from a small and generally inconsequential revolutionary group to the rulers of China in a decade and then again transformed to discredited and seemingly doomed exiles in Taiwan in another twenty years. The reasons for the failure of the Republic obviously included both the overwhelming problems facing the country and the considerable shortcomings of the KMT regime itself, with extreme disagreement existing among historians and, especially, political partisans over how much weight should be given each factor.

The KMT probably should not be given too much blame for their failures to unify China and end humiliation and exploitation at the hands of foreign imperialists, since they simply were not strong enough to bring the warlords to heel or to resist Japanese threats. In the realm of restructuring the government and polity, the Nationalists appear much more culpable in not living up to the ideals of the *San Min Chu I*. Modest progress, at least at times, was made toward constitutionalism and reforming the bureaucracy, but the regime remained essentially authoritarian, repressive and even terroristic, highly factionalized, and marked by bureaucratic indifference and contempt toward the people that differed little from the Ch'ing dynasty. Judgment in the realm of promoting economic development or "people's livelihood" is even more ambiguous. Significant economic progress was made under government auspices during the 1930s, which might even be considered remarkable, given the objective problems facing China. On the other hand, no coherent economic strategy emerged; attempts at "state-building" destroyed the traditional social fabric and alienated much of the population; there was little effort to help peasants and workers; the ever-increasing demands for taxes placed an impossible burden on most Chinese; and government corruption and bureaucratism clearly contributed to the disaster of the 1940s.

Portents

On the surface, Taiwan faced a rather bleak situation at the time of the R.O.C.'s evacuation to the island in 1949. Much of the economic transformation and development that had occurred in the brief period of self-strengthening and during the colonial administration had been destroyed. The Nationalist regime appeared defeated and discredited, and moreover, it had earned the enmity of the Taiwanese because of the February 28 uprising. Thus Taiwan seemed an exceedingly unpromising site for an "economic miracle."

There were other, less obvious factors regarding both the island's past development and the history of Chiang Kai-shek and the KMT that suggested a more optimistic picture. A base had been laid for a more integrated economy and industrialization pattern than exist in most developing countries. If anything were to come of such "structural" potentials, however, a major revolution was needed in the "behavioral" dimension of providing leadership in the formulation and implementation of a successful development strategy. Here, the KMT had some potential, if they could survive the threat of Communist conquest. The KMT leadership included the skilled administrators and entrepreneurs who could fill the void left by Japanese exclusion of Taiwanese from these fields. The party, in addition, was based on a strongly developmentalist ideology committed to nationalism, democracy, and people's livelihood. The question, therefore, was whether the KMT leaders were capable of learning from their past mistakes and returning to their roots.

Notes

1. The R.O.C. continues to use the traditional Wade-Giles system for rendering Chinese into the Roman alphabet, whereas the P.R.C. has introduced the new "pin-yin" system of Romanization, which is much closer phonetically to English than Wade-Giles. Because this book is about Taiwan, Wade-Giles spelling will generally be used. The one exception is current political leaders and major places in the P.R.C. for whom or which the pin-yin spelling is much more familiar now (e.g., Zhao Ziyang or Beijing). For other people or places associated with the P.R.C., the Wade-Giles spelling is used with the pin-yin in parentheses after the first usage. Also, general usage is followed for a few common terms, (e.g., Taiwan or Taiping Rebellion instead of T'aiwan or T'ai-p'ing) or spellings used in proper names.

2. Chiao-min Hsieh, *Taiwan–Ilha Formosa: A Geography in Perspective* (Washington, D.C.: Butterworth's 1964), pt. I.

3. George W. Barclay, *Colonial Development and Population in Taiwan* (Princeton, N.J.: Princeton University Press, 1954), pp. 15–16.

4. Richard L. Walker, "Taiwan's Movement into Political Modernity, 1945–1972," in Paul K. T. Sih, ed., *Taiwan in Modern Times* (New York: St. John's University Press, 1973), p. 362. For a broader discussion of differences among ethnic groups see Hill Gates, "Ethnicity and Social Class," in Emily H. Ahern and Hill Gates, eds., *The Anthropology of Taiwanese Society* (Stanford, Calif.: Stanford University Press, 1981), pp. 241–281.

5. George M. Beckman, "Brief Episodes—Dutch and Spanish Rule," in Paul K. T. Sih, ed., *Taiwan in Modern Times* (New York: St. John's University Press, 1973), pp. 31–57; Hsieh, *Taiwan—Ilha Formosa*, ch. 11; and Wen-hsiung Hsu, "From Aboriginal Island to Chinese Frontier: The Development of Taiwan Before 1683," in Ronald G. Knapp, ed., *China's Island Frontier* (Honolulu: University Press of Hawaii, 1980), pp. 3–29.

6. Parris H. Chang, "Cheng Cheng-kung (Koxinga) and Chinese Nationalism in Taiwan, 1662–1683," in Paul K. T. Sih, ed., *Taiwan in Modern Times* (New York: St. John's University Press, 1973), pp. 59–86; Ralph C. Crozier, *Koxinga and Chinese Nationalism* (Cambridge, Mass.: East Asian Research Center, Harvard University, 1977); and W. G. Goddard, *The Makers of Taiwan* (Taipei: China Publishing Company, 1963), chs. 1 and 2.

7. Thomas B. Gold, *State and Society in the Taiwan Miracle* (Armonk, N.Y.: M. E. Sharpe, 1986), ch. 2; Wen-hsiung Hsu, "Frontier Social Organization and Social Disorder

in Ch'ing Taiwan," in Ronald G. Knapp, ed., *China's Island Frontier* (Honolulu: University Press of Hawaii, 1980), pp. 87–105; Ting-yee Kuo, "The Internal Development and Modernization of Taiwan, 1683–1891," in Paul K. T. Sih, ed., *Taiwan in Modern Times* (New York: St. John's University Press, 1973), pp. 171–240; and Edwin A. Winckler, "Mass Political Incorporation, 1500–2000," in Edwin S. Winckler and Susan Greenhalgh, eds., *Contending Approaches to the Political Economy of Taiwan* (Armonk, N.Y.: M. E. Sharpe, 1988), pp. 47–53.

8. Gold, *State and Society*, ch. 2; Samuel P. S. Ho, *Economic Development of Taiwan, 1860–1970* (New Haven, Conn.: Yale University Press, 1978), ch. 2; Hsieh, *Taiwan—Ilha Formosa*, ch. 12; Ramon H. Myers, "Taiwan Under Ch'ing Imperial Rule, 1684–1895: The Traditional Economy," *Journal of the Institute of Chinese Studies of the Chinese University of Hong Kong* 5:2 (No. 2, 1972), pp. 373–409; and Sophia Su-fei Yen, *Taiwan in China's Foreign Relations, 1836–1874* (Hamden, Conn.: Shoe String Press, 1965), pt. II.

9. Ho, *Economic Development of Taiwan*, pp. 20–21.

10. Samuel Chu, "Liu Ming-ch'uan and the Modernization of Taiwan," *Journal of Asian Studies* 23:1 (November 1963), pp. 37–53; Goddard, *Makers of Taiwan*, ch. 4; Kuo, "Internal Development and Modernization of Taiwan," pp. 184–237; William M. Speidel, "The Administration and Fiscal Reforms of Liu Ming-ch'uan in Taiwan, 1884–1891: Foundation for Self-strengthening," *Journal of Asian Studies* 35:3 (May 1976), pp. 441–459; and Yen, *Taiwan*, pt. III.

11. The Japanese did reduce the preexisting three-tier land tenure system to two tiers, but this had little effect on the actual economic and social relations is rural areas. Edgar Wickberg, "Continuities in Land Tenure, 1900–1940," in Emily Martin Ahern and Hill Gates, eds., *The Anthropology of Taiwanese Society* (Stanford, Calif.: Stanford University Press, 1981), pp. 212–238.

12. Han-yu Chang and Ramon Myers, "Japanese Colonial Development Policy in Taiwan," *Journal of Asian Studies* 22:4 (August 1963), pp. 433–449; Ho, *Economic Development of Taiwan*, chs. 3 and 4; Hsieh, *Taiwan—Ilha Formosa*, ch. 13; Teng-hui Lee, *Intersectoral Capital Flows in the Economic Development of Taiwan, 1895–1960* (Ithaca, N.Y.: Cornell University Press, 1971), chs. 2–4; Eric Thorbecke, "Agricultural Development," in Walter Galenson, ed., *Economic Growth and Structural Change in Taiwan: The Postwar Experience of the Republic of China* (Ithaca, N.Y.: Cornell University Press, 1979), pp. 133–138; and E. Patricia Tsurumi, *Japanese Colonial Education in Taiwan, 1895–1945* (Cambridge, Mass.: Harvard University Press, 1977).

13. Barclay, *Colonial Development and Population*, ch. 3; and Lee, *Intersectoral Capital Flows*, chs. 2 and 5.

14. Ho, *Economic Development of Taiwan*, p. 72.

15. Barclay, *Colonial Development and Population*, ch. 2; Ho, *Economic Development of Taiwan*, ch. 5; and Ching-yuan Lin, *Industrialization in Taiwan, 1946–72: Trade and Import-Substitution Policies for Developing Countries* (New York: Praeger, 1973), ch. 2.

16. Ho, *Economic Development of Taiwan*, pp. 29–32; and Lin, *Industrialization in Taiwan*, p. 3.

17. Gold, *State and Society*, ch. 3; Hyman Kublin, "Taiwan's Japanese Interlude, 1895–1945," in Paul K. T. Sih, ed., *Taiwan in Modern Times* (New York: St. John's University Press, 1973), pp. 317–335.

18. Bruce Cumings, "World System and Authoritarian Regimes in Korea, 1948–

1984," in Edwin A. Winckler and Susan Greenhalgh, eds., *Contending Approaches to the Political Economy of Taiwan* (Armonk, N.Y.: M. E. Sharpe, 1988), pp. 257–258.

19. Ian M. D. Little, "An Economic Reconnaissance," in Walter Galenson, ed., *Economic Growth and Structural Change in Taiwan: The Postwar Experience of the Republic of China* (Ithaca, N.Y.: Cornell University Press, 1979), p. 453.

20. Edward I-te Chen, "Formosan Political Movements Under Japanese Colonial Rule, 1914–1937," *Journal of Asian Studies* 31:3 (May 1972), pp. 477–497; Thomas B. Gold, "Colonial Origins of Taiwanese Capitalism," in Edwin A. Winckler and Susan Greenhalgh, eds., *Contending Approaches to the Political Economy of Taiwan* (Armonk, N.Y.: M. E. Sharpe, 1988), pp. 101—117; Gold, *State and Society*, ch. 3; Ho, *Economic Development of Taiwan*, pp. 86–90; George H. Kerr, *Formosa: Licensed Revolution and the Home Rule Movement, 1895–1945* (Honolulu: University Press of Hawaii, 1974); Kublin, "Japanese Interlude," pp. 317–335; and Winckler, "Political Incorporation," pp. 54–58.

21. Gustav Ranis, "Industrial Development," in Walter Galenson, ed., *Economic Growth and Structural Change in Taiwan: The Postwar Experience of the Republic of China* (Ithaca, N.Y.: Cornell University Press, 1979), p. 209.

22. George H. Kerr, *Formosa Betrayed* (Boston: Houghton Mifflin, 1965); and Douglas Mendel, *The Politics of Formosan Nationalism* (Berkeley: University of California Press, 1970), provide the most detailed accounts but are extremely critical of KMT oppression of the Taiwanese. For a more balanced summary see Gold, *State and Society*, ch. 4.

23. Maurice Meisner, "The Development of Formosan Nationalism," in Mark Mancall, ed., *Formosa Today* (New York: Praeger, 1964), pp. 147–162; and Mendel, *Formosan Nationalism*, ch. 1.

24. John F. Copper with George P. Chen, *Taiwan's Elections: Political Development and Democratization in the Republic of China* (Baltimore: School of Law, University of Maryland, 1984), ch. 2.

25. Myers, "Taiwan Under Ch'ing Imperial Rule, 1684–1895: The Traditional Society," *Journal of the Institute of Chinese Studies of the Chinese University of Hong Kong* 5:2 (No. 2, 1972), pp. 413–451.

26. O. Edmund Clubb, *20th Century China*, 3rd ed. (New York: Columbia University Press, 1975), ch. 1; Immanuel C. Y. Hsu, *The Rise of Modern China*, 3rd ed. (New York: Oxford University Press, 1983), pts. II–IV; and Frederic Wakeman, Jr. *The Fall of Imperial China* (New York: Free Press, 1975), especially chs. 7–11.

27. Hsu, *Rise of Modern China*, ch. 10; and Yu-win Jen, *The Taiping Revolutionary Movement* (New Haven, Conn.: Yale University Press, 1973).

28. Joseph W. Esherick, *The Origins of the Boxer Uprising* (Berkeley: University of California Press, 1987); and Victor Purcell, *The Boxer Uprising: A Background Study* (Cambridge: Cambridge University Press, 1963).

29. Wellington K. K. Chan, *Merchants, Mandarins, and Modern Enterprise in Late Ch'ing China* (Cambridge, Mass.: Harvard University Press, 1977); Albert Feuerwerker, *China's Early Industrialization: Sheng Hsuan-huai, 1844–1916, and Mandarin Enterprise* (Cambridge, Mass.: Harvard University Press, 1958); and Hsu, *Rise of Modern China*, ch. 11.

30. Hao Chang, *Chinese Intellectuals in Crisis: Search for Order and Meaning (1890–1911)* (Berkeley: University of California Press, 1987), ch. 2; Jerome B. Grieder, *Intellectuals and the State in Modern China* (New York: Free Press, 1981), ch. 4; and

Luke S. K. Kwong, *A Mosaic of the Hundred Days: Personalities, Politics, and Ideas of 1898* (Cambridge, Mass.: Harvard University Press, 1984).

31. Harold Z. Schiffrin, *Sun Yat-sen and the Origins of the 1911 Revolution* (Berkeley: University of California Press, 1968); and C. Martin Wilbur, *Sun Yat-sen, Frustrated Patriot* (New York: Columbia University Press, 1976).

32. Sun Yat-sen, *San Min Chu I: Three Principles of the People* (Taipei: China Publishing Co., 1958). For analytic interpretations see Robert E. Bedeski, *State-Building in Modern China: The Kuomintang in the Prewar Period* (Berkeley: Institute of East Asian Studies, University of California, 1981), ch. 7; A. James Gregor with Maria Hsia Chang, and Andrew B. Zimmerman, *Ideology and Development: Sun Yat-sen and the Economic History of Taiwan* (Berkeley: Institute of East Asian Studies, University of California, 1981), especially ch. 1; and Wilbur, *Sun Yat-sen*, pp. 197–207, 243–245.

33. Jerome Ch'en, *Yuan Shih-k'ai*, 2nd ed. (Stanford, Calif.: Stanford University Press, 1972); Hsi-sheng Ch'i, *Warlord Politics in China, 1916–1928* (Stanford, Calif.: Stanford University Press, 1976); Joseph W. Esherick, *Reform and Revolution in China: The 1911 Revolution in Hunan and Hubei* (Berkeley: University of California Press, 1976); Andrew J. Nathan, *Peking Politics, 1918–1923: Factionalism and the Failure of Constitutionalism* (Berkeley: University of California Press, 1976); Lucian W. Pye, *Warlord Politics: Conflict and Coalition in the Modernization of Republican China* (New York: Praeger, 1971); James E. Sheridan, *China in Disintegration: The Republican Era in Chinese History, 1912–1949* (New York: Free Press, 1975), chs. 2 and 3; Mary Clabaugh Wright, ed., *China in Revolution: The First Phase, 1900–1913* (New Haven, Conn.: Yale University Press, 1968); and George T. Yu, *Party Politics in Republican China: The Kuomintang, 1912–1924* (Berkeley: University of California Press, 1966), chs. 1–5.

34. Tse-tsung Chow, *The May Fourth Movement: Intellectual Revolution in Modern China* (Cambridge, Mass.: Harvard University Press, 1960); and Vera Schwarcz, *The Chinese Enlightenment: Intellectuals and the Legacy of the May Fourth Movement of 1919* (Berkeley: University of California Press, 1986).

35. Brian Crozier, *The Man Who Lost China: The First Full Biography of Chiang Kai-shek* (New York: Charles Scribner's Sons, 1976), chs. 3–6; Richard B. Landis, "Training and Indoctrination at the Whampoa Academy," in F. Gilbert Chan and Thomas Etzold, eds., *China in the 1920s: Nationalism and Revolution* (New York: Franklin Watts, 1976), pp. 73–93; Sheridan, *China in Disintegration*, ch. 5; Martin Wilbur, *The Nationalist Revolution in China, 1923–1928* (Cambridge: Cambridge University Press, 1983), chs. 1 and 2; and Yu, *Party Politics in Republican China*, chs. 6 and 7.

36. Bedeski, *State-Building in Modern China*, ch. 3; George F. Botjer, *A Short History of Nationalist China, 1919–1949* (New York: G. P. Putnam, 1979), ch. 2; Tuan-sheng Ch'ien, *The Government and Politics of China* (Cambridge, Mass.: Harvard University Press, 1950), chs. 6–8; Crozier, *The Man Who Lost China*, chs. 7–10; Donald A. Jordan, *The Northern Expedition: China's National Revolution of 1926–1928* (Honolulu: University Press of Hawaii, 1976); and Wilbur, *Nationalist Revolution*, chs. 3–7.

37. Sheridan, *China in Disintegration*, ch. 6.

38. Edgar Snow, *Red Star over China* (New York: Random House, 1938); Richard C. Thornton, *China, the Struggle for Power, 1917–1972* (Bloomington: Indiana University Press, 1973), chs. 1–4; and Dick Wilson, *The Long March: The Epic of Chinese Communism's Survival 1935* (New York: Viking Press, 1971).

39. Botjer, *History of Nationalist China*, ch. 5; and John Israel, *Student Nationalism in China, 1927–1937* (Stanford, Calif.: Stanford University Press, 1966).

40. Botjer, *History of Nationalist China*, ch. 4; Clubb, *20th Century China*, ch. 6; and Alvin D. Coox and Hilary Conroy, eds., *China and Japan: A Search for Balance Since World War I* (Santa Barbara, Calif.: ABC-Clio, 1978), pt. II.

41. Lloyd E. Eastman, *The Abortive Revolution: China Under Nationalist Rule, 1927–1937* (Cambridge, Mass.: Harvard University Press, 1974), especially chs. 2 and 4; Sterling Seagrave, *The Soong Dynasty* (New York: Harper & Row, 1985), chs. 10–15; and Hung-mao Tien, *Government and Politics in Kuomintang China, 1927–1937* (Stanford, Calif.: Stanford University Press, 1972), especially ch. 3.

42. Parks M. Coble, *The Shanghai Capitalists and the Nationalist Government, 1927–1937* (Cambridge, Mass.: Harvard University Press, 1980), especially chs. 5 and 7; Eastman, *Abortive Revolution*, ch. 5; Joseph Fewsmith, *Party, State, and Local Elites in Republican China: Merchant Organizations and Politics in Shanghai, 1890–1930* (Honolulu: University Press of Hawaii, 1985); Sheridan, *China in Disintegration*, ch. 7; and Arthur N. Young, *China's Nation-Building Effort, 1927–1937: The Financial and Economic Record* (Stanford, Calif.: Stanford University Press, 1971).

43. Coble, *Shanghai Capitalists*; Eastman, *Abortive Revolution*, ch. 5; and Fewsmith, *Party, State, and Local Elites*.

44. Prasenjit Duara, *Culture, Power, and the State: Rural North China, 1900–1942* (Stanford, Calif.: Stanford University Press, 1988).

45. Paul K. T. Sih, ed., *The Strenuous Decade: China's Nation-Building Efforts, 1927–1937* (New York: St. John's University Press, 1970), represents the most optimistic conclusion that the KMT's "nation-building efforts" had succeeded by 1936 and that only the Japanese invasion caused the regime's ultimate failure. Even such a skeptic as Eastman, *Abortive Revolution*, ch. 6, however, agrees that the situation in China and the KMT's popularity had improved considerably by 1936. Hsu, *Rise of Modern China*, pp. 565–573, provides a good short summary of the KMT's relative successes and failures.

46. Clubb, *20th Century China*, pp. 202–210; and Tein-wei Wu, *The Sian Incident: A Pivotal Point in Modern Chinese History* (Ann Arbor: Michigan Monographs in Chinese Studies, 1976).

47. Botjer, *History of Nationalist China*, ch. 6; Alvin D. Coox, "Recourse to Arms: The Sino-Japanese Conflict, 1937–1945," in Coox and Conroy, *China and Japan*, pp. 295–321; Frank Dorn, *The Sino-Japanese War: From Marco Polo Bridge to Pearl Harbor* (New York: Macmillan, 1974); and Dick Wilson, *When Tigers Fight: The Story of the Sino-Japanese War, 1937–1945* (New York: Viking Press, 1982).

48. Chalmers Johnson, *Peasant Nationalism and Communist Power: The Emergence of Revolutionary China, 1937–1945* (Stanford, Calif.: Stanford University Press, 1962). However, also see Robert A. Kapp, "The Kuomintang and Rural China in the War of Resistance, 1937–1945," in F. Gilbert Chan, ed., *China at the Crossroads, 1927–1949* (Boulder, Colo.: Westview Press, 1980), pp. 151–182, for the argument that images that the KMT lost the support of the peasantry because of their ties to the rural gentry are too simplistic. Kapp's conclusions, though, do stress the responsibilities of the central government.

49. Lloyd Eastman, *Seeds of Destruction: Nationalist China in War and Revolution, 1937–1949* (Cambridge, Mass.: Harvard University Press, 1984), chs. 1, 2 and 5; Kapp, "Kuomintang and Rural China," pp. 151–182; and Arthur N. Young, *China's Wartime Finance and Inflation, 1937–1945* (Cambridge, Mass.: Harvard University Press, 1965).

50. Crozier, *Man Who Lost China*, pt. III; Herbert Feis, *The China Tangle: The American Effort in China from Pearl Harbor to the Marshall Mission* (Princeton, N.J.: Princeton University Press, 1953); Michael Schaller, *The U.S. Crusade in China, 1938–1945* (New York: Columbia University Press, 1979); Tang Tsou, *America's Failure in China, 1941–50* (Chicago: University of Chicago Press, 1963); Barbara W. Tuchman, *Stilwell and the American Experience in China, 1911–45* (New York: Macmillan, 1971), pt. II; and Arthur N. Young, *China and the Helping Hand, 1937–1945* (Cambridge, Mass.: Harvard University Press, 1963).

51. Forrest C. Pogue, *George C. Marshall: Statesman* (New York: Viking Press, 1987), pp. 141–142. The Marshall mission is described in detail in chs. 3–6.

52. Shun-hsien Chou, *The Chinese Inflation, 1937–1949* (New York: Columbia University Press, 1964); Eastman, *Seeds of Destruction*, especially chs. 3 and 8; Suzanne Pepper, *Civil War in China: The Political Struggle, 1945–1949* (Berkeley: University of California Press, 1978), pt. I; and Seagrave, *Soong Dynasty*, chs. 17–20.

53. Botjer, *History of Nationalist China*, ch. 7; and Hsu, *Rise of Modern China*, ch. 25. Steven A. Levine, *Anvil of Victory: The Communist Revolution in Manchuria, 1945–1948* (New York: Columbia University Press, 1987), provides an excellent case study of a critical region in the war. For detailed discussions of Sino-American relations see Dorothy Borg and Waldo Heinrichs, eds., *The Uncertain Years: Chinese-American Relations, 1947–1950* (New York: Columbia University Press, 1980); June Grasso, *Truman's Two-China Policy, 1948–1950* (Armonk, N.Y.: M. E. Sharpe, 1987); and Nancy Bernkopf Tucker, *Patterns in the Dust: Chinese-American Relations and the Recognition Controversy, 1949–1950* (New York: Columbia University Press, 1983).

PART II

PERFORMANCE

The Republic of China in the International Arena: Conflict, Clientelism, and the Search for Stability

Despite its history as the "Middle Kingdom" and its view of foreigners as barbarians coming to pay tribute to its court, China had never attained even medium power status in the global international system before 1950. The nineteenth century witnessed the Western imposition of semicolonial status through the "unequal treaties." The Revolution of 1911–1912 did little to improve matters as the warlord-dominated "phantom Republic" was too chaotic and disunited to have much of a foreign policy. Even the Kuomintang's (KMT's) coming to power in 1928 with an explicitly nationalist program did not help China's international position much, as detailed in chapter 3. The weakness of China's economy prevented Chiang Kai-shek from moving against foreign capital; much more important, China's external environment was essentially defined by the increasingly aggressive encroachments of the much more powerful Japan. China's alliance with the United States during World War II stimulated Roosevelt's inclusion of China among "the big five" that, he hoped, would preside over the postwar international order. However, the chasm that had opened between the KMT and the Chinese Communist party (CCP) meant that such hopes were pipedreams, even after the defeat of Japan.

Thus, when the government of the Republic of China (R.O.C.) was forced to flee to Taiwan at the end of 1949, any expectations that it could develop a successful foreign policy would have appeared rather dismal. The R.O.C. was now confined to a few islands with a population of less than 2 percent of China's total. The economy of Taiwan was a former colonial one with a low per capita income and agricultural focus—precisely the conditions that, according to dependency theory, should promote the confining linkages to the world economy that ensure continued stagnation. Moreover, Taiwan's diplomatic condition was such that extreme political and military dependency appeared inevitable. It was threatened by the much more powerful Communist regime, which had inflicted a total and humiliating defeat on the mainland. Thus its only hope for even physical survival lay in the provision of support and protection by the United States.

Despite these extremely unsalubrious conditions, the R.O.C. prospered. Its economic growth became legendary; it navigated a largely independent path through the shoals of international politics; and it even survived international ostracism to become stabler economically and politically. Yet, if from one perspective Taiwan appears an extraordinary small-state "success story," it also points up the limitations inherent in weakness in global politics. Thus history has demonstrated that the R.O.C. cannot take any of its temporary "successes" (whether they be penetration of the U.S. polity through the "China lobby," protection of national interests in economic negotiations, or achievement of an "armed truce" with the People's Republic of China [P.R.C.]) for granted. Rather, evolving political and economic circumstances confront Taiwan with new challenges almost as soon (if not sooner) as an old crisis is solved.

For almost the entire postwar period the centerpiece of the R.O.C.'s foreign policy has been its conflict with the P.R.C. over which government represents China. Initially this conflict had a strong potential for a "hot war," with a Communist invasion appearing imminent after the KMT evacuated to Taiwan in 1949. The outbreak of the Korean War, however, led to the extension of America's security umbrella to Taiwan and the evolution of "cold war" competition between the Nationalists and Communists. This entailed the R.O.C.'s becoming a client-state of the United States. During the 1950s and 1960s this alliance was quite stable as the political and economic objectives of the two countries remained in concert. In fact, the R.O.C. appeared to manipulate its clientelistic position quite successfully in the pursuit of its own goals, indicating that weakness and dependency are not necessarily deleterious in the international realm. Over the 1970s and 1980s, though, major policy divergencies developed, owing to America's rapprochement with the P.R.C. and growing economic conflict between Taiwan and its patron. The search for stability in its international position, hence, became increasingly strained for Taiwan as its client-state status began to be threatened by the changing international environment.

This chapter provides an overview of the diplomatic history of the R.O.C. during the postwar period. The first section describes the creation of the alliance with the United States in the early 1950s that has provided the undergirding of Taiwan's international position ever since and the stabilization of its relationship with the P.R.C. after the two Taiwan Strait crises in 1954 and 1958. The second discusses the R.O.C.'s participation in two very different types of competition over the next two decades: a losing rivalry for diplomatic status with the P.R.C. and a successful manipulation of trade and economic negotiations to stimulate domestic growth. The final substantive section, titled "The World Turned Upside Down," examines Taiwan's successful recovery from the breaking of diplomatic relations by its patron coupled with new challenges in economic relations with the United States and political relations with mainland China.

Setting the Parameters of Alignment with the United States

The road to the Sino-American alliance of the 1950s was anything but smooth and straight. The strains of the Stilwell mission in World War II were exacerbated as the Chinese civil war broke out while the United States tried to pursue a mediatory policy. As total Communist victory loomed, the Truman administration refused to intervene, despite growing domestic pressures from the "China lobby." The outbreak of the Korean War led to an immediate change in policy and an American commitment to protect Taiwan in a rather delayed application of the containment doctrine to Asia. However, the relations between the U.S. government and the Chiang Kai-shek regime remained far from completely harmonious, even after the much friendlier Eisenhower administration took office in 1953.

The initial Roosevelt policy toward China as the "light at the end of the tunnel" appeared in World War II assumed a postwar order based on an entente among the Allies. Roosevelt believed that a unified China would emerge as the dominant power in East Asia after the war with the destruction of Japanese power and the withering away of European colonial systems. Thus, in addition to the central military goal of defeating the Japanese, American policy toward China aimed at promoting national reconciliation and a strong government and at obtaining recognition of great power status for postwar China. These efforts (along with growing realization of China's weaknesses) culminated in the agreements at Yalta in February 1945. In the general bargaining over the Soviet Union's entry into the war against Japan after the conclusion of the war in Europe, the Soviet Union agreed to support the KMT government in return for concessions for special rights in Manchuria's major harbors and ports. Although critics of U.S.-China policy later termed Yalta a sellout, this appeared quite reasonable, given the military realities in Asia. It was certainly greeted at the time with less despondency in Chungking (the KMT was angered that Chiang Kai-sek was not included in the negotiations) than in Yenan by the two parties directly competing to control China; a Sino-Soviet Treaty was signed along these general lines in August, just before Japan's surrender.[1]

In line with the logic of Yalta that both the United States and USSR would support a China led by Chiang Kai-shek, Patrick Hurley, the American ambassador to China, made some efforts to create a coalition government that would be dominated by the KMT that proved fruitless. After the Japanese surrender both sides tried to claim as much territory as possible, with the United States providing much more assistance to the KMT than the USSR did to the CCP; by the autumn of 1945 major fighting had erupted. The failure of U.S. policy was signaled by Hurley's dramatic resignation in November on a trip to Washington when he blamed his failure on pro-Communist diplomats in China—charges that were to reverberate much more loudly in the early 1950s than they did when they were made.

After Hurley's resignation President Truman appointed General George C. Marshall to lead a peace mission to China. Marshall succeeded in arranging a truce and made some progress toward a political agreement. The United States placed an arms embargo on China in the hope of promoting the peace process. Yet the talks ultimately fell apart—probably inevitably, given the basic irreconcilable political goals of the KMT and CCP—and the Chinese civil war was in full swing by late 1946. Marshall, blaming hardliners in both parties for the civil war, returned to Washington in January 1947 to become secretary of state. U.S. policy, for its part, seemed to suggest the adage "cursed be the peacemakers," since both the KMT and Communists felt betrayed by the Americans.[2]

Thus, when the Chinese civil war was being decided in 1947 and 1948, official American policy was clearly ambivalent. The State Department under Marshall and presumably President Truman had little love for Mao Zedong's Communist party and no wish that it would emerge as the new ruler of China. On the other hand, the KMT was viewed with suspicion and contempt as a corrupt and inefficient regime that did not deserve U.S. support. The result was that America did little, providing only limited aid to the Nationalist government and forces; as the tide of battle turned decisively against the Nationalists in 1948, the realistic determination was made that the United States could not affect the outcome short of actions (e.g., the major commitment of U.S. troops) that the administration was quite unwilling to undertake.[3]

This dilemma of what to do about the rapidly deteriorating position in China gave rise to the probably wishful expectation that the impending CCP victory might not represent a major disaster if a reconciliation could be worked out with Mao's regime. Furthermore, advocacy for establishing relations with the Communists, especially as their victory appeared increasingly inevitable, came from a variety of external and internal sources. Several allies, in particular Britain, wanted to establish relations with the P.R.C. to ensure that "business as usual" would continue; many Asian countries saw the Chinese Communists as anticolonial heroes; businessmen and missionaries in China hoped for an accommodation with the new rulers; and many scholars and diplomats viewed the Communists as nationalists who were sweeping out a corrupt and repressive regime that was little better than the preceding warlords.

Thus, especially after Dean Acheson became secretary of state in January 1949, United States seemingly hoped that the Chinese Communists would follow the Titoist model of independence from the USSR (American diplomats were well aware of Stalin's penchant for sacrificing Mao's interests for his own in negotiations). As the last Nationalist defenses on the mainland crumbled during 1949, and as the Communist forces built up for an amphibious invasion of Taiwan in the first half of 1950, therefore, American policy was to provide token aid to the KMT and wait for a propitious time to recognize the P.R.C. America's backing away from Chiang Kai-shek and the KMT was perhaps best symbolized by the *China White Paper* issued by the State Department in August 1949, which blamed the "loss of China" on the ineffectiveness, policy mistakes, and corruption of the Nationalist regime. Although much of this criticism was certainly justified, the *White Paper* was just as certainly rather self-serving for the United States. However, the attempt to influence the CCP in a Titoist direction was undermined by the somewhat hostile attitude that the United States adopted in public toward the CCP both because it did not want to be seen as undermining the Nationalists and because it hoped to pressure the Chinese Communists into assuming more nationalist positions. Consequently, the CCP continued to view America as pro-KMT and harassed Americans in the "liberated" areas of China, which made rapproachement even harder.[4]

This drift in U.S.-China policy became quite controversial, as might well have been expected. In terms of domestic policy, the Truman administration's acquiescence to a Communist victory in China stood in sharp contrast to its proclamation of a global policy of "containment" directed against communism and the Soviet Union, and its major commitment of resources to an anti-Soviet crusade in Europe dating from 1947. Within the government, for instance, the Defense Department and the military generally favored the greatly expanded support for the KMT necessary to prevent a Communist takeover in China.

There was, of course, an obvious answer to the question of why the administration was not applying its containment policy in Asia—that the strategic competition with the Soviet Union was centered in Europe, making it unwise for America to waste its finite resources in a nonessential region. Although this logic was strongly believed by most of the key foreign policymakers, the administration's attempt to sell "containment" in terms of global anti-communism made a discussion of regional priorities difficult. By the late 1940s China had also become a major partisan issue that inflamed the rhetoric to say the least. The Republicans, shocked by Truman's upset win in the 1948 presidential election, saw the China debacle as an easy target for excoriating the administration in terms of its own rhetoric for "coddling Communists."[5]

The leaders of the R.O.C. were the ones most affected by the drift of American policy toward the malign neglect of their cause. By early 1948 it had become clear that the very survival of the regime depended on massive American aid. Yet Chiang Kai-shek was far from a U.S. puppet; in fact, the American reluctance to support the KMT was derived in large part from past strains that emanated from the somewhat divergent goals of the two countries. America's policy toward China was primarily directed toward defeating the Japanese in World War II and creating a viable central government in the postwar period. Chiang, in contrast, believed, with a good deal of justification, that the rivalry between the KMT and CCP would determine China's political fate. These different perspectives, in turn, provide a partial explanation for Chiang's conflicts with Stilwell, the overextension of KMT deployments in North China and Manchuria after the war, and Chiang's toleration of inept generals and corrupt bureaucrats that did so much to poison Sino-American relations and weaken the KMT regime itself during the mid–1940s.

The KMT leadership evidently believed that whatever the individual disputes between the two countries, the United States would ultimately provide the aid needed for their regime's survival simply because of the logic of cold war "containment." In particular, they felt that the anticipated Dewey victory of 1948 would result in the immediate reorientation of American policy. Truman's victory, coupled with the loss of North China, led instead to a significant re-orientation of Chinese policy. Before the presidential election Chinese policy had focused on normal diplomatic interaction with the administration and fairly limited support of what came to be called the "China lobby"—outspoken critics of Truman's and Marshall's China policy. After the election it was clear that normal diplomacy was doomed. Thus the major effort of the R.O.C.'s policy toward the United States turned to generating external political pressure on the Truman administration that would force it to reverse its policy in China.[6]

This switch to using the "China lobby" as the major vehicle for Chinese diplomacy was signaled by the return of Madame Chiang Kai-shek, a popular figure in the United States, to New York in December 1949, where she coor-dinated much of the R.O.C.'s increasingly desperate efforts to secure massive American aid. The China lobby itself was composed of a diverse lot of American influentials. Some were strong supporters of Chiang and the KMT; others viewed China from the perspective of cold war competition; and others seemed primarily concerned with finding a handy stick with which to beat the incumbent admin-istration. Some of its most prominent figures included military leaders (e.g., Douglas MacArthur and Claire Chennault), publishers (e.g., Henry Luce and William Randolph Hearst), businessmen with ties to China (e.g., Alfred Kohl-berg), several religious groups, and some prominent conservative Republicans in Congress (e.g., Walter Judd). The China lobby argued that China was essential to American interests and that the Truman administration was foolhardy to allow a hostile regime to come to power. As time passed the China lobby became increasingly strident, emphasizing the "betrayal" of Chiang Kai-shek by pro-Communist figures in the administration and shifting the blame for the loss of China to American blunders and subversion; China figured prominently in the advent of McCarthyism in early 1950.[7]

Despite the later power of the China lobby to destroy the careers and lives of its enemies, it was clearly ineffectual before the outbreak of the Korean War as the United States continued its disengagement from China. President Truman issued an official statement on "United States Policy toward Formosa" on Jan-uary 5, 1950, that confirmed America's belief that Taiwan was part of China and intention of not providing military support to the Nationalist government. As late as early June, Acheson and the State Department continued in their policy of awaiting the fall of Taiwan and anticipating the ultimate recognition of the P.R.C. There was the assumption that the shrill cries of the China lobby could not dispel that the general public was not greatly concerned with China and opposed American military intervention there.[8] Contrariwise, although several historians have argued that America strongly considered forcing Chiang Kai-shek's abdication and replacing him with a government of native Taiwanese, the evidence here appears fairly tenuous.[9]

North Korea's invasion of South Korea brought an immediate and radical change to America's China policy. Now, Asia was seen as the source of a direct Communist threat; the containment logic was applied to Taiwan post haste; and the U.S. Seventh Fleet was ordered to protect Taiwan, which effectively ended the threat of a Communist invasion. This policy reversal, however, did little to improve the relations between the Truman administration and the R.O.C.:

"Truman's unfavorable attitude toward Chiang Kai-shek," . . . as well as the fear that Chiang would drag America into World War III if given half the chance, led the State Department to stress to Nationalist representatives the "very tentative" nature of America's defense commitment to them. If any large package of credits was to be considered for the island, it was intimated, Chiang would have to go. The Nationalists, for their part, reciprocated this pressure upon their bureaucratic enemies in Washington, seeking to ultimately tie the United States tightly to their cause. Unsurprisingly, this scenario led to bitter feelings between the two reluctant allies. As Dulles commented to [Chinese Ambassador] Koo on 25 July, "he found it extremely strange that although Nationalist China and the United States were engaged in the same struggle against the Communist danger, they were hardly on speaking terms."[10]

The Chinese intervention in the Korean War and the vicious fighting that followed changed the situation dramatically. The P.R.C. was seen as an implacable enemy; the United States made a strong commitment to the Chiang Kai-shek regime. Diplomatically, the United States used its considerable power to ostracize the P.R.C. and secure recognition for the R.O.C. as the sole legitimate government of China. For example, America supported the R.O.C.'s membership in the United Nations and U.N. Security Council and concluded the Peace Treaty with Japan with the understanding that Japan would "recognize" the R.O.C. by concluding a separate treaty with the R.O.C. but not the P.R.C.[11] Moreover, the United States provided massive military and economic support that guaranteed the island's security and laid the basis for its economic recovery (see chapter 6 for a discussion of U.S. aid). The U.S. aid program brought a large number of American officials into contact with the Taipei government with several implications for Sino-American relations and for the internal evolution of Taiwan's politics. Military cooperation and aid missions, starting with General McArthur's visit to Taiwan in early August 1950, reinforced America's commitment to the R.O.C.'s security and promoted the military modernization of Taiwan's armed forces. U.S. aid officials participated in many of the decisions about restructuring the domestic economy; although there is some controversy about the extent of their influence, they evidently helped to push through several important policies, such as land reform in the 1950s and externally oriented economic liberalization in the early 1960s.[12]

Domestic political change in America in the early 1950s improved Sino-American relations substantially. The election of Dwight Eisenhower as president in 1952 brought in an administration that was much more favorably disposed toward the R.O.C., and the wildfire of anti-Communist McCarthyism that swept the American political landscape made advocating the abandonment of Chiang Kai-shek a political impossibility. Yet even the advent of the Eisenhower administration and the purge of the State Department's Far Eastern specialists did not produce complete harmony between Washington and Taipei. For example, Eisenhower's famous "unleashing of Chiang Kai-shek" by ordering the Seventh Fleet to stop preventing R.O.C. attacks on the mainland was accompanied by the clear message that Taiwan's armed forces had better remain "leashed."[13]

Taipei and Beijing, accordingly, settled down to what Ralph Clough has called their "unfinished civil war."[14] The Seventh Fleet protected Taiwan; the overwhelming power of the Communists on the mainland made the unleashing of Chiang Kai-shek an unrealizable slogan. However, although both governments were secure and implacably hostile toward each other, they did share one common position—that Taiwan was an integral part of China, that each represented the sole legitimate government, and that a "two-China" or "one-China, one-Taiwan" situation was totally unacceptable.

The P.R.C. challenged the status quo twice during the 1950s with attacks on the "offshore islands" near the mainland that the R.O.C. still controlled in 1954–1955 and 1958. The CCP provoked these two "Taiwan Strait" crises presumably out of frustration over the consolidation of the R.O.C.'s position and continued U.S. diplomatic ostracism. Chinese military aggressiveness proved rather counterproductive, though, since it resulted in the reaffirmation of American support for Taiwan. Thus, although Taiwan withdrew from several smaller offshore islands in 1955, Communist attacks speeded up the adoption of the R.O.C.-U.S. Mutual Defense Treaty in December 1954 and the Joint Formosa Resolution of January 1955, which committed the United States to the protection of Taiwan and made military support of the two major offshore islands of Quemoy (Kinmen) and Matsu much more likely. The second Taiwan Strait crisis in the late summer of 1958 was shorter and more intense; it resulted in a strong and explicit American commitment to protect Quemoy and Matsu, as well as adding to the burgeoning Sino-Soviet split because of the USSR's reluctance to extend the full support expected by its Chinese allies.

The second Strait crisis also produced significant tensions between Taiwan and the Eisenhower administration as U.S. military support for the Nationalist cause did not go to the length that Chiang desired and as the administration's commitment to the offshore islands was unpopular, both internationally and domestically:

Dulles commented privately to his colleagues that Chiang Kai-shek must be made to realize that the US government had been forced to strain its relations with both Congress and its allies almost to the breaking point in order to save him and that such a situation could not be permitted to arise again.[15]

The results of such strains, however, yielded only cold comfort to the CCP. First, after the 1954–1955 offshore island crisis, the United States and the P.R.C. began ambassadorial talks in Geneva (later moved to Warsaw) in August 1955, much to the discomfort of the R.O.C. Yet these talks quickly stagnated, and their suspension helped to foment the second clash. Second, the apparent willingness of the American administration, including Secretary of State Dulles and President Eisenhower, to consider a "two-China" policy of recognizing and dealing with both Taipei and Beijing from the mid–1950s on brought consternation to both sides of the Taiwan Strait. For example, the Committee of One Million Against the Admission of Communist China to the United Nations, which had disbanded in August 1954, reorganized less than a year later amid fears of reconciliation with the P.R.C. Perhaps not so coincidently, Communist Premier Chou En-lai offered to open direct negotiations for the reintegration of Taiwan into China and warned against America's "two-China" policy in July 1955. The R.O.C. government for its part hunkered down, refusing to deal with the "Communist bandits" and relying on the China lobby to deter a reorientation in U.S. policy.[16]

The establishment of a stable alliance with the United States, in sum, occurred only after the Chinese intervention in the Korean War. This long delay in America's applying the logic of containment to Asia resulted from several factors: the European focus of top foreign policy–makers, strains with Chiang Kai-shek's government, (probably unrealistic) hopes about the attitudes of CCP leaders, and a willingness to let China policy drift. Once the alliance was established, Taiwan's position was secured, and the regime could turn its attention to economic and political reconstruction. The stability of the R.O.C.'s international position was subject to continuing challenge, however, since it was by far the smaller and weaker of the two governments claiming to represent China. In addition, its position as a client-state certainly held potential disadvantages. The conflict with the United States during the Truman era showed that American policy could be made with little regard for its effect on a weaker ally, such as the R.O.C. Thus, although America's military support was vital to Taiwan's security, the existence of such dependency was far from desirable.

Diplomatic and Trade Competition

After the 1958 crisis in the Taiwan Strait, relations between the R.O.C. and P.R.C. became frozen in an armed but nonaggressive hostility, in part because a military stalemate existed and in part because they must have realized that a new crisis might result in the imposition of a "two-China" solution that they both abhorred. Over the next decade, then, Taiwan's foreign policy focused on three major issues: (1) a diplomatic contest with the P.R.C. for status and recognition as the rulers of China, (2) negotiations aimed at protecting the island's trade as the international economy became increasingly "managed" by larger and more powerful nations, and (3) maintaining a favored client-state position in its relations with the United States. These three issue areas were strongly intertwined. The maintenance of Taiwan's trade negotiations focused on the United States. Thus this section is organized chronologically with a brief conclusion that compares the three types of diplomatic outcomes.

The status quo that had resulted from the resolution of the 1958 Taiwan Strait crisis and the fading of a direct Communist military threat to Taiwan proved short-lived. The next challenge came in the realm of diplomatic recognition and involved the R.O.C.'s holding of China's seat in the United Nations and the U.N. Security Council. At the time of the Korean War the United States had been able to mobilize a huge majority (forty-three to eleven with six abstentions in 1954) in support of a moratorium on Soviet and Communist demands to have the P.R.C. replace the R.O.C. in the United Nations. As memories of Korea faded and more nations, primarily from the Third World, joined the United Nations, however, there was increasing pressure to reconsider the China issue, since after all the Communist government controlled most of China's territory and population. By 1960 support for the moratorium had fallen to forty-two to thirty-four with twenty-two abstentions, and it seemed almost certain to be defeated within a few years.

A P.R.C. victory in the United Nations would have been rather unwelcome for the new Kennedy administration in the United States both because it feared the domestic political backlash of the China lobby and because the Communist Chinese had already rejected tentative moves to warm relations unless the United States abandoned the R.O.C. American efforts to save China's seat for their allies were complicated by the politics of admitting two other new members, Mongolia and Mauritania. The prime goal of several African nations whose votes were needed was Mauritania's admission, which the USSR threatened to veto unless the candidacy of its ally Mongolia was successful. The R.O.C., however, planned to use its power as a permanent member of the Security Council to veto the admission of Mongolia because it regarded Mongolia as an integral part of China and a lackey of the Soviet Union.

In the end the Kennedy administration worked things out nicely. The R.O.C. agreed to forego a Pyrrhic veto in return for a secret American pledge to veto the P.R.C.'s membership if necessary and to abandon a diplomatic initiative toward Mongolia. At the United Nations, the United States changed its tactics from supporting a moratorium on the China seat to having it declared an "important question" that required two-thirds approval. In 1961 this resolution easily passed sixty-one to thirty-four with seven abstentions, while the Soviet resolution to replace the R.O.C. with the P.R.C. (which now required a two-thirds majority) lost thirty-seven to forty-eight with nineteen abstentions.[17]

Still, the battle over diplomatic status was far from won. Support for the P.R.C. continued to grow gradually until the mid–1960s. In 1965, for instance, there was a tie vote for the first time on who should hold China's seat; the majority for considering this an "important question" had shrunk to seven. The P.R.C. also made some gains in bilateral diplomatic recognitions, although the R.O.C. maintained the lead in total number (fifty-eight to forty-two in 1963 and sixty to fifty in 1965). A major victory for China occurred in 1964 when France recognized the P.R.C. Moreover, P.R.C. objections negated what might have been a feeler toward a "two-China" policy on the part of Taiwan (the R.O.C., for the first time, did not break relations with a country when it recognized its rival, and France made no move to do so until pressured by Communist China). Fortunately for Taiwan the P.R.C. withdrew into xenophobic isolation during the Cultural Revolution in the latter part of the 1960s, but the stage has certainly been set for a major diplomatic reversal.[18]

Relations with the United States also came under some strain in the summer of 1962 when Chiang Kai-shek initiated the third (and final) confrontation between Taipei and Beijing in the Taiwan Strait. Mao's Great Leap Forward of the late 1950s and early 1960s had resulted in economic disaster and chaos, which gave hope to the Nationalists that an invasion might spark a broad-based popular uprising against the Communists. The United States, with memories of the Bay of Pigs debacle still fresh, were hardly supportive, but trips to Taipei by Averell Harriman and Allen Dulles to restrain Chiang apparently inflamed suspicion on the mainland. Finally, the crisis evaporated after the Americans made it clear to the P.R.C. that they would not support an invasion that again could only have been viewed with suspicion on Taiwan.[19]

The negotiating front in the early 1960s was not entirely bleak, though, since it was at this time that Taiwan began its economic bargaining with advanced industrial states that was to prove quite effective for several decades. The growing competitiveness of many developing countries in industrial production, commencing with textiles, whose production is highly standardized and labor-intensive, created escalating pressures for protectionism in the developed industrial nations from the 1950s on.[20] Taiwan's first major negotiations in this economic realm resulted in an October 1963 agreement for voluntary export restraint in cotton textiles with the United States under the so-called Long-term Agreement on trade in cotton textiles. The negotiated quotas for the R.O.C. were not particularly good compared with other exporters, but the agreement reflected other, much more positive aspects that were to mark Taiwan's successful response to Western protectionism over the next two decades: delay in negotiations until an export surge produced a much higher "base" for the quotas, an upgrading and diversification of production into categories not covered by the agreement (e.g., synthetic fibers), and the ability to cheat significantly on the quotas without bringing down economic retaliation. As a result, Taiwan's textile exports skyrocketed from $38 million in 1962 to over $200 million in 1969.[21]

The respite of the P.R.C.'s self-destructive Cultural Revolution proved short-lived; by the end of the decade a new and more ominous threat had arisen on the diplomatic front in terms of a nascent rapprochement between the P.R.C.

and the United States. Since the outbreak of the Korean War, China had viewed America with strong hostility. On the United States' part, although the Eisenhower, Kennedy, and Johnson administrations had all evidenced some interest in warming relations with the P.R.C. and perhaps moving toward a "two-China policy," they had never seriously wavered in their support of the R.O.C. By the end of the 1960s, however, changes in the "strategic triangle" among the United States, USSR, and P.R.C. were beginning to affect Sino-American relations. Armed conflict between Chinese and Soviet troops on Damansky Island and Soviet threats of a preemptive attack against China's nuclear facilities made the Chinese willing to consider seeking American support against the "polar bear." In America the new president, Richard Nixon, and his national security advisor, Henry Kissinger, seemed eager, at least in private, to improve relations with the P.R.C., both for short-run gains in Viet Nam and for long-run abilities to manipulate the strategic triangle. Consequently a variety of harbingers of diplomatic realignment appeared in 1969–1970. Ambassadorial talks resumed between Washington and Beijing; Chinese troop withdrawal from Viet Nam continued apace; America initiated "feelers" toward Mao's regime through France, Pakistan, and Romania; and perhaps most dramatically in terms of Chinese relations per se, President Nixon discontinued the Seventh Fleet's permanent patrol of the Taiwan Strait on November 7, 1969.[22]

These initiatives came to a head during the summer of 1971 when, after "Ping-Pong diplomacy" and Henry Kissinger's secret visit to Beijing, President Nixon announced in July that he would visit China the next February. This dramatic breakthrough in U.S.-P.R.C. relations, furthermore, doomed the R.O.C.'s attempt to save its seat in the United Nations. In 1970, for the first time, a slim majority (fifty-one to forty-nine with twenty-five abstentions) had voted to seat Beijing in place of Taipei, but the "important question" resolution had been supported by a comfortable majority of sixty-six to fifty-two with seven abstentions. As the fall 1971 U.N. session approached, America announced that it would support the seating of the P.R.C. but would also try to prevent the R.O.C.'s expulsion, while the P.R.C., for its part, stated that it would not participate if Taiwan's membership were to be continued. Despite heavy lobbying that looked for a time as if it might succeed, America failed to retain Taiwan's seat as the "important question" resolution failed by four votes and the resolution to replace the R.O.C. by the P.R.C. carried by more than two-to-one (seventy-six to thirty-five with seventeen abstentions).[23]

The loss of the R.O.C.'s seat in the United Nations was diplomatically devastating because many of its bilateral ties and memberships in multilateral organizations had depended on its U.N. status. Thus Taiwan's expulsion from the United Nations was almost immediately followed by a massive switch in diplomatic recognition to the Beijing government, as shown by the data in Table 4.1, with the United States, Saudi Arabia, and South Korea being some of the major countries that retained diplomatic ties with the R.O.C. The P.R.C. was also fairly successful in forcing Taiwan's expulsion from many international

Table 4.1
Number of Countries Recognizing the R.O.C. and P.R.C.

	R.O.C.	P.R.C.
1950	53	26
1963	58	42
1966	60	50
1970	68	53
1973	39	85
1977	23	111

Source: Ralph N. Clough, *Island China* (Cambridge, Mass.: Harvard University Press, 1978), pp. 153–54.

organizations. Taiwan lost its membership in the organizations that were affiliated with the United Nations; Chinese pressure even excluded the R.O.C. from compendia of U.N. statistics. The R.O.C. gradually was excluded from many other multilateral organizations as well, although it was able to retain its membership in the principal international financial institutions (e.g., the World Bank, International Monetary Fund, and Asian Development Bank) throughout the 1970s.[24]

Perhaps the most devastating loss of bilateral recognition was Japan's establishment of diplomatic relations with the P.R.C. in September 1972. However, this "defeat" also helped to create an institutional model for informal relations between Taipei and Tokyo that undergirded Taiwan's later efforts to re-emerge diplomatically. Japan clearly wanted to protect its extensive economic relations with Taiwan, and neither the P.R.C. or R.O.C. objected too vehemently. In December 1972, then, Taiwan and Japan signed an agreement creating "private organizations" (called the Interchange Association for Japan and the East Asian Relations Association for the R.O.C.) that conducted bilateral relations between the two countries and were primarily staffed by government officials temporarily detached from their official positions. Thus the "Japanese model" created "informal" diplomatic relations that, in reality, differed from formal ones in name only but that proved sufficient to save face in Beijing, Taipei, and Tokyo; despite some hostility when derecognition was announced, there seemed to be little impact on the growing links between Japan and Taiwan.[25]

American relations with Beijing reached a high point with Nixon's visit, but the United States refused to back away from its support of Taiwan. Strategic cooperation between the two countries as stated in the famous Shanghai Communique of February 28, 1972, was possible because the Chinese leaders did not press the Taiwan issue. However, the Shanghai Communique also contained a strong difference on Taiwan, with the P.R.C. claiming Taiwan as one of its provinces and the United States taking a more ambiguous position that Taiwan was part of China but that its ultimate fate rested on the Chinese themselves:

The Chinese side reaffirmed its position: The Taiwan question is the crucial question obstructing the normalization of relations between China and the United States; the Government of the People's Republic of China is the sole legal government of China; Taiwan is a Province of China which has long been returned to the motherland; the liberation of Taiwan is China's internal affair in which no other country has the right to interfere; and all U.S. forces and military installations must be withdrawn from Taiwan. The Chinese Government firmly opposes any activities which aim at the creation of ''one China, one Taiwan,'' ''one China, two governments'' or advocate that ''the status of Taiwan remains to be determined.''

The U.S. side declared: The United States acknowledges that all Chinese on either side of the Taiwan Strait maintain that there is but one China and that Taiwan is part of China. The United States Government does not challenge that position. It reaffirms its interest in a peaceful settlement of the Taiwan question by the Chinese themselves. With this prospect in mind, it affirms the ultimate objective of the withdrawal of all U.S. forces and military installations from Taiwan. In the meantime, it will progressively reduce its forces and military installations on Taiwan as the tension in the area diminishes.[26]

The P.R.C. then set three conditions for normalization of relations with the United States: (1) derecognition of the R.O.C. (2) abrogation of the Mutual Defense Treaty between Taiwan and America, and (3) withdrawal of all U.S. forces. The United States refused to meet these conditions, and issued over fifty reassurances of its continued support to the R.O.C. during the next few years, contributing to the stagnation in relations between America and the P.R.C. during the mid–1970s.[27]

These developments certainly left the R.O.C. government in quite a quandary. Its attempts to maintain support through diplomacy and foreign aid had proved fruitless, as did its attempts in the early 1970s to sabotage America's rapprochement with the P.R.C. by increasing guerrilla attacks on the mainland. Even with continued American pledges of support the R.O.C.'s position was becoming increasingly shaky. The pressure on Taipei was exacerbated by the ''peace offensive'' that emanated from Beijing for most of the mid–1970s. China began to call for people-to-people contacts with Taiwan, considerably cut back on criticisms of Chiang Kai-shek and the Nationalist government, even proposed peace talks with the KMT, and for the first time began to appeal to the native Taiwanese residents of the island (although the latter could not have been received too kindly by the mainlander-dominated KMT). Given the disparity of power between the two sides and the existing international situation, the R.O.C. had little choice but to remain silent, stridently refuse to have any interaction with the mainland, and hope that time really was not on the side of the Communists.[28]

Thus the government took a hard line in international affairs and based its foreign policy on the ''four firm and unyielding principles'' enunciated by Premier Chiang Ching-kuo (Chiang Kai-shek's son) in September 1972:

1. The system of the state of the Republic of China as established under article 1 of the Constitution will never be changed. . . .

2. The overall goals of anti-Communism and national recovery of the Republic of China will never be changed.

3. The Republic of China will always remain with the democratic bloc and its dedication to the upholding of righteousness and justice and safeguarding peace and security of the world will never be changed.

4. The resolute stand of the Republic of China in never compromising with the Chinese Communist rebel group will never be changed.[29]

Taipei evidently assumed, probably quite rightly, that the massive disparities between itself and Beijing in terms of domestic resources and international status meant that any discussion of Taiwan could only be a step toward negotiated surrender. Thus, although this position made the R.O.C. appear rather dogmatic and ostrich-like, it probably represented the only viable strategy of hunkering down and waiting for more propitious times.

Again, the R.O.C.'s diplomacy in the economic realm proved a welcome counterpoint to its declining diplomatic position. For example, Taiwan negotiated agreements with the United States on textiles in 1971 and shoes in 1977 that were fairly successful for a number of reasons. First, Taiwan's bargaining position was maximized because of coordination with other Asian exporters and "transnational allies" within the United States. Second, America was willing to trade off quotas that appealed to the domestic constituencies demanding protection for flexibility, which greatly reduced the burden on the exporters (e.g., "pipeline" clauses that allowed substantial increases in first-year exports or transferring products between categories, such as rubber and nonrubber footwear). Third, the government raised the threat of U.S. protectionism against existing exports to force upgrading within an industry that produced new markets and higher profits in the long run.[30]

During the two decades from the late 1950s through the late 1970s diplomatic outcomes for the R.O.C. differed vastly from the escalating defeat in the diplomatic realm to its highly successful negotiating strategy on economic matters. Relations with the United States fell somewhere in between. American rapprochement with the P.R.C. represented a major setback, but the United States maintained its alliance and support of Taiwan's cause. These contrasting outcomes reflected America's varying stakes in international economics and politics. In the former, America's primary goal was to buy off domestic constituencies without threatening diplomat ties or the "liberal" world economy. In the latter, unfortunately for Taiwan, an alliance that was satisfactory in bilateral terms was increasingly subordinated to broader strategic concerns. Thus Taiwan's search for stability began to be threatened by its client-state status.

The World Turned Upside Down

The status quo in the R.O.C.'s international position that emerged after the P.R.C. backed down in the 1958 Taiwan Strait crisis was gradually undermined by the flow of events in the global diplomatic arena. In contrast, the more precarious status quo that seemed to be taking hold in the late 1970s was abruptly shattered by the announcement of the United States on December 15, 1978, that it was establishing diplomatic relations with the P.R.C. on January 1, 1979, and terminating official ties with the R.O.C. Truly, Taiwan's world had been turned upside down. In the subsequent decade, however, the R.O.C.'s diplomatic situation compared with previous trends was turned upside down in another (and probably more positive) sense. In direct contrast to the 1958–1978 period Taiwan recovered quite nicely in terms of solidifying an autonomous position in world politics but found its economic position increasingly threatened by a rapidly deteriorating bargaining position vis-à-vis the United States.

Although the Carter administration in the United States, elected in 1976, showed some interest in normalizing relations with the P.R.C., little progress was made until 1978 (a visit of Secretary of State Cyrus Vance to China in September 1977 ended in well-publicized failure). The key factor that pushed Carter toward a more accommodating position evidently was deteriorating relations with the Soviet Union, since there was little domestic pressure for a reversal of China policy and the Chinese Communists appeared satisfied with the existing relationship. Thus, ironically, although the activities of the China lobby during the 1950s had fostered a significant amount of hostility toward the R.O.C. on the part of "liberal" and "dovish" State Department professionals, the final nails in Taiwan's diplomatic coffin were driven by anti-Communist hawks, exemplified by National Security Advisor Zbigniew Brzezinski, whose visit to China in May 1978 set in motion the normalization negotiations.

During these negotiations the United States basically accepted all three of the P.R.C.'s basic conditions with several provisos that somewhat softened them: (1) that the Mutual Defense Treaty would be canceled with a year's notice according to its stipulations, (2) that the United States could continue to furnish Taiwan with defensive arms, (3) that the P.R.C. would not contradict American statements that the Taiwan question should be settled peacefully, and (4) that America's commercial and cultural relations with Taiwan would be continued under nongovernmental auspices. In addition, although it was not noticed at the time, the United States was careful to state that it "acknowledged" the P.R.C.'s position on Taiwan, which it later interpreted as meaning "cognizance of, but not necessarily agreement with."[31]

In essence, therefore, Carter evidently wanted to follow the Japanese model of having formal relations with the P.R.C. and informal ones with the R.O.C. The problem was that America had been Taiwan's principal patron and that the Chinese could always challenge the "informal" understandings in the future by citing the formal accords of recognition (an ironic reversal of the normal differences between American and Chinese cultures in their devotion to "legalism").

Carter's announcement sent shockwaves through Taipei. Understandably there was substantial fear that the withdrawal of American support could lead to the end of the island's independence and prosperity. For example, a demonstration against the American delegation that was sent in late December to discuss the "new" relationship between Taiwan and America turned quite ugly and violent, manifesting the depth of popular fears. A most pressing question obviously was to whom the R.O.C. could turn for the provision of its security needs in deterring the P.R.C. Rumor suggests that some discussion may have occurred at the very highest levels concerning improving (or, more accurately, establishing) relations with the Soviet Union (Chiang Ching-kuo, who had become Taiwan's top leader after his father's death in 1975, spent twelve years in the Soviet Union in the 1920s and 1930s and had a Russian wife).[32] However, Sino-Soviet rapprochement, the KMT's staunchly anti-Communist ideology, and adverse reaction to derecognizing the R.O.C. in the United States all combined to make such a potentially radical realignment both impractical and unnecessary.

Most fortunately for Taiwan, Carter's China policy stirred up strong domestic opposition, not primarily to normalizing relations with Beijing, but much more to abandoning Taipei. Thus the U.S. Congress objected to the administration's initial proposal for conducting relations with Taiwan because security issues were generally ignored, rewrote it extensively, and passed the final Taiwan Relations Act (TRA) by veto-proof majorities of more than two-thirds. President Carter signed the revised bill on April 10, 1979.

The TRA established informal mechanisms along the lines of the Japanese model for maintaining government-to-government ties between the United States and the R.O.C., albeit by another name, through the American Institute in Taiwan and Taiwan's Coordination Council for North American Affairs. In the important area of national security the TRA stated that any change in the situation of Taiwan by other than peaceful means would constitute "a threat to the peace and security of the Western Pacific area and [a] grave concern to the United States." In order to protect Taiwan's autonomy, Section 3 of the Act included the following provisions:

A. In the furtherance of the policy set forth in section 2 of this Act, the United States will make available to Taiwan such defense articles and defense services in such quantity as may be necessary to enable Taiwan to maintain a sufficient self-defense capability.

B. The President and Congress shall determine the nature and quality of such defense articles and services based solely upon their judgment of the needs of Taiwan. . . .

C. The President is directed to inform the Congress promptly of any threat to the security or the social or economic system of the people on Taiwan and any danger to the interests of the United States arising therefrom.[33]

The P.R.C.'s reaction to the TRA was relatively restrained. As early as December 16, 1978, the Chinese had publicly denied that they accepted continued arms sales, and they expressed concern that it maintained an official nature in U.S. relations with Taiwan. However, the Chinese government appeared satisfied

with Carter's reassurances, including his message when signing the TRA that
the Act was consistent with the normalization agreement and with the recognition
of Beijing as "the sole legal government of China." Consequently the P.R.C.
did not challenge the TRA, and the United States successfully implemented the
Japanese model for maintaining relations with both Chinas. Thus, largely through
pressures from supporters in the United States, the R.O.C.'s immediate security
problems were brought under control, and the political and military situation in
the Taiwan Strait remained stable.[34]

Again, however, the stability of a seemingly secure position for Taiwan proved
short-lived. The key factor was a basic reorientation in the P.R.C.'s strategic
orientations during 1980 from viewing the United States as a partner in containing
the Soviet Union to concluding that China could pursue a more "independent"
foreign policy balancing off the two superpowers. This resulted from changed
Chinese perceptions that the threat of direct Soviet encroachments on major
Chinese interests had receded and that the hostility between the United States
and USSR had reached the point where they would check each other. Thus Deng
Xiaoping and the Chinese leadership evidently concluded that they could replicate
the Nixon-Kissinger strategy of acting as the "balance" in the strategic triangle.[35]

Consequently the P.R.C. felt freer to assume a harder line with America on
the Taiwan issue. The Chinese soon found some provocation in statements by
Republican presidential candidate Ronald Reagan during the summer of 1980
that he would restore official relations with Taipei, although Reagan later mod-
erated his position and sent his vice-presidential candidate to Beijing to reaffirm
his support for strategic cooperation with China in August. Thus, after Reagan's
election, the P.R.C. became increasingly critical of U.S. policy and warned that
the Taiwan issue, especially continued American arms sales to the R.O.C.,
represented a major obstacle to further improvements in Sino-American relations.
For example, early in 1981 the P.R.C. downgraded its diplomatic relations with
the Netherlands to the charge d'affaires level in retaliation for selling two sub-
marines to Taiwan in what was generally seen as a warning directed toward the
United States.

The central issue soon turned on the planned sale of an advanced fighter
aircraft, called the FX, to Taiwan that would replace a previous generation
airplane, the F–5E. The R.O.C. had first requested to buy the FX during the
middle of the Carter administration, but the decision had been postponed because
of political factors. Proponents argued that this represented the normal technological development of Taiwan's military forces and was necessary to maintain
a credible deterrent as stipulated by the TRA while opponents contended that
China no longer posed a military threat to Taiwan and that the FX sale would
needlessly strain relations with the P.R.C. Initially the Reagan administration
appeared favorably inclined. However, after growing domestic opposition and
increasingly strident denunciations by the P.R.C., the United States announced
on January 11, 1982, that it would not approve the FX sale, but only allow the
continued coproduction of the F–5E.

The expectation that this would mollify the Chinese Communists turned out to be totally misplaced. The P.R.C. strongly denounced the decision, demanded that all arms sales end by 1986, threatened to downgrade diplomatic relations over a routine sale of spare parts, and even began to hint that the TRA itself was unacceptable. The United States for its part began to respond to Chinese threats in kind, commenting that downgraded relations would extend to the economic and technological cooperation highly valued by the P.R.C. and proposing a joint communique that justified American policy.

The result was the joint communique of August 17, 1982, which contained the following major provisions:

1. That the P.R.C. constituted the sole legitimate government of China, which included Taiwan, but "within that context" the United States would maintain "unofficial relations with the people of Taiwan." However, the United States would not adopt a policy of "two Chinas" or "one China, one Taiwan."

2. That relations between the two countries would continue to be guided by the Shanghai Communique and the Joint Communique on the Establishment of Diplomatic Relations, including "respect for each other's sovereignty and territorial integrity."

3. That "the Chinese government reiterates that the question of Taiwan is China's internal affair" but that the 1979 Message to Compatriots in Taiwan and 1981 Nine-Point Proposal [see below] "represented a further major effort under this fundamental policy to strive for a peaceful solution to the Taiwan question."

4. That the "United States Government states that it does not seek to carry out a long-term policy of arms sales to Taiwan, that its arms sales to Taiwan will not exceed, either in qualitative or quantitative terms, the level of those supplied in recent years since the establishment of diplomatic relations between the United States and China, and that it intends to reduce gradually its sales of arms to Taiwan, leading over a period of time to a final resolution."

If diplomacy is meant to paper over differences, this joint communique failed in the short term but succeeded in the long term. Almost immediately all concerned publicized radically different interpretations. The United States argued that the communique was consistent with the TRA and that China was committed to a peaceful resolution of the Taiwan question; claimed the right to "index" future arms sales by inflation, technological development, and even the threat represented by the P.R.C.; and reassured the R.O.C. that America's relations with Taiwan would not be materially affected. Beijing, in sharp contrast, contended that the TRA was inconsistent with basic agreements between the United States and P.R.C., that policy toward Taiwan was an internal Chinese issue, and that no link existed between the arms sales and peaceful resolution issues. The government of Taiwan and many American conservatives fretted, moreover, that the R.O.C. had been sold out and that the communique would be used to justify abandoning Taiwan.[36] However, American policy continued to support two basic principles that were certainly advantageous to the R.O.C.: (1) that the

Taiwan issue should be settled peacefully and (2) that it was up to the Chinese people themselves to find the solution.[37]

Despite the sharp conflict indicated by these contrasting interpretations, and despite continued jousting between Washington and Beijing for another year or so (especially over a spate of arms sales, including final approval of the F–5E agreement), the joint communique did represent a turning point in Sino-American relations. President Reagan's visit to China in the spring of 1984 solidified relations between the United States and P.R.C., and there was increasing emphasis on cooperation in technology transfer and military cooperation as China became only the second Communist nation eligible for government arms sales and credits. Thus a status quo tolerable to (though not particularly desirable for) all parties was gradually established.[38]

The FX issue, however, did highlight the severe security questions facing Taiwan. As the comparative data on the R.O.C. and P.R.C. in Table 4.2 demonstrate, China possesses an overwhelming advantage in total forces, although the balance in the Taiwan Strait is more even. With the declining commitment of America's strategic umbrella over the 1970s, Taiwan's deterrent in a strictly military sense came to depend on maintaining a technological lead in aircraft and naval vessels that would make a Chinese attack prohibitively expensive. American security support during the 1980s, then, switched to helping the R.O.C. upgrade its own defense industries, and Taiwan has made substantial progress in this regard (for example, the production of tanks and a new advanced fighter). Still, clearly the major obstacle to a Chinese attack—especially in the forms of a submarine blockade or invasion of Quemoy and Matsu, rather than full-scale war—is the political cost of disrupting valuable political and economic relations with the West, especially the United States. Although this situation has seemed stable, it is not one that military planners in Taipei or their allies among American conservatives relish or even accept as viable in the long run. In addition, the cost of supporting the military establishment—now estimated at 9 percent of GNP and 40 percent of the budget—is high enough to represent a potential drain on the civilian economy.[39]

In addition to the muted security threat (at least for the short term), the R.O.C. has made a considerable comeback from what appeared to be the onset of stark diplomatic isolation in 1979. Although the number of formal diplomatic relations dropped to twenty-three in the early 1980s, by the mid–1980s Taiwan had "substantive" relations (e.g., commercial, cultural, educational) with almost 150 countries; R.O.C. passports were almost universally accepted, which by itself indicates a significant acceptance of "sovereignty." In fact, in the aftermath of America's passage of the TRA, quite a few countries (including France, Japan, Singapore, and West Germany) that recognized the P.R.C. moved to expand and upgrade their ties with the R.O.C., using the U.S. precedent to shield themselves from Chinese retaliation.

Taiwan made significant gains in terms of memberships in international organizations. Although the R.O.C. belonged to only ten "intergovernmental"

Table 4.2
R.O.C.-P.R.C. Military Balance, 1983

	R.O.C.	P.R.C.
Total Military		
Regular forces	464,000	4,000,000
Nuclear forces (ICBMs, IRBMs, MRBMs)	0	115
Army troops	310,000	3,250,000
Navy personnel	77,000	360,000
Submarines	2	106
Destroyers	23	10
Missle craft	49	230
Air Force personnel	77,000	490,000
Total aircraft	485	5,300
Taiwan Strait Area		
Army troops	340,000	535,000
Tanks	2,000	1,700
Artillery	1,750	1,450
Submarines	2	40
Destroyers	23	2
Missle craft	49	90
Coastal craft	23	290
Bombers	0	215
Fighter-bombers	0	100
Fighters	370	1,100

Source: Martin L. Lasater, *The Taiwan Issue in Sino-American Strategic Relations* (Boulder, Colo.: Westview Press, 1984), pp. 124–127.

organizations in 1984 (it lost membership in the International Monetary Fund and World Bank in the early 1980s), its memberships in nongovernmental organizations expanded greatly from 254 in 1979 to 630 in 1982 as the government clearly used nongovernmental organization membership to boost international status. Moreover, by the mid–1980s, it belonged to over 100 organizations that the P.R.C. had also joined. The two most important were probably the International Olympic Committee, which Taiwan rejoined in 1981 under the name

"Taipei, China," and the Asian Development Bank, where Taiwan was assigned the same name after the P.R.C. joined in 1985. In protest, the R.O.C. did not attend the Asian Development Bank's 1986 meeting, but has subsequently moved toward a more active role in the organization and attended the Bank's April 1988 meeting. Taiwan dubbed these new initiatives "flexible diplomacy" and in early 1989 the Foreign Minister even expressed an interest in re-entering the U.N.[40]

Thus, the R.O.C. and P.R.C. seem to be moving toward something of a modus vivendi on the question of Taiwan's international status. Although P.R.C. still applies diplomatic pressures on issues concerning Taiwan's international participation, it has been willing to accept Taiwan's "informal" treatment as a separate entity. Even though the second-class status inherent in most of these "informal" arrangements is galling to Taipei, the R.O.C. government has been increasingly willing to accept them—probably because of the realization that the inertia of time is now giving greater legitimacy to Taiwan's international status and making it harder for its rival to openly challenge the "informal" linkages that have been created. In fact, the R.O.C. can now credibly claim to meet generally recognized conditions of sovereignty in terms of its position in international relations.[41]

Political ties with the United States also improved somewhat under the Reagan administration, albeit not to the extent that might have been expected, given candidate Reagan's sharp criticism of Jimmy Carter for breaking relations with the R.O.C. Normal diplomatic contacts became much warmer once Reagan assumed office, and a stability emerged in America's relations with Taipei and Beijing that, although far from completely satisfactory to the R.O.C., quieted the fears of the late 1970s in Taiwan. In particular, the United States has resisted pressures from China in the late 1980s to become involved in settling the Taiwan question by using its influence to bring the R.O.C. to the negotiating table.[42] Thus, the R.O.C. appears well satisfied with the "six" reassurances that it received from the Reagan administration at the time of the August 17 communique, although its periodic public reassertion of them probably betokens a significant degree of uneasiness. For example, on the one hand, arms sales were continued at quite significant levels (e.g., over $700 million per year) and the United States was willing to cooperate in Taiwan's upgrading its defensive forces, while on the other hand, Taipei regularly clamored for the sale of more advanced weaponry, which America denied on political grounds, and viewed with growing alarm the beginning of U.S. technology and military transfers to the P.R.C.

U.S.-R.O.C. relations were also threatened by several untoward incidents, but their effects proved transitory. First, a Chinese newspaperman in San Francisco, Henry Liu, was murdered by Chinese gangsters at the behest of the head of Taiwan's Defense Intelligence Bureau, provoking a considerable outcry in the United States, particularly among Taiwan's opponents in Congress. However, the crisis soon passed for a variety of reasons: Taiwan's rapid bringing to trial of those involved, the lack of evidence of broader involvement by R.O.C. officials, and the major domestic democratization reforms that began in 1986.

Second, early in 1988 the deputy director of Taiwan's Institute for Nuclear Energy Research left the country under mysterious circumstances, allegedly with the help of the Central Intelligence Agency, and apparently charged that nuclear weapons materials could be extracted from Taiwan's largest reactor. This issue was resolved quickly and quietly, though, when the R.O.C. announced in March that the reactor was being closed down for "economic reasons."[43] Both these incidents indicate a significant concern by both sides to maintain a stable relationship by smoothing over individual irritants.

Still, Taiwan appeared to be taking out some insurance in its relations with its patron in late 1988 by extending some feelers toward the Soviet Union. Thus a highly publicized trade delegation of private businessmen in late 1988 may well have had broader political significance as it brought the resignation of the secretary general to the president's office and Central Standing Committee member Shen Chang-huan, a former foreign minister who was seen as still exerting a conservative influence on foreign policy, in protest against it.[44] The R.O.C. appeared confident enough to apply its own logic of the "strategic triangle." Certainly, "flexible diplomacy" was in style.

In contrast to the growing stability and status in Taiwan's diplomatic relations over the 1980s, however, its performance in economic negotiations, particularly with the United States, which took almost half of its exports, dropped drastically in the second half of the decade. The principal factor here was the deteriorating position of America in the international economy, which led to a major change in its negotiating strategy. By the mid–1980s America's dominant economic position of the 1950s and 1960s was clearly a thing of the past; the United States was running trade deficits of well over $100 billion annually, which became a heated domestic political issue. Consequently the dominant aim of trade policy changed from negotiating the minimum protection that would satisfy key constituencies in "declining industries" to assuming harsh negotiating positions to do everything possible to beat back the trade deficit.[45]

Taiwan was certainly an inviting target for this more aggressive negotiating strategy, since its trade surplus with America had rapidly escalated from $2 billion in 1980 to $13.6 billion in 1986 and America's market was probably substantially more open to Taiwan than vice versa. Thus trade negotiations between the United States and the R.O.C. have become much more acrimonious over the past few years, and the United States has forced a series of major concessions, some of which were politically embarrassing to the Taipei government. For example, Taiwan appreciated its currency over 40 percent against the U.S. dollar during 1987–1988, more than twice as much as the other "little dragons." The R.O.C.'s opening of its markets to America liquor and tobacco products, previously a state monopoly, in 1987 was widely viewed as an affront to sovereignty and stimulated cries of new "unequal treaties," harkening back to the Opium War of the nineteenth century. Finally, in the late summer of 1988 the government reversed itself and allowed the import of turkey parts, an issue of high domestic visibility because of its role in stimulating the massive demonstration of May 20, 1988 (see chapter 5).[46] Thus the system of ad hoc negotiations on single trade issues, which had served Taiwan well until the trade deficit became the overriding issue for America, now became increasingly a detriment to the R.O.C. because concessions in one set of negotiations were forgotten when the next issue arose.

Relations (or perhaps more accurately nonrelations) with the P.R.C. became more salient and probably troublesome as well. Again, as in the early 1970s, the P.R.C. initiated what might be called a "peace offensive." Although the Chinese never fully committed themselves to a peaceful resolution of the Taiwan issue, claiming that this was a matter of domestic politics, they did indicate generally peaceful intentions and suggested that they would resort to military force only in the face of such provocation as (a) Taiwan's acquisition of nuclear weapons, (b) an alliance between Taiwan and the USSR, or (c) a declaration that Taiwan was a country independent of China. Beijing also took the much more positive approach of offering Taiwan ostensibly quite favorable terms for unification, such as Ye Jianying's Nine-Point Proposal of September 1981:

1. Direct negotiations between the CCP and KMT should commence.
2. Direct economic and human contacts between the Mainland and Taiwan should be developed.
3. Taiwan would retain a high degree of autonomy including separate military forces.
4. Taiwan's socioeconomic system, including property rights, would remain unchanged.
5. Taiwan leaders could assume national posts.
6. If necessary, the central government could subsidize Taiwan.
7. Residents of Taiwan could settle on the Mainland without discrimination or restrictions on travel.
8. Investments by Taiwan businessmen in the Mainland would be encouraged.
9. All Chinese should work toward "the reunification of the motherland."

With the conclusion of the agreement between the P.R.C. and the United Kingdom for the retrocession of Hong Kong to China in 1997 under the formula of "one country, two systems," furthermore, the P.R.C. began to argue that this could serve as a precedent for reunification with Taiwan along the lines of the Nine-Point Proposal.

The R.O.C. government viewed these Chinese Communist proposals with extreme suspicion for several reasons. It would clearly be negotiating its own surrender from a position of weakness; previous agreements for a "United Front" in the 1930s and 1940s had not prevented a vicious civil war; the Communists had reneged on their promise of autonomy for Tibet; the CCP could not offer Taiwan anything that it did not already have; and just as important (if not more so), any attempt to talk with mainlander Communists could push islander nationalists toward open insurrection. Thus the regime announced a "Three-No" policy for dealing with the P.R.C. (no contacts, negotiations, or compromises).[47]

This adamant policy did not prove tenable, though. Even in the realm of no official contacts, negotiations were held between the national airlines of the R.O.C. and P.R.C. in May 1986 over the return of a cargo plane that had been hijacked to the mainland. Although this did not set a precedent for more official contacts, it was part of a much broader process of growing interactions that by 1988 had blossomed into a "China fever" in Taiwan.

Throughout the 1980s, commercial contacts between the two countries had been growing spurred by their highly complementary economies. Trade conducted through third countries, especially Hong Kong, and via fishing boats grew rapidly into a multibillion-dollar business (estimated at $2.4 billion in 1988, up 60 percent from 1987, making the P.R.C. the R.O.C.'s fifth largest trade partner) as China's cheap raw materials were exchanged for Taiwan's manufactures. By the late 1980s this trade had become quite open, and intermittent harassment by the Taipei authorities had almost ceased. There was even public discussion of Taipower, a state corporation, purchasing coal from the mainland—by way of a third country of course. Moreover, Taiwan businessmen began to invest in the mainland (estimated at $400 million in 1988) as Taiwan's rising wages eradicated the island's comparative advantage in labor-intensive production. During the summer of 1988, for example, Taiwan's newspapers ran stories about the comparative price of goods in China and Taiwan, and there were worker protests against the loss of jobs from offshore production in the P.R.C. There was a rapid escalation in human contacts too. Responding to domestic political pressure, the R.O.C. in 1987 allowed mainlanders who were not officials to visit relatives in China; this set off a massive tourist business that reached the level of tens of thousands per month in the summer of 1988 and that was manifestly not limited to "visiting relatives." A trickle of visitors and "guest workers" from the mainland to Taiwan also began. Pressure grew for liberalization of this "human contact" policy that included (almost) direct mail linkages, scientific delegations, access to mainland materials, and so forth. These contacts were also quite positive in the political sense that the government's relaxation was popular and that many visitors to China were far from impressed by the much lower standard of living there. Finally, China fever and flexible diplomacy came together dramatically in April 1989 when Taiwan announced that it was sending a delegation headed by Finance Minister Shirley Kuo to an ADB meeting held in Beijing.

In fact, the P.R.C. evidently began to worry about these burgeoning ties somewhat since it tried to disrupt some of the trade and denied permission for a leading Chinese intellectual dissident to visit Taiwan late in 1988. Moreover, these policies were accompanied by a Deng Xiaoping statement that the P.R.C. had not renounced the use of force against Taiwan; and by growing Chinese pressure against Taiwan's regaining membership in international organizations, implying Beijing's growing frustration as Taiwan's international status becomes more secure.[48]

This "China fever" presents the regime with a basic dilemma. In the short term at least, these escalating contacts are highly popular and, for the economic linkages, profitable, and there is certainly strong pressure on Taiwan to expand them. However, there is also the danger that in the long-run they may undermine the legitimacy of the R.O.C. as an autonomous polity. This underlines the nature of the past decade as one in which Taiwan's world has been turned upside down—from diplomatic isolation to a much more secure international situation that may, in turn, be challenged by the successful "China fever" of the late 1980s and from successful economic bargaining to the danger of "unequal treaties" being imposed by its prime patron and ally.

Overall, therefore, Taiwan's search for stability appeared fairly successful as the 1980s came to an end. Its conflict with the P.R.C. had become more manageable and institutionalized, somewhat to the frustration of its rival. In the political sphere its client-state relations with the United States were quite good, and the danger that America would sacrifice its smaller ally to broader strategic interests seemingly had passed. Economic conflict between the United States and the R.O.C. had increased but was still manageable, at least in the short run. Certainly, Taiwan became more active and assertive in international affairs in the late 1980s.

Dependency and Taiwan as a Small State in the Global Arena

The R.O.C. is clearly a small state in the international order. Conventional wisdom holds that small states become political and economic dependencies that are pushed around and exploited by large powers. Taiwan's postwar historical experience provides mixed evidence in this regard. In one sense, Taiwan's political fate has been highly dependent. The very survival of the R.O.C. in the early 1950s depended on decisions made by the Truman administration in the United States that was far from sympathetic toward it. Moreover, its position changed greatly in the wake of global events over which it had no control—positively from the outbreak of the Korean War and negatively from the changing "strategic triangle" and from America's declining economic hegemony during the 1970s and 1980s.

Yet, in another sense, Taiwan has been surprisingly independent along a variety of dimensions. It successfully resisted international pressure, including that coming from its patron, to compromise its basic position on its status as the government of China. In the late 1940s and 1950s it had "penetrated" the American polity through the China lobby much more than the United States was able to effect its own political decision making. From the early 1960s through the early 1980s it almost certainly won more than it lost in trade negotiations with the United States. Its status as a political dependency of the United States was associated with substantial aid flows and rapid growth rather than with exploitation and stagnation. Thus Taiwan's experience suggests that even weak and dependent states can achieve considerable success in the international arena.[49]

The R.O.C. to sum, has been quite successful on the international stage, given the considerable disadvantages it faces. However, whenever it seemed to have reached a secure equilibrium by solving some major political or economic crisis, its environment changed, presenting new threats and challenges. Lately past economic success has brought growing pressure from the United States, past diplomatic success has raised the "China question" again in a more convoluted and ambiguous manner. Thus, a more nationalistic stance toward Taiwan by Deng Xiaoping (compared, ironically, to the R.O.C.'s old archenemy Mao) has been offset by changes in the strategic triangle that reduced U.S. need for the P.R.C. as an ally and enhanced China's need for Western good will.[50] Internally on Taiwan, the commitment to "Mainland recovery"—which dominated foreign policy and the regime's legitimacy claims in the 1950s—has almost completely waned. However, the relationship between the two emerging foreign policy trends of "China fever" and "reasserting autonomy" through "flexible diplomacy" is almost certain to become somewhat contradictory in the near future.

Notes

1. Herbert Feis, *The China Tangle: The American Effort in China from Pearl Harbor to the China Mission* (Princeton, N.J.: Princeton University Press, 1953), chs. 22 and 23.

2. Forrest C. Pogue, *George C. Marshall: Statesman* (New York: Viking Press, 1987), chs. 3–6; and Tang Tsou, *America's Failure in China, 1941–50* (Chicago: University of Chicago Press, 1973), chs. 9 and 10.

3. Kenneth S. Chern, *Dilemma in China, America's Policy Debate, 1945* (Hamden, Conn.: Archon, 1980); Ernest R. May, *The Truman Administration and China, 1945–1949* (Philadelphia: J. B. Lippincott, 1975); and Tang, *America's Failure in China*, chs. 11 and 12.

4. Warren I. Cohen, "Acheson, His Advisors, and China, 1949–1950," in Dorothy Borg and Waldo Heinrichs, eds., *Uncertain Years: Chinese-American Relations, 1947–1950* (New York: Columbia University Press, 1980), pp. 13–52; Nancy Bernkopf Tucker, *Patterns in the Dust: Chinese-American Relations and the Recognition Controversy, 1949–1950* (New York: Columbia University Press, 1983), ch. 1; and U.S. Department of State, *United States Relations with China: With Special Reference to the Period 1944–1949* (New York: Greenwood Press, 1968).

5. June M. Grasso, *Truman's Two-China Policy, 1948–1950* (Armonk, N.Y.: M. E. Sharpe, 1987); and Tucker, *Patterns in the Dust*.

6. George F. Botjer, *A Short History of Nationalist China, 1919–1949* (New York: G. P. Putnam, 1979), ch. 7; and Immanuel C. Y. Hsu, *The Rise of Modern China*, 3rd ed. (New York: Oxford University Press, 1983), ch. 25.

7. Ross Y. Koen, *The China Lobby in American Politics* (New York: Octagon Books, 1974). Tucker, *Patterns in the Dust*, ch. 5, provides a more balanced overview.

8. Cohen, "Acheson"; David Allan Mayers, *Cracking the Monolith: U.S. Policy Against the Sino-Soviet Alliance, 1949–1955* (Baton Rouge: Louisiana State University Press, 1986), chs. 1 and 2; and Tucker, *Patterns in the Dust*, ch. 10.

9. Grasso, *Truman's Two China Policy*; and Thomas E. Stolper, *China, Taiwan, and the Offshore Islands* (Armonk, N.Y.: M.E. Sharpe, 1985).

10. Leonard A. Kusnitz, *Public Opinion and Foreign Policy: America's China Policy, 1949–1979* (Westport, Conn.: Greenwood Press, 1984), p. 45.

11. Foster Rhea Dulles, *American Policy Toward Communist China, 1949–1969* (New York: Thomas Y. Crowell, 1972), chs. 7 and 8; J. H. Kalicki, *The Pattern of Sino-American Crises: Political-Military Interactions in the 1950s* (Cambridge: Cambridge University Press, 1975), pt. I; Mayers, *Cracking the Monolith*, ch. 3; and Glenn D. Paige, *The Korean Decision: June 24–30, 1950* (New York: Free Press, 1968).

12. Thomas B. Gold, *State and Society in the Taiwan Miracle* (Armonk, N.Y.: M. E. Sharpe, 1986), pp. 58–59, 68–78; and Neil H. Jacoby, *U.S. Aid to Taiwan: A Study of Foreign Aid, Self-help, and Development* (New York: Praeger, 1966), especially ch. 10.

13. Kusnitz, *America's China Policy*, pp. 55–56.

14. Ralph N. Clough, *Island China* (Cambridge, Mass.: Harvard University Press, 1978), ch. 4.

15. Ibid., pp. 19–20.

16. Dulles, *American Policy Toward Communist China*, chs. 10 and 11; Dennis Van Vranken Hickey, "America, the Offshore Island Crisis of 1954–55, and Calculated Ambiguity," *Issues and Studies* 24:8 (August 1988), pp. 120–152; Kalicki, *Pattern of Sino-American Crises*, chs. 6 and 8; Stolper, *Offshore Islands*; and Kenneth T. Young, *Negotiating with the Chinese Communists: The United States Experience, 1953–1967* (New York: McGraw-Hill, 1968), pt. III.

17. Kusnitz, *America's China Policy*, pp. 97–101; and Young, *Negotiating with the Chinese Communists*, ch. 9.

18. Hungdah Chiu, "The Question of Taiwan in Sino-American Relations," in Hungdah Chiu, ed., *China and the Taiwan Issue* (New York: Praeger, 1979), pp. 174–177; and Clough, *Island China*, pp. 149–155.

19. Kusnitz, *America's China Policy*, pp. 103–109.

20. Vinod K. Aggarwal, *Liberal Protectionism: The International Politics of Organized Textile Trade* (Berkeley: University of California Press, 1985).

21. David B. Yoffie, *Power and Protectionism: Strategies of the Newly Industrializing Countries* (New York: Columbia University Press, 1983), pp. 107–116.

22. A. Doak Barnett, "The Changing Strategic Balance in Asia," in Gene T. Hsiao, ed., *Sino-American Detente and Its Policy Implications* (New York: Praeger, 1974), pp. 22–45; John W. Garver, *China's Decision for Rapprochement with the United States, 1968–1971* (Boulder, Colo.: Westview Press, 1982); A. James Gregor, *The China Connection: U.S. Policy and the People's Republic of China* (Stanford, Calif.: Hoover Institution Press, 1986), ch. 9; and Robert G. Sutter, *China-Watch: Toward Sino-American Reconciliation* (Baltimore: Johns Hopkins University Press, 1978), chs. 5 and 6.

23. Chiu, "Taiwan in Sino-American Relations," pp. 178–179.

24. Clough, *Island China*, ch. 6.

25. Ibid., ch. 7.

26. Martin L. Lasater, *The Taiwan Issue in Sino-American Strategic Relations* (Boulder, Colo.: Westview Press, 1984), p. 155.

27. Sutter, *China Watch*, ch. 7.

28. Robert G. Sutter, *The China Quandary: Domestic Determinants of U.S. China*

Policy, 1972–1982 (Boulder, Colo.: Westview Press, 1983), pp. 42–46. King C. Chen, "Taiwan in Peking's Strategy," in Hungdah Chiu, ed., *China and the Taiwan Issue* (New York: Praeger, 1979), pp. 127–146, discusses the P.R.C.'s strategy to undermine the KMT regime.

29. Lasater, *Taiwan Issue*, p. 111.

30. Yoffie, *Power and Protectionism*, chs. 4 and 5.

31. Dennis Van Vranken Hickey, "America's Two-Point Policy and the Future of Taiwan," *Asian Survey* 28:8 (August 1988), p. 883.

32. John W. Garver, "Taiwan's Russian Option: Image and Reality," *Asian Survey* 18:7 (July 1978), pp. 751–766.

33. Lasater, *Taiwan Issue*, pp. 161–162.

34. For an overall history of normalization and the TRA see Robert L. Downen, *The Taiwan Pawn in the China Game: Congress to the Rescue* (Washington, D.C.: Center for Strategic and International Studies, Georgetown University, 1979); Gregor, *China Connection*, pp. 127–136; Lasater, *Taiwan Issue*, ch. 8; Edwin K. Snyder, A. James Gregor, and Maria Hsia Chang, *The Taiwan Relations Act and the Defense of the Republic of China* (Berkeley: Institute of International Studies, University of California, 1980); Sutter, *China Quandary*, chs. 3–5; and Lester L. Wolff and David L. Simon, *Legislative History of the Taiwan Relations Act* (New York: American Association for Chinese Studies, 1982).

35. Lasater, *Taiwan Issue*, pp. 164–177; and Jonathan D. Pollock, "China and the Global Strategic Balance," in Harry Harding, ed., *China's Foreign Relations in the 1980s* (New Haven, Conn.: Yale University Press, 1984), pp. 158–169.

36. A. Doak Barnett, *U.S. Arms Sales: The Chinese-Taiwan Tangle* (Washington, D.C.: Brookings Institution, 1982); Lasater, *Taiwan Issue*, chs. 9 and 10; and Sutter, *China Quandary*, ch. 6.

37. Hickey, "America's Two-Point Policy," pp. 881–896.

38. Hong N. Kim and Jack Hammersmith, "U.S.-China Relations in the Post-Normalization Era, 1979–1985," *Pacific Affairs* 59:1 (Spring 1986), pp. 83–91; and Stephen Uhalley, Jr., "The Reagan Administration Turnaround on China," in James C. Hsiung, ed., *Beyond China's Independent Foreign Policy: Challenges for the U.S. and Its Asian Allies* (New York: Praeger, 1985), pp. 55–70.

39. A. James Gregor and Maria Hsia Chang, *The Iron Triangle: U.S. Security Policy for Northeast Asia* (Stanford, Calif.: Hoover Institution Press, 1984), ch. 6; Lasater, *Taiwan Issue*, pp. 122–132; Snyder et al., *The Defense of the Republic of China*; and Robert G. Sutter, *Taiwan: Entering the 21st Century* (Lanham, Md.: University Press of America, 1988) pp. 13, 38. & 63.

40. Gerald Chan, "The Two-Chinas' Problem and the Olympic Formula," *Pacific Affairs* 58:3 (Fall 1985), pp. 473–490; Byron S. J. Weng, "Taiwan's International Status Today," *China Quarterly* 99 (September 1984), pp. 462–480; and "ROC Takes Aim at Old U.N. Seat." *Free China Journal* 6:26 (April 13, 1989), p. 1.

41. Thomas B. Lee, "Quasi-Diplomatic Relations of the Republic of China: Their Development and Status in International Law," *Issues and Studies* 24:7 (July 1988), pp. 104–117.

42. Hickey, "America's Two-Point Policy," pp. 886–890.

43. John F. Copper, "Politics in Taiwan, 1985–86: Political Developments and Elections," in Hungdah Chiu, ed., *Survey of Recent Developments in China (Mainland and Taiwan), 1985–1986* (Baltimore: School of Law, University of Maryland, 1987), pp.

29–30; "Taiwan to Close Nuclear Reactor," *Washington Post* 111:110 (March 24, 1988) p. A32; and "US will Maintain ROC Ties," *Free China Journal* 6:8 (February 2, 1989), p. 1.

44. Cindy M. Benedicto, "Trade Visitors Say, USSR Eager to Deal," *Free China Journal* 5:72 (December 12, 1988), p. 7; and "Secretary General Resigns," *Free China Journal* 5:57 (October 20, 1988), p. 1.

45. I. M. Destler, *American Trade Politics: System Under Stress* (New York: Twentieth Century Fund, 1986).

46. Susan Chira, "Taiwan Shift Jolts U.S. on Trade," *New York Times* 137:47,505 (May 14, 1988), pp. B1 & B18; John F. Copper, "Taiwan: A Nation in Transition," *Current History* 88:537 (April 1989), pp. 174–175; K. T. Li, *The Evolution of Policy Behind Taiwan's Development Success* (New Haven: Yale University Press, 1988), pp. 137–138; James D. Seymour, "Taiwan in 1988: No More Bandits," *Asian Survey* 29:1 (January 1989), p. 62; and "US Wins Turkey Fight, ROC Gets Bird Parts," *Free China Journal* 5:41 (August 25, 1988), p. 1.

47. Thomas J. Bellows, "Taiwan's International Relations," in Hungdah Chiu, ed., *Survey of Recent Events in China (Mainland and Taiwan), 1985–1986* (Baltimore: School of Law, University of Maryland, 1987), pp. 153–175; Gregor and Chang, *Iron Triangle* ch. 6; and Yu-ming Shaw, "Taiwan: A View from Taipei," *Foreign Affairs* 63:5 (Summer 1985), pp. 1050–1063.

48. Bellows, "Taiwan's International Relations," pp. 171–173; Katherine L. Chen, "Taiwan Action on China Meeting Called Prelude to Easing Control on Universities," *Chronicle of Higher Education* 35:3 (September 14, 1988), pp. A45–46; Susan Chira, "For Taiwan, China Looms Even Larger," *New York Times* 137:47,513 (May 22, 1988), pg. 15; Copper, "Nation in Transition" pp. 198–199; John Frankenstein, "China's Foreign Trade in the 1980's," *Current History* 87:530 (September 1987), pp. 273–274; Thomas B. Gold, "The Status Quo Is Not Static: Mainland-Taiwan Relations," *Asian Survey* 27:3 (March 1987), pp. 300–315; James McGregor, "Taiwan's Entrepreneurs Moving Quietly to Reap Once-Forbidden Profit in China," *Wall Street Journal* 211:89 (May 6, 1988), p. 16; James D. Seymour, "Taiwan in 1987: A Year of Political Bombshells," *Asian Survey* 28:1 (January 1988), pp. 71–77; Seymour, "Taiwan in 1988," pp. 60–62; "Ball's in Peking Court," *Free China Journal* 5:76 (December 26, 1988), p. 1; "M'land Coal May Soon Provide Taiwan Power," *Free China Journal* 5:38 (August 15, 1988), p. 8; "Mainland Fifth in R.O.C. Trade," *Free China Journal* 6:1 (January 9, 1989), p. 1; and "ROC Officials Going to Mainland Meet," *Free China Journal* 6:25 (April 10, 1989), p. 1.

49. Davis B. Bobrow and Steve Chan, "Assets, Liabilities, and Strategic Conduct: Status Management by Japan, Taiwan, and South Korea," *Pacific Focus* 1:1 (Spring 1987), pp. 23–56; Steve Chan, "Developing Strength from Weakness: The State in Taiwan," *Journal of Developing Societies* 4:1 (Spring 1988), pp. 38–51; and Steve Chan, "The Mouse That Roared: Taiwan's Management of Trade Relations with the U.S.," *Comparative Political Studies* 20:2 (July 1987), pp. 251–292.

50. Sutter, *Taiwan*, ch. 6.

CHAPTER 5

Political Development in Taiwan: An Intertwining of Institutionalization and Democratization

As suggested in chapter 2, the conception of what actually constitutes political development is ambiguous and controversial. Developmentalists are split over whether "democratization" or "institutionalization" represents the core; *dependencistas* would argue that neither provides the systemic transformation necessary for "real" development; and statists would probably focus on institutionalization in the form of effective state policies. The Republic of China (R.O.C.) represents an interesting case study of the relation between these two dimensions. Clearly, the Republican era on the mainland was a failure because neither democratization nor institutionalization advanced much. The stereotype of the R.O.C. in the postwar period has been one of successful institutionalization coupled with the lack of democratization, in the sense that an authoritarian regime has overseen rapid state-led economic development and transformation, although this system finally seemed to be undergoing fundamental change with the far-reaching political reforms of the mid–1980s. The reality, however, appears more complex. As argued below, economic development from the 1950s on was conditioned by significant political changes and, in turn, created pressures for more extensive political change and liberalization. Thus, over time, mutually reinforcing relations evolved between political change and economic change and between the institutionalization and democratization dimensions of political development.

This chapter considers the R.O.C.'s political development. The first section describes the basic political institutions (government and party) and the next three examine basic periods in the island's political history: (1) the 1950s and 1960s, when many of the basic policy parameters were developed; (2) 1971–1985, when Chiang Ching-kuo, first as premier and then as president, introduced a gradual (and somewhat cyclical) set of reforms that cumulatively transformed Taiwan's political system; and (3) the major democratization reforms of the late 1980s. The concluding section summarizes the major dimensions of reform and briefly considers the interrelations that emerged between democratization and institutionalization in the R.O.C.

Basic Political Institutions

The polity in the R.O.C. is structured around the 1947 Constitution, which was based on earlier constitutional and institutional developments in the interwar Republican period.[1] The Constitution created the institutions for a liberal democracy based on the five branches of government proposed by Sun Yat-sen and on constitutional guarantees of civil rights and liberties. Thus, at the national level, there were five basic governmental organizations: the Executive Yuan, the Legislative Yuan, the Judicial Yuan, the Control Yuan, and the Examination Yuan. An indirectly elected president stood above these five branches of government and served as the top political official in the country. Freedom of speech and other political rights were guaranteed, and universal suffrage and the secret ballot were mandated.[2]

This liberal political edifice was undercut, however, by several important factors. First, the system created the possibility of a strong president who could dominate the system even within the constitutional framework; Chiang Kai-shek used his personal political clout to do so. Second, the extraconstitutional fact that the R.O.C. has essentially been a one-party state meant that many of the democratic elements envisioned by the constitution were drastically curtailed. Third, the Constitution contained an "emergency" clause that constitutional provisions could be restricted by law "for reasons of averting an imminent crisis, maintaining social order, or advancing the general welfare" (an admittedly catch-all set of categories). Based on this, the R.O.C. adopted in 1948 the "Temporary Provisions Effective During the Period of Communist Rebellion," under which martial law was declared in 1949 and continued until 1987. Finally, the conditions of open civil war that existed when the Constitution was adopted created less than optimum conditions for the exercise of democratic rights.[3]

The keystone of the R.O.C.'s government is the president, who is indirectly elected for six-year terms by the National Assembly. The National Assembly itself was originally conceived as a major representative body that, in addition to electing the president and vice-president, was charged with adopting and amending the Constitution. Assembly members were originally elected by constituencies of 500,000 for six-year terms; the Assembly also included members of occupational groups, racial minorities, and overseas Chinese.[4] Thus, as initially conceived, the National Assembly functioned analogously to the Electoral College in America for selecting the president.

The power of the president in the R.O.C. derives from both constitutional and extraconstitutional factors. Constitutionally, he appoints the leaders of three of the five branches of government, which certainly provides considerable leverage and serves as the focus for coordination among the different branches. More informally, the president has been the focal point for a number of important decision-making bodies, such as the somewhat shadowy National Security Council, created by Chiang Kai-shek in 1967 and composed of some of the top officials in the regime, which at times has seemingly served as a "super Cabinet,"[5] and important ad hoc committees. In addition, the president has always been the leader of the Kuomintang party (KMT) (with the exception of three years after the death of Chiang Kai-shek), which provides the most significant power base in Taiwan's politics. Finally, presidential power in Taiwan has also been a function of the personal characteristics of its two strongest incumbents, Chiang Kai-shek (1950–1975) and his son, Chiang Ching-kuo (1978–1988).

The most important branch of government has been the executive or administrative. The president appoints a premier to head the Executive Yuan with the consent of the legislature. The premier, in turn, selects a Cabinet to administer the eight ministries (e.g., Communications, Defense, Economic Affairs, Education, Finance, Foreign Affairs, Interior, and Justice), Ministers Without Portfolio, and Councils and Commissions (e.g., Agriculture, Atomic Energy, Central Bank, Economic Planning and Development, Government Information, Overseas Chinese Affairs, Science, and Youth). It is somewhat ambiguous, therefore, whether Taiwan possesses a presidential or Cabinet system, since the exact division of labor between the president and premier is unclear and depends to a considerable extent on their personal power positions. For example, although the president has almost always been the supreme leader, Chiang Ching-kuo, who was premier when his father died, assumed the mantle of leadership directly, while Vice-President Yen Chia-ken served out the rest of the presidential term.

The Legislative Yuan is a directly elected body, constituted much like the National Assembly. It passes budgets and legislation and exercises oversight of the executive (e.g., the Executive and Legislative Yuans have vetoing and overriding powers fairly similar to those exercised by the president and Congress in the United States). In reality, however, the Legislative Yuan has been fairly weak throughout most of its history. Although it is probably fair to describe it as a "rubber stamp" in regard to major policies at least until recently, legislators do exercise considerable initiative in such important areas as amending legislation, constituent service, local development projects, and overseeing the executive in public interpellation sessions.[6] Traditional Chinese emphasis on administration and the dominant role of the KMT in Taiwan's politics explain much of this subservient position, but another key factor has devolved from the R.O.C.'s claim to be the sole legitimate government of China.

Members of the Legislative Yuan (as well as the National Assembly and Control Yuan) were chosen for three-year terms in nationwide elections on the mainland (including Taiwan) in 1947 and 1948. With the Communist victory in the civil war, it was impossible to hold new elections at the periods specified in the Constitution. Thus, for almost two decades, these bodies basically atrophied

Table 5.1
Composition of Elected Bodies

	National Ass	Legis Yuan	Control Yuan
Year Original Election	1947	1948	1948
Number Original Members	2,961	760	180
Orig Mems Active 1967	1,521	493	84
Orig Mems Active 1975	1,281	376	57
Members Elected 1969	15	11	2
Members Elected 1972-73	53	51	15
Total Members 1975	1,349	438	74
% Directly Elct Mems	5%	14%	23%
Orig Mems Active 1986	899	222	35
Mems Elct in Supplmt Elects	91	74	24
Overseas Chinese Aptd by Pres	0	27	10
Total Members 1986	990	323	69
% Directly Elct Mems	9%	23%	35%
% Members Under 70	24%	31%	39%
Ave Deaths per year, 1981-86	44	14	1

Sources: Yangsun Chou and Andrew J. Nathan, ''Democratizing Transition in Taiwan,'' *Asian Survey* 27:3 (March 1987), p. 279; Ralph N. Clough, *Island China* (Cambridge, Mass.: Harvard University Press, 1978), p. 35; and Hung-chao Tai, ''The Kuomintang and Modernization in Taiwan,'' in Samuel P. Huntington and Clement H. Moore, eds., *Authoritarian Politics in Modern Society: The Dynamics of Established One-Party Systems* (New York: Basic Books, 1970), p. 417.

and increasingly lost their representative character in relation to the territory actually governed by the R.O.C. However, to replace them with popularly elected assemblies would deny the political legitimacy that the regime was desperately seeking to maintain both externally and internally. By the late 1960s, as shown in Table 5.1, these elected bodies had fallen to about half of their original memberships, and the passing of time had made many of the ''active members'' far from active. When coupled with the pressure to make the elected organs more representative and democratic, these demographic trends led the regime to hold ''supplementary'' elections, beginning in 1969, to rejuvenate the ''representative'' parts of the national government. The death of incumbents and increased number of Taiwan constituencies has gradually increased the proportion of directly elected members to about a tenth of the National Assembly, a quarter of the Legislative Yuan, and a third of the Control Yuan (these do not count the replacements appointed by the president to the Legislative and Control Yuans); given the advanced age of many of the original incumbents, the ''newly elected'' members form a much higher percentage of those who actively participate.

Consequently these elective bodies have become much more assertive over the 1980s. Still, as discussed in the section on recent democratization, reform of the legislative bodies has become a major issue on the current political agenda.[7]

The other three branches are less salient in Chinese politics, although their stature and powers are increasing as part of the process of political liberalization. This is especially true of the Control Yuan, whose members are indirectly elected by provincial assemblies (and municipalities granted provincial status) for six-year terms. Its primary function is to exercise oversight over the other parts of the government (e.g., it holds general auditing powers, must consent to appointments to the Judicial and Examination Yuans, and can censure or, with approval of the National Assembly, impeach government officials), and by the late 1980s it was becoming increasingly assertive and public in its activities. The Judicial Yuan, whose members are appointed by the president, interprets the Constitution and serves as the Supreme Court for the R.O.C. Finally, the Examination Yuan, which is also appointed by the president, oversees the system of civil service examinations and serves as a personnel agency for the government.

As originally established on the mainland, the governmental structure was a federal one with three levels—national, provincial, and county. The retreat from the mainland left essentially one province (Taiwan) that encompassed almost all the territory governed by the R.O.C. (the offshore islands are under military administration). The provincial administration is directed by the governor, who is appointed by the president. There is a directly elected Provincial Assembly, whose relation with the governor and provincial executive parallels that of the Legislative and Executive Yuans. In the past at least, legislative politics at the provincial level have been considerably livelier than in the Legislative Yuan, reflecting the nature of its selection.[8] Counties and municipalities have elected executives (magistrates and mayors) and councils. In addition, the two largest cities, Taipei in 1967 and Kaohsiung in 1979, were made "special municipalities" directly under the Executive Yuan, ostensibly to give them greater autonomy. Their structure is now fairly similar to the provincial government, with an appointive mayor (which probably provides the real reason for the institutional change, given the rising strength of opposition candidates in mayoral elections) and elected councils. As part of the current democratization reforms, though, these two mayorships are slated to become elective offices. Generally, over time, there has been a devolution of power from the central to the lower levels of government.[9]

Figure 5.1 outlines these basic governmental bodies and their relation to the electorate (the special municipalities are omitted). Solid arrows indicate the formal power to select and dashed arrows show check-and-balance relations. The major features suggested by this diagram are (a) that the electorate has substantial powers but that these can be circumscribed in practice by the indirect method of choosing the central and provincial administrations; (b) that the institutional structure certainly exists for a strong presidency; (c) that the system

Figure 5.1
Government Structure of R.O.C.

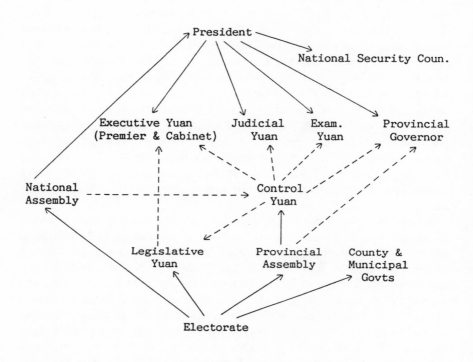

———→   Responsibility for selection

- - -→   Check and balance relationship

provides, at least in theory, a significant number of checks and balances; and (d) that democracy will probably be strongest at the lowest levels of government.

How formal institutions of government operate depends to a large extent on the more informal political practices and institutions that exist in a society. The most salient feature of Taiwan's politics has been the dominant position of the KMT. Not only do KMT members win most of the elections in Taiwan and hold almost all of the significant administrative positions, but the party per se has exercised the major role in policymaking. Thus major policy and personnel decisions are approved, if not made, by the top party organs (e.g., the premier formally submits his Cabinet choices to the party's Central Standing Committee for approval); at least until recently, the Executive Yuan has been viewed as much more of a policy implementer than an initiator.[10] Furthermore, the most powerful governmental official in the country has also maintained the position of party leader as well: Chiang Kai-shek served as director general of the KMT from 1938 until his death in 1975; Chiang Ching-kuo served as party chairman from 1975 until his death in 1988; and the new president, Lee Tung-hui, became party chairman as well.

The KMT falls somewhere between a small, tightly organized "cadre" party and a "mass" electoral party. In the early 1980s it had approximately two million members, almost a fifth of the adult population (up from a ninth in 1963). About two-thirds of its members are native islanders and under the age of forty, reflecting the party's strong efforts to garner popular support.[11] Because of the Russian influence on its organizational heritage in the 1920s, the KMT is structured along typical Leninist lines, moving upward from small basic units to regional organizations to the national party. Above the lowest level the party organizations are headed by central committees, advisory committees (generally composed of "retired" party elders), and executive structures. A Provincial Party Congress is held every two years to select the provincial leadership; a National Party Congress is held every five years (the Thirteenth Party Congress was held in July 1988).

At the national level the Congress elects a Central Committee (now 180 members) and a chairman. Elections for the Central Committee have become increasingly open. For example, at the Thirteenth Congress, Party Chairman Lee Tung-hui nominated 180 candidates; another 180 candidates were nominated by Congress participants; and the Central Committee was chosen in a highly competitive election. The Central Committee meets infrequently, though. Thus the major party body is the Central Standing Committee, which now has thirty-one members plus the KMT chairman. According to party statutes, the Central Standing Committee is elected by the Central Committee, but in practice a slate is nominated by the chairman and approved by acclamation. Under Chiang Ching-kuo the Central Standing Committee did not appear to be that major a decisional forum for the party, since Chiang worked with more informal councils and presented major policies to the Central Standing Committee for fairly pro forma approval.[12] The KMT chairman also appoints the secretary general of the party, who supervises the party's extensive administrative structure and is usually one of the most powerful politicians in the country.

The KMT has fairly extensive ties with the broader society, although they are much less pervasive and monopolistic than for Leninist parties in Communist systems. First, given its electoral success, the party's nominating power is an important political resource, although central control over nominations has decreased markedly over time.[13] Second, the party coordinates or directs a variety of groups supportive of the regime. The most important include the China Youth Corps, which serves an important political recruitment function, and Farmers' Associations, which are closely associated with KMT politics, as described in the next section. Third, although the party does not monopolize the mass media, it owns major outlets in all the media, which certainly helps its political efforts. Finally, in something of a patronage-style mode, the KMT operates over 400 centers around the island that provide a variety of services to the general citizenry.[14].

The "Temporary Provisions" and martial law have also affected Taiwan's politics in several significant ways. First, they permitted the suspension of constitutional rights, giving rise to an extensive security apparatus and censorship activities (e.g., many opposition political journals have been suspended or harassed even in the 1980s). Second, the formation of new political parties, in addition to the KMT and two politically inconsequential parties that came to Taiwan from the mainland, was prohibited, although opposition candidates ran as independent candidates and by the 1980s had formed a quasi-formal party structure. Third, martial law provisions have been used in periodic crackdowns on crime, which has proved quite popular.[15] The "Emergency Decree" for Taiwan was finally abolished in July 1987. Although some critics of the regime argued that the National Security Law that replaced it was just as restrictive, this clearly marked a significant step forward in Taiwan's democratization (e.g., in the institutionalization of opposition parties).

Setting the Basic Political Contours, 1950–1971

When the R.O.C. re-established its basic political institutions in Taipei in 1949–1950, its political prospects were quite dim. Even excluding the threat of a Communist invasion, which was vitiated by the outbreak of the Korean War, the problems facing the regime were quite daunting: the government itself was disorganized and depressed after the disaster of the civil war; the population of Taiwan was sullen and hostile after the tragedy of February 1947; and the island's economy remained poor and agriculturally oriented. Despite (or perhaps, more accurately, because of) these daunting problems, Chiang Kai-shek and the KMT quickly made a strong commitment to fundamental political change. Consequently, over the 1950s and 1960s, the KMT implemented a policy package of party reform, economic development, economic and political appeals for popular support, and strong security controls that produced a much stabler polity than had existed on the mainland and, in turn, transformed the nature of the KMT elite.

The regime, therefore, both applied the stick and offered the carrot in its relationship with its subjects. In terms of the stick of a massive security crackdown, considerable threats to internal security certainly existed in the early 1950s. The Communists had begun infiltrating agents in the late 1940s; support existed for deposing the KMT and establishing an "independent" Taiwan; and dissident elements of the KMT constituted a significant coup potential. To counter these threats, a strong security apparatus was created under Chiang Ching-kuo that essentially operated outside the law during the early 1950s and only gradually relaxed over the next two decades:

The Nationalist leadership decided that survival and eventual return to the mainland were possible only through rigorous ideological reindoctrination and the elimination of dissidents. Turning to one he knew he could trust, the Generalissimo put Ching-kuo in charge of a massive crackdown in both the military and civilian sectors. An all-pervasive secret police system was employed to root out individuals and groups regarded as subversive and to expose conspiracies. The regime executed hundreds and imprisoned thousands more.[16]

In terms of the allegiances of the internal opposition, the threat from the Communist-controlled mainland faded fairly rapidly, as the Chinese Communist party (CCP) evidently came to be seen by Taiwanese islanders as the representative of another alien set of mainlanders with an even more alien ideology. What came to be called the Taiwan Independence Movement (TIM) constituted a stronger and more lasting challenge, however. Anti-KMT Taiwanese leaders who left the island in the late 1940s split into two groups, one settling in the mainland and the other in Japan. The former quickly faded from the Taiwan political scene, but the latter seemingly exerted some external influence on the island; additionally, a much younger set of Taiwanese nationalists emerged in the United States, centered on student groups. The appeal that TIM exerted in Taiwan during the 1950s and 1960s is hard to estimate, given the degree of repression directed toward it. There clearly was significant support among intellectuals and students as demonstrated by such incidents as the arrests of Lei Chen in 1960 for trying to organize an opposition party and Professor Peng Ming-min in 1964 for writing pamphlets advocating the overthrow of the KMT. Mass interest in Taiwan independence, though, seemed rather limited at best.[17]

Unlike many authoritarian regimes in similar circumstances, however, the KMT did not try to hang onto power simply through repression and terror. Rather, Chiang Kai-shek, who had been primarily interested in military matters (including extracting resources for the army) on the mainland, evidently took his defeat in the civil war to heart and concluded that the KMT needed to reform itself and appeal to the people in terms of Sun Yat-sen's original precepts (nationalism, democracy, and people's livelihood).

A major problem for the Republic on the mainland had been the extreme factionalism and corruption of the KMT. There had been several strong factions led by leaders opposed to Chiang Kai-shek; regional warlords had shifted alliances to promote their own independence and power; and even Chiang's followers were split into several distinct groups, such as the conservative CC clique (named for the Ch'en brothers who led it) that controlled the party, the Whampoa faction in the military, and the Political Study Group of professionals and businessmen. Such factionalism, in turn, promoted corruption by minimizing central control and responsibility.[18]

The evacuation to Taiwan reduced these problems significantly. Corrupt officials took their ill-gotten gains to Hong Kong, the United States, or other parts of the world beyond the reach of the Chinese Communists; opposing leaders and factions within the KMT had no incentive to follow Chiang to almost certain defeat and annihilation; and Chiang's dispirited followers were certainly in the

mood to re-evaluate their past practices. Chiang Kai-shek moved rapidly, therefore, to reform the party. In July 1950 he formed a Central Reform Committee,
largely composed of younger and less tainted leaders, such as his son, Chiang
Ching-kuo, and Taiwan provincial governor Ch'en Ch'eng. The Central Reform
Committee replaced the leading organs of the KMT for two years, until the
Seventh Party Congress in 1952, and allowed Chiang Kai-shek to both shake
up the party (e.g., a Central Advisory Committee was established to which "out-
of-date" leaders, such as the Ch'en brothers, could be retired without a great
"loss of face") and to commit it to a policy of economic development and
popular reconciliation.[19]

The land reform programs under Governor Ch'en Ch'eng of rent reductions
for tenants in 1949 and enforced land sales in 1953 (which are discussed in detail
in chapter 6) formed a major initiative in both economic development and popular
appeal. The reasons behind the land reform were probably both enlightened and
cynical. On the one hand, land reform was a clear appeal to the peasantry that
had been mandated by Sun Yat-sen's *San Min Chu I*. On the other, it undoubtedly
did not escape KMT policymakers that radical agricultural reform would destroy
the social power of the one elite group on Taiwan, the rural gentry, who could
potentially challenge mainlander control over the island. The land reform and
the increased agricultural investment, and creation of a sophisticated agricultural
extension system that accompanied it, resulted in increased output and rising
peasant incomes, as discussed in more detail in the next chapter.

The changed economic situation in the countryside affected social and political
relations as well, as the landlords were deprived of their basis for exerting social,
economic, and political control over their villages, resulting in vastly increased
socioeconomic mobility for rural residents and more equalitarian relations in
agricultural areas. These socioeconomic changes were also reflected in the political realm. First, land reform and the growing agricultural prosperity that it
produced greatly enhanced the regime's popularity in the countryside (e.g., the
KMT has traditionally done significantly better in elections in rural areas than
in urban ones[20]). Second, the Farmers' Associations that were created to promote
new technology and cropping techniques and to organize credit and marketing
cooperatives became significant patronage bodies that assumed an increasingly
important role in local KMT politics. Finally, rural local politics revolved around
competition among cliques and factions, particularly kinship ones, so that the
mainlander central and regional party leaders were adroitly able to assume "balance wheel" positions among competing islander groups.[21]

The Nationalist state in Taiwan, therefore, engaged in much the same "state-
building" intrusion into rural communities in Taiwan as it had on the mainland
in the 1930s. Some of the results were quite similar. The traditional lineage and
mediation systems eroded considerably; village society broke down significantly;
traditional leaders among the gentry lost power; and because of such changes it
became hard at times to even recruit local political leaders. Yet the ramifications
of these changes for regime-society relations were far different than the alienation

and loss of legitimacy on the mainland. Land reform brought growing prosperity as opposed to rapacious tax farming. The subsequent urbanization and industrialization of Taiwan meant that the breakdown of village life was associated with growing prosperity, not poverty. The erosion of the gentry's leadership opened the way for new leaders to emerge and for entrepreneurial ability to be rewarded among the broad class of peasantry. As suggested above, the KMT party organizations and Farmers' Associations that assumed leadership roles in rural communities were integrated into traditional social and political networks. Finally, over time, traditional linkages and organizations re-emerged. Thus the major difference from the interwar period was not the intrusion of state-building activities per se, but their contribution to social and economic development, in contrast to their earlier concentration on "revenue extraction" to support the KMT's continuous warfare.[22]

The KMT also moved almost immediately to garner popular support by promoting democratization in local affairs and by bringing substantial numbers of islanders into the government and party. Although almost all local officials had been appointed during the colonial period, the Chiang Kai-shek government moved rapidly to create a viable system of local elected governments once it moved to Taipei; local elections were held in 1950–1951. The KMT dominated these elections, except at the local level, as demonstrated by the data in Table 5.2 on election winners in the mid–1960s. However, electoral competition for local offices was quite intense among different KMT factions in many localities. In addition, "independents" were able to win important elections (e.g., they won mayoral elections in three of the five largest cities in 1964). Thus local officials were forced to become responsive to their constituencies, although the less salubrious phenomena of corruption and vote-buying were also fostered.[23]

Such democratization almost inevitably led to considerable "Taiwanization" of the lower levels of the government and party, since native islanders had a large advantage at the polls. Thus the KMT began a major recruitment drive among the Taiwanese; by the early 1970s islanders composed over two-thirds of the party. They also soon came to hold most of the elective and appointive positions at the provincial and local levels (excluding the provincial governor); as Table 5.3 shows, Taiwanese were well represented in the civil service, at least at the lower levels, even immediately after the large-scale influx of mainlander administrators in 1950. To be sure, mainlanders still predominated in the national government, which exercised most of the power, but even early in its rule on Taiwan the KMT took substantial steps toward integrating the local citizenry into the polity.[24]

Ultimately the most momentous attempt to reach out for popular support probably was the almost immediate decision to assign a high priority to economic development despite the continuing security threat and staunch ideological commitment to "mainland recovery." This high priority on economic development by what at the time was a strongly military regime—which, incidentally, was almost the polar opposite of Chiang Kai-shek's position in the interwar

Table 5.2
KMT Strength in Local Elected Office, 1967*

	Total Offices	KMT Members	KMT Per Cent
Provincial Assembly	74	61	82%
County Magistrates & City Mayors	21	17	81%
County & City Assemblies	907	670	74%
Village & Township Heads	319	295	92%
Village & Township Assemblies	4776	2355	46%

*Especially for Village and Township Assemblies, non-KMT elected officials should not necessarily be assumed to be anti-KMT.

Source: Hung-chao Tai, "The Kuomintang and Modernization in Taiwan," in Samuel P. Huntington and Clement H. Moore, eds., *Authoritarian Politics in Modern Society: The Dynamics of Established One-Party Systems* (New York: Basic Books, 1970), p. 417.

Table 5.3
Islander Representation in Civil Service, June 1950

	Total Positions	Islander Officials	Islander Per Cent
Senior Civil Sevice	316	55	17%
Second Class Civ Serv Posts	3,118	780	25%
Third Class Civ Serv Posts	24,635	15,476	63%
Provincial Government	81,006	53,024	65%
Teaching Positions	22,130	15,929	72%

Source: Fred W. Riggs, *Formosa Under Chinese Nationalist Rule* (New York: Octagon Books, 1972), p. 49.

Republic[25]—evidently stemmed from several factors. First, the KMT concluded that development and reform were necessary to expand its popular appeal, especially to the peasantry, whose alienation was seen as a key factor in the loss of the Chinese civil war. Second, there was considerable American pressure for liberalization and for following the example of the U.S. occupation in Japan. In addition to U.S. interest in promoting land reform, American advisors pressured the R.O.C. to expand the private sector of the economy and to facilitate the activities of Taiwanese businessmen in order to give the islanders a larger stake in the system. Third, industrialization was viewed as necessary for building a defense industry. Finally, the *San Min Chu I* certainly called for economic growth and liberalization.[26]

This concern with development was reflected in a series of strategic decisions about the nature of Taiwan's fundamental economic orientations and structures. Two such decisions were made in the early 1950s: the land reform and an "import substitution'' approach to industrialization (i.e., the imposition of protectionist controls to stimulate the domestic production of goods, especially light industry and consumer items, that had previously been imported). Both decisions, discussed in more detail in the next chapter, proved to be quite felicitous in terms of their economic results. They also contributed to the R.O.C.'s political development by broadening the political leadership. In addition to the democratization of local politics noted above, the push for rapid economic growth necessitated bringing technocrats and administrators, many of whom had been educated at leading American universities, into the top levels of government. On the other hand, the state retained a strong influence over the credit available to the private-business sector during the import-substitution phase through its control of foreign aid and the banking sector. Consequently the major beneficiaries were managers of state corporations and businessmen (mostly mainlanders, but a few Taiwanese as well) who had access to the political authorities—which was at least a little reminiscent of the interwar ''bureaucratic capitalism.''[27]

These technocrats then played the central role in making the much more controversial decision to switch to export-led growth in the late 1950s and early 1960s as they formed an alliance with Taiwan's American advisors to push through this drastic policy reorientation against the opposition of conservative elements in the regime. This change in economic strategy was controversial for several reasons. Many cautious leaders did not believe that the R.O.C.'s labor-intensive light industries could become competitive on international markets; they feared that the opening of the Taiwan economy would simply result in a wave of imports that would fuel inflation and create a horrendous balance-of-trade and balance-of-payments position. The liberalizing of Taiwan's economy, moreover, would mean the dismantling of many economic controls and the giving up of the dominant position of state corporations in the industrial sector, which threatened the power of many bureaucrats in the government and party. Finally, an emphasis on light industry for export meant foregoing, at least in the short term, the heavy industry necessary for defense production, which obviously created much concern in the still powerful military sector. Despite these powerful bases of opposition, the leading economic technocrats (such as K. Y. Yin, C. K. Yen, and K. T. Li) won the backing of President Chiang Kai-shek and Premier Ch'en Ch'eng; the result was a rapid economic reorientation that produced a spectacular growth spurt in the late 1960s and early 1970s.[28]

The government's policy of rapid, export-led industrialization was centered on the private-business sector and opened up another avenue for advancement and mobility for native Taiwanese who possessed the skills and resources to become entrepreneurs. For example, many former landlords used the compensation paid to them by the Land-to-the-Tiller program to start up dynamic ventures. Thus islanders dominated the private-business sector from the early 1960s onward and became the prime beneficiaries of rapid growth, high profit rates, and escalating land prices during the export surge decade of 1963–1973. In fact, by the early 1970s private entrepreneurs, most of whom were islanders, had

Table 5.4
Educational Progress in Taiwan, 1944–1970

	1944	1970	Ratio 1970/1944
College Education			
Number of Colleges	5	75	15
Number of Students (1000s)	2	139	64
High School Education			
Number of Schools	75	778	10.4
Number of Students (1000s)	47	961	23
Elementary Education			
Number of Schools	1,079	2,176	2
Number of Students (1000s)	898	2,166	2.4
Per cent School-age Children Enrolled in Primary Schools	71%	98%	1.4

Source: Yung Wei, "Taiwan: A Modernizing Chinese Society," in Paul K. T. Sih, ed., *Taiwan in Modern Times* (New York: St. John's University Press, 1973), p. 467.

surpassed all but the top political officials in terms of income, standard of living, and perhaps even social status. They also had begun to assume a significant political role in terms of economic initiatives and of acting as a link between the still mainlander-dominated national regime and the general citizenry, although they remained subordinated to the KMT regime. By the 1970s, hence, Taiwan had evolved something of a dual elite structure in which mainlanders dominated the top government and party positions and islanders dominated the business establishment.[29]

A final important policy of the R.O.C. for promoting the economic advancement of its citizenry was in the field of education. Reflecting the traditional Chinese emphasis on education (e.g., the 1947 Constitution stipulated that the central government should spend at least 15 percent of its budget on education, science, and culture), the R.O.C. instituted a policy of compulsory primary education that was expanded from six to nine years in 1968. Beyond the compulsory education, opportunities for secondary and higher education were vastly expanded over the colonial period, as demonstrated by the date in Table 5.4. The regime's considerable investment in education produced several salutatory results. The literate and increasingly well educated population both formed a reservoir of human capital that could be mobilized for labor-intensive industrialization and allowed individuals to benefit from industrialization in terms of rapid upward socio-economic mobility. Furthermore, the "National Language Movement" of using Mandarin as the language of instruction, it is generally agreed, helped to promoted social integration between mainlanders and islanders.[30]

To sum, the KMT regime assumed a much different orientation after it arrived in Taipei than it had adopted in the mainland. Although stringent security controls were imposed and only gradually relaxed, Chiang Kai-shek realized that the party had to reform itself and appeal to a much greater extent to the broader society. These positive appeals took a variety of forms—a reform of the party organization, a strong commitment to economic development (despite the continued ideological stress on "mainland recovery"), major investments in education, an internationally acclaimed land reform program that benefited a large proportion of the islander population, and a movement toward grass-roots democratization. Still, as the 1970s began, economic and social modernization had clearly outstripped political development; a significant degree of estrangement remained between mainlanders and islanders. Thus, in addition to the growing threat on the international scene described in chapter 4, the stability that rapid development had seemingly produced on the domestic front was certainly vulnerable to challenge.

The Chiang Ching-kuo Liberalization

The R.O.C. responded by adopting a major series of political reforms during the 1970s and first half of the 1980s under the leadership of Chiang Ching-kuo, who became premier in 1972, party chairman in 1975 after his father's death, and president in 1978. Chiang Ching-kuo's reforms embraced three principal dimensions: (1) bringing younger and more professionally oriented leaders into top government and party positions, (2) increasing the importance of elections and popular participation in Taiwan's politics, and (3) promoting a "Taiwanization" of first middle-level and then top-level political positions. This reform movement was certainly cyclical, in the sense that domestic and international crises periodically produced significant retrenchments and crackdowns, but the reforms cumulated over time and transformed political life in the R.O.C.

By the early 1970s the R.O.C. government was facing growing pressures from both international and domestic sources. Externally, the country's deteriorating diplomatic status, as dramatized by the loss of its U.N. seat in 1971, produced growing concern among the bulk of the population at home that their growing prosperity might be threatened. Internally, the KMT's success in promoting land reform and rapid industrialization had created general support for increased participation and democratization among the citizenry, while islander entrepreneurs and intellectuals began to demand entree into policymaking positions. These pressures produced two interacting processes throughout the decade: a bubbling up of political activities and dissent from below, on the one hand, and efforts toward reform and popular outreach by the regime from above on the other.

The first signs of organized dissent (excepting the underground activities of the TIM) occurred in 1971, initially as nationalistic protests that were at least partially encouraged by the government against America's decision to return the Senkaku or Tiao Yu Ti Islands to Japan along with Okinawa despite the R.O.C.'s claim to them and against the R.O.C.'s expulsion from the United Nations. The shock caused by the latter event stimulated the formation of study groups among intellectuals and students that discussed Taiwan's deteriorating position, criticized the government for its domestic as well as foreign policies, and issued the first of what might be considered dissident publications in Taiwan. In contrast, the regime benefited from a major change in the position of the TIM, which now perceived Beijing to constitute the primary threat to Taiwan and, thus, became much less rabid in its attacks on Taipei.[31]

This new movement from below advocated more effective foreign policies and more democratization internally. These positions implied a subtler type of "Taiwanization" in terms of establishing a separate identity from the People's Republic of China (P.R.C.) and changing the composition of the R.O.C.'s central political institutions than the TIM's calls for ousting the KMT and declaring Taiwan's "independence" from China. Such reformist criticism was much more acceptable to the regime; thus the scope of political debate was gradually allowed to expand. In fact, there was not a great political divide between mainlanders and islanders on many central political issues. Both strongly opposed any move to incorporate Taiwan into the P.R.C. and supported the R.O.C.'s free-market development policies. Ironically, in view of the KMT's staunchly conservative image, many Taiwanese criticized the government from what would normally be considered a conservative perspective for not declaring Taiwan's separation from the Communist mainland and for preserving too large a role in the economy for state corporations, which were viewed as inefficient and as patronage plums for mainlanders. Rather, the key question centered on who exactly would hold office—which can be extremely important for a political system like Taiwan's in which personal networks and patronage are vital for advancement. The KMT responded to this "bubbling up" with a combination of tolerance for increasing freedom of speech and repressive actions against its most outspoken critics, becoming significantly more liberal and less coercive over time.[32]

A major reason for the containing of dissent in the early 1970s was that the government proved ready to sponsor significant political change and liberalization itself. This reform process was sparked by the appointment of Chiang Ching-kuo as premier in 1972. Chiang had been an idealistic youth committed to revolutionizing Chinese society and politics. At sixteen he both joined the KMT and went to Moscow, where he was forced to stay for more than a decade because of his father's falling out with the Communists during the Northern Expedition. With the second "United Front" between the KMT and CCP, he was allowed to return to China in 1936 and held increasingly major positions under Chiang Kai-shek during the 1940s in which he gained a reputation for strong administration, opposition to corruption, and at least some sympathy for the common people. In Taiwan, in addition to spearheading the security drive, he also formed the China Youth Corps, which allowed him to sponsor some younger and more liberal leaders. His climb up the ladder of official positions—minister without portfolio in 1958, vice-minister of defense in 1960, minister of defense in 1965, and vice-premier in 1969—probably understated his actual power position (e.g., he had become heir apparent to Chang Kai-shek after Ch'en Ch'eng's death in 1965). In addition to his father's extremely important sponsorship, he had skillfully built his own power bases in the major party, governmently, and security bureaucracies. Thus he was certainly well placed to make a major impact on Taiwan's politics when he assumed the premiership.[33]

Chiang Ching-kuo moved quickly once he assumed the premiership. First, he instituted a highly popular crackdown on official corruption that included the jailing of a former personal secretary to Chiang Kai-shek, members of the feared Taiwan Garrison Command (i.e., the security forces), and wealthy businessmen. Most officials soon got the message that no one was immune; the anti-corruption campaign appeared fairly successful. Furthermore, he put pressure on officials to be more responsive to the public and greatly reduced the secrecy surrounding government and party activities. Second, he showed an interest in promoting economic growth as he reduced the size of the military and sponsored the Ten Major Development Projects aimed at expanding Taiwan's transportation infrastructure and heavy industry capabilities in response to the rapid economic expansion of the previous decade. Third, he had a much more populist demeanor, emphasizing informal contacts with common people, in sharp contrast to his father's austere and distant leadership style, which appeared to be quite attractive to Taiwan's citizenry.[34]

Perhaps most dramatically, Chiang Ching-kuo sought to revitalize the regime's leadership by bringing younger technocrats and islanders into top positions. Although the leadership transition had begun in the late 1960s, 1972 marked a major turning point—new governments were installed at both the central and provincial levels, the first large-scale elections for the Legislative Yuan and National Assembly were held, provincial and local elections were held, and changes occurred in the top party leadership. As Table 5.5 shows, substantial turnover occurred in all these positions except the KMT CSC and senior administrative cadre. In general, the new leadership group was younger and more likely to be Taiwanese (a clear exception was the Examination Yuan, for which appointment appeared to be "honorific retirement"). Taiwanese remained grossly underrepresented in the top KMT organs (although they registered further gains later in the 1970s) and still only constituted a third of the Cabinet, but Ching-kuo's new appointments put many more islanders in "the pipeline" for future advancement. In addition, a native Taiwanese was appointed provincial governor for the first time. Many important party and KMT appointments went to U.S.-trained technocrats, both mainlanders and islanders, which was seen as pushing the regime in a more liberal and pragmatic direction. Beyond the move toward "Taiwanization" in the political leadership, fairly close ties evolved

Table 5.5
Leadership Changes, 1972

	% New Members	% Islander Members	Average Age	Number
KMT Cent Standing Com				
Old	--	10%	66	21
New	14%	14%	64	21
KMT Central Administrators				
Old	--	10%	61	20
New	25%	19%	57	16
Executive Cabinet				
Old	--	17%	65	18
New	47%	32%	61	19
Legislative Yuan				
KMT Nominees	--	88%	45	32
National Assembly				
KMT Nominees	--	91%	47	44
Judicial Yuan				
Appointees	--	60%	55	5
Examination Yuan				
Old	--	5%	62	21
New	48%	5%	60	21
Provincial Gov Council				
Old	--	65%	59	20
New	68%	58%	51	19
Provincial Assembly				
Old	--	94%	51	71
KMT Nominees	70%	97%	45	60
County Executives				
Old	--	100%	49	20
KMT Nominees	83%	100%	44	18

Source: J. Bruce Jacobs, "Taiwan 1972: Political Season," *Asian Survey* 13:1 (January 1973), p. 109.

between the KMT and the Taiwanese business community, which considerably dampened the support for Taiwanese nationalism among the richest and most politically active islanders. In fact, younger islander businessmen became increasingly important in electoral politics because of their financial resources.[35]

By the second half of the 1970s considerable progress had been made in bringing younger, more educated, and more liberal politicians, many of them Taiwanese, into positions of power under the aegis of Lee Huan, the director of the KMT's Organization Department and of the China Youth Corps and a close associate of Chiang Ching-kuo. This alienated many in the party's conservative and mainlander-dominated old guard; they used the problems associated with the 1977 elections to strike back. The November 1977 elections caused the regime considerable embarrassment for several reasons. First, several of Lee's liberal proteges defected from the party when they were not slated for high office; second, a surprisingly large number of KMT candidates lost (twelve of sixty-nine for the Provincial Assembly, four of twenty for county/municipal executives, and two of forty-five for Taipei City Council); and third, a political riot broke out in Chung-li over alleged election fraud that involved supporters for one of the leading opposition candidates, Hsu Hsin-liang, who had defected from the KMT earlier. After the elections Lee Huan resigned both his KMT and China Youth Corps posts in an obvious victory for the conservatives (although the party also changed its method of slating candidates from "nominating" to "recommending" in a loosening of controls). This conservative reaction then continued apace when the December 1978 elections were abruptly cancelled after the U.S. derecognition.[36] Fairly tight control of workers was also continued, using "martial law prohibitions against strikes, party-manipulated unions, and security offices run by retired military officers in the factories."[37]

External uncertainty and internal conservatism, in turn, sparked increasing dissent inside Taiwan centered on the *Formosa* magazine. The opposition became increasingly vocal in calling for democratization and, at least implicitly, for Taiwan to strike out on its own as an autonomous state in international affairs; despite the prohibition against the formation of new political parties, a *Tangwei* (literally, "outside the party") Campaign Assistance Corps was formed to coordinate the opposition. This challenge to the regime reached a head when a large demonstration in Kaohsiung sponsored by the *Formosa* group to commemorate Human Rights Day on December 10, 1979, broke up in a riot in which most of the people beaten up were policemen. Although who started the riot was never firmly established (accusations were hurled at the *Formosa* group, undercover agent provocateurs from the security police, or gangsters seeking revenge against the police), the leaders of the *Formosa* group were arrested. Eight of them (christened the Kaohsiung Eight) received stiff sentences; the mother and twin daughters of one were murdered under mysterious circumstances. On the other hand, the trials were surprisingly open, in that the defendants advocated their political beliefs; the crackdown on the dissidents seemed fairly popular with the public, who evidently thought that the government should be supported in a time of crisis.[38]

Just when it appeared that political reaction had set in, however, the regime launched another round of liberalization in the hope of unifying the nation, with the reforms this time being focused on expanding electoral democracy. A major reason for this was that Chiang Ching-kuo had continued his trend of replacing older KMT leaders with younger and more progressive ones during the late 1970s, despite the sacrifice of Lee Huan (who himself re-entered the top leadership as minister of education in 1984). In 1978, when Chiang assumed the presidency, a Taiwanese, Shieh Tung-min, was chosen as vice-president for the first time; Sun Yun-suan, a leading technocrat, was selected premier and subsequently appointed a substantially younger and more pragmatic Cabinet. In the next year Chiang engineered a significant turnover in the KMT's CSC that included the promotion to membership of three younger Taiwanese, who now hold top leadership positions in the R.O.C. (Lee Tung-hui, Lin Yang-kang, and Ch'iu Ch'uang-huan).[39]

The elections were rescheduled for December 1980 based on behind-the-scenes bargaining between the regime and the *tangwei* in which the former agreed not to harass the opposition in return for the latter's agreement not to publicly air certain emotional issues (e.g., Taiwan Independence, sympathy for the Kaohsiung Eight, or Communist appeals). The opposition was able to campaign fairly freely and effectively, although some tacit limitations on freedom of speech and issues that could be raised clearly existed:

Judging from what independent candidates have said in recent years, the government is able to tolerate charges of corruption and undemocratic practices, election fixing (when there is some substance to the comments), government policy on a wide range of domestic (especially local) issues, and the age of government officials. Even human rights can be discussed openly within certain limits. On the other hand, the top hierarchy of the government will not tolerate criticism that may be construed to mean changing or overthrowing the system, anything that might be pro-Communist or suggest negotiating with Peking, or anything aimed directly at individuals in the top leadership hierarchy. Similarly it will not tolerate Taiwanese who run strictly as Taiwanese or who advocate Taiwanese independence.[40]

The 1980 elections proved highly successful for the KMT, as the party garnered slightly over 70 percent of the votes and 80 percent of the seats in contests for the Legislative Yuan and National Assembly. Clearly, the citizenry gave the KMT credit for Taiwan's economic success and feared political instability. The next elections were held on schedule in December 1983. The ruling party again won slightly over 70 percent of the vote and actually captured an even higher percentage of the seats (e.g., K'ang Ning-hsing, the "unofficial" leader of the opposition in the Legislative Yuan, was defeated). This resulted both from the Nationalists' greater sophistication in maximizing its vote in Taiwan's unique single-vote, multimember districts (e.g., the number of renegade KMT candidates was reduced greatly) and from growing competition within the *tangwei* between "moderates" and "radicals." These elections also helped to open the political system, since the legislators elected in the 1980s were much more assertive and active than previous incumbents, especially those elected on the mainland in the late 1940s. In addition, many KMT candidates began to distance themselves from the government by calling for more democracy and for greater efforts in combating pollution and social problems. Thus both the opposition and "electoral politicians" within the KMT helped to increase the impetus for further liberalization.[41]

The *tangwei* used the growing liberal atmosphere to become more outspoken and to stretch the limits of political discourse, using three primary techniques: (1) publishing dissident journals that were fairly successful in avoiding the regime's attempts at censorship (i.e., by changing their names when closed down), (2) conducting vigorous and highly critical election campaigns, and (3) using legislative interpellation sessions to ask embarrassing questions. Although the opposition was composed of a loosely connected set of personalistic factions, two major groupings or orientations could be discerned. One, called the "Action" faction and associated with such leaders as the Kaohsiung Eight and Hsu Hsin-liang, emphasized Taiwan nationalism and suggested the need for radical changes in social and economic policies, whereas the other, led by K'ang Ning-hsing, was much more reformist and emphasized democratization and incremental policy changes. In the wake of the turmoil of the Kaohsiung incident the latter was more powerful, but the Action group became more assertive over time (e.g., the *tangwei*'s poor showing in 1983 partially resulted from their contesting seats held by "moderates").[42]

The *tangwei* received considerable encouragement from the fact that the regime suffered a series of embarrassments in the mid–1980s that brought on a brief bout of self-doubt, malaise, and seeming paralysis. Diplomatic decline brought nothing except the "three nos." The economic growth rate fell sharply and unemployment rose. The involvement of top military intelligence officers in the murder of newsman Henry Liu in the United States gave rise to "conspiracy theories" (e.g., including the president's son Hsiao-wu) that were highly embarrassing even though lacking in firm evidence. Finally, the country was rocked by its largest financial scandal in history, involving the Tsai family's Cathay Group, whose assets totaled over $3.5 billion and whose creditors lost over $300 million, as well as several leading KMT politicians. The government responded to its problems with a renewed swing toward conservatism. When the highly popular Premier Sun suffered a stroke in February 1984 he was replaced with the more conservative Yu Kuo-hwa, whose primary approach appeared to be hunkering down in the face of challenge (although this appointment was somewhat counterbalanced by the selection of liberal Taiwanese technocrat Lee Teng-hui as vice-president for Chiang's second term and the "exiling" of General Wang Sheng, the most powerful member in the conservative military and security factions, as ambassador to Paraguay). Harassment of the opposition also increased. For example, several publishers of dissident journals were convicted of libel (although the charges seemed justified, the fines and jail sentences that were meted out appeared rather excessive). Even this proved counterproductive, though, since political martyrs or symbols were created, while other opposition figures appeared far from intimidated.[43]

As the provincial and local elections of November 1985 approached, something of a crisis atmosphere prevailed within the KMT, as serious losses were feared that could challenge the political status quo on the island. The 1985 elections, however, went well for all concerned. The KMT won its usual 70 percent of the popular vote, while the *tangwei* won some satisfying victories. "Gentlemen's agreements" between the two parties generally held, and both sides seemed satisfied with the way the elections were conducted. Finally, President Chiang personally intervened when the Election Commission seemed ready to press charges against an opposition candidate for defaming him. Thus the 1985 elec-

tions showed that democratic progress and competition were possible in the
R.O.C. and set the stage for the more far-reaching reforms described in the next
section.[44]

In the decade and a half after his appointment to the premiership of the
Executive Yuan, Chiang Ching-kuo transformed the nature of Taiwan's politics.
In the early 1970s the R.O.C. essentially had a one-party authoritarian regime
with significant responsiveness to the populace and limited democratization at
the lower levels. By the mid–1980s, in contrast, the KMT had proved that it
could win majority support on a continuing basis, had greatly relaxed its strictures
on political freedoms, and had made its leadership both more representative of
the general population and more pragmatic and capable. It had, thus, moved a
long way down the path of democratization with the remaining authoritarian
features primarily being the continuance of martial law and the ''Temporary
Provisions,'' the accompanying restrictions on political activities that were being
increasingly unenforced, and the nature of the central government institutions
that would deny the opposition effective political power if they were to gain
majority support. Thus President Chiang could take considerable pride in what
John Copper has called the ''quiet revolution'' in the political development of
the R.O.C.[45] Furthermore, the confidence that the regime regained after the 1985
elections set the stage for Chiang to move from a ''quiet revolution'' to a more
dramatic stride toward democratization.

The Democratic Revolution of 1986–1988

The cumulative movement toward political liberalization and democratization
over the 1972–1985 period reached a more dramatic crescendo in 1986–1988.
Three major dimensions of political change occurred: (1) the formation and
institutionalization of an opposition party in 1986, (2) the abolition of martial
law and absorption of open dissent and public demonstrations in 1987 and 1988,
and (3) leadership change and liberalization after the death of President Chiang
Ching-kuo in 1988. Together these changes produced a radical transformation
in the nature of politics in the R.O.C. that can truly be considered a ''democratic
revolution.''

The first major event in the afterglow of the successful 1985 elections was a
speech by President Chiang commemorating the anniversary of the R.O.C. Constitution in which he explicitly stated that the political succession in Taiwan
would be carried out according to the Constitution. That is, current political
rumors to the contrary, succession to the presidency or top leadership position
by a member of the Chiang family or a military coup ''cannot happen and will
not happen.'' This strong speech was followed up by significant personnel
changes. The president's allegedly most ambitious relative, son Chiang Hsaio-
wu, was dispatched to Singapore as deputy commercial counselor; a civilian was
appointed minister of defense; Vice-President Lee's rank in the CSC was upgraded, marking him as the heir apparent; and the president's well-respected

younger brother, General Chiang Wei-kuo, was named secretary of the National Security Council which was seen as providing a further guarantee for a "normal" transition.[46]

At a March 1986 plenum of the KMT's Central Committee, Chiang announced that the time had come to implement the KMT's goal of constitutional democracy; after the plenum he appointed a special Task Force of twelve CSC members that included both leading liberals and conservatives in the party to draw up a reform package (reminiscent of the Central Reform Committee in the early 1950s). In June the Task Force proposed a "bold, but vague" six-point program that was remarkable for addressing almost all the outdated KMT shibboleths:

1. Large-scale supplementary elections for the central representative bodies
2. Reform of local self-government (e.g., direct election of the provincial governor and Taipei and Kaohsiung mayors)
3. Simplification of national security laws
4. Legalization of new civic associations, most importantly political parties
5. Strengthening public order
6. Strengthening party work[47]

The president also directed the KMT to open negotiations with the *tangwei*, with the apparent goal of allowing the opposition to operate a research and campaign-aid organization but not a full-fledged political party in the upcoming elections for the Legislative Yuan and National Assembly. The negotiations failed, though, as KMT conservatives believed that this was going too far, and *tangwei* leaders did not want to be perceived as a "tame" opposition. The opposition then seemingly threw down the gauntlet to the regime when it declared the formal formation of the Democratic Progressive party (DPP) on September 28 at a meeting that had been called to slate candidates. A political crisis seemed imminent as the Ministry of Justice filed charges against the DPP under the "Temporary Provisions," but President Chiang defused it by announcing that martial law would be ended and that new political parties could be formed as long as they supported the R.O.C. Constitution and renounced communism and Taiwan Independence. The DPP then held a Congress in early November (despite renewed government warnings that it would be illegal) that adopted a party charter (creating a complex organizational structure to ensure representation for its many subfactions) and program that advocated "self-determination" and readmittance to the United Nations for Taiwan in vague enough language to stop just short of a direct challenge to the regime.

The campaign itself in late November and early December was certainly lively and competitive. Although polls indicated that the citizenry was most concerned with such mundane problems as crime, pollution, and traffic congestion (which both parties could easily oppose),[48] the candidates generally castigated each other over broader and more symbolic issues:

KMT candidates generally espoused a more conservative position, supporting the government's record on economic growth and opportunity, while stressing political stability. They advocated slow steps toward full democracy, a cautious foreign policy, and greater attention to national security. DPP candidates demanded more press freedom and freedom of speech, fewer restrictions on campaigning (including spending), increased social welfare, and a more aggressive foreign policy that would get Taiwan back into some of the international organizations from which it had been expelled during the 1970s and early 1980s.[49]

The campaign was also stirred up by the attempt of Hsu Hsin-liang to return from the United States, where he had gone into exile and formed the Taiwan Revolutionary party, causing the R.O.C. to issue a warrant for his arrest in 1981. This proved embarrassing for both the KMT (which did not want to arrest Hsu) and the DPP (which viewed Hsu as too radical but felt constrained to welcome his return because of his domestic popularity). In the end the R.O.C. denied him entry, but there were several violent confrontations between his supporters and the police at Chiang Kai-shek International Airport (both sides produced videotapes showing that the other was to blame).

The elections themselves went off with few problems, and the results closely paralleled previous contests in the 1980s. The KMT won about 68 percent of the vote (down slightly from previous elections), and their proportion of seats dropped to about 80 percent. The DPP received about 20 percent of the votes and 15 percent of the seats (for example, doubling the *tangwei*'s previous representation in the Legislative Yuan), with the balance of votes and seats going primarily to independents rather than to the two minor pro-KMT parties. Thus almost everyone seemed happy with the election outcome. The KMT could claim continued widespread popular support, and the DPP could claim an impressive electoral debut. More important, the election was almost universally seen as a major step toward democratization and liberalization. The opposition party had been institutionalized, and the KMT and DPP proved that they could compete within mutually acceptable "rules of the game."[50]

Yet, despite the accommodations that were worked out between the KMT and DPP, the two sides still did not totally accept the legitimacy of the other. That is, in Ramon Myers' terms, "increasing political pluralism was combined with a certain political impasse."[51] More philosophically, opposition intellectuals challenged the *San Min Chu I* with doctrines of "Chinese humanism" (or an emphasis on development combined with traditional Confucian values) and "Chinese liberalism" (or a concern with democratization). Although many of these ideas would theoretically appear little different from Sun's doctrine, their proponents argued that the *San Min Chu I* had degenerated into a ritualistic rationale for the KMT's power and, thus, implicitly challenged the regime's basis of legitimacy.[52]

The next step was the formal abolition of martial law and the "Emergency Decree" that had been applied to Taiwan ever since the R.O.C.'s seat of government had moved to Taipei. After some evident lobbying of KMT conservatives by the president, the Emergency Decree was formally repealed in July 1987 (although the offshore islands still remained under its provisions) and replaced by a National Security Act approved by the Legislative Yuan. Although the abolition of martial law had little direct impact on Taiwan's politics, it certainly marked a symbolic break with the past and opened the way for many of the reforms of the preceding years to be institutionalized. The break with the past was not total, though, as critics charged (with some but far from total justification) that the National Security Act simply provided for martial law in another guise. For example, several of the most outspoken dissidents were arrested and given long sentences for advocating "Taiwan independence."[53]

The lifting of the Emergency Decree and the continuation of the reform in a "politics-as-usual" style by the R.O.C. government were especially significant because the opposition was becoming increasingly strident, perhaps in frustration over its inability to achieve real power both because of the country's political institutions and because of their lack of popular support. At the elite level legislative assemblies became quite raucous, in sharp contrast to the normal Chinese concern with decorum and ritual. Microphones were regularly smashed in battles over them; open fistfights even broke out among deputies; at the Constitution Day ceremonies in December 1987 a group of DPP legislators engaged in an unprecedented protest before President Chiang Ching-kuo against the slowness of legislative reform. The press became quite lively and free, but there was much less change in the state-controlled radio and television media. In terms of popular activities, mass rallies and demonstrations became a regular occurrence, although they generally remained orderly. Although such demonstrations had been unthinkable before 1986, the public soon became fairly blasé about them, except perhaps to complain with at least some spontaneity about increased traffic jams:

On a sultry Saturday night in the busy Westgate market, a taxi-driver stands on a flag-bedecked truck and shouts his anti-Government protests to the crowd. Nearby, shoppers continue haggling over the price of shoes and snake blood, while worshipers crowd into an open-air temple holding burning incense sticks aloft and bowing before the gods. Not so long ago, such a protest would not have met with such public calm nor police indifference.[54]

One reason that the burgeoning protest movement did not disrupt Chiang Ching-kuo's reform strategy was simply that the opposition remained too weak to constitute a real political challenge to KMT domination. Certainly the disruptive behavior unleashed by the liberalization and the continuing popularity of such radical leaders as Hsu Hsin-liang demonstrated alienation from the regime on the part of a considerable minority of Taiwan's citizenry. Still, at least two-thirds of the electorate continued to support the KMT and opt for political stability. Just as important, the opposition was far from unified. Although the

DPP fielded a unified slate of candidates in 1986, strong tensions still existed between moderates and radicals, especially over the question of Taiwanese nationalism (e.g., the DPP's flag contained both a map of Taiwan and a green background representing the universally popular environmentalist movement). The power relations between the different factions and political tendencies within the DPP appeared somewhat unstable. For example, "Radicals" won the party chairmanship in 1986 and 1987 but lost it in 1988. The opposition was also fragmented into personalistic factions, as indicated by the formation during 1987 of other parties (e.g., the China Democratic Justice, the Democratic Freedom, the Democratic Liberal, and the Labor parties) that ranged along a wide liberal-to-conservative ideological spectrum.[55]

More important perhaps, the opposition was frustrated by the continuing liberalization process carried out by the KMT. The regime's democratization reforms had met some of the *tangwei*'s central demands, and although there was general frustration (even within the KMT) over the slowness in reforming the national legislative bodies and provincial and special municipality governments, the regime certainly seemed to be moving in the right direction. The KMT also co-opted some of the most popular issues of the DPP, such as environmentalism, and young Turk KMT legislators (e.g., Chao Shao-kang, who was the top vote-getter for the Legislative Yuan in Taipei City in the 1986 elections, and Jaw Shau-kong) differed little from many DPP moderates in their outspokenness and aggressiveness, which caused some KMT conservatives to complain that their party was sacrificing its principles. The government also moved to appeal to the awakening labor movement, which was being generally ignored by the DPP, whose leaders were primarily drawn from the intelligentsia; a Cabinet-level Labor Council was formed in August 1987. The power of the National Security Council evidently declined somewhat as well. Additionally, President Chiang continued to push the top party leadership in a more liberal direction, which guaranteed the policy changes. In the spring of 1986 there was a turnover of four members in the CSC which made it slightly younger and almost one-half Taiwanese in composition (as opposed to only a quarter five years earlier). Then in July 1987 Lee Huan was appointed secretary general of the party, indicating the growing strength of the liberals.[56]

Chiang Ching-kuo's sudden death on January 14, 1988, threw the leadership and its liberal trend into some question. Initially the conservatives, with Chiang Kai-shek's widow as their spokeswoman, appeared ready to counterattack in the form of denying the party chairmanship to the new president, Lee Teng-hui. After some controversy Lee was proclaimed acting chairman, pending the KMT's Thirteenth Party Congress in July, in what was seen as a victory for the liberals. Lee clearly did not have the power of Chiang Ching-kuo (e.g., he was successfully defied at the ministerial level over a plan for reforming the financial system). However, he moved to consolidate his position as party chair and continued to enunciate the KMT's commitment to further reforms. Moreover, leading administrative officials, such as Vice-Minister of Economics Wang

Chien-shien, received laudatory treatment in the popular press simply for being competent, hardworking, and honest, suggesting the strong appeal that relatively "nonpolitical" technocrats have.

The Party Congress in early July was a landmark in KMT politics in several regards. The party itself clearly moved toward more democratization; liberals became significantly stronger at the top levels; and the "Taiwanization" of the party took a significant step forward as islanders for the first time received a majority of seats on the CSC. Lee Teng-hui was elected party chairman by acclamation, and Madame Chiang Kai-shek addressed the Congress in what was seen as an implicit endorsement by the old guard. The Congress itself was conducted in a much more open and lively manner than ever before, reaching its height in the strongly competitive scramble during the election for the Central Committee. The election results themselves showed strong support for such leading liberal figures as Lee Yuan, former premier Sun Yun-suan (who is not active in day-to-day politics), and Lin Yang-kang, who finished first, second, and fourth, respectively (Party Chairman Lee was not included in the election), and indicated several rising young stars in the party, such as James Soong, John Chang, Frederick Chien, and Lawrence Li-an Chen (third, sixth, ninth, and sixteenth). The changing nature of the party was also indicated by the fact that Taiwanese were four of the top ten vote-getters; in addition to Lin, Interior Minister Wu Poh-hsiung finished fifth, Provincial Governor Ch'iu Ch'uang-huan seventh, and Control Yuan President Hwang Tzuen-chiou tenth. In contrast, among the leading conservative figures General Hau Pei-tsun, the chief of the General Staff, finished a highly respectable fourteenth, but Premier Yu Kuo-hwa was an embarrassing thirty-fifth. Overall, a tremendous turnover in Central Committee membership occurred, as less than half (seventy-one) of the previous 150 members were re-elected. The average age of Central Committee members fell precipitously from seventy-eight to fifty-nine; the proportion of Taiwanese members doubled from 17 percent to 38 percent.

The CSC that Lee Teng-hui named, listed in Table 5.6, conformed to this younger and more liberal trend. For example, the average age of the CSC fell from seventy to sixty-three, and for the first time ever, Taiwanese constituted a majority (seventeen of the thirty-two members, including Lee Teng-hui). There was a forty percent turnover (twelve of the thirty-one appointees) in the CSC's membership, which is especially significant because of the more fluid situation in the top party leadership (see below). The Cabinet reshuffling that followed the Congress brought more mixed results, though (see Table 5.7 for the composition of the new Cabinet). Despite some expectations to the contrary, Yu Kuo-hwa retained the premiership. The new ministers were generally respected technocrats and included the first woman minister (and CSC member) and first Taiwanese foreign minister; the changes produced the first islander majority in the major Cabinet positions. Yet, unlike the new CSC, there was little real "new blood," as prominent government officials were basically reshuffled; the average age of the Cabinet only declined from fifty-eight to fifty-five; and several of the

Table 5.6
KMT Central Standing Committee, July 1988*

	Age	Native Province	Position	Rank in CC Elec
Shieh Tung-min	82	Taiwan	Former Vice-President	13
Li Kwoh-ting	79	Nanking	Senior Advisor to President	31
Nieh Wen-ya	84	Chekiang	Pres Leg Yuan***	50
Yu Kuo-hwa	75	Chekiang	Premier	35
Lee Huan	71	Hankow	Sec-Gen KMT	1
Shen Chang-huan	75	Kiangsu	Presidential Sec-Gen***	81
Lin Yang-kang	62	Taiwan	Pres Judicial Yuan	4
Chiu Chuang-huan	63	Taiwan	Provincial Governor	7
Hwang Tzuen-chiou	65	Taiwan	Pres Control Yuan	10
Hau Pei-tsun	69	Kiangsu	Chief General Staff	14
Irwine Ho	77	Fukien	Nat Assembly Sec-Gen	53
James Soong**	47	Hunan	Dep Sec-Gen KMT	3
Wu Poh-hsiung	50	Taiwan	Taipei Mayor	5
Fredrick Chien**	54	Chekiang	Dir Council Ec Plan & Dev	9
Lawrence Chen Li-an	52	Chekiang	Economics Minister	16
Lien Chan	52	Taiwan	Foreign Minister	27
Shih Chi-yang	54	Taiwan	Vice Premier	23
Cheng Wei-yuan**	76	Anhui	Defense Minister	17
Mao Kao-wen**	53	Chekiang	Education Minister	24
Hsu Li-nung**	68	Anhui	Chiar Voc Ast Rtd Srvcmen	25
Koo Chen-fu	62	Taiwan	Chr Brd Taiwan Cement Corp	77
Kao Yu-jen	54	Taiwan	Speaker Prov Assembly	26
Hsu Shiu-teh	57	Taiwan	Interior Minister	21
Clement Chang	59	Taiwan	Speaker Taipei City Coun	29
Chao Tze-chi**	73	Jehol	Sec-Gen KMT Policy Coord Com	84
Tseng Kwang-shun**	64	Kwangtung	Chair Com Overseas Chin Afs	47
Shirley Kuo**	58	Taiwan	Finance Minister	86
Su Nan-cheng**	52	Taiwan	Kaohsiung Mayor	43
Chien Tien-mao**	60	Taiwan	Speaker Kaohsiung City Coun	68
Hsui Sheng-fa**	63	Taiwan	Chr Brd Prince Moters Corp	88
Hsieh Shen-shan**	49	Taiwan	Pres Chinese Labor Fed	62

*In order of official ranking, which reflects both political power and respect for older leaders. The positions for new Cabinet members are their current ones, not the ones they held when appointed to the Central Standing Committee.

**New member of Central Standing Committee.

***Resigned from position but not Central Standing Committee in late 1988.

Source: *China Post* 35:13,273 (July 15, 1988), p. 12.

Table 5.7

R.O.C. Cabinet, July 1988

	Position	Native Province	Age
Yu Kuo-hwo	Premier	Chekiang	75
Shih Chi-yang*	Vice Premier	Taiwan	53
Kuo Nan-hung	Communications Min	Taiwan	53
Cheng Wei-yuan	Defense Ministry	Anhui	76
Chen Li-an*	Economics Ministry	Chekiang	52
Mao Kao-wen	Education Ministry	Chekiang	54
Shirley Kuo*	Finance Ministry	Taiwan	59
Lien Chan*	Foreign Ministry	Taiwan	52
Hsu Shui-teh*	Interior Ministry	Taiwan	57
Hsiao Tien-tzang*	Justice Ministry	Taiwan	54
Tseng Kwang-shun	Ovseas Chinese Afs	Kwangtung	65
Wu Hua-peng	Mong & Tib Afs	Mongolia	64
Chang Feng-hsu	State Minister	Taiwan	61
Fredrick Chien*	State Min & CEPD	Chekiang	54
Chow Hong-tao	State Minister	Chekiang	73
Huang Kun-hui*	State Minister	Taiwan	53
Henry Yu-shu Kao	State Minister	Taiwan	76
Shen Chun-shan*	State Minister	Kiangsu	56
Wang You-tsao*	State Minister	Fukien	64
Robert Chien*	Cabinet Sec-Gen	Chekiang	60
Yen Chen-hsing	Atomic Energy Com	Honan	77
Chang Chi-cheng	Cent Bank of China	Szechwan	71
Chen Kuei-hwa	Cent Personnel Adm	Kwangtung	71
Yu Yu-hsien*	Coun of Agriculture	Taiwan	54
Kuo Wei-fan*	Coun Cul Plan & Dev	Taiwan	51
Cheng Shui-chih	Council of Labor	Taiwan	63
Yu Chien-min	Dir-Gen Bud, Act, St	Honan	65
Eugene Y.H. Chien	Environtl Prot Adm	Taiwan	43
Shaw Yu-ming	Govt Information Off	Heilungkiang	51
Shih Chun-jen	Natl Health Adm	Taiwan	66
Chin Hsiao-yi	Natl Palace Museum	Hunan	68
Hsia Han-min*	Natl Science Council	Fukien	58
Jeanne T.K. Li	Natl Youth Com	Kiangsu	51
Ma Ying-jeou*	Resh, Dev & Eval Com	Hunan	39
Hsu Li-nung	Voc Ast Rtd Svcmen	Anhui	69
Wu Poh-hsiung*	Taipei Mayor	Taiwan	50
Su Nan-cheng	Kaohsiung Mayor	Taiwan	53
Ding Mou-shih*	Ambass to U.S.	Yunnan	63

*New position.

Sources: *China Post* 35:13,279 (July 21, 1988), p. 11; and *Republic of China, 1988: A Reference Book*. Taipei: Hilit, 1988, pp. 519–20.

new Cabinet members were given portfolios outside their major areas of expertise (although in the case of Fredrick Chien, former ambassador to the United States who became chairman of the Council of Economic Planning and Development, this seemed to represent a grooming for higher office).[57]

The KMT itself, therefore, is in the middle of a significant generational and political transformation. The various elite factions in the KMT have traditionally been seen as forming three major groupings with different primary issue emphases and orientations: military security, economic development, and democratization through electoral politics.[58] The leadership changes in the party and government during the summer of 1988 suggest that the economic technocrats are now the strongest. However, the continuation of General Hau Pei-tsun's term as chief of the General Staff beyond the normal tenure indicates the continuing power of the military sector; the democratization reforms will almost inevitably bring greater power to the electoral politicians. Generational change is perhaps most important; there is almost a palpable sense of the younger (in reality middle-aged) leaders emerging from the shadows of and ending their deference to the old-generation KMT. What this generational change should produce is probably less of a fundamental policy reorientation than a much more pragmatic and nonideological style of government and public discourse. To the extent that this permits the open (and hopefully rational) discussion of several fundamental issues that have been taboo because of regime sensitivities, the R.O.C. will be a major beneficiary.

Of course, Chinese politics turns to a goodly extent on personal ambition and competition, perhaps more so than in many other nations, given the centrality of factional politics in the Chinese culture.[59] Thus Taiwan's short-term political future depends on the interactions among several top leaders, whose calculations about personal power are probably just as important as ideological or generational factors. Three of them are generally viewed as liberals:

- President Lee Teng-hui is a highly popular technocrat and obvious protege of Chiang Ching-kuo, but he suffers from never having developed a personal political or bureau-cratic base. After President Chiang's death, though, he showed a facility for forming high-level political coalitions.

- Secretary-General of the KMT Lee Huan is a long-time reformer and associate of Chiang Ching-kuo. He now seemingly controls the KMT organization and was rumored to be a strong candidate for the Premiership at the 13th Congress. However, in late 1988 he began to suffer health problems.

- President of the Judicial Yuan Lin Yang-kang probably is the Taiwanese with the largest political machine and popular following. In the past, his career was seemingly hampered by perceptions that he was too capable and ambitious, but he now seems ready to assume a major leadership position.

The conservatives are somewhat hampered by the fact that neither of their two top leaders appears highly popular.

- Premier Yu Kuo-hwa, another long-time associate of the Chiang family, retained his post in 1988 despite liberal attacks. His biggest political asset appears to be that he is the most visible representative for party conservatives.
- Chief of the General Staff Hau Pei-tsun retains a strong position as the most powerful figure in the security sector, but the military's position suffers from growing popular enthusiasm for "China fever" and disenchantment with high defense budgets.

Finally, the late president's family still has considerable political clout, as indicated by the fact that three of his sons were among the top fifteen vote-getters in the 1988 Central Committee elections. Thus another important figure still may be:

- General Chiang Wei-kuo, the Secretary General of the powerful National Security Council, who was favored to win a position on the Central Standing Committee at the 13th Congress when he suddenly retired to the Central Advisory Committee.

Taiwan's politics in the next few years, thus, will be largely shaped by whether these top leaders can cooperate in making policy and apportioning the major government and party posts among themselves, or whether disagreements over ideology and personal power drive them into conflict and stalemate.[60]

The KMT is certainly facing significant pressure for unity and reform. Although Chiang Ching-kuo clearly sponsored the reform movement, his death was evidently seen by many as depriving the regime of its "strong man" and was followed by burgeoning popular restiveness and "decompression." Thus, there was a great increase in popular demonstrations (for example, over 700 were recorded in the first four months of 1988, about two-thirds of them directed against the regime), culminating in the mass demonstration by farmers protesting against trade and agricultural policies on May 20. The demonstration attracted large numbers of opposition political supporters and students, and erupted into an eighteen-hour melee that resulted in several hundred injuries (about half among the police) and arrests (few of them involving farmers). Labor unrest grew, perhaps most dramatically indicated by widescale conflict with business in early 1989 over demands for Chinese new year bonuses of up to three-to-four months' wages. Government restrictions on contacts with the P.R.C. were honored in the breach or openly defied. Events from the past (for example, the February 1947 revolt) were dragged out for public discussion. Many formerly sacrosanct policies, (for example, the defense budget and KMT-owned businesses) came in for strong public criticism. And so on, and so on, and so on. Clearly a new day had dawned in Taiwan's politics.[61]

The growing political conflict both within the KMT and between the regime and the opposition is well illustrated by the recent battle over how to treat the "senior legislators" elected on the mainland in the late 1940s. The opposition is demanding their immediate retirement both because it would increase their power in the assemblies and give more legitimacy to the Taiwanization of the political system and because it appears quite popular with the general public. Many liberals among the Nationalists probably agree, but the party is hesitant to embarrass senior members or to undermine the legitimacy of the 1947 Constitution. Thus the regime has taken a temporizing position of trying to bribe the senior legislators to retire with huge pensions ($3.5 million NT, or about $125,000) and of enlarging the elected bodies. The increasingly raucous nature of Taiwan's politics and the lack of legitimacy politicians accord to their opponents is well illustrated by the opposition's response to the KMT's introducing the bill on senor legislators without the lengthy and politically embarrassing debate that they desired:

Only then did the DPP lawmakers realize that they had been outwitted. Protesting the sneaky act, they smashed all the microphones and threw the rule book at the staffer who read the report. The DPP supporters in the spectators' gallery also shouted protests at the top of their voices. The acting speaker put an end to the scene by declaring a 10-minute recess and retiring to a room outside. DPP lawmakers who tried to force their way in were blocked by the police. They vented their anger by kicking at the door.[62]

Early in 1989, the Legislative Yuan passed the bill encouraging the retirement of senior legislators, along with two other laws of central importance to democratization in Taiwan. The first on Civic Organizations legalized the formation and registration of political parties without the prior approval of the government, and the second on the Election and Recall of Public Officials broadened candidate rights in elections, in particular permitting access to radio and television, and ended the KMT's monopoly over the Central Election Commission. The bill on reforming legislative bodies was quite controversial, and in seeming recognition that few senior legislators would retire the National Security Council subsequently approved a plan to radically increase the number of directly elected members of the National Assembly, Legislative Yuan, and Control Yuan over the next few elections. The bills on parties and elections represented more of a compromise between the KMT and DPP, suggesting that agreement on the "rules of the game" had been reached, as did the subsequent announcement that both the DPP and KMT would hold primary elections for their 1989 nominations.[63]

In particular, the regime appears to be facing challenges in three major areas. First is the continuation of democratization in terms of reforming the central governmental institutions and guaranteeing political rights. Second, growing political activism by farmers and labor, two constituencies that have traditionally supported the KMT, shows that economic discontent can arise even in the midst of general prosperity. Finally, the extreme popularity of "China fever" indicates that the government must come up with a comprehensive policy toward the P.R.C. in the near future. However, the regime can take some comfort from the fact that, except for the first, these issues present dilemmas for the opposition as well. The DPP is based on the intelligentsia and has yet to make a concerted appeal to farmers or workers. Moreover, the association of the opposition with

Taiwanese nationalism creates a quandary over how to respond to the escalating "China fever." In fact, if anything, both a greater sense of Taiwan autonomy (e.g., growing emphasis by intellectuals on Taiwan's historical distinctiveness from China) and interest in "China fever" seem to be growing simultaneously in a "dialectical contradiction" that presents a challenge to all the players in the R.O.C.'s game of politics.

During his last two years of life, then, President Chiang Ching-kuo oversaw a "democratic revolution" in the R.O.C. that has seemingly institutionalized a much more open political system in which the KMT and opposition have worked out a mutually acceptable set of "rules of the game," although the failure of both sides to fully accept the other's legitimacy may create problems for democratic politics. Given the continuing strength of the ruling KMT, the R.O.C. appears headed toward Japanese-style democracy with one dominant party composed of several distinct factions. For the moment, therefore, the central aspect of Taiwan's politics revolves around the ability of the top KMT figures to work out a "collective leadership" arrangement, since none of them evidently is now capable of assuming Chiang's dominant position. The DPP and other non-KMT organizations have a key role to play, though, since their very existence forces the ruling party to continue its liberalization and to face, rather than evade, the central political issues on Taiwan.

Political Development, Sunist Doctrine, and Chinese Culture

Writing in the 1970s, Arthur Lerman conceptualized the R.O.C. as a "fledgling Western-style electoral democracy" with three basic characteristics:

1. A "relatively democratic subsystem" at the lower levels;
2. A "governing elite" at the top whose positions did not depend directly on competition within this electoral subsystem; and
3. Widespread perceptions by the top elite that many of the electoral politicians were "immoral and incompetent" because of their preoccupation with patronage politics rather than the "national interest."[64]

To restate this in terms of the two dimensions of political development, strong political institutionalization coexisted with limited democratization and probably was successful precisely because of the limits on popular influence.

The nature of the regime did not remain static, but changed considerably over time as new elites with valuable skills for development were sequentially incorporated into the top leadership. The initial military regime transformed itself by bringing in technocrats at the central level to lead economic development and by breaking the stranglehold of landlords at the local level, which allowed the emergence of a new set of political and economic entrepreneurs. The technocrats, for their part, did not devise a development strategy maximizing their own interests, but fostered a strong private sector of primarily islander businessmen.

The success of businessmen and local politicians, in turn, created growing pressures for the Taiwanization of central political institutions and also led to the emergence of the final "sector" of the political leadership—electoral politicians primarily concerned with winning and maintaining popular support.

In addition to elite change, furthermore, political structures and practices evolved significantly. As described in the last two sections, President Chiang Ching-kuo instituted major democratization reforms that transformed the entire polity.[65] Thus the antithesis that many developmentalists assume to exist between institutionalization and more than limited democratization does not appear to hold for the R.O.C. In fact, over the past decade considerable democratization has probably been necessary to preserve the R.O.C.'s political stability and to provide a conducive environment for further economic growth and social development. Another partial antithesis between political development at the macro and micro levels is worth a brief note too. At the macro level elite change and development strategy have meshed in almost perfect unison and transformation. At the micro level of government operations, though, mindless bureaucratism and corruption continue, demonstrating that political change is far from coherent and unidimensional even under a "strong and autonomous state."

The nature and evolution of this polity can be explained by Sun Yat-sen's broad doctrine of the Three Principles of the People. The idea of tutelary democracy involved a "vanguard" party's gradually educating the people so that they could exercise self-government. The evolution of democracy from the local to the national levels and the gradual yielding of the regime to popular influences clearly fall within this framework. Sunist doctrine also emphasized that the state should play a leading role in promoting economic development, controlling capital (especially foreign enterprise) to ensure its contribution to the development project, and promoting a rising standard of living and a decent "people's livelihood." Again, this is quite consistent with the evolution of the political and economic policies after World War II. The state, therefore, has a powerful role in directing society, but one that should be devoted to the national welfare and should become more "inhibited" and "accommodating" over time.[66] This is not to say that the *San Min Chu I* provided an operational guideline for Taiwan's policies. However, it certainly did constitute a broad guidepost and legitimating motif for the considerable political and economic reforms that the regime implemented on Taiwan (and that might be considered quite surprising, given the record of the interwar Republic).

The R.O.C.'s political institutions and Sunist doctrine may also be related to the basic Confucian culture, which stresses benevolent paternalism on the part of leaders and deference and acceptance by subjects. Although Lucian Pye has quite aptly noted the "sweet and sour" nature of Confucianism in terms of its degeneration into oppressive authoritarianism, the Confucian model seemingly applies to Taiwan.[67] The rulers, somewhat surprisingly in view of their record during the interwar Republic, manifested a strong commitment to the national interest, the people's livelihood, and economic development. The citizenry, for its part, acquiesced to authoritarian rule and then showed positive support for the regime once the fruits of the government's economic policies began to alter life on the island. In the words of Edwin Winckler:

Taiwan's formal political institutions are relatively recent imports from abroad, grafted onto traditional Chinese values of deference to age, cultivations of networks and preference for mediation over confrontation.[68]

The moral nature of Confucian government has another "sweet and sour" characteristic, though. On the one hand, leaders may feel greater responsibility for "national welfare," but they also see opponents as illegitimate. Ramon Myers states this problem for Taiwan quite insightfully:

The prospects for further expansion of political pluralism in the ROC, therefore, are considerable, but the impasse noted above [between contending parties] will hardly be resolved in the foreseeable future. On the contrary, political pluralism will probably remain within the context of the "inhibited center." Yet, every step taken by the center to promote real democracy creates new conditions which inhibit the center even more. Herein lie the seeds of uncertainty.[69]

To sum, complex interactions appear to have occurred between institutionalization and democratization and between economic and political development in the R.O.C. Initially, as in many developing countries, institutionalization was primarily provided by authoritarian rule. This institutionalization was not simply used to protect the power of a stagnant regime, however. Rather, it was used to provide a foundation for developing a highly successful economic strategy. Economic growth, in turn, proved instrumental in stimulating democratization and liberalization in three separate but interdependent areas: (1) integrating native Taiwanese into the economic and political elites, (2) increasing the scope of electoral competition and making the regime more directly responsible to the people, and (3) bringing new people with relevant skills into top policymaking positions. Now, the regime faces growing restiveness among the intelligentsia and the emerging middle class over authoritarian practices, international isolation, and the search for national identity and pride.[70] Thus, the movement toward democratization seems a central force in maintaining political stability and promoting more effective decision making (in other words, institutionalization), which are requisites for continued economic growth and transformation.

The R.O.C.'s economic success has been widely recognized. Political development in Taiwan has received much less attention, perhaps because it clearly lagged behind economic change during much of the postwar period. In fact, several analysts believe that the authoritarian state has been an important contributor to the R.O.C.'s enviable record in economic development.[71] This chapter, in contrast, argues that significant (albeit still somewhat limited) political development has occurred in terms of both institutionalization and democratization. Furthermore, the highly interdependent nature of these two developmental processes may be an important factor in the creation of long-term economic well-being.

Notes

1. Tuan-sheng Ch'ien, *The Government and Politics of China* (Cambridge, Mass.: Harvard University Press, 1950), chs. 10–19, describes the constitutional arrangements and political institutions of the interwar Republic in considerable detail. For a shorter summary discussion see Robert E. Bedeski, *State-Building in Modern China: The Kuomintang in the Prewar Period* (Berkeley: Institute of East Asian Studies, University of California, 1981), ch. 4.

2. The institutional description in this section is (unless otherwise cited) generally based on Ch'ien, *Government and Politics of China*, ch. 21; John Franklin Copper, "Political Development in Taiwan," in Hungdah Chiu, ed., *China and the Taiwan Issue* (New York: Praeger, 1979), pp. 40–49; John F. Copper with George P. Chen, *Taiwan's Elections: Political Development and Democratization in the Republic of China* (Baltimore: School of Law, University of Maryland, 1984), ch. 2; Thomas E. Greiff, "The Principle of Human Rights in Nationalist China: John C. H. Wu and the Ideological Origins of the 1946 Constitution," *China Quarterly* 103 (September 1985), pp. 441–461; and Edwin A. Winckler, "Institutionalization and Participation on Taiwan: From Hard to Soft Authoritarianism?" *China Quarterly* 99 (September 1984), pp. 481–499.

3. Suzanne Pepper, *Civil War in China: The Political Struggle, 1945–1949* (Berkeley: University of California Press, 1978), pp. 137–147, provides a good critique of the shortcomings of constitutionalism in the late 1940s.

4. A. Doak Barnett, *China on the Eve of Communist Takeover* (New York: Praeger, 1963), describes the lively opening session of the National Assembly in Nanking in 1948.

5. Melvin Gurtov, "Taiwan: Looking to the Mainland," *Asian Survey* 8:1 (January 1967), p. 16. "Besides enhancing the President's powers . . . , the National Security Council itself has been given broad functions embracing national reconstruction, planning, strategy and defense, post-recovery [of the mainland] political administration, and mobilization." *Republic of China 1988: A Reference Book* (Taipei: Hilit, 1988), p. 125, gives the membership of the National Security Council.

6. Bih-er Chou, Cal Clark, and Janet Clark, "Role Perceptions of Female Legislators in Taiwan." Paper presented at the Annual Meeting of the Midwest Political Science Association, Chicago, April 9–11, 1987.

7. Yangsun Chou and Andrew J. Nathan, "Democratizing Transition in Taiwan," *Asian Survey* 27:3 (March 1987), pp. 277–299; and Richard L. Engstrom and Chu Chi-hung, "The Impact of the 1980 Supplementary Election on Nationalist China's Legislative Yuan," *Asian Survey* 24:4 (April 1984), pp. 446–458.

8. Arthur J. Lerman, *Taiwan's Politics: The Provincial Assemblymen's World* (Washington, D.C.: University Press of America, 1977), provides a rich and detailed case study of politics in the Provincial Assembly.

9. Richard L. Walker, "Taiwan's Movement into Political Modernity, 1945–1972," in Paul K. T. Sih, ed., *Taiwan in Modern Times* (New York: St. John's University Press, 1973), pp. 373–378.

10. Bedeski, *State-Building in Modern China*, ch. 7; and Hung-chao Tai, "The Kuo-

mintang and Modernization in Taiwan," in Samuel P. Huntington and Clement H. Moore, eds., *Authorization Politics in Modern Society: The Dynamics of Established One-Party Systems* (New York: Basic Books, 1970), pp. 407–411, discuss the party's "tutelary" role.

11. John F. Copper, *A Quiet Revolution: Political Development in the Republic of China* (Washington, D.C.: Ethics and Public Policy Center, 1988), pp. 13–14. The 1963 estimate of KMT membership comes from Tai, "Kuomintang and Modernization in Taiwan," p. 367.

12. Parris H. Chang, "Evolution of Taiwan's Political Leadership After Chiang Ching-kuo," *AEI Foreign Policy and Defense Review* 6:3 (No. 3, 1986), pp. 11–12.

13. Tai, "Kuomintang and Modernization in Taiwan," pp. 426–428.

14. Ralph N. Clough, *Island China* (Cambridge, Mass.: Harvard University Press, 1978), pp. 49–54.

15. Copper, "Political Development in Taiwan," p. 42, describes a crackdown in the mid–1970s. Another one aimed primarily at organized crime occurred in 1984–1985.

16. Tillman Durdin, "Chiang Ching-kuo and Taiwan: A Profile," *Orbis* 18:4 (Winter 1975), p. 1031.

17. Clough, *Island China*, pp. 37–44, 58–60; and Hung-mao Tien, "Taiwan in Transition: Prospects for Socio-Political Change," *China Quarterly* 64 (December 1975), pp. 628–632. Mark Mancall, ed., *Formosa Today* (New York: Praeger, 1963), and Douglas Mendel, *The Politics of Formosan Nationalism* (Berkeley: University of California Press, 1970), discuss Taiwanese nationalism and KMT repression in detail.

18. For descriptions of factionalism within the KMT see Lloyd Eastman, *Seeds of Destruction: Nationalist China in War and Revolution, 1937–1949* (Cambridge, Mass.: Harvard University Press, 1984), ch. 5; Tang Tsou, *America's Failure in China, 1941–50* (Chicago: University of Chicago Press, 1963), pp. 376–384; Hung-mao Tien, "Factional Politics in Kuomintang China: An Interpretation," in F. Gilbert Chan, ed., *China at the Crossroads, 1927–1949* (Boulder, Colo.: Westview Press, 1980), pp. 19–35; and Hung-mao Tien, *Government and Politics in Kuomintang China, 1927–1937* (Stanford, Calif.: Stanford University Press, 1972), ch. 3.

19. Fred W. Riggs, *Formosa Under Chinese Nationalist Rule* (New York: Octagon Books, 1972), pp. 37–40; and Walker, "Taiwan's Movement into Political Modernity," pp. 366–367.

20. Wen Lang Li, "Structural Correlates of Emerging Political Pluralism in Taiwan," *Journal of Asian and African Studies* 23:3–4 (July-October, 1988), pp. 305–317; and Tai, "Kuomintang and the Modernization of Taiwan," pp. 419–423.

21. Bernard Gallin, *Hsin Hsing, Taiwan: A Chinese Village in Change* (Berkeley: University of California Press, 1966), especially chs. 3 and 6; Lerman, *Taiwan's Politics*, especially pt. II; and Martin M. C. Yang, *Socio-economic Results of Land Reform in Taiwan* (Honolulu: East-West Center Press, 1970), especially chs. 9–12.

22. Chung-min Chen, "Government Enterprise and Village Politics," in Emily Martin Ahern and Hill Gates, eds., *The Anthropology of Taiwanese Society* (Stanford, Calif.: Stanford University Press, 1981), pp. 38–49; Gallin, *Hsin Hsing*, especially ch. 9; Bernard Gallin and Rita S. Gallin, "Socioeconomic Life in Rural Taiwan: Twenty Years of Development and Change," *Modern China* 8:2 (April 1982), pp. 205–246; Stevan Harrell, *Ploughshare Village: Culture and Context in Taiwan* (Seattle: University of Washington Press, 1982); P. Steven Sangren, *History and Magical Power in a Chinese Community* (Stanford, Calif.: Stanford University Press, 1987); and Edwin A. Winckler, "Roles

Linking State and Society," in Emily Martin Ahern and Hill Gates, eds., *The Anthropology of Taiwanese Society* (Stanford, Calif.: Stanford University Press, 1981), pp. 50–86.

23. Riggs, *Formosa Under Chinese Nationalist Rule*, pp. 48–53; and Tai, "Kuomintang and the Modernization of Taiwan," pp. 419–430. Copper with Chen, *Taiwan's Elections*, ch. 4, emphasize the theoretical importance of democratization at the local level.

24. Clough, *Island China*, pp. 49–57.

25. Parks M. Coble, *The Shanghai Capitalists and the Nationalist Government, 1927–1937* (Cambridge, Mass.: Harvard University Press, 1980).

26. Alice H. Amsden, "The State and Taiwan's Economic Development," in Peter B. Evans, Dietrich Rueschemeyer, and Theda Skocpol, eds., *Bringing the State Back In* (Cambridge: Cambridge University Press, 1985), pp. 78–106; Clough, *Island China*, chs. 2 and 3; Thomas B. Gold, *State and Society in the Taiwan Miracle* (Armonk, N.Y.: M. E. Sharpe, 1986), ch. 5; A. James Gregor with Maria Hsia Chang and Andrew B. Zimmerman, *Ideology and Development: Sun Yat-sen and the Economic History of Taiwan* (Berkeley: Institute of East Asian Studies, University of California, 1981); and Denis Fred Simon, "External Incorporation and Internal Reform," in Edwin A. Winckler and Susan Greenhalgn, eds., *Contending Approaches to the Political Economy of Taiwan* (Armonk, N.Y.: M. E. Sharpe, 1988), pp. 138–150.

27. Gold, *State and Society*, pp. 68–72; Simon, "Internal Reform," pp. 138–150; and Edwin A. Winckler, "Elite Political Struggle, 1945–1985," in Edwin A. Winckler and Susan Greenhalgh, eds., *Contending Approaches to the Political Economy of Taiwan* (Armonk, N.Y.: M. E. Sharpe, 1988), pp. 161–168.

28. Samuel P. S. Ho, "Economics, Economic Bureaucracy, and Taiwan's Economic Development," *Pacific Affairs* 60:2 (Summer 1987), pp. 226–247.

29. Allan B. Cole, "Political Roles of Taiwanese Enterprisers," *Asian Survey* 7:9 (September 1967), pp. 645–654; and Ichiro Numazaki, "Networks of Taiwanese Big Business: A Preliminary Analysis," *Modern China* 12:4 (October 1986), pp. 487–534. Hill Gates, "Ethnicity and Social Class," in Emily Martin Ahern and Hill Gates, eds., *The Anthropology of Taiwanese Society* (Stanford, Calif.: Stanford University Press, 1981), pp. 241–281, presents an excellent and comprehensive analysis of the social, economic, and political statuses of mainlanders and islanders.

30. Theodore E. Chen, "The Educational System: A Commentary," in James C. Hsiung, ed., *Contemporary Republic of China: The Taiwan Experience, 1950–1980* (New York: Praeger, 1981), pp. 65–77; and Yung Wei, "Taiwan: A Modernizing Chinese Society," in Paul K. T. Sih, ed., *Taiwan in Modern Times* (New York: St. John's University Press, 1973), pp. 465–471. For a more critical perspective on the impact of educational policies see Sheldon Appleton, "The Social and Political Impact of Education on Taiwan," *Asian Survey* 16:8 (August 1976), pp. 703–720.

31. Copper, "Political Development in Taiwan," pp. 61–62; and Tien, "Taiwan in Transition," pp. 630–632.

32. Clough, *Island China*, pp. 37–42, and 60–66; Gerald McBeath, "Taiwan in 1976: Chiang in the Saddle," *Asian Survey* 17:1 (January 1977), pp. 18–20; and Lucian W. Pye, *Asian Power and Politics: The Cultural Dimensions of Authority* (Cambridge, Mass.: Harvard University Press, 1985), pp. 227–233.

33. Durdin, "Chiang Ching-kuo and Taiwan," pp. 1023–1042; Tillman Durdin,

"Chiang Ching-kuo's Taiwan," *Pacific Community* 7:1 (October 1975), pp. 92–117; and Winckler, "Political Struggle," pp. 152–161.

34. Copper, "Political Development in Taiwan," pp. 68–69; and Durdin, "Chiang Ching-kuo and Taiwan," pp. 1024–1025, 1033–1035.

35. Copper with Chen, *Taiwan's Elections*, pp. 26, 122; and Winckler, "Political Struggle," pp. 168–169. Winckler, "Roles," pp. 50–86, presents the most detailed analysis of political networks and coalitions during the 1970s.

36. Copper, "Political Development in Taiwan," pp. 67–69; J. Bruce Jacobs, "Recent Leadership and Political Trends in Taiwan," *China Quarterly* 45 (January/March 1971), pp. 129–159; J. Bruce Jacobs, "Taiwan 1972: Political Season," *Asian Survey* 13:1 (January 1973), pp. 102–112; and J. Bruce Jacobs, "Taiwan 1978: Economic Successes, International Uncertainties," *Asian Survey* 19:1 (January 1979), pp. 20–24.

37. Gold, *State and Society*, p. 89. Also see Frederick C. Deyo, "State and Labor: Modes of Political Exclusion in East Asian Development," in Frederic C. Deyo, ed., *The Political Economy of the New Asian Industrialism* (Ithaca, N.Y.: Cornell University Press, 1987), pp. 182–202; Walter Galenson, "The Labor Force, Wages, and Living Standards," in Walter Galenson, ed., *Economic Growth and Structural Change in Taiwan: The Postwar Experience of the Republic of China* (Ithaca, N.Y.: Cornell University Press, 1979), pp. 425–432; and Hill Gates, *Chinese Working-Class Lives: Getting By in Taiwan* (Ithaca, N.Y.: Cornell University Press, 1987), pp. 62–63.

38. John F. Copper, "Taiwan in 1980: Entering a New Decade," *Asian Survey* 21:1 (January 1981), pp. 52–55; Jurgen Domes, "Political Differentiation in Taiwan: Group Formation Within the Ruling Party and Opposition Circles, 1979–1980," *Asian Survey* 21:10 (October 1981), pp. 1017–1020; and Gold, *State and Society*, pp. 114–117.

39. Winckler, "Institutionalization and Participation on Taiwan," pp. 486–487.

40. Copper, "Political Development in Taiwan," p. 52.

41. Parris H. Chang, "Taiwan in 1983: Setting the Stage for Power Transition," *Asian Survey* 24:1 (January 1984), pp. 122–126; John F. Copper, "Taiwan's Recent Election: Progress Toward a Democratic System," *Asian Survey* 21:10 (October 1981), pp. 1029–1039; Copper with Chen, *Taiwan's Elections*, chs. 5–7; Engstrom and Chu, "Nationalist China's Legislative Yuan," pp. 447–458; and Edwin A. Winckler, "After the Chiangs: The Coming Political Succession on Taiwan," in Richard C. Bush, ed., *China Briefing, 1982* (Boulder, Colo.: Westview Press, 1983), pp. 103–121.

42. Yangsun Chou and Andrew J. Nathan, "Democratizing Transition in Taiwan," *Asian Survey* 27:3 (March 1987), pp. 280–282; Domes, "Political Differentiation in Taiwan," pp. 1017–1020; Alexander Ya-li Lu, "Future Democratic Developments in the Republic of China on Taiwan," *Asian Survey* 25:11 (November 1985), pp. 1085–1092; and Lucian W. Pye, "Taiwan's Development and Its Implications for Beijing and Washington," *Asian Survey* 26:6 (June 1986), pp. 611–626. Gates, *Chinese Working-Class Lives* ch. 4, discusses the political, ethnic, and class conflicts underlying the opposition movement.

43. Copper, *Quiet Revolution*, pp. 17–30; and James C. Hsiung, "Taiwan in 1985: Scandals and Setbacks," *Asian Survey* 26:1 (January 1986), pp. 93–101.

44. Copper, *Quiet Revolution*, pp. 30–33; John F. Copper, "Taiwan in 1986: Back on Top Again," *Asian Survey* 27:1 (January 1977), pp. 81–91; and Pye, "Taiwan's Development," pp. 611–626.

45. Copper, *Quiet Revolution*.

46. Chou and Nathan, "Democratizing Transition in Taiwan," p. 284.

47. Ibid., pp. 285–286.

48. Ramon H. Myers, "Political Theory and the Recent Political Developments in the Republic of China," *Asian Survey* 27:9 (September 1987), pp. 1016–1018.

49. Copper, *Quiet Revolution*, p. 40.

50. Chou and Nathan, "Democratizing Transition in Taiwan," pp. 287–293; Copper, *Quiet Revolution*, ch. 4; Copper, "Taiwan in 1986," pp. 81–84; Myers, "Recent Political Developments," pp. 1003–1022; and Robert G. Sutter, *Taiwan: Entering the 21st Century* (Lanham, Md.: University Press of America, 1988), pp. 46–51.

51. Myers, "Recent Political Developments," pp. 1007–1010.

52. Thomas A. Metzger, "Developmental Criteria and Indigenously Conceptualized Options: A Normative Approach to China's Modernization in Recent Times," *Issues and Studies* 23:2 (February 1987), pp. 19–81.

53. James D. Seymour, "Taiwan in 1987: A Year of Political Bombshells," *Asian Survey* 28:1 (January 1988) pp. 74–76; and James D. Seymour, "Taiwan in 1988: No More Bandits," *Asian Survey* 29:1 (January 1989), p. 59.

54. Susan Chira, "In Taiwan: Change Sweeps Out Taboos," *New York Times* 137:47,495 (May 4, 1988), p. 1. Also see Seymour, "Taiwan in 1988," p. 59; and Donald Southerland, "Taiwan's Ruling Party Eases Grip on Politics," *Washington Post* 111:21 (December 26, 1987), p. 23.

55. Julia Leung, "Taiwan's Brassy Opposition Poses Little Threat to Ruling Party," *Wall Street Journal* 210:7 (July 9, 1987) p. 24; and Seymour, "Taiwan in 1987," pp. 74–76.

56. Copper, *Quiet Revolution*, pp. 33–36; and Seymour, "Taiwan in 1987," pp. 74–76.

57. Selig S. Harrison, "Taiwan After Chiang Ching-kuo," *Foreign Affairs* 66:4 (Spring 1988), pp. 791–796; Seymour, "Taiwan in 1988," pp. 56–58; "Cabinet Revamp Approved," *China Post* 35:13,279 (July 21, 1988), p. 1; "KMT Congress Ends with Pledge of Reform," *China Post* 35:13,272 (July 14, 1988), p. 16; "In Wake of KMT Congress: Echoes of Change," *Free China Journal* 5:30 (July 18, 1988), p. 1; and "More Diverse Leadership Named to Standing C'tee," *China Post* 35:13,273 (July 15, 1988), p. 1.

58. Domes, "Political Differentiation in Taiwan," pp. 1021–1026; Winckler, "After the Chiangs," pp. 103–121; and Winckler, "Institutionalization and Participation," pp. 481–499.

59. Lucian Pye, *The Dynamics of Chinese Politics* (Cambridge: Oelgeschlager, Gunn & Hain, 1981). For applications to politics on Taiwan see, J. Bruce Jacobs, "A Preliminary Model of Particularistic Ties in Chinese Political Alliances: *Kan-ch'ing* and *Kuan-hsi* in a Rural Taiwanese Township," *China Quarterly* 78 (June 1979), pp. 237–273; Lerman, *Taiwan's Politics*, pt. II; Winckler, "Political Struggle," pp. 151–171; and Winckler, "Roles," pp. 50–86.

60. Parris H. Chang, "Evolution of Taiwan's Political Leadership After Chiang Ching-kuo," *AEI Foreign Policy and Defense Review* 6:3 (No. 3, 1986), pp. 12–18; and Harrison, "Taiwan After Chiang Ching-kuo," pp. 791–796 describe these contending leaders and factions.

61. Chira, "Changes Sweeps Out Taboos," pp. 1, 17; Angus Deming, "Taiwan's Age of Democracy," *Newsweek*, Asian Ed. (June 6, 1988), p. 24; James McGregor, "Taiwan Ruling Party's Many Businesses are Beginning to Be an Embarrassment," *Wall*

Street Journal 212:13 (July 20, 1988), p. 18; Seymour, "Taiwan in 1988," pp. 55 & 60; and "Workers Told to Cool It," *Free China Journal* 6:9 (February 6, 1989), p.1.

62. "KMT Scores Tactical Victory over DPP," *China Post* 40:155 (December 3, 1988), p. 12.

63. Wen-cheng Wu and I-hsin Chen, "Entering the Age of Party Politics, *Free China Review* 39:4 (April 1989), pp. 52–57; and "Primaries a Milestone," *Free China Journal* 6:24 (April 6, 1989), p. 1.

64. Arthur J. Lerman, "National Elites and Local Politicians in Taiwan," *American Political Science Review* 71:4 (December 1977), pp. 1406–1422; and Lerman, *Taiwan's Politics*, pt. IV.

65. Copper with Chen, *Taiwan's Elections*, especially chs. 1, 2, 8, and Myers, "Recent Political Developments," pp. 1003–1022, construct models of democratization in the R.O.C.

66. Gregor with Chang and Zimmerman, *Sun Yat-sen and the Economic History of Taiwan*; K. T. Li, *Economic Transformation of Taiwan, ROC* (London: Shepheard-Walwyn, 1988), Chp. 7; Metzger, "Developmental Criteria and Indigenously Conceptualized Options," pp. 19–81; and Myers, "Recent Political Developments," pp. 1003–1022.

67. Pye, *Asian Power and Politics*, chs. 2, 3, 11, 12. Gates, *Chinese Working-Class Lives*, presents a complex case study of the relationship between popular cultural values and regime stability, albeit one that is highly critical of the Nationalist government. Also see Gerald A. McBeath, "Roots of Regime Stability in the Taiwanese Family," *Journal of Chinese Studies* 4:1 (April 1987), pp. 1–18.

68. Winckler, "Institutionalization and Participation," p. 484.

69. Myers, "Recent Political Developments," pp. 1021–1022.

70. Sutter, *Taiwan*, pp. 30–31.

71. Amsden, "State and Taiwan's Economic Development," pp. 78–106; and George T. Crane, "The Taiwanese Ascent: System, State, and Movement in the World Economy," in Edward Friedman, ed., *Ascent and Decline in the World System* (Beverly Hills, Calif.: Sage, 1982), pp. 91–113.

CHAPTER 6

Rapid Economic Growth in the Republic of China

Cold economic statistics certainly imply that an "economic miracle" has occurred in the Republic of China (R.O.C.) on Taiwan since 1950. Real gross national product (GNP) has grown by almost 9 percent annually for three and a half decades; the economy has been transformed from an agricultural to an industrial one; once growth took off in the early 1960s the savings rate has been one of the highest in the world; Taiwan's industrial exports have become highly competitive on world markets; the standard of living of the general population has increased considerably; and income inequality on the island fell significantly during the early stages of development and is now similar to the levels found in advanced industrial states.

In comparative terms, Taiwan's growth trajectory has been much steeper and faster than those exhibited by many of the earlier developing nations, as shown by Figure 6.1. This chart compares the growth rate of Taiwan's real (i.e., inflation-adjusted) industrial production between 1952 and 1969 (this growth index is plotted on a semilogarithmic scale) with industrial growth in nine advanced industrial states during the 1860–1913 period. The much steeper slope for Taiwan's growth shows that similar industrial growth occurred much more rapidly than for the European and North American countries and even somewhat more quickly than for Japan.

The R.O.C.'s economic strategy has certainly been a "capitalist" one, in the sense that the private-business sector has predominated and that the economy has been primarily based on responding to market forces, both internal and international. Yet the state has played a significant role in formulating development strategy and in guiding the economy through a series of policy changes and structural transformations that have proved vital to its economic dynamism.

Figure 6.1
Comparison of Speed of Industrialization of R.O.C. (1952–1969) with Other Countries (1860–1913)

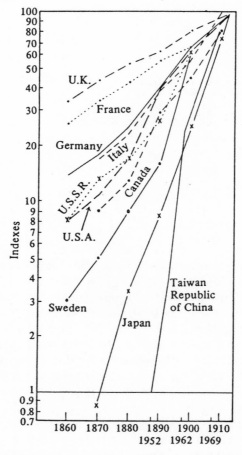

Source: Shirley W. Y. Kuo, Gustav Ranis, and John C. H. Fei, *The Taiwan Success Story: Rapid Growth with Improved Distribution in the Republic of China, 1952–1979* (Boulder, Colo.: Westview Press, 1981), p. 9.

In particular, five key strategic decisions may be discerned that created different policies and periods in Taiwan's developmental history: (1) the radical agricultural reform policies that were adopted when the Nationalists evacuated to the island; (2) the import substitution era of the 1950s; (3) the domestic and international liberalization policies that created an export surge and rapid overall growth in the 1963–1973 period; (4) the adjustment to international shocks associated with skyrocketing oil prices during the 1970s; and (5) the transformation of the economy to more capital-intensive and high-technology production that began in the 1970s and has been increasingly stressed in the 1980s. The next five sections, hence, describe Taiwan's rapid growth in terms of these five strategic decisions and the economic periods that they created.

The many details of economic growth described in this chapter may well seem overwhelming and could obscure the general dynamics of Taiwan's rapid economic growth and structural transformation. Thus a brief listing of the central features of the R.O.C.'s development pattern appears appropriate as an introduction to the specific sections. First, Taiwan's economy has been marked by extreme flexibility and by a continuous restructuring. Second, the country has consistently moved from lower to higher "value-added" production activities, thereby capturing greater profits for the domestic economy. Finally, the strong state role in the economy has generally been directed toward providing incentives for the private sector to engage in activities reflecting the island's "comparative advantage" as defined by international markets.

Agricultural Reform and Growth

Perhaps the most commonly cited reason for the Kuomintang's (KMT's) defeat on the mainland was its alienation of the peasantry, who composed over 80 percent of China's population, although the reasons adduced for this failure by different scholars vary significantly: lack of control over much of China, especially the countryside; reliance on landlords for support and revenues, especially after the retreat to Chungking; bureaucratic arrogance and independence; and/or the need to raise monies to support an endless series of military campaigns. Whatever the reasons, the Communists won over the peasantry, "encircled the cities," and ultimately sent the Nationalists packing across the Taiwan Strait. Once they arrived in Taiwan, however, the KMT took a much different tack. The regime controlled all the territory on a relatively small island and had few ties with either the local population or gentry. Thus, unlike the situation on the mainland, it certainly had the power and autonomy to implement whatever agricultural policies it desired. General Ch'en Ch'eng, who had had some experience with land reform on the mainland, was appointed governor of Taiwan at the beginning of 1949. Almost immediately he initiated a series of reform policies that provided the first step in the economic transformation of the island. The agricultural reform proceeded through three major stages. First, within three months of taking office Ch'en Ch'eng decreed a major rent reduction for tenant farmers on Taiwan. Rent was set at 37.5 percent of the production of main crops grown calculated according to a standard yield based on the quality of land. Because rents had previously averaged about 50 percent of production, this constituted a rent reduction of 25 percent. Second, the government conducted a series of sales of public farmland between 1948 and 1958 (the government had acquired about a fifth of the island's cultivated area in confiscations from the Japanese at the end of World War II). Current cultivators of these public

lands were given the first priority to buy them; other tenant farmers had the
second. The price was set at 2.5 times the annual yield of principal crops, which
made it affordable; limits were set on the amount that could be purchased to
prevent new concentrations of landholding. The third and capstone phase of the
agricultural reform was the land redistribution program that was implemented
in 1953. Under the Land-to-the-Tiller Act landlords were forced to sell agricultural holdings over about three hectares (depending on the quality of land) to
the government for 2.5 times the annual yield—which was significantly under-
priced (in 1937, for example, farmland was priced at between 4.5 and 8 times
the annual yield). Payment was made 70 percent in commodity bonds and 30
percent in stocks in four government corporations. The land was then sold for
the same price to tenant farmers, who had to make repayments over a ten-year
period.

The agricultural reform had considerable impact on rural life. Both the rent
reduction and the land redistribution affected about a quarter of the farmland
and almost half of the agricultural households on the island. One major effect
was on land ownership. As a result of the Land-to-the-Tiller Act the proportion
of full owners jumped from 38 percent to 55 percent between 1952 and 1953,
while the proportion of tenants fell from 36 percent to 21 percent. Over the
subsequent thirty years the proportion of owners gradually rose to 83 percent
full owners and 12 part owners in 1986.[2] Thus the land reform clearly had the
intended effect of turning Taiwan's agriculture into a smallholder economy.

The reform also had a significant impact on the incomes of the peasants
receiving land, as illustrated by Samuel Ho's reconstruction of tenant income
measured in terms of rice produced. The first row in Table 6.1 reports the actual
rice yield in kilograms per chia (1 chia = 0.97 hectares), and the second lists
the cost of seed and fertilizer used in production. The next three rows measure
the effect of rent reduction and land redistribution. The first is the rent that would
have been paid if the 50 percent level had continued; the second is the actual
rents (assuming redistribution in 1953 by the Land-to-the-Tiller Act); and the
third is the difference between them, or the rent reduction for the tenant. After
redistribution the new owners were responsible for land repayments and taxes,
so that these payments must be subtracted from the reduced rents to give the
"net income gain." The net income gain is also subdivided into the components
attributable to the rent reduction and to the land redistribution. Total income
from the rice crop, therefore, is actual production minus seed and fertilizer
expenses, rent, and land repayment and taxes, and is calculated in terms of both
actual values and levels that would have occurred without the reform. Finally,
the table includes the percentage of actual income that the net gain contributed
and growth indices for total production, actual income, and income without
reform (based on their 1948 value as 100).

Ho's detailed and complex calculations lead to several interesting conclusions.
Land reform certainly produced a major increment in peasant incomes. The net
income gain was 18 percent of total income in 1949 and jumped to 38 percent

Table 6.1

Impact of Land Reform on Tenant Income in Terms of Distribution of Rice Produced (in kg/chia)

	1948	1949	1952	1953	1955	1959
Actual Yield	4,649	4,860	5,530	5,717	6,283	7,258
Spending for Fert & Seed	164	426	827	831	1,030	1,127
Rent with no Reform	2,324	2,430	2,765	2,859	3,142	3,629
Actual Rent	2,324	1,995	1,995	0	0	0
Rent Reduction	0	435	770	2,859	3,142	3,629
Land Repaymt & Tax	0	0	0	1,639	1,639	1,639
Net Income Gain	0	435	770	1,220	1,503	1,990
From Rent Reduc	0	435	770	864	1,147	1,634
From Land Redist	0	0	0	356	356	356
Total Income	2,161	2,439	2,708	3,247	3,614	4,492
Income without Gain	2,161	2,004	1,938	2,027	2,111	2,502
Net Gain % Total Inc	0%	18%	28%	38%	42%	44%
Production Index	100	105	119	123	135	156
Actual Income Index	100	113	125	150	167	208
Inc without Gain Index	100	93	90	94	98	116

Source: Samuel P. S. Ho, *Economic Development of Taiwan, 1860–1970* (New Haven, Conn.: Yale University Press, 1978), p. 169.

in 1953 and 44 percent in 1959. Most of this gain (over 70 percent) resulted from the rent reductions rather than the land redistribution, but this balance changed greatly when land repayments were completed in the mid–1960s (repayments constituted 84 percent of repayments and taxes). The termination of the land repayments also produced a major increase in the income gains accruing to the former tenants. Without these income gains, total income per chia (or hectare) would have in fact been slightly lower in 1955 than in 1948, despite the fact that the yield was 35 percent higher. With the reforms, however, income actually increased 67 percent, almost double the increase in production. Finally, both production and income spurted in the late 1950s, with income again growing significantly faster.[3]

Land reform per se was not the only important facet of the R.O.C.'s policy of upgrading agriculture during the 1950s. The radical change in land tenure was complemented and supported by a program of increased investment and a widespread and aggressive program of agricultural extension work to stimulate

Table 6.2
Annual Growth Rates of Agricultural Inputs

	1947-53	1954-67	1968-74
Labor: Total Man-Days	6.4%	1.7%	-0.9%
Land: Crop Area	3.8%	0.9%	-0.7%
Working Capital: Chem Fert	--	5.7%	3.7%
Fixed Capital: Total Value	4.7%	3.5%	5.9%*

*1968–72 average.

Source: Erik Thorbecke, "Agricultural Development," in Walter Galenson, ed., *Economic Growth and Structural Change in Taiwan: The Postwar Experience of the Republic of China* (Ithaca, N.Y.: Cornell University Press, 1978), p. 151.

the introduction of new techniques. This program was directed by the Sino-American Joint Commission on Rural Reconstruction (JCRR), which assumed the primary responsibility for developmental projects itself and stimulated the formation of a comprehensive and extensive set of Farmers' Associations (over 300 at the local level) that promoted technology application, participated in agricultural planning, created marketing and credit cooperatives that were vital for agricultural activities and seemingly constituted a successful grass-roots approach to stimulating agricultural growth.[4] Because of this extensive organization, new technology could be introduced rapidly, which greatly helped production. For example, the utilization of a new type of sugar cane skyrocketed from 1 percent of all planting in 1952–1953 to 43 percent in 1953–1954 to 82 percent in 1955–1956.[5]

The JCRR programs were particularly important because of a basic change that occurred in the forces behind agricultural growth in the 1950s, as indicated by Erik Thorbecke's data on the growth of agricultural inputs in Table 6.2. During the "recovery period" before 1953 agricultural growth primarily resulted from increased labor and land (i.e., through multicropping) inputs. These resources reached their limits by the early 1950s, so that production increases depended on greater inputs of working and fixed capital, particularly fertilizers and better seeds and the expansion of irrigation projects. Finally, after the late 1960s, increased mechanization became the principal source of agricultural inputs as land and labor actually decreased slightly. For example, mechanical labor rose rapidly as a percentage of total energy inputs in agriculture from 2 percent in 1961 to 21 percent in 1970 to 41 percent in 1974.[6]

The R.O.C. clearly made a substantial financial commitment to agricultural modernization. During the 1950s agriculture accounted for about a fifth of Taiwan's total investment and averaged a 14 percent growth rate in ''real'' (i.e., inflation-adjusted) terms, although agricultural investment began to tail off in the early 1960s (averaging 18 percent of total investment and a real 6.5 percent growth rate for 1960–1965). The application of fertilizer, one of the principal working capital inputs, grew rapidly during the 1950s, increasing by almost 50 percent between 1952 and 1958 before leveling out in the late 1950s and early 1960s before another growth spurt in the mid–1960s.[7] As a result, fertilizer application per hectare in 1955–1959 was much higher than during the last normal half decade of the colonial period, in 1935–1939 (e.g., 38 percent for chemical fertilizers and 64 percent for farm-producted fertilizers).[8]

Land reform created a nation of smallholders with greater individual incentive to innovate and produce (note in Table 6.1 that tenants would not have received any benefits from the 35 percent increase in productivity between 1948 and 1955 if the land reform measures had not been implemented), and government programs, building on the model of the colonial period, generated more investment, local involvement, and technological innovation. It is impossible to separate the effects of these two factors on agriculture, since they were interrelated and complementary to a goodly extent. In combination, though, they produced steady, if not almost spectacular, agricultural growth for two decades. Total agricultural production grew by 4.6 percent a year during the 1950s and 4.1 percent during the 1960s, as compared with 4.0 percent annual growth during the peak 1923–1937 period under the Japanese.[9]

Another important facet of Taiwan's agricultural development was an increasing diversification of production away from the traditional main crops, such as rice, sugar, and sweet potatoes, to new crops, such as soybeans and citrus fruits, and livestock production. This diversification is indicated by the comparative growth percentages and traditional and nontraditional crops presented in Table 6.3. The ''nontraditional'' products, such as fruits, vegetables, livestock, and fish, generally grew much faster than the island's traditional crops, indicating a significant diversification of agricultural production. The output of rice, the traditional staple, displayed particularly modest growth, and a boom in sugar production in the late 1950s was clearly on the wane by the mid–1960s.

Increased agricultural production and productivity and diversification into fruits, vegetables, livestock, and dairy products produced a corresponding growth in the general population's food consumption. Both the quantity, as indicated by caloric intake, and quality, as indicated by protein consumption, rose steadily and somewhat in tandem. Daily consumption of calories increased from 2,078 to 2,662, or 28 percent, and daily protein intake from 49.0 to 72.2, or 47 percent, between 1952 and 1970. The greater increase in protein consumption occurred mostly in the latter part of the 1960s and reflected a changing emphasis from improving quantity to quality of diets as the developmental processes proceeded.[10] In comparative terms, food consumption in Taiwan was generally superior to that of other developing societies and only slightly lower than in Japan during the 1960s.[11] It was also significantly above normally recognized

Table 6.3
Growth Indices for Volumes of Agricultural Production

	1952	1955	1960	1965	1968
Traditional					
Rice	100	103	122	150	160
Sugar	100	141	149	193	163
Brown Sugar	100	185	222	420	243
Sweet Potatoes	100	117	142	150	153
Wheat	100	116	274	141	103
Tea	100	127	150	179	211
Nontraditional					
Soybeans	100	165	360	449	499
Citrus Fruits	100	109	190	412	632
Pineapples	100	112	266	368	496
Hogs Slaughtered	100	141	170	214	280
Chickens Slgtd	100	109	124	160	224
Chicken Eggs	100	103	154	215	418
Fish	100	148	213	314	436

Source: Council for Economic Planning and Development, *Taiwan Statistical Data Book, 1987* (Taipei: Council for Economic Planning and Development, 1987), pp. 69–72, 79–81.

standards of dietary adequacy by the World Health Organization of about 2,200 calories of energy and thirty-three grams of protein per day.

Agriculture also supplied the bulk of Taiwan's exports during the 1950s, which was especially valuable, given the country's chronic negative trade balance during that period (see next section). Raw and processed agricultural products constituted 90 percent of the R.O.C.'s exports through 1955 and were still at the 85 percent level in 1958 before falling swiftly to about 50 percent in the early 1960s. Overall, total agriculturally related exports averaged over 10 percent annual increases between 1953 and 1964, thereby making a major contribution to Taiwan's economic stability until the country's industrialization drive was well under way.[12] For a decade, however, Taiwan's trade clearly depended on its ability to produce enough agricultural products to create a surplus for exporting. Although exports as a proportion of total food supplies averaged only 6 percent during the 1950s, as opposed to 20 percent to 40 percent during the colonial era (see Table 6.4), this was enough to support export growth well in excess of increases in agricultural production.

Agriculture, furthermore, generated a considerable surplus that was used to finance industrialization. Table 6.4 presents Teng-hui Lee's estimates of the net capital outflows taken from the agricultural sector during the 1950s (unfortunately his study ends at 1960), with the 1931–1935 data being presented for comparative purposes. This table corresponds to Table 3.2 in the discussion of agriculture's

Table 6.4

Indicators of Agriculture's Contribution to Taiwan's Development

	1950-55	1956-60	1931-35
Product (Mil T$ in 1935-37 prices)			
Net Domest Product	$795	$1,119	$706
Total Ag Product	$327	$468	$334
Real Capital Outflow from Ag	$113	$96	$89
Ag Terms of Trade* (1935-37=100)	126	120	107
Ag Role (%)			
Ag Prod/NDP	41%	42%	47%
Outflow/Ag Prod	35%	21%	27%
Outflow/NDP	14%	9%	13%
Rice Sold/Total Output	50%	46%	74%
Food Exports/Total Food Supply	6%	5%	38%
Govt % Farm Income	13%	12%	8%

*The lower this index, the more favorable the terms of trade are for agriculture.

Source: Teng-hui Lee, *Intersectoral Capital Flows in the Economic Development of Taiwan* (Ithaca, N.Y.: Cornell University Press, 1971), pp. 19–20, 29, 72, 75, 174.

role during the colonial period. There were some significant differences from the colonial period. Farmers retained much more of their crops (a half as opposed to a quarter), and the proportion of food that was exported fell drastically, as noted above. Still, the proportionate rate of resource flows out of the agricultural sector rivaled that of the Japanese era—about 25 percent of total agricultural production and 12 percent of net domestic product. Moreover, the share of farm income that was taken by the government rose by approximately a half, from 8 percent in the 1930s to 12 percent in the 1950s, indicating a significantly increased role for the state in transferring resources from agriculture to other areas of development. Because much of the outflow of capital from agriculture during the colonial period was siphoned off to Japan, these figures imply that agriculture's contribution to the expansion of other domestic sectors was much greater than during the Japanese era.

The government played a central and direct role in this extraction of resources from the agricultural sector. To some extent this was based on tax collections, land repayments, and other direct collections from the rural sector (e.g., the government directly received 12 percent of farm income in the 1950s as opposed to 8 percent in the 1930s). The principal outflow was caused by the "hidden

Table 6.5
Indicators of Importance of Agriculture

	1965	1970	1975	1980	1985
Ag Pop % Total Pop	45%	41%	35%	30%	22%
Ag Prod % NDP	27%	18%	15%	9%	7%
Ag Invst % Tot Invst	17%	8%	5%	4%	4%
Farm income p.c./Nonfarm income p.c.*	70%	60%	67%	64%	69%

*This data series is for 1966, 1970, 1978, and 1985.

Source: Council for Economic Planning and Development, *Taiwan Statistical Data Book, 1987* (Taipei: Council for Economic Planning and Development, 1987), pp. 41, 50, 65; and Eldon L. Johnson, Frederick C. Fliegel, John L. Woods, and Mel C. Chu, *The Agricultural Technology System of Taiwan* (Urbana: Office of International Agriculture, University of Illinois, 1987), p. A4.

rice tax'' that resulted from the government's acquiring a large share of the rice crop (slightly over 60 percent in the 1950s and 50 percent in the 1960s[13]) at artificially depressed prices, while selling fertilizer to the farmers at inflated ones. This resulted in the terms of trade for agriculture worsening by about 20 percent in comparison with the 1930s; these decreased terms of trade or ''invisible net outflow'' accounted for about half of the funds leaving agriculture in the 1950s, according to Lee's calculations.[14]

An evaluation of Taiwan's agricultural policies in the late 1960s, therefore, would have rated them as highly successful. Land reform, investment, and intensive extension work brought increased productivity and production. These, in turn produced rising incomes and decreasing inequality in the agricultural sector, a more than adequate supply of cheap food, exports to help mitigate balance-of-payments problems, and a significant surplus that was transferred to support industrialization. Everybody seemed to be benefiting!

The past two decades, however, have not been kind to agriculture and the rural population in the R.O.C. Total overall agricultural production has stagnated, growing by less than 3 percent a year between 1969 and 1976 and by only 1.6 percent annually since then, despite the strong performance in the livestock, which grew at over 7 percent annually.[15] Consequently, as shown in Table 6.5, agriculture's share in population and production dropped sharply in the two decades after the mid–1960s, from 45 percent to 22 percent and from 27 percent to 7 percent, respectively. Perhaps more ominously, agriculture's share in total investment fell from 17 percent to 5 percent in the decade between 1965 and 1975 and has shown no signs of recovery. In addition, the farmers' disadvantage in income remained fairly constant, as farm income per capita has averaged only 60 percent to 70 percent of nonfarm income over the past twenty years. Thus agriculture is clearly a declining sector.[16]

I. S and I
price substitution
successful

The R.O.C. government responded to the growing stagnation of agriculture by reversing the invidious terms of trade in favor of the sector and by trying to promote increased productivity through mechanization. The mechanisms supporting the hidden rice tax were ended in the early 1970s, and by the 1980s the government was actually indirectly subsidizing agriculture through supporting prices for many major crops that are significantly above world market prices. For example, in 1987 the farm prices for rice and sugar were NT$14 and $21 per kilogram, respectively, compared with their prices on the international market of $6.5 and $15.[17] As discussed earlier, mechanization has proceeded apace in Taiwan's agriculture, and the government has tried to overcome the problems for mechanized agriculture of the smallholdings created by the land reform by promoting joint and cooperative farming. Still, as the data on yield per hectare increases since 1970 show, mechanization has produced only modest gains in most crop yields, especially when compared with the rapidly rising productivity of the 1950s and 1960s.[18]

Agricultural policy and land reform were quite successful in stimulating agricultural growth and creating resources for Taiwan's industrialization during the 1950s and 1960s. Since then, however, agriculture has clearly been in a decline and has seemingly become increasingly marginalized in the R.O.C.'s economy. The recent demonstrations of farmers against concessions opening the domestic market to American agricultural imports, which were briefly noted in chapter 5, therefore, are quite understandable both in terms of farmers' rising frustration in general and as a threat to the price support system in particular. Agriculture, then, may become more of a political than an economic problem for the regime.

Import-Substitution Industrialization

The R.O.C.'s economic strategy in the 1950s was not limited to just reviving and stimulating the agricultural sector. In addition, the regime hoped to spark industrialization by promoting the production of light industrial goods that were being imported (hence the term "import substitution"). Because Taiwan had developed a significant amount of small-scale and geographically dispersed light industry (see chapter 3) before the devastation of World War II, the initial industrialization policy was much more a case of utilizing a "backlog of unexploited production opportunities," as occurred in the postwar reconstruction of Europe, than of starting from scratch.[19] However, given the primarily agricultural nature of the economy and the political and economic chaos of the late 1940s, promoting industrial development must have appeared a rather daunting task.

Raging inflation in the late 1940s (about 500 percent annually during 1946–1948 and a stupendous thirtyfold in the first half of 1949) presented the regime with an extreme challenge that had to be overcome before any growth policies could be implemented, especially in view of the widespread perception that uncontrolled inflation on the mainland had played a major role in the KMT's defeat there. The regime, hence, implemented a stringent stabilization program in the late 1940s and early 1950s. This package included currency reform and a policy of high "preferential" interest rates, as well as the imposition of tight governmental controls over the financial system (the state dominated the banking sector), aimed at controlling money supply and credit availability. Additionally, the government began to follow a conservative fiscal policy of maintaining balanced budgets. The R.O.C. also benefited from massive infusions of American aid.[20]

These stabilization policies proved to be highly successful. The inflation rate "fell" to 300 percent in 1950 and about 30 percent in 1951–1952 and then averaged under 10 percent for the rest of the 1950s. The attempt to control money supply and credit worked as the "velocity of money" (i.e., the ratio of national income to money supply) dropped sharply in the early 1950s. Tibor Scitovsky, furthermore, has argued that the anti-inflation policy produced several important spin-offs that promoted industrialization. High interest rates spurred savings and created incentives for labor-intensive production, which, in turn, created competitive small-scale industries that could adjust more easily to market conditions.[21]

The government was also able to maintain a balanced budget during the 1950s, as public spending remained stable at slightly over 20 percent of gross domestic product (GDP) and budget priorities centered on defense and administration. Controls over labor kept real wage increases low; rising agricultural productivity stimulated by the land reform also helped to repress demand inflation (see Table 6.8 for data on most of these socioeconomic indicators after 1952). Compared with most other less developed countries at that time, this was an enviable record.[22]

The R.O.C. also moved aggressively to promote "import substitution" in a variety of light consumer industries by sealing off the domestic market. The end of the colonial relationship with Japan followed by the loss of mainland markets reinforced this decision because of lost special treatment for Taiwan's agricultural exports and the opportunity to replace previously imported Japanese manufactures. Tariffs were substantially raised, with the average minimal rate doubling from about 20 percent in 1948 to over 40 percent in 1955; "effective" tariff rates were estimated to be significantly higher than nominal ones. Import quotas for specific goods, especially luxury items, were also implemented and expanded over the 1950s. Foreign exchange rates were also manipulated to discourage imports and dampen inflation (e.g., multiple exchange rates were introduced in April 1951 and the New Taiwan dollar, or NT$, was overvalued). As would be expected, nondurable consumer goods received the greatest protection under these various devices, while imports of plant equipment received the most favored treatment.[23]

This import substitution was quite successful, at least in the short run. As shown by Table 6.6, which presents the ratio of Taiwan's domestic wholesale to world prices as a measure of the cumulative protectionism afforded by the R.O.C.'s import substitution package, most basic industrial goods were priced 50 percent or more above nominal import costs. This certainly provided a strong financial incentive to develop "infant industries." The result was that rapid

Table 6.6
Ratio of Domestic Wholesale to World Prices, 1953

Wheat flour	168	Leather	147
Soybeans	255	Sheet glass	215
Dried cuttlefish	271	Sulfur black	222
Powdered Milk	174	Soda ash	408
		Ammonium sulphate	210
Cotton yarn	141		
Cotton piece goods, gray	178	Gasoline	205
Cotton piece goods, poplin	289	Ink	206
Woolen yarn	480	Diazine	163
Gunny bags	244	Toothpaste	268
		Galvanized iron wire	151
		Steel plate	155
		Primemovers	184

Source: Ching-yuan Lin, *Industrialization in Taiwan, 1946–72: Trade and Import-Substitution Policies for Developing Countries* (New York: Praeger, 1973), p. 51.

Table 6.7
Imports as a Percentage of Domestic Supply

	1948	1950	1952	1954	1958
Flour	46%	83%	73%	5%	0%
Cotton yarn	79%	22%	4%	1%	0%
Cotton fabric	71%	59%	9%	3%	0%
Synthetic yarn	--	100%	100%	100%	1%
Iron & steel sht, bar, plate	**	59%	37%	31%	25%
Bicycles	100%	100%	55%	1%	0%
Electric bulbs	59%	72%	59%	48%	31%
Ammonium sulfate	100%	100%	97%	98%	95%

**Probable error in source.

Source: Samuel P. S. Ho, *Economic Development of Taiwan, 1860–1970* (New Haven, Conn.: Yale University Press, 1978), p. 188.

import substitution occurred in many light industries, as demonstrated by the data in Table 6.7 on the share of imports in total domestic supply. For example, imports dropped precipitously from 83 percent to 5 percent of consumption for flour between 1950 and 1954, from 79 percent to 4 percent for cotton yarn between 1948 and 1952, from 100 percent to 1 percent for synthetic yarn between 1954 and 1958, and from 100 percent to 1 percent for bicycles between 1950 and 1954. For all manufacturing except for food processing (where imports only constituted 9 percent before the war), imports had fallen to 23 percent of total supply in 1954, in marked contrast to their dominant share of 60 percent in 1937.[24]

The R.O.C.'s import substitution program, therefore, had a major impact on Taiwan's economic and, especially, industrial structure. First, it provided a primary stimulus for industrial expansion. For example, Ching-yuan Lin calculated with sophisticated econometric techniques that import substitution produced 91 percent of the increase in non–food manufacturing production between 1937 and 1954.[25] Second, Tawian was able to expand its industrial base from primarily food processing to other light industries (e.g., textiles, bicycles, rubber and leather goods, chemicals, and wood products) and to the beginnings of machinery and metals production. Thus these industries grew much faster than food processing during the 1950s.[26] Third, most of the island's industry remained concentrated in labor-intensive production, which was seemingly in line with Taiwan's comparative advantage.[27] Finally, the state maintained a strong hand over economic activity through state corporations (many of which were based on expropriated Japanese assets), which accounted for about half of industrial production during the 1950s, and through strong influence over the allocation of credit and foreign exchange.

The effects of these import substitution policies can readily be discerned in the aggregate data on Taiwan's economy and society during the 1952–1961 period, presented in Table 6.8. Between 1952 (after import substitution had been well under way) and 1955, for example, the ratio of imports to GDP fell from 14 percent to 12.6 percent and the share of consumer goods in total imports was more than halved, falling from 20 percent to 9 percent. This was associated with an economic dynamism that must have been quite surprising given the chaotic conditions of the late 1940s, as real GNP growth averaged 10 percent annually during the first half of the 1950s. Total energy consumption, a leading indicator of economic development, more than tripled between 1952 and 1961. The industrial sector began to take off, as this strategy intended. Although growth rates fluctuated wildly, industrial production averaged a strong expansion of 11.5 percent annually between 1952 and 1959; over this period manufacturing's share of net domestic product rose by a half, from 11 percent to 18 percent. The savings rate averaged about 9 percent of GNP during the 1950s, just below the 10 percent level usually seen as necessary for economic takeoff, but because of foreign aid the investment rate averaged almost 15 percent. Unemployment was significant but averaged only 4 percent (or 6 percent, using a "broader" definition of unemployment) during the 1950s, which was quite good by the standards of most developing countries. However, the popular standard of living as depicted by the last set of indicators in Table 6.8 was much slower to show marked improvements with the exception of the significant gains in diet quality.

Another central aspect of the R.O.C.'s development during the 1950s was its extreme dependence on foreign aid received from the United States. America extended approximately $1.5 billion in economic aid, slightly over 80 percent of which was in the form of direct grants, and $2 billion in all-grant military aid before the aid program was terminated in 1965 owing to mutual agreement between the United States and R.O.C. that Taiwan's development had become self-sustaining. American aid, for example, financed Taiwan's balanced budgets, which would have had deficits of 25 percent of expenditures in the absence of American support (especially for the huge defense budget). Just as important, if not more so, aid flows during the 1950s averaged over 40 percent of the R.O.C.'s gross domestic capital formation and accounted for 74 percent of the net investment in infrastructure projects and 59 percent of agricultural investment, allowing a substantial increment in Taiwan's investment rate. As a result, it has been estimated that Taiwan's growth rate would have been cut in half during the 1950s and early 1960s in the absence of American aid.[28]

Such a policy of import substitution is usually associated with a series of long-term difficulties, however, and Taiwan proved to be no exception. The very success of import substituting indicated by the precipitous fall of imports' share in the supply of many light industrial goods (see Table 6.6) meant that the domestic market was becoming saturated with Taiwan-produced goods and that there was little opportunity to expand production at the expense of imports. For example, domestic demand accounted for 90 percent of increased non-food production during 1954–1961, in stark contrast to a similar domination of import substitution for the 1937–1954 period.[29] The lagging standard of living indicators in Table 6.8 imply that domestic demand was somewhat constrained at best. The strong protectionist walls indicated by Table 6.7 encouraged inefficiency and created monopoly profits. Consequently the economy began to slow down appreciably in the latter part of the 1950s. Real GNP growth fell to 6 percent to 7 percent a year during the late 1950s and early 1960s; manufacturing's contribution to national product stagnated at 15 percent to 17 percent; there was little increase in the savings rate; inflation began to rise again, averaging 15 percent in 1959 and 1960; and unemployment increased slightly but significantly.

A second major problem for import substitution is that light industry generally requires the importation of both capital goods and industrial raw materials, so that successful import substitution in the light and consumer industries requires increasing imports of other items that create balance-of-trade and balance-of-payments difficulties. The aggregate date in Table 6.8 show that this was certainly the case for Taiwan. The R.O.C. had a consistent trade deficit of $75 million each year throughout the 1950s, which amounted to over 50 percent of exports and a significant 4 percent to 8 percent of GDP and which could only be sustained

Table 6.8
Socioeconomic Indicators during Import Substitution[1]

	1952	1953	1954	1955	1956	1957	1958	1959	1960	1961
Population										
Total Pop (mil)	8.1	8.4	8.7	9.1	9.4	9.7	10.0	10.4	10.8	11.1
Pop Growth (%)	4.1	3.8	3.7	3.8	3.4	3.2	3.6	3.9	3.5	3.3
Economic Growth										
Real GNP Grth (%)	12.1	9.3	9.6	8.1	5.5	7.3	6.6	7.7	6.5	6.8
GNP p c. (NT$)[2]	2009	2591	2764	3147	3483	3936	4254	4754	5571	6046
GNP p.c. (US$)[2]	195	167	177	203	139	157	170	131	153	151
Real Ind Grth (%)	--	25.1	5.8	13.1	3.5	12.8	8.6	11.7	14.1	15.7
Real Ag Grth (%)	--	9.5	2.1	0.5	7.7	7.1	6.7	1.7	1.4	8.9
Energy (mil KWH)	1076	1225	1402	1497	1770	2084	2416	2770	3136	3528
Econ Structure										
Ind % NDP	18.0	17.7	22.2	21.1	22.4	23.9	23.9	25.7	24.9	25.0
Manf % NDP	10.9	11.3	14.5	13.8	14.5	15.7	15.5	17.7	16.8	17.0
Serv % NDP	46.1	44.0	46.1	46.0	46.0	44.6	45.1	43.9	42.3	43.6
Ag % NDP	35.9	38.3	31.7	32.9	31.6	31.7	31.0	30.4	32.8	31.4
Ag % Emplymt	56.1	55.6	54.8	53.6	53.2	52.3	51.1	50.3	50.2	49.8
State % Ind Prod	56.6	55.9	52.7	51.1	51.0	51.3	50.0	48.7	47.9	48.2
Savings & Invstmt										
Savings % GNP	9.2	8.9	7.7	9.0	9.2	10.6	9.9	10.3	12.7	12.8
GDCF % GNP	15.4	14.1	16.1	13.4	16.1	15.9	16.7	18.9	20.3	20.1
Real Sav Grth (%)	--	5.3	-5.3	27.1	7.6	23.7	-0.7	12.0	31.1	8.0
Real GDCF Grth (%)	--	0.1	25.2	-10.1	27.1	5.9	12.1	21.8	14.1	5.7
Manf % GDCF	19.5	22.9	23.9	20.5	24.2	26.6	24.1	20.6	23.5	22.5
State % GDCF[3]	55.7	43.4	36.3	47.6	48.4	54.3	62.6	53.1	45.3	41.8
Inflation										
Cons Prc Grth (%)	--	18.8	1.7	9.9	10.5	7.5	1.3	10.6	18.5	7.8
Whlsl Prc Grth (%)	--	8.8	2.4	14.1	12.7	7.2	1.4	10.3	14.2	3.2
Employment										
Tot Emplyd (1000s)	2929	2964	3026	3108	3149	3229	3340	3422	3473	3505
Unempl Rate (%)[4]	4.4	4.1	4.0	3.7	3.6	3.7	3.8	3.8	4.0	4.2
Emplyd w/ Wk Ins (%)	6.7	9.1	9.2	10.0	11.9	13.6	13.8	14.3	15.2	15.3
Public Finance[5]										
Govt Expd % GDP	--	--	21.4	21.9	22.1	22.3	24.0	--	19.6	21.4
Real Grth Gvt Exp (%)	--	--	--	10.9	6.3	8.6	14.4	--	--	10.1
Budget Bal (mil US$)	--	--	-3.5	9.9	-7.4	7.7	6.6	--	-2.3	-1.0
Adm & Def % Bud	--	--	60.7	63.6	59.3	61.8	62.4	--	60.5	60.8
Ed & Cul % Bud	--	--	13.8	13.6	13.9	14.3	13.4	--	13.5	14.6
Soc Relief % Bud	--	--	6.0	6.7	7.0	6.1	6.9	--	6.9	6.5
Trade										
Export % GDP	8.6	8.7	5.8	6.4	8.6	9.2	8.7	11.1	9.6	11.2
Import % GDP	14.8	12.0	13.2	10.5	14.0	13.2	12.6	16.4	17.4	18.5
Trd Bal (mil US$)	-71	-64	-118	-78	-76	-64	-70	-74	-133	-127
Trd Bal % GDP	-6.2	-3.4	-7.4	-4.1	-5.5	-4.0	-3.9	-5.3	-7.8	-7.3
Trd Bal % Exports	-73	-39	-128	-64	-64	-43	-45	-48	-81	-65
Real Expt Grth (%)	--	10.9	-27.0	20.1	40.7	15.4	0.3	38.0	-8.0	24.9
Real Impt Grth (%)	--	-10.8	19.8	-13.5	40.4	0.8	1.8	40.2	12.8	13.9
% Capt Gds Impts	14.2	15.6	15.1	16.5	18.7	20.6	21.8	25.1	27.9	26.4
% Cons Gds Impts	19.9	17.3	12.6	8.8	7.4	6.9	6.4	7.4	8.1	10.1
% Ind Expts	8.1	8.4	10.6	10.4	17.0	12.6	14.0	23.6	32.3	40.9
% Expts to US	3.5	4.2	5.4	4.4	5.6	3.5	6.2	8.6	11.5	21.9
% Expts to Jap	52.6	45.6	50.8	59.5	37.2	35.2	41.9	41.5	37.7	29.0

Table 6.8 (Continued)

	1952	1953	1954	1955	1956	1957	1958	1959	1960	1961
% Impts from US	45.7	38.7	46.4	47.5	42.0	39.9	37.3	36.1	38.1	40.6
% Impts from Jap	31.2	30.6	33.4	30.5	36.3	33.2	39.6	40.3	35.3	31.0
Foreign Capital										
US Aid (mil US$)	87	107	120	132	102	108	82	129	101	94
US Aid % GDCF	44	49	46	52	46	42	27	48	29	27
For Inv (mil US$)[6]	1	4	2	5	4	2	3	1	16	14
✓For Invst % GDCF[6]	0.5	1.6	0.9	1.8	1.6	0.6	0.8	0.4	4.5	4.2
Net Fr Cp (ml US$)[7]	80	80	135	83	95	85	123	122	130	126
NFC % GDCF[7]	40.0	36.9	52.2	32.5	42.8	33.2	40.9	45.6	37.5	36.6
Standard of Living										
Income Ratio[8]	--	20.47	--	--	--	--	--	--	--	11.56
Gini Coeff	--	.56	--	--	--	--	--	--	--	.46
Food % Consptn[9]	55.6	54.4	54.1	53.3	53.1	52.2	51.7	51.3	53.1	51.2
Rl Mnf Wg Inc (%)[10]	--	--	10.8	1.5	3.2	1.6	4.3	-2.4	-1.6	12.7
Hlth Pers (1000s)	--	--	10.4	10.3	10.6	10.3	10.8	11.7	12.4	12.7
Commc Disease Rate	14.1	20.9	12.7	11.4	16.5	26.3	22.7	22.3	11.5	6.5
Energy Cons (cal)	2078	2283	2176	2247	2262	2369	2359	2339	2390	2430
Protein Cons (gm)	49.0	53.4	51.9	53.2	53.6	56.8	56.9	56.6	57.1	60.3
% Prim Grads to Jr HS	--	33.8	35.6	38.7	43.0	46.7	48.5	50.3	50.7	51.2
Real Expd per Prim Stdt (1981 NT$)	3297	2901	3468	2962	3674	2733	2789	3229	3048	3368

1. Several data series reported in current NT$s in the *Taiwan Statistical Data Book* were converted to constant 1981 NT$s by using the ratio between current and constant GDP series. Likewise, several conversions were made between figures reported in NT$s and US$s.

2. The stagnation of GNP per capita in US$ terms results from the rapidly deteriorating NT$/US$ ratio from $13.21/$1 in 1952 to $36.41/$1 in 1959.

3. Includes investment both by the government and by state corporations.

4. Official unemployment rate determined by people "seeking jobs." A broader definition in terms of people "willing to work" produces estimates about 50 percent higher. See Shirley W. Y. Kuo, *The Taiwan Economy in Transition* (Boulder, Colo.: Westview Press, 1983), p. 57.

5. There are no public fiscal data for 1959 because the government changed the definition of the fiscal year.

6. Foreign investments are reported in terms of project approvals by the R.O.C. rather than in terms of actual investment flows, so that these figures somewhat overstate actual foreign investment.

7. This includes inflows of aid, investment, and loans and outflows of repayments and foreign investments and loans coming from the R.O.C.

8. This is the ratio of the income of the richest fifth of the population to the poorest fifth.

9. Source: *National Income in the Taiwan Area, Republic of China: National Accounts for 1951–1983 and Preliminary Estimates for 1984* (Taipei: Directorate-General of Budget, Accounting, and Statistics, 1985), pp. 146–147.

10. Source: Walter Galenson, "The Labor Force, Wages, and Living Standards," in Walter Galenson, ed., *Economic Growth and Structural Change in Taiwan: The Postwar Experience of the Republic of China* (Ithaca, N.Y.: Cornell University Press, 1979), p. 415.

Source: Taiwan Statistical Data Book, 1987 (Taipei: Council for Economic Planning and Development, 1987), passim.

because of the receipt of large amounts of American aid.[30] This balance-of-trade problem began to escalate in the late 1950s. Imports as a percentage of GDP rose markedly from 10.5 percent in 1955 to 16.4 percent in 1959, driven by a rising demand for capital goods whose share in total imports almost doubled from 15 percent to 28 percent between 1954 and 1960. Taiwan's protected industrial products, in turn, were not competitive on international markets, as indicated by the overwhelmingly agricultural nature of the R.O.C.'s export mix. Thus agricultural production's inability to keep up with escalating import needs caused a near doubling of Taiwan's trade deficit to about $130 million annually in the early 1960s.

The R.O.C.'s import substitution strategy of promoting economic development and industrialization during the 1950s was quite successful in the short term. However, within a few years import substitution was clearly running out of steam. The government, hence, faced a choice among three economic strategies as the 1950s ended. It could continue as before and hope that the deteriorating economic situation would not get out of hand; it could attempt to move to "second-stage" import substitution in heavy and capital-intensive industry; or it could open its economy in the hope of becoming internationally competitive in its current labor-intensive industries and of promoting development through the large-scale export of these products. This strategic decision was a momentous one, and Taiwan's "economic miracle" essentially resulted from selecting the right strategy.

The Export-led Surge

The decision to follow the strategy of promoting growth through labor-intensive export industries was not an easy one, as discussed in chapter 5. Few other developing countries had taken this path in the recent past; many leaders doubted that Taiwan's light industries could become internationally competitive and feared that the new strategy would be economically disasterous (e.g., worsening the balance of trade, rekindling inflation, and bringing back the external dependence of the era of "unequal treaties"). Moreover, this strategy challenged the interests of the military sector, which wanted to develop defense-related heavy industries, and of bureaucrats, who were forced to yield much of their direct power over the economy. Yet the R.O.C. made this decision quickly and decisively; the results were probably more rapid and spectacular than even the most ardent advocates of the reform had dared hope.[31]

The R.O.C., thus, adopted several major policies in the late 1950s and early 1960s aimed at promoting exports and domestic investment and industrialization. The most important of these measures were the Nineteen-Point Program of Economic and Financial Reform, the Statute for the Encouragement of Investment, and the establishment of Export Processing Zones (EPZs).[32] This new policy package provided a variety of incentives for exporting. Exchange rates were made more realistic (i.e., the dual exchange rates were abolished and the overvalued NT$ was depreciated), which made foreign trade and exporting more profitable. In addition, cheap credit and rebates on imported components and raw materials were made available to exporters; trade associations were formed to promote and subsidize exporting; and the establishment of EPZs stimulated assembly work by low-cost Taiwan labor for export. Domestically, tax reform and decreased regulation encouraged private enterprise, and foreign investment was encouraged rather than restricted. Concomitantly, the protectionist trade system was substantially liberalized, since most export industries needed to import various components. Tariffs were cut substantially, and other types of import restrictions were reduced.[33] As a result, the nominal rate of protection for manufactured goods fell dramatically from 53.5 percent in 1961 to 30.0 percent in 1971, and variations in the degree of protectionism offered specific industries narrowed considerably, although export-oriented sectors continued to receive the most protection.[34] Another indicator of declining protectionism was that the ratio of customs revenues to total imports fell sharply from 25 percent to 30 percent for 1954–1958 to 15 percent to 18 percent during the decade of the 1960s.[35]

This new economic strategy proved to be phenomenally successful, as shown by the aggregate data in Table 6.9. Real GNP growth accelerated to a very high average of 11 percent annually during 1963–1973. This rapid growth resulted from a fundamental industrial transformation in the nature of the R.O.C.'s economy, spurred by an increase in manufacturing's share of total investment from 22 percent in the early 1960s to 33 percent in the early 1970s. Industrial production rose by 18 percent a year over the 1963–1973 period, and the substantial underutilization of manufacturing capacity that reached 50 percent or more during the 1950s was alleviated (e.g., production as a percentage of productive capacity jumped by more than a half for goods in a wide variety of industries between 1961 and 1966).[36] As a result, manufacturing's share of net domestic product doubled from about 17 percent to 35 percent between the late 1950s and early 1970s. Conversely, agriculture ceased to be the dominant economic sector during the 1960s, as agriculture's proportions of national product and employment dropped from about 30 percent to 15 percent and 50 percent to 35 percent, respectively, over the decade. Energy consumption escalated as well, doubling between 1962 and 1968 and doubling again between 1968 and 1972.

Industrial expansion also created a large number of jobs. For example, although total employment rose by only 23 percent between 1952 and 1963, it jumped 48 percent over the next decade. The unemployment rate was cut by 60 percent between 1964 and 1968, dropping to 1.7 percent of those "seeking work" and 2.8 percent of those "willing to work." Since then unemployment has almost always been below 2 percent on the former index and 3 percent on the latter, denoting a situation of labor shortage.[37] Inflation, which seemed to be re-emerging in the the 1950s, was well under control as well. Between 1962 and 1972, for example, consumer prices rose by 2.9 percent a year and wholesale prices by 2.1 percent. Finally, the population growth rate dropped steadily from

Table 6.9
Socioeconomic Indicators during Export Surge*

	1962	1963	1964	1965	1966	1967	1968	1969	1970	1971	1972
Population											
Total Pop (mil)	11.5	11.9	12.3	12.6	13.0	13.3	13.7	14.3[1]	14.7	15.0	15.3
Pop Grth (%)	3.3	3.2	3.1	3.0	2.9	2.3	2.7	5.0[1]	2.4	2.2	2.0
Economic Growth											
Real GNP Grth (%)	7.9	9.4	12.3	11.0	9.0	10.6	9.1	9.0	11.3	12.9	13.3
GNP p. c. (US$)	161	178	202	216	236	266	302	343	387	441	519
Real Ind Grth (%)	7.9	9.1	21.2	16.2	15.6	16.7	22.3	19.8	20.1	23.6	21.2
Real Ag Grth (%)	2.6	0.2	11.9	6.6	3.2	6.3	6.9	-2.0	5.4	0.5	2.2
Energy (bil KWH)	4.1	4.4	5.2	5.7	6.5	7.5	8.8	10.1	12.0	13.8	16.1
Econ Structure											
Ind % NDP	25.7	28.2	28.9	28.6	28.8	30.8	32.5	34.6	34.7	36.9	40.4
Manf % NDP	17.0	19.7	20.9	20.1	20.3	22.2	24.1	26.2	26.4	28.9	32.4
Serv % NDP	45.1	45.1	42.9	44.1	45.0	45.4	45.4	44.6	47.4	48.2	45.5
Ag % NDP	29.2	26.7	28.2	27.3	26.2	23.8	22.1	18.8	17.9	14.9	14.1
Ag % Emplymt	49.7	49.4	49.5	46.5	45.0	42.5	40.8	39.3	36.7	35.1	33.0
State % Ind Prod	46.2	44.8	43.7	41.3	38.2	34.7	31.1	29.4	27.7	20.5	19.1
Savings & Invst											
Savings % GNP	12.4	17.1	19.6	19.6	21.5	22.5	22.1	23.8	25.5	28.8	32.1
GDCF % GDP	17.9	18.4	18.8	22.8	21.3	24.7	25.2	24.6	25.6	26.4	25.8
Real Sav Grth (%)	4.2	50.9	28.5	11.3	19.5	15.5	7.3	17.1	19.1	27.8	26.2
Real GDCF Grth (%)	-3.8	12.3	14.8	34.8	1.8	28.4	11.2	6.3	16.0	16.0	10.7
Manf % GDCF	21.6	22.7	31.0	29.8	29.8	33.7	33.4	32.4	36.1	31.1	32.8
State % GDCF*	46.8	36.0	34.4	31.3	34.6	37.5	36.6	41.8	40.1	40.4	39.3
Inflation											
Cons Prc Grth (%)	2.4	2.2	-0.2	-0.1	2.0	3.4	7.9	5.1	3.6	2.8	3.0
Whsl Prc Grth (%)	3.0	6.5	2.5	-4.6	1.5	2.5	3.0	-0.3	2.7	0.0	4.4
Money Sup Grth (%)	5.0	28.1	35.0	15.9	12.2	30.1	11.5	15.6	15.0	30.6	34.1
Employment											
Tot Emplyd (1000s)	3541	3592	3658	3763	3856	4050	4225	4390	4576	4378	4948
Unempl Rate (%)*	4.1	4.3	4.4	3.3	3.0	2.3	1.7	1.9	1.7	1.8	1.4
Empl w/ Wk Ins (%)	15.5	15.3	15.5	16.8	17.6	17.8	18.3	19.2	20.5	21.8	23.1
Public Finance											
Govt Expd % GDP	21.3	20.0	19.5	21.1	20.4	22.9	21.3	22.8	23.5	22.5	22.2
Rl Gth Gvt Exp (%)	7.3	3.2	7.8	22.0	3.6	23.3	0.6	19.2	13.5	8.2	9.7
Bud Bal (mil US$)	-9.3	-15.4	14.2	24.8	33.8	22.8	55.7	79.3	51.5	62.8	67.4
Adm & Def % Bud	59.1	59.3	58.4	53.8	61.3	51.0	54.4	48.7	48.7	47.7	43.3
Ed & Cul % Bud	14.2	14.1	13.8	12.5	14.5	13.2	14.7	16.3	16.3	17.6	17.3
Soc Relief % Bud	7.2	7.6	8.1	7.6	4.7	7.2	7.8	8.9	9.6	10.4	12.7

Table 6.9 (Continued)

	1962	1963	1964	1965	1966	1967	1968	1969	1970	1971	1972
Trade											
Export % GDP	11.4	15.3	17.1	16.1	17.1	17.7	18.7	21.4	26.3	31.4	38.0
Import % GDP	15.9	16.7	16.9	19.9	19.9	22.3	21.5	24.8	27.1	28.2	32.1
Trd Bal (mil US$)	-86	-30	5	-106	-86	-165	-114	-164	-43	216	474
Trd Bal % GDP	-4.5	-1.4	0.2	-3.9	-2.8	-4.6	-2.8	-3.4	-0.8	3.2	6.0
Trd Bal % Exports	-39.4	-9.0	1.2	-24.0	-16.3	-26.1	-14.7	-15.9	-3.1	10.3	15.7
Real Expt Grth (%)	9.5	47.0	25.4	4.3	16.0	14.3	15.3	24.9	36.5	34.9	37.0
Real Impt Grth (%)	-7.5	15.0	13.7	30.8	8.9	23.9	5.0	26.1	21.5	17.4	28.8
% Capt Goods Impts	23.4	21.4	22.1	29.3	29.4	32.1	32.5	34.7	32.3	32.0	31.1
% Cons Goods Impts	8.3	6.5	6.1	5.1	5.1	4.7	4.6	4.5	4.9	5.1	5.7
% Ind Exports	50.5	41.1	42.5	46.0	55.1	61.6	68.4	74.0	78.6	80.9	83.3
% Expts to US	24.4	16.3	18.6	21.3	21.6	26.2	35.3	38.0	38.1	41.7	41.9
% Expts to Jap	23.9	31.7	30.9	30.6	24.0	17.9	16.2	15.0	14.6	11.9	12.6
% Impts from US	38.0	41.6	32.5	31.7	26.7	30.7	26.5	24.1	23.9	22.1	21.6
% Impts from Jap	34.1	29.7	34.8	39.8	40.4	40.5	40.0	44.2	42.8	44.9	41.6
Foreign Capital											
US Aid (mil US$)	66	115	84	57	4	4	29	--	--	--	--
US Aid % GDCF	19	29	18	9	1	1	3	--	--	--	--
For Inv (mil US$)*	5	18	20	42	9	57	90	109	139	163	127
For Inv % GDC*	1.5	4.5	4.2	6.5	4.4	6.4	8.4	9.1	9.6	9.4	6.3
Net Fr Cap (ml US$)*	106	28	-20	89	-6	83	132	42	13	-159	-495
NFC % GDCF*	30.8	7.0	-4.2	14.0	-1.0	9.2	12.4	3.4	0.9	-9.2	-24.4
Standard of Living											
Income Ratio*	--	--	5.33	--	5.25	--	5.28	--	4.58	--	4.49
Gini Coeff	--	--	.36	--	.36	--	.36	--	.32	--	.32
Food % Conspt*	50.1	48.8	49.3	48.7	47.9	46.4	44.8	43.6	42.7	42.0	42.0
Rl Manf Wg Inc (%)*	2.9	1.6	3.7	7.8	4.4	8.6	2.6	-3.7	5.2	13.6	4.2
Hlth pers (1000s)	12.7	13.0	13.3	13.0	14.2	13.7	12.5	12.3	13.6	18.2	19.1
Commc Disease Rate	8.3	6.5	6.5	8.0	7.6	8.2	6.3	4.3	2.1	1.6	1.1
Energy Cons (cal)	2317	2326	2364	2411	2433	2504	2545	2639	2662	2674	2738
Protein Cons (gm)	57.8	58.8	59.5	61.2	62.3	64.5	64.9	69.1	72.2	72.4	74.6
% Prim Grads to Jr HS	52.5	54.4	53.5	55.1	57.4	59.0	62.3	74.7[2]	76.0	79.8	81.3
Real Expd per Prim Stdt (1981 NT$)	3502	3690	4058	4471	3669	3815	4778	4976	7209	6981	7490

1. This large increase resulted from a change in the definition of total population to include military servicemen, who had not previously been counted.

2. Before 1968, based on number of students in graduating class; after 1968, based on number of actual graduates.

*See Table 6.8 for explanatory notes.

Source: *Taiwan Statistical Data Book, 1987* (Taipei: Council for Economic Planning and Development, 1987), passim.

Table 6.10
Structure of Manufacturing Production (in percentage of total manufacturing output)

	1951	1960	1970	1979
Food, bevs, tob	33.4%	31.8%	16.5%	8.5%
Textiles & apparel	19.0%	16.1%	18.1%	15.5%
Chemicals	15.6%	6.6%	12.2%	11.4%
Wood & furniture	4.2%	5.2%	4.7%	4.5%
Paper & printing	7.5%	8.5%	4.9%	5.2%
Petroleum & Coal	3.7%	5.4%	9.1%	4.5%
Basic Metals	0.4%	4.1%	2.5%	7.5%
Electronics*	0.7%	2.1%	10.7%	12.6%
Other Mach & Metals*	4.5%	9.2%	10.7%	13.5%

*Disaggregated with data from primary source.

Source: Gary S. Fields, "Industrialization and Employment in Hong Kong, Korea, Singapore, and Taiwan," in Walter Galenson, ed., *Foreign Trade and Investment: Economic Development in the Newly Industrializing Asian Countries* (Madison: University of Wisconsin Press, 1985), p. 363.

over 3 percent in the early 1960s to just over 2 percent in the early 1970s, which was certainly helpful, given the crowded condition of a country that has the second highest population density in the world.

The nature of Taiwan's industry changed significantly as well as development proceeded. First, the country began to produce a wider range of manufactured goods that became increasingly sophisticated over time, as shown by the data in Table 6.10 on the relative share of industries in total manufacturing output. The food-processing industry rapidly lost its dominant position during the 1960s as its share plummeted from 32 percent in 1960 to 17 percent in 1970 and 8.5 percent in 1979. In contrast, the largest gains were scored by chemicals, metal products, and machinery, while the position of the textile industry remained fairly constant. Thus the dominant industries progressed from food products to textiles to electronics assembly and chemicals over the 1950s and 1960s in the normal pattern of transformation from "early" to "middle" to "late" industries.[38]

Second, industrial growth in Taiwan was not, as in many other developing countries, concentrated in a few urban areas. Rather, because of the legacy of industrial siting during the Japanese colonial period, the excellent transportation system developed during the postwar period, the R.O.C.'s rural electrification program, and a fairly well educated population, a wide dispersal of manufacturing enterprises occurred in smaller cities and rural areas. For example, between 1951 and 1971 the proportion of industrial firms located in Taipei increased only slightly, from 15.1 percent to 17.8 percent, whereas the proportion of firms located in the next four largest cities actually decreased from 19.2 percent to

17.1 percent.[39] This dispersion represented a pattern of small, decentralized, labor-intensive enterprises that reflected the R.O.C.'s international comparative advantage of low-cost labor and rapid flexibility to meet international demand. It also promoted income equality by providing ready parttime employment for underemployed people in the rural sector that is not available in economies with urban concentrations of industry.[40]

Third, the reforms were also quite successful in stimulating private enterprise. Because the Japanese had not permitted native Taiwanese to own any large-scale businesses, the transfer of Japanese assets to the R.O.C. after World War II resulted in government-owned enterprises dominating industrial production; as was seen in the last section, the import substitution industrialization of the 1950s produced little change in this situation. The rapid growth of the 1950s and 1960s, however, was predominantly based on expanding private enterprise as the private sector's share of industrial production rose from 52 percent in 1961 to 81 percent in 1972. The development of the banking sector, in addition, meant that direct government controls over business finance were drastically curtailed.[41] As a result, most of the private entrepreneurs who led and benefited from this boom were native Taiwanese.[42]

The export-led nature of this economic growth and structural transformation is clear in the aggregate data in Table 6.9, since the growth in exports was phenomenal, averaging 15 percent a year through 1968 and over 30 percent for 1969–1972 in real terms. Consequently exports skyrocketed as a percentage of GDP from 9 percent in 1958 to 17 percent in 1964 to 26 percent in 1970 and to 38 percent in 1972. Taiwan's export mix became overwhelmingly industrial, proving that its manufactured products were internationally competitive. In 1958 industrial products composed only 14 percent of the R.O.C.'s exports, but the island's export structure underwent rapid transformation, as their share in total exports jumped to 50 percent in 1962, 68 percent in 1968, and 83 percent in 1972. The nature of industrial exports also changed in line with the advance of Taiwan's leading industries from food processing to textiles to electronics, heavy chemicals, and machinery. For example, between 1960 and 1970 processed agricultural products fell from 56 percent to 13 percent of total exports (sugar alone plummeted from 44 percent to 5 percent), whereas textiles grew from 14 percent to 32 percent, electronics goods from 0.5 percent to 12 percent, and machinery and metal products from 4 percent to 10 percent.[43]

A dramatic change in the country's balance of trade also occurred. Through most of the 1960s the R.O.C. continued to run substantial negative deficits averaging $100 million (the small surplus in 1964 was caused by a boom in the price of sugar) as the rapidly expanding export industries necessitated increased imports as well. For example, capital goods rose from just over 20 percent to just over 30 percent of total imports between the first half and second half of the decade. However, this negative trade balance declined somewhat to about 3 percent of GDP and dropped dramatically to only about 15 percent of total exports (compared with about 60 percent in the 1950s), making its management much easier. Moreover, in the early 1970s rapid export growth finally caught up with import needs (e.g., in 1973 only 48 percent of export proceeds went for the purchase of imported raw materials and components[44]); Taiwan recorded strong trade surpluses of $216 million in 1971 and $474 million in 1972.

Sophisticated econometric analysis indicates that exports had a leading role in the growth of Taiwan's economy during the 1960s and 1970s, in contrast to the predominant role of import substitution between 1937 and 1954 and domestic demand during 1954–1961. Table 6.11 presents results that decompose the sources of output expansion into increases in (a) domestic demand, (b) exports, (c) import substitution, and (d) technical changes in the input-output coefficients used in the calculations (the last two had almost no effect on production expansion after 1960). These data reveal the considerable and growing importance of exports in fueling Taiwan's economic dynamism. For 1961–1966 they produced a respectable 35 percent of the growth in the R.O.C.'s economy; for 1966–1971 this rose to 46 percent; and for the first half of the 1970s exports accounted for over two-thirds of Taiwan's growth. As might be expected, the importance of exports varied considerably by industry even within the manufacturing sector, as shown by the data in Table 6.12 on the percentage of production being exported in various industries over the 1960s. The food-processing industry, which had one of the highest export ratios at the beginning of the 1960s, maintained a stable export proportion in the 20 percent to 25 percent range, which explains its declining relative position in the increasingly export-driven Taiwan economy. In contrast, textiles, electronics, wood, rubber, plastics, and leather all increased their export percentages dramatically to between a third and a half of total production; substantial gains were also registered in the machinery and the metals industries. Most of these were labor-intensive industries, and even the "late" industries among them (for example, electronics and machinery) primarily involved assembly work.[45]

The fact that labor-intensive industries displayed the fastest growth implies that Taiwan had been able to find a niche in the global economy based on a comparative advantage in low-cost labor. This logic of comparative advantage suggests that the R.O.C. should import capital-intensive and export labor-intensive products and that, in terms of export markets, labor-intensive goods should be sent to developed countries and capital-intensive products to other developing nations. Table 6.13 indicates that this in fact occurred. In 1961, just before the export boom started, the differences between the capital intensities of exports and import-oriented industries and between exports to developed and developing countries were fairly small, on the order of 5 percent. Once the export surge started, these gaps quickly became quite pronounced, reaching 15 percent to 20 percent differentials.

Despite this general emphasis on labor-intensive production, small and medium industry in Taiwan did become more capital intensive over the 1960s as domestic entrepreneurs significantly upgraded their production techniques.[46] Moreover, investment in Taiwan was much more productive than elsewhere in the world

Table 6.11
Relative Contributions to Output Expansion

	Domestic Demand	Exports	Import Substitution	Changes in I/O Coeffs
1961–1966	63.2%	35.0%	0.5%	1.3%
1966–1971	51.4%	45.9%	5.7%	-3.0%
1971–1976	34.7%	67.7%	-2.4%	--

Source: Shirley W. Y. Kuo and John C. H. Fei, "Causes and Roles of Export Expansion in the Republic of China," in Walter Galenson, ed., *Foreign Trade and Investment: Economic Development in the Newly Industrializing Asian Economies* (Madison: University of Wisconsin Press, 1985), p. 68.

Table 6.12
Exports as a Percentage of Production

	1961	1966	1969
Food	21%	25%	24%
Textiles & apparel	20%	26%	39%
Wood products & furniture	23%	45%	50%
Paper & pulp	6%	13%	7%
Leather	2%	17%	35%
Rubber	17%	21%	37%
Fertilizers	5%	6%	9%
Pharmaceuticals	3%	3%	8%
Plastics	12%	27%	44%
Other chemicals	15%	8%	6%
Petroleum products	5%	4%	12%
Nonmetallic Minerals	9%	19%	15%
Iron and Steel	11%	16%	16%
Aluminum	12%	14%	18%
Other metals	5%	34%	25%
Machinery	3%	15%	28%
Electronics	10%	20%	36%
Transport Equipment	1%	7%	10%

Source: Samuel P. S. Ho, *The Economic Development of Taiwan, 1860–1970* (New Haven, Conn.: Yale University Press, 1978), p. 201.

as measured by the ratio of increased investment to increased GDP (the lower this ratio, the more productive investment is because a given amount of investment produces greater growth). For the R.O.C. this ratio was 2.2 during the 1950s, 2.3 during the 1960s, and 2.9 during the 1970s, compared with 5.1, 4.4, and 7.0 for all industrial countries and 4.5, 3.4, and 6.5 for Japan.[47] Thus Taiwan clearly seemed to be following a path of comparative advantage; as a result, the cost of exporting in Taiwan fell dramatically compared with that in other nations between the late 1950s and the late 1960s.[48]

Table 6.13
Capital Intensity of Exports and Import-Oriented Industries* (in 1,000 NT$ per worker)

	Import-Ort Industries	All Exports	Exports to Devd States	Exports to LDCs
1961	$88.3	$84.8	$82.8	$87.8
1966	$98.9	$88.5	$80.2	$100.7
1971	$113.6	$98.3	$92.8	$110.1

*Import-oriented industries are those for which imports compose over 10 percent of final demand.

Source: Shirley W. Y. Kuo and John C. H. Fei, "Causes and Roles of Export Expansion in the Republic of China," in Walter Galenson, ed., *Foreign Trade and Investment: Economic Development in the Newly Industrializing Asian Countries* (Madison: University of Wisconsin Press, 1985), p. 66.

This comparative advantage in labor-intensive exports affected Taiwan's markets in several ways. Exports to developed countries soared (rising from 42 percent to 70 percent of Taiwan's total industrial exports between 1962 and 1970),[49] whereas those to developing nations stagnated, indicating that Taiwan had assumed a position in the global division of labor based primarily on manufacturing for markets in the capitalist industrial world. This is strongly reflected in exports to the United States, the largest market in advanced industrial societies. The United States had taken less than 10 percent of Taiwan's exports during most of the 1950s. This doubled to just over 20 percent during the early and mid–1960s and then jumped again in the late 1960s, averaging almost 40 percent from 1968 to 1972. Conversely, exports to Japan, which had taken agricultural products but used protectionism to limit industrial imports, fell drastically from over 50 percent in the early 1950s to just over 10 percent in the early 1970s. On the other hand, just the opposite pattern occurred in imports as the Japanese began to outcompete America in industrial products. Taiwan imported more from America than from Japan during the 1950s and early 1960s, but by the 1970s imports from Japan were twice as great as those from the United States.

A principal reason for Taiwan's industrial transformation and growth was the country's strong investment record. Savings as a proportion of GNP, which had averaged 9 percent in the mid–1950s and 11 percent in the late 1950s and early 1960s, rose dramatically as export-led growth produced more resources, from 12.4 percent in 1962 to 17.1 percent in 1963 to 25.5 percent in 1970 and to 32.1 percent in 1972—perhaps the highest in the world. This great jump in the savings rate, in turn, permitted the investment rate to rise from 18 percent in the early 1960s to 25 percent over the rest of the decade, despite the termination of U.S. aid, which had financed over 40 percent of the R.O.C.'s investment during the import-substitution period. Industry was the primary beneficiary of growing investment. For example, machinery and equipment as a proportion of fixed capital formation jumped from 32 percent in 1951–1955 to 55 percent in

1971–1973; the number of industrial firms using power equipment leaped from 34 percent to 81 percent between 1954 and 1966.[50]

One reason for this extremely high savings rate was the high profit rate in manufacturing, which skyrocketed from 9 percent in the early 1950s to 28 percent in the early 1960s to 34 percent in the late 1960s, thus allowing substantial reinvestment.[51] In addition, unlike most developing countries, household savings played an important role as well, generally averaging well over a third of total capital formation. For example, there was a fairly high rate of household savings (which includes some small business savings as well) that was estimated at 16.6 percent for 1967–1972 at the peak of the export boom, compared with about 7 percent in the United States.[52] The R.O.C.'s remarkable record for savings and investment derived from a variety of factors. In terms of the government's economic policy, the tax structure rewarded savings, and many incentives were provided for both domestic and foreign investment. More indirectly, the government used its control of the banking sector to perpetuate realistic interest rates that provided financial incentives to save, and the very low social security net made saving for old age almost mandatory. The expansion of financial markets after the early 1960s also made channeling investment into the private-business sector easier and less subject to governmental control. In addition, the widespread use of bonus payments, the limited availability of consumer credit, and the popularity of opening small businesses all contributed to the Chinese "cultural" propensity to save.[53]

This tremendous increase in the savings and investment rates occurred, despite a decline in the "enforced" savings, through government taxing and investment; for example, the share of gross domestic capital formation accounted for by the government and public corporations shrank from 50 pecent in the late 1950s to 35 percent to 40 percent in the late 1960s and early 1970s. This reflected the continuing fiscal conservatism of the R.O.C. There was no great expansion in the size of government or accumulation of debt. Government expenditures as a percentage of GNP remained fairly constant, in the 20 percent to 23 percent range, and the government ran a significant cumulative budget surplus of over $300 million for 1960–1972. Taiwan in fact seemingly represented a successful case of "supply side" economics. The tax cuts, investment incentives, and import rebates of the 1960s had the potential to reduce government revenues by almost 20 percent, but rapid economic expansion actually produced an increase in collections.[54]

The increased domestic savings were augmented by the R.O.C.'s generally successful measures to stimulate and manage foreign investment. Private foreign investment, which had averaged less than 1 percent of gross domestic capital formation during the 1950s, rose to over 4 percent during 1960–1967 and to 9 percent at the beginning of the 1970s. Foreign investment varied considerably by industry, as shown in Table 6.14. Foreign investment was concentrated in the electronics, textile, and chemical industries during the 1960s, which accounted for two-thirds of all foreign capital. In the 1970s the proportion of

Table 6.14
Foreign Investment by Industry

	Per cent of Total Foreign Investment		Per Cent Foreign Investment of All Investment	
	1962-69	1973-79	1962-69	1973-79
Electrical Mach	33.6%	44.5%	18.9%	33.6%
Textiles	20.9%	4.8%	4.3%	2.2%
Chemicals	12.9%	14.9%	4.5%	6.1%
Machinery	6.8%	8.7%	11.6%	22.8%
Basic Metals	6.5%	5.6%	5.5%	3.4%
Footwear	5.5%	1.3%	5.1%	8.0%
Food Processing	4.7%	2.1%	1.5%	2.9%
Rubber & Petroleum	4.5%	3.0%	14.5%	15.9%
Nonmetallic Mins	2.0%	12.0%	1.1%	20.2%
Paper	1.6%	1.1%	2.7%	2.8%
Wood	0.9%	1.3%	1.0%	3.9%
Leather	0.1%	0.7%	1.5%	13.7%
All Manufacturing	100%	100%	--	7.9%

Source: Shirley W. Y. Kuo, Gustav Ranis, and John C. H. Fei, *The Taiwan Success Story: Rapid Growth with Improved Distribution in the Republic of China* (Boulder, Colo.: Westview Press, 1981), pp. 32–33.

foreign investment in electronics rose markedly from 34 percent to 44.5 percent, while foreign investors lost most of their interest in textiles. In terms of foreign capital's role within a particular industry, electronics was the only sector with a particularly large foreign presence (19 percent in the 1960s and 34 percent in the 1970s), although foreign investment reached a fifth of total gross domestic capital formation in machinery and nonmetallic mineral products in the 1970s.

Considerable controversy surrounds the activities of foreign capital and multinational corporations (MNCs) in developing countries. On the one hand, developmentalists argue that foreign capital contributes needed capital, technology, and marketing networks. On the other hand, *dependencistas* contend that MNCs denationalize the local economy, create enclaves that do not benefit most of society, use "inappropriate" capital-intensive production techniques in labor-surplus societies, and ultimately extract a "surplus" from a dependent economy.[55] Foreign capital in Taiwan does not seem to have brought most of the problems posited by dependency theory. First, the R.O.C.'s economy does not appear to have been denationalized. Electronics was the only sector in which foreign firms even approached a dominant position. Moreover, the ratio of direct foreign investment, which provides the strongest controls, to other forms of foreign capital (i.e., portfolio and loans) was fairly low, and decreased over time from 36 percent in the 1960s to 22 percent in the 1970s. Overall, direct foreign investment never constituted more than 10 percent of total manufacturing investment. There was some potential problem for dependency, though, in the concentration of the sources of foreign capital (i.e., the United States, Japan, and overseas Chinese provided 75 percent of foreign investment). Second, MNCs did not form enclaves, but became increasingly linked to the domestic economy. For example, in the early 1970s foreign firms purchased about half their goods locally. Third, MNCs were, on average, more capital intensive than domestic enterprises, but this difference narrowed appreciably over time.[56]

The reasons that the R.O.C. escaped the problems associated with the operations of MNCs in many other developing societies include both the timing of Taiwan's industrialization surge and the explicit efforts of the government to manage foreign capital. Foreign investment did not really begin to flow into Taiwan until the early 1960s both because of the barriers erected as part of the import-substitution strategy and because of the poor investment climate created by the island's uncertain political and economic status. Thus domestic industrialization was well under way when the foreign presence started to escalate, which made "denationalization" and foreign domination much harder to achieve.

The regime, with its memories of "unequal treaties" and foreign enclaves, was quite sensitive to the need to control MNCs so that their activities helped, rather than hindered, the nation's developmental efforts. In particular, it moved to channel foreign capital into the new dynamic export sector,[57] to ensure its integration with the overall economy through domestic content legislation and limitations on the number of expatriate managers, and to maintain the monopolies of state corporations in the heavy and capital-intensive industries usually dominated by foreigners. The government's ability to regulate foreign capital depended on the high profits that could be obtained in the rapidly expanding export sector, but the attractive economic environment meant that foreign firms could be successfully harnessed to Taiwan's developmental objectives. In terms of the three major contributions that foreign capital can make (funds, technology, and marketing networks), the first was relatively minor, given the country's strong record on domestic savings after the early 1960s, while the second was probably less important than normal in developing countries because of the successful strategy of channeling foreign investment into labor-intensive export production. Still, foreign companies were much more likely to use imported technology than domestic ones, and the MNCs made a major technology contribution to the upgrading of such export industries as microelectronics, synthetic fibers, and plastics. Finally, international groups, such as large Japanese trading firms and American retail chains, assumed a leading role in marketing Taiwan's exports (e.g., in 1970 about half of all exports were marketed through foreign companies).[58]

Rapid economic growth in Taiwan had a profound effect on improving living standards and reducing socioeconomic inequality for the population at large. Several aspects of this improved standard of living can easily be discerned in the aggregate data in Table 6.8 and 6.9. First, food consumption and especially dietary quality rose substantially, as indicated by a 15 percent increase in caloric intake and a 30 percent jump in protein consumption between 1960 and 1972.

Second, the number of health personnel nearly doubled betwewen 1958 and 1973, while the communicable disease rate fell from 22.7 to 1.1 per 100,000 persons during this period. In education real expenditures per primary school student, which had remained constant during the 1950s, doubled between 1962 and 1972, and the number of primary students going on to junior high rose from about a half in the early 1960s to over 80 percent a decade later (although changed statistical procedures accounted for some of this increase). This investment in education is generally credited with producing the skilled and trainable workforce that was central to Taiwan's development strategy (e.g., in 1979 51 percent of the workforce had a secondary education, two and a half times the 20 percent in 1950) and with providing broad opportunities for upward social mobility.[59] Finally, despite the pronounced fiscal conservatism, government spending patterns did move in a slightly liberal direction. Between 1958 and 1972, for example, the share of the budget devoted to defense and administration fell from 62 percent to 43 percent, while there was a gradual rise in the priorities accorded to education and social relief.

In addition, the R.O.C. differed markedly from the normal developmental pattern in which industrialization and growth first produce increased inequality in wealth and lead to greater equality only over extended periods of time. In Taiwan, in contrast, income inequality fell sharply during the 1950s, primarily because of the land reform program. During the 1960s and 1970s rapid industrialization produced a tight labor market and rising real wages that averaged a 5.5 percent annual growth between 1960 and 1972 (concomitantly, the proportion of household income spent on food fell from 53 percent to 42 percent, implying a substantial increase in disposable income). Consequently the ratio of the income of the richest fifth to the poorest fifth of the population fell from 5.33 in 1964 to 4.49 in 1972. Thus income inequality in Taiwan had been reduced to approximately the levels found in advanced industrial societies by the early 1970s.[60]

In the late 1950s and early 1960s, therefore, the R.O.C. government took a fateful gamble that Taiwan could become internationally competitive in the production of labor-intensive manufactures based on a low-cost labor force that was comparatively well educated and skilled. This strategy turned out to be tremendously successful. Exports soared and pulled the economy to extremely high growth without significant inflation. Rapid growth, in turn, produced the resources both for a very high savings rate and for appreciable gains in the popular standard of living. The tight labor market and rising wages, however, suggested that this strategy might face some long-term constraints because Taiwan was gradually pricing itself out of the low-cost labor niche in the international economy.

Inflation, Crisis, and Governmental Response

The Arab oil embargo and accompanying escalation of energy prices shook the economies of most countries in both the developed and developing world. Taiwan certainly appeared to be a prime candidate for economic devastation. It imported almost all of its energy products, and as a highly trade-dependent economy, it was vulnerable to global inflation and instability in international markets for its manufactured products. On the other hand, the R.O.C.'s economy was seemingly quite strong as the result of its switch to export-led growth in the mid–1960s. Thus, while the R.O.C. was severely affected by the oil crisis, the domestic economy in 1973 appeared strong enough to absorb some of these disruptive pressures if the government could devise and implement a coherent strategy for managing the crisis.

Table 6.15 certainly demonstrates that the surge in oil prices sent major shockwaves through Taiwan's economy. As would be expected, the oil price explosion created massive inflationary pressures. Both wholesale and consumer prices, which had increased by under 5 percent a year for the preceding decade, leaped to almost 30 percent average inflation for 1973–1974, with 1974 seeing increases in the 40 percent to 50 percent range. There was more behind Taiwan's inflation than simply the Organization of Petroleum Exporting Countries (OPEC) revolution, however, since prices began to rise considerably in mid–1973, well before the Arab oil embargo (see Table 6.16). Thus sophisticated analysis of input-output tables indicates that oil price increases per se accounted for slightly over half of these jumps in the price indices. Ironically, the nation's trade success contributed significantly to the inflation problem. The large trade surpluses that Taiwan began to accumulate in the early 1970s stimulated a rapid expansion of money supply that rose by 30 percent in 1971–1972 and 50 percent in 1973 after much more moderate increases of 15 percent annually during the 1960s, thus transmitting a considerable inflationary pressure.[61]

The global and local inflation put an immediate damper on Taiwan's export performance, which had been outstanding in the early 1970s (e.g., real exports had grown by 30 percent annually during 1970–73; by the end of this period Taiwan was running a very healthy trade surplus equal to 15 percent of exports). First, the global economic crisis was quickly transferred to the R.O.C.'s externally oriented and dependent economy. Exports declined in real terms by over 6 percent per year in 1974–1975, as the proportion of GNP being exported fell from 42 percent to 35 percent between 1973 and 1975. Furthermore, real foreign investment, which (while erratic) had averaged increases of 20 percent per year over the previous decade, fell precipitously by 40 percent annually in these two years, dropping from 8 percent to 2.5 percent of total investment. Second, the import bill of energy-dependent Taiwan skyrocketed by 38 percent in real terms in 1974, creating a trade deficit of $1.3 billion (compared with a surplus of $0.7 billion in 1973) that equalled almost a quarter of total exports.

Poor performance in foreign trade, in turn, had a major adverse impact on the domestic economy, as would certainly be expected in a country that exported 40 percent to 50 percent of its domestic product. Real industrial production fell by 4.5 perent in 1974; Taiwan's GNP growth dropped to a minuscule 1.1 percent that year after the effects of inflation were controlled. Industry was particularly hard hit as manufacturing's share of net domestic product dropped from 36

Table 6.15
Socioeconomic Indicators during Oil Crisis*

	1973	1974	1975	1976
Population				
Total Pop (mil)	15.6	15.9	16.2	16.5
Pop Growth (%)	1.8	1.8	1.9	2.2
Econ Grth				
Real GNP Grth	12.8	1.1	4.3	13.9
GNP p.c. (US$)	695	913	956	1122
Real Ind Grth (%)	16.2	-4.5	9.5	23.3
Real Ag Grth (%)	2.7	1.9	-1.2	10.0
Energy (bil KWH)	17.9	18.9	21.2	24.7
Econ Structure				
Ind % NDP	43.8	41.2	39.2	42.7
Manf % NDP	36.3	32.9	29.3	32.6
Serv % NDP	42.1	44.3	45.9	43.9
Ag % NDP	14.1	14.5	14.9	13.4
Ag % Emplymt	30.5	30.9	30.4	29.0
State % Ind Prod	18.9	19.6	18.8	20.2
Savings & Invst				
Savings % GNP	34.6	31.7	26.9	32.5
GDCF % GDP	29.3	39.5	30.6	30.8
Real Sav Grth (%)	21.7	-7.5	-11.4	37.2
Real GDCF Grth (%)	28.2	36.4	-18.7	14.4
Rl Pv Inv Gth (%)	38.0	29.2	-44.4	26.3
Rl St Invst Grth (%)	12.9	49.9	23.0	5.7
Rl Pv Bk Ln Gth (%)	30.3	9.9	24.2	2.1
Rl Pub Bk Ln Grth (%)	7.0	34.3	42.5	8.8
Manf % GDCF	34.0	38.1	39.0	37.0
State % GDCF*	34.7	38.1	57.7	53.3
Inflation				
Cons Price Grth (%)	8.2	47.5	5.2	2.5
Whsl Prc Grth (%)	22.9	40.6	-5.1	2.8
Money Sup Grth (%)	50.4	10.5	28.8	25.1
Employment				
Tot Emplyd (1000s)	5327	5486	5521	5669
Unempl Rate*	1.3	1.5	2.4	1.7
Empl w/ Wk Ins (%)	25.9	26.3	28.4	30.5

Table 6.15 (Continued)

	1973	1974	1975	1976
Foreign Capital				
For Inv (mil US$)*	249	189	118	142
For Invst % GDCF*	7.9	3.3	2.5	2.5
Rl For Inv Grth (%)*	63.0	-42.7	-39.0	13.5
Net Fr Cap (ml US$)*	-567	1125	596	-270
NFC % GDCF*	-18.2	19.8	12.7	-4.7
Public Finance				
Govt Expd % GDP	23.0	18.2	23.0	23.6
Rl Gth Gvt Exp (%)	9.2	-14.8	37.4	12.4
Bud Bal (mil US$)	256	681	200	424
Bud Bal % Gov Revs	10.9	22.4	5.6	9.7
Adm & Def % Bud	41.4	41.0	39.2	36.6
Ed & Cul % Bud	16.9	16.7	16.4	15.9
Soc Relief % Bud	10.8	10.8	10.0	11.3
Trade				
Expt % GDP	41.9	39.2	34.7	44.5
Impt % GDP	35.6	48.7	39.0	41.5
Trd Bal (mil US$)	691	-1321	-643	567
Trd Bal % GDP	6.3	-9.5	-4.3	3.0
Trd Bal % Exports	15.0	-24.2	-12.4	6.7
Real Exp Grth (%)	24.3	-5.3	-7.8	45.7
Real Imp Grth (%)	25.3	38.3	-16.6	21.0
% Capt Goods Impts	28.6	30.7	30.6	29.1
% Cons Goods Impts	5.6	6.9	6.8	6.2
% Ind Exports	84.6	84.5	83.6	87.6
% Expts to US	37.4	36.1	34.3	37.2
% Expts to Jap	18.4	15.0	13.1	13.4
% Impts from US	25.1	24.1	27.8	23.7
% Impts from Jap	37.7	31.8	30.6	32.3
Standard of Living				
Income Ratio*	--	4.37	--	4.18
Gini Coeff	--	.32	--	.31
Food % Conspt*	41.3	44.3	44.2	42.1
Rl Manf Wg Inc (%)	1.1	-9.0	11.3	15.0
Hlth Pers (1000s)	20.4	22.5	26.6	32.0
Commc Disease Rate	1.3	1.0	0.8	1.0
Energy Cons (cal)	2754	2780	2722	2771
Protein Cons (gm)	73.7	74.2	74.7	75.9
% Prim Grads to Jr HS	83.9	84.3	88.6	90.1
Rl Ex/Pr St (1981 $)	7857	10158	11176	12646

*See Table 6.8 for explanatory notes.

Source: *Taiwan Statistical Data Book, 1987* (Taipei: Council for Economic Planning and Development, 1987), passim.

Table 6.16
Monthly Changes in Bank Deposits and Wholesale Prices (in current NT$)

	Bank Deposits	Wholesale Prices
1973		
May	3.2%	0.9%
June	2.3%	2.0%
July	2.1%	3.1%
Aug	3.0%	4.5%
Sept	0.8%	4.6%
Oct	-0.4%	4.3%
Nov	-0.2%	2.8%
Dec	0.4%	4.6%
1974		
Jan	-1.6%	12.9%
Feb	1.6%	12.9%
Mar	3.2%	-1.8%
Apr	3.2%	-3.0%
May	3.2%	-1.8%
June	3.9%	-1.1%
July	3.6%	-0.9%
Aug	4.0%	-0.1%
Sept	3.2%	-0.9%
Oct	3.0%	-1.4%
Nov	1.8%	-1.5%
Dec	3.5%	-0.1%

Source: Shirley W. Y. Kuo, *The Taiwan Economy in Transition* (Boulder, Colo.: Westview Press, 1983), p. 213.

percent in 1973 to 29 percent just two years later (although the manufacturing sector's priority in total investment remained constant). As would be expected, the rapid increase in energy consumption leveled off too. For example, energy use rose 20 percent between 1972 and 1975, compared with 60 percent for the preceding three-year period. Even agricultural production showed some slippage, falling from 2.5 percent to 0.5 percent growth between 1972–1973 and 1974–1975. Economic distress was reflected in a significant cutback in domestic savings as well. Real savings, which had grown by 20 percent a year in the early 1970s, fell by 7.5 percent in 1974 and 11.4 percent in 1975. Despite the drop off in foreign capital, total private investment remained buoyant in 1974 (i.e., it grew by 29 percent versus 38 percent in 1973) as domestic businessmen evidently tried to reinvest their profits to stay ahead of inflation. The effects of the deteriorating economy caught up with private-sector investment in 1975, though, as it plummeted 44.5 percent in that year and led to an overall drop of 14.5 percent in gross domestic capital formation (GDCF).

Not surprisingly, rapidly deteriorating economic performance hurt the popular standard of living as well. The growth rate in the number of jobs, which had expanded by 6 percent in 1972–1973, fell to 3 percent in 1974 and 0.6 percent in 1975 as unemployment almost doubled from 1.3 percent in 1973 to 2.4 percent two years later. The economic slowdown affected wages as well. Real monthly wages in the manufacturing sector, which had grown by 4 percent in 1972, only increased 1 percent the next year and then fell sharply by 9 percent in 1974. Falling income would be expected to hurt the quality of life for the average citizen. Atlhough there were only slight absolute dips in the standard of living as measured by calorie and protein consumption, long-term trends of increasing food quality and consumption were clearly interrupted. There was a larger blip in the trend for households to spend smaller proportions of their income on food (which dropped sharply from 48 percent in 1966 to 35 percent in 1980). Spending on food actually increased from 41 percent to 44 percent of family budgets between 1973 and 1974, implying a significant drop in discretionary income. Unlike in many developing countries, however, the poor did not have to bear a disproportionate share of the ill effects of the economic crisis, since Taiwan's low ratio of the richest to the poorest fifths of the population actually decreased further, from 4.5 to 4.2, between 1972 and 1976.

This externally induced economic crisis produced a strong challenge to the R.O.C., and the government responded quickly and actively to control it. In particular, four principal components of Taiwan's successful response can be delineated: (1) applying conservative fiscal measures to counter inflation, (2) managing inflationary pressures and psychology through a one-time major price increase, (3) using government spending and investment to reinvigorate the economy, and (4) enhancing international export competitiveness to stimulate another economic growth spurt.

The R.O.C. has always been highly sensitive to inflation and saw its containment of inflation during the early 1950s as a major reason for its economic success. Thus the government's first reaction to the oil price explosion was to institute stabilization measures to dampen inflation. A major component of the stabilization program, as in the 1950s, was a sharp increase in interest rates. After more moderate increases in interest rates proved ineffective, the "Stabilization Measures" of January 1974 imposed radical jumps averaging 33 percent for deposit rates and 25 percent for loan rates with greater rises for short-term rates.[62] This interest-rate policy proved successful in its deflationary aims of discouraging spending and promoting saving. Bank deposits, which had declined by 2 percent in current NT dollars between September 1973 and January 1974, grew by 3 percent a month for the rest of 1974 (see Table 6.16), and the rate of increase in loans to private corporations, measured in constant 1981 dollars, tumbled precipitously from 30 percent in 1973 to 10 percent in 1974 (see Table 6.15).

The state also used fiscal policy to dampen the inflationary pressures set off by the OPEC revolution. Real government expenditures that had grown by 9.5 percent in 1972 and 1973 were cut by 14.8 percent in 1974 as spending fell from 23 percent to 18 percent of GNP. In particular, the general area of administration and defense was cut (e.g., its proportion of the budget fell from 43.3 percent in 1972 to 36.6 percent in 1976). On the other hand, whereas education's share of the budget declined slightly, the government's investment in basic education, as indicated by real spending per primary student, continued its previous rapid escalation. This then created a significant surplus in the government budget, which rose as a proportion of total revenues from 4 percent in 1972 to 11 percent in 1973 to a high of 22 percent in 1974. Thus fiscal policy was clearly used in a deflationary manner.

The government also tried to control inflation by managing price increases through the monopolies exercised by government corporations, such as the China Petroleum Corporation and the Taiwan Power Company. Initially, the highly profitable China Petroleum Corporation tried to absorb the escalating oil prices, but when this proved impractical the R.O.C. opted for a one-shot major price increase. Thus the "Stabilization Measures" enacted in January 1974 included price hikes of 88 percent for oil products and 79 percent for electricity.[63] The government also moved quickly to control the inflationary pressures of the rapidly expanding money supply as its growth rate was cut back sharply from 50 percent in 1972 to 10.5 percent in 1973.

These measures, along with the stabilization of global energy prices, proved highly successful in bringing inflation under control in Taiwan. Although wholesale prices had increased by about 4 percent a month for the second half of 1973 and then leaped by 13 percent for each of the first two months of 1974, they actually fell slightly in every remaining month in 1974 and then dropped another 5 percent in 1975. Increases in consumer prices were somewhat higher, but they, too, were clearly under control by the end of 1974.

The regime's response to the economic crisis went far beyond conservative stabilization policies, though. As detailed above, the inflationary surge had undermined the R.O.C.'s growth, investment, and export competitiveness. Thus Taiwan faced the problems of inflation and recession simultaneously in a "stagflation" for which traditional Keynesian countercyclical remedies were insufficient. The government evidently composed a sophisticated policy package that coupled its deflationary measures with targeted economic stimuli. The early 1970s had seen the beginning of the "Ten Major Development Projects" in heavy industry and infrastructure. Thus their augmentation in the mid–1970s served several important purposes: providing a countercyclical stimulus to the economy, helping the structural transformation away from labor-intensive industry, and overcoming transportation and supply bottlenecks. In addition, significant cuts were enacted in 1974 in income and commodity taxes and in customs duties to provide an economic stimulus.[64]

In 1974, then, Taiwan simultaneously applied both the brake of fiscal conservatism and the accelerator of greatly increased public investment, mostly by state corporations. State investment, which had grown by 10 percent annually in 1972–1973, was increased by 50 percent in real terms to offset drops in foreign investment and growing pressures on the private sector. In part this was paid for by a reorientation in financial policy, as a large increase of 34 percent in bank loans to public corporations occurred in 1974 (compared with 6 percent to 7 percent in the previous two years). Because private investment was still expanding, as noted above, this resulted in only a modest increase of 35 percent to 38 percent in the public share of GDCF.

By 1975 the economic situation had changed considerably. Inflation had clearly been tamed, but the effects of the crisis were still quite evident in sluggish growth and export performance and in a disastrous drop of 44 percent in private investment. The government responded by removing the fiscal brake but keeping the investment accelerator pushed down. Government spending shot up by 37 percent in real terms, returning to its precrisis level of 23 percent of GNP, as the huge 1974 budgetary surplus of 22 percent of total revenues dropped to under 6 percent. The investment stimulus continued as well. Real state investment grew by 23 percent, and bank loans to public corporations jumped 42.5 percent, almost twice the rate for private loans. Coupled with the precipitous drop in private investment, the state's share of GDCF rose to 57.7 percent, indicating that the state had assumed a major role in supporting future economic growth on the island.

Simply acting to reinvigorate the economy, of course, was not enough for a country so export-dependent as Taiwan. If investment, production, and growth were to rebound, external markets had to be found. The tremendous drop in the R.O.C.'s trade performance during 1974–1975 described above certainly reflected disruptions in global demand stemming from the oil price explosion, but it was also caused to a significant extent by a marked decline in the competitiveness of Taiwan's exports. The government's successful stabilization and stimulation program, though, might have been expected to improve the competitive position of Taiwan's products in international trade.

Shirley Kuo has devised a measure of export competitiveness based on relative prices and foreign exchange rates between the R.O.C. and its trade partners that she terms the "real effective exchange rate" (REER). This index is based on a norm of 100 for the year 1980, when Taiwan was again feeling the effects of an oil price surge and of a large accumulated trade balance. Increases in this index, thus, indicate decreased trade competitiveness, since this means that the prices of Taiwan's goods are rising in foreign markets; conversely, decreases demonstrate increased competitiveness.[65] The movement of this index during 1972–1977 is reported in Table 6.17, along with several other indicators of trade performance, some of which are repeated from Table 6.15 for comparative purposes.

Clearly, export competitiveness had a large impact on trade performance (although it was not the only factor at work); just as clearly the R.O.C.'s strong anti-inflation policies had major positive impact on the nation's ability to compete

Table 6.17
R.O.C. Export Performance

	1972	1973	1974	1975	1976	1977
Export Competitiveness						
Expt Rl Eff Ex Rate*	86.3	94.1	112.7	99.6	97.8	93.4
Real Export Grth	37.0%	24.3%	-5.3%	-7.8%	45.8%	7.7%
Real Import Grth	28.8%	25.3%	38.3%	-16.6%	21.0%	5.2%
Exports/GNP	38.0%	41.9%	39.2%	34.7%	44.5%	43.6%
Trd Bal/Expts	15.7%	15.0%	-24.2%	-12.4%	6.7%	8.8%
Export Markets						
United States	41.9%	37.4%	36.1%	34.3%	37.2%	38.8%
Japan	12.6%	18.3%	15.0%	13.1%	13.4%	12.0%
Asian Deving**	16.8%	16.1%	16.6%	19.0%	16.3%	15.6%
Devd Countries**	17.1%	17.5%	20.6%	20.4%	18.5%	17.8%
Oil Producers**	2.2%	1.7%	2.2%	4.4%	3.6%	4.6%
Export Goods						
Food Products	15.5%	14.4%	14.8%	15.4%	11.7%	12.5%
Txt, Clth, Ftwr	33.1%	33.4%	31.9%	34.8%	34.8%	30.6%
Elec Eqmt & Mac	15.7%	16.6%	16.4%	13.2%	14.6%	15.0%
Iron, Stl, Metal Prds	4.8%	3.5%	4.7%	4.8%	4.4%	4.6%
Ind Mach	3.2%	3.2%	4.5%	4.2%	4.0%	4.1%
Import Goods						
Minerals	8.3%	4.2%	13.1%	13.6%	17.2%	18.7%
Chemicals	10.5%	10.9%	10.7%	11.6%	11.5%	10.6%
Iron, Stl, Met Prds	9.4%	9.9%	10.7%	9.2%	9.1%	9.9%
Elec Eqmt & Mac	14.6%	16.0%	10.6%	9.3%	11.1%	11.1%
Ind & Trans Mach	18.0%	16.9%	21.9%	22.5%	19.5%	15.8%

*Based on an index of 1980 value = 100.

**Asian Developing Countries include Hong Kong, Indonesia, Malaysia, Philippines, Singapore, South Korea, and Thailand. Developed Market Economies (Devd Countries) include Australia, Belgium, Canada, France, Italy, Netherlands, Sweden, United Kingdom, and West Germany. Oil Producers include Iran, Kuwait, Nigeria, and Saudi Arabia.

Source: *Monthly Statistics of Exports and Imports, The Republic of China, June 1986* (Taipei: Department of Statistics, Ministry of Finance, 1986), passim; *Taiwan Statistical Data Book, 1987* (Taipei: Council for Economic Planning and Development, 1987), passim; and Shirley W. Y. Kuo, *The Taiwan Economy in Transition* (Boulder, Colo.: Westview Press, 1983), p. 307.

in the international marketplace. Rising inflation in 1973 and 1974 strongly undercut Taiwan's international economic position as its REER index for exports leaped by an astounding 30 percent from 86.3 in 1972 to 112.7 in 1974, leading to the very marked decline in trade performance discussed earlier. The R.O.C.'s ability to move decisively and effectively against inflation, however, meant that the country's prices stabilized more quickly than those in most of its trade partners, thereby greatly increasing the competitiveness of its exports as the REER index dropped sharply in 1975 to 99.6 and more slowly over the next two years to 93.4 in 1977—approximately what it had been in 1973.

Trade performance improved accordingly, but in a slightly different pattern. Despite Taiwan's improved competitiveness in 1975, exports actually did worse than in the preceding year, falling by 8 percent in real terms as opposed to 5 percent in 1974, reflecting both the uncertain international market and a time lag before price changes affect trade. Real imports, however, were cut by nearly 17 percent, which resulted in the trade deficit, expressed as a proportion of exports, being halved from 24 percent to 12 percent. Taiwan's major improvement in export competitiveness and stabilizing world markets came together in 1976 to create a remarkable trade resurgence. Exports shot up 46 percent in real terms, over twice the increase in imports, thereby restoring a healthy trade balance and moving up to 44.5 percent of GNP.

These changes in Taiwan's export competitiveness were also reflected somewhat in the changes in the country's composition of trade, depicted in Table 6.17. Taiwan's traditional major export partners in the United States and Japan suffered the most in the downturn of the mid–1970s as both dropped significantly in their share of total exports, indicating a special loss of competitiveness in these markets (also note Taiwan's breaking into the lucrative markets in the oil-producing countries). In contrast, the United States took the preponderant share of Taiwan's expanding exports in 1976–1977, while trade with Japan stayed stable in percentage terms and trade with other developing countries in Asia suffered the most. This implies that Taiwan's increased competitiveness was greatest in goods sold to developed countries, as well as indicating the United States' declining economic position vis-a-vis Japan.

In terms of the commodity composition of exports, the R.O.C.'s export decline in 1974–1975 was most pronounced both in the traditional textile, clothing, and footwear industries and in the emerging electronics sector, indicating special problems in labor-intensive production. Heavy industries, such as iron and steel and industrial machinery, actually increased their share slightly (but still remained fairly unimportant in the overall export structure). In contrast, electronics led the export recovery, while the position of the traditional light industries began to slip noticeably, reflecting the country's strategy of emphasizing more capital- and technology-intensive production. The changes in the import mix were fairly predictable. Rising energy prices created a fourfold increase in minerals' percentage of total imports from 4 percent to 17 percent between 1973 and 1976. The economic crisis of 1974–1975 was accompanied by a significant drop in the percentage of electronics imports, probably reflecting decreased consumer purchases. Finally, the regime's support of investment in heavy industry and infrastructure brought a substantial increase in the importation of industrial and transportation machinery during 1974–1976.

The recovery of foreign trade, in turn, stimulated a new spurt of economic growth. Real GNP growth shot up to "double digits" of 14 percent in 1976 and 10 percent in 1977; real industrial production increased even faster; and even agricultural production jumped by 10 percent in 1976 and 4 percent in 1977. Savings and investment responded to the new growth spurt as well. Real savings jumped by 37 percent in 1976 and again surpassed 30 percent of GNP. Private domestic investment increased by 26 percent and foreign capital inflows by 13 percent as well. As a result, total employment grew at 4 percent for each of these two years, and the unemployment rate fell below 2 percent again. More spectacularly, real wages in manufacturing averaged increases of 13 percent during 1975–1977—by far the largest three-year spurt in the history of Taiwan—and the various indicators of the popular standard of living resumed their upward trends.

In response to the revived economy and growing private investment, the government cut back on its own stimulative activities and policies. The growth rate in real government expenditures was cut in half from the high of 37 percent in 1975, and its share of GNP stabilized at 23 percent to 25 percent. The cutbacks in state investment and bank loans to public corporations were even more pronounced, as the regime seemed willing to allow the private sector to reassert economic predominance.

In sum, the strong external economic shock resulting from the OPEC revolution had only a fleeting impact on the R.O.C., unlike its more devastating consequences for many other countries in both the developed and especially the developing worlds. This occurred partly because Taiwan already had created a strong and expanding economic base that was able to absorb the shock. Considerable credit must be given to the Chiang Kai-shek government, though, for responding with a sophisticated and subtle program. Even before the debate on "stagflation" had really commenced, the regime successfully blended deflationary and stimulative policies and fine-tuned the degree of government activities to rapidly changing macroeconomic conditions.

The 1980s: Economic Cycles, Dynamism, and Dilemmas

In the late 1970s, then, Taiwan's economy seemed ready to resume its dynamic expansion. The R.O.C. still faced the problem of transforming its economic structures, however, as it was pricing itself out of the low-cost labor niche in the global economy. Moreover, economic progress put increasing stress on some of its institutions, such as the conservative financial system; a new inflationary surge of oil prices occurred during 1979–1980; and the R.O.C.'s very success in expanding exports led to major trade conflicts, especially with the United States, during the mid-1980s. Thus the economy had passed through several pronounced cycles over the past decade, and despite its continued dynamism, it faced several important dilemmas about how to adjust to new challenges in order to maintain its vitality.

The late 1970s witnessed another round of extremely rapid growth. Real GNP averaged 12 percent annual growth for the three-year period of 1976–1978 as Taiwan's per capita income rose by more than half, from $956 to $1,628. Export-based industrialism clearly formed the central thrust as exports skyrocketed by 26 percent a year and industry by 20 percent a year in real terms over this three-year period. Consequently manufacturing's share of net domestic product rebounded from 29 percent in 1975 to 34 percent in 1978, and the trade surplus grew to $1.7 billion in 1978, which amounted to a very healthy 6 percent of GDP and 13 percent of exports. Inflation also remained in check, averaging under 5 percent a year. In addition, savings and investment remained quite high at over 30 percent of GNP. Finally, the state continued to decrease the economic activities that it had undertaken to counter the downswing in the business cycle in the mid–1970s. The state's share of total investment fell from 58 percent in 1975 to 39 percent in 1979 as public-sector investment only increased by 1 percent a year during 1976–1978; bank loans to the private sector grew faster than those to the public sector.

The second oil price explosion of 1979–1980 that followed the outbreak of the Iran-Iraq war brought this growth surge to an end, however. The aggregate data in Table 6.18 reveal a pattern of deja vu, although the effects were not as extreme as those produced by the first crisis. The inflation rate jumped to 17 percent for both wholesale prices in 1979–1980 and consumer prices in 1980–1981. The import bill jumped as oil rose from 15 percent to 25 percent of total import costs,[66] wiping out the strong trade surplus of 1978. However, in contrast to 1974–1975, exports continued to increase in real terms (11 percent in 1979 and 6 percent in 1980) and did not fall appreciably as a percentage of total national product, and the country did not fall into a trade deficit. This squeeze in the foreign trade sector, in turn, produced a deceleration in economic growth, although, again, this was not as severe as during the first oil crisis. Real GNP growth dropped from 14 percent in 1978 to 8.5 percent in 1979 to 7 percent in 1980; industrial output growth fell more sharply, from 22.5 percent in 1978 to 6.5 percent in 1979–1980, but this did not lead to increased unemployment. The savings and investment rates were not affected by the economic downturn, however, providing another indication that it was not as severe as the recession of the mid–1970s.

Given the almost spectacular success of the policies described in the preceding section, it is hardly surprising that the R.O.C. implemented a similar strategy in the 1980s. Conservative fiscal and monetary policies were quickly imposed to dampen inflation. Government spending was held almost constant in real terms in 1979 as the budget surplus rose more than fourfold, from $182 million to $908 million, which constituted 11.4 percent of revenues; the annual increase in money supply was cut dramatically from 35 percent in 1977–1978 to 8 percent in 1979; and interest rates were increased substantially.[67] In addition, energy policies were formulated aimed at promoting greater conservation, alternate sources, and a transformation to less energy-intensive production. As in the

Table 6.18
Socioeconomic Indicators during 1980s*

	1977	1978	1979	1980	1981	1982	1983	1984	1985	1986
Population										
Total Pop (mil)	16.8	17.1	17.5	17.8	18.1	18.5	18.7	19.0	19.3	19.5
Pop Growth (%)	1.8	1.9	2.0	1.9	1.9	1.8	1.5	1.5	1.3	1.0
Econ Growth										
Real GNP Grth (%)	10.1	13.9	8.5	7.1	5.7	3.3	7.9	10.5	5.1	10.8
GNP p.c. (US$)	1288	1628	1895	2311	2548	2540	2748	3048	3143	3748
Real Ind Grth (%)	13.3	22.5	6.4	6.8	3.5	-0.6	14.1	12.2	1.4	14.9
Real Ag Grth (%)	4.1	-1.8	5.2	0.0	-0.7	1.0	1.6	1.9	2.0	-1.6
Energy (bil KWH)	27.6	31.9	35.3	37.9	37.4	38.1	42.3	45.8	47.9	53.8
Hvy Ind Grth (%)	20.5	27.2	6.8	9.2	5.0	-2.1	21.9	14.6	-0.8	19.7
Lt Ind Grth (%)	7.1	21.1	4.5	3.2	2.2	5.2	8.7	10.8	3.5	11.8
Econ Structure										
Ind % NDP	43.5	45.1	45.3	45.0	44.6	43.0	43.7	45.4	45.2	47.3
Manf % NDP	32.8	34.3	34.8	34.2	33.9	33.4	34.0	36.2	36.0	39.0
Serv % NDP	44.0	43.7	44.4	45.8	46.7	47.8	47.5	47.0	47.9	46.1
Ag % NDP	12.5	11.2	10.3	9.2	8.7	9.2	8.8	7.6	6.9	6.6
Ag % Emplymt	26.7	24.9	21.5	19.5	18.8	18.9	18.6	17.6	17.5	17.0
State % Ind Prod	20.5	19.3	19.0	18.7	17.9	18.0	17.4	16.4	16.1	14.8
Savings & Invst										
Savings % GNP	32.9	34.9	34.5	33.0	32.0	30.4	32.1	33.7	33.5	37.8
GDCF % GDP	28.4	28.6	33.3	34.3	30.3	25.2	23.0	21.5	17.9	16.7
Real Sav Grth (%)	11.3	20.8	7.2	2.4	2.5	-1.8	13.8	16.1	4.5	25.1
Real GDCF Grth (%)	1.2	14.0	26.4	10.4	-6.2	-14.6	-1.6	2.4	-13.3	2.9
Rl Pv Invst Gth (%)	6.8	27.2	39.0	-6.1	-7.9	-21.7	8.4	14.5	-19.0	8.7
Rl St Inv Gth (%)	-3.7	1.2	10.8	35.8	-4.4	-7.4	-10.2	-10.2	-5.6	-3.7
Rl Pv Bk Ln Gth (%)	4.2	16.7	-3.8	-0.0	-3.4	6.1	11.6	12.3	-1.4	-0.0
Rl Pb Bk Ln Gth (%)	12.6	3.6	16.5	29.9	1.2	15.9	2.9	-3.8	-2.5	-4.8
Manf % GDCF	29.3	24.0	27.2	29.2	29.9	24.9	24.7	30.3	27.6	33.3
State % GDCF*	50.7	45.0	39.4	48.5	49.4	53.6	48.9	42.8	46.7	43.6
Inflation										
Cons Prc Grth (%)	7.0	5.8	9.8	19.0	16.3	3.0	1.4	-0.0	-0.2	0.7
Whsl Prc Grth (%)	2.8	3.5	13.8	21.5	7.6	-0.2	-1.2	0.5	-2.6	-3.4
Money Sup Grth (%)	33.6	37.0	7.7	22.7	13.8	14.6	18.4	9.3	12.2	51.4
Public Finance										
Govt Expd % GDP	25.6	25.6	23.6	26.2	26.9	27.3	25.7	23.9	24.0	25.0
Rl Gvt Expd Gth (%)	20.6	11.9	0.8	16.9	11.9	10.2	-1.0	3.3	8.4	8.8
Bud Bal (mil US$)	35	182	908	589	122	-69	121	166	271	94
Bud Bal % Gov Revs	0.7	2.9	11.4	6.4	1.0	-0.6	0.6	2.8	2.1	0.6
Adm & Def % Bud	36.1	37.1	37.5	39.1	33.9	34.4	38.0	34.1	35.0	35.3
Ed & Cul % Bud	14.7	17.2	16.2	15.3	17.5	17.8	19.5	19.0	19.8	20.5
Soc Relief % Bud	10.6	10.8	11.4	11.1	11.8	14.5	15.2	15.7	15.7	15.6

Table 6.18 (Continued)

	1977	1978	1979	1980	1981	1982	1983	1984	1985	1986
Employment										
Tot Emplyd (1000s)	5980	6228	6424	6547	6672	6811	7070	7308	7428	7733
Unempl Rate*	1.9	1.7	1.2	1.2	1.4	2.1	2.7	2.3	2.9	2.6
Empl w/ Wk Ins (%)	31.5	33.8	35.7	38.9	41.8	43.4	47.1	50.6	55.9	62.4
Trade										
Expt % GDP	43.6	47.9	49.0	48.5	47.7	46.5	49.2	52.9	51.0	54.9
Impt % GDP	39.7	41.8	45.1	48.5	44.8	39.6	39.8	38.2	33.4	33.4
Trd Bal (mil US$)	850	1660	1329	78	1411	3316	4836	8497	10621	15624
Trd Bal % GDP	3.9	6.1	3.9	0.1	2.9	6.9	9.4	14.7	17.6	21.4
Trd Bal % Exports	8.8	12.8	8.0	0.1	6.2	14.8	19.0	27.7	34.4	39.1
Real Exp Grth (%)	7.7	25.2	11.0	6.0	3.9	0.7	14.1	18.8	1.3	19.2
Real Imp Grth (%)	5.2	19.8	17.2	15.0	-2.4	-8.6	8.5	6.1	-8.1	10.8
% Capt Gds Impts	25.8	24.7	24.6	23.4	25.7	24.8	23.6	23.7	23.8	26.9
% Cons Gds Impts	7.8	6.8	6.4	5.8	6.1	7.9	7.6	7.5	8.5	8.6
% Ind Exports	87.5	89.2	90.5	90.8	92.2	92.4	93.1	93.9	93.8	93.5
% Expts to US	38.8	39.5	35.1	34.1	36.1	39.4	45.1	48.8	48.1	47.7
% Expts to Jap	12.0	12.4	14.0	11.0	10.9	10.7	9.9	10.5	11.3	11.4
% Impts from US	23.1	21.5	22.9	23.7	22.5	24.1	22.9	23.0	23.6	22.4
% Impts from Jap	31.1	33.4	30.9	27.1	28.0	25.3	27.5	29.3	27.6	34.2
Foreign Capital										
For Inv (mil $US)*	164	213	329	466	396	380	405	559	703	770
For Invst % GDCF*	2.7	2.8	3.0	3.3	2.7	3.2	3.5	4.6	6.6	6.5
Rl For Inv Gth (%)*	8.8	20.1	35.1	22.0	-22.7	-1.5	7.4	35.4	26.2	1.0
Net Fr Cp (ml US$)*	-929	-1667	-386	552	-724	-2494	-4651	-7152	-9605	-15588
NFC % GDCF*	-15.2	-22.0	-3.5	3.9	-5.0	-20.8	-39.7	-58.5	-90.9	-131.9
Standard of Living										
Income Ratio*	--	4.18	4.34	4.17	4.21	4.29	4.36	4.40	4.50	--
Food % Consumption	41.1	39.8	36.8	34.7	34.3	33.9	33.5	32.3	--	--
Rl Manf Wg Inc (%)	12.4	5.3	10.3	3.0	2.1	6.6	4.8	15.5	-1.7	6.2
Hlth Pers (1000s)	34.7	36.2	39.6	42.4	45.7	50.0	52.6	57.4	66.3	69.8
Commc Disease Rate	0.7	0.5	0.5	1.0	0.5	1.4	1.7	1.1	2.1	0.9
Energy Cons (cal)	2805	2822	2845	2812	2729	2749	2721	2811	2874	2890
Protein Cons (gm)	76.6	77.0	78.7	78.2	75.3	76.6	77.0	80.2	83.1	84.0
% Prim Grads to Jr HS	91.0	94.2	94.7	96.2	96.8	97.4	98.6	98.6	99.3	99.4
Real Expd per Prim Stdt (1981 NT$)	11993	12972	14775	16735	18353	19373	18914	24358	24518	24526

*See Table 6.8 for explanatory notes.

Source: *Taiwan Statistical Data Book, 1987* (Taipei: Council for Economic Planning and Development, 1987), passim.

previous crisis, the state also moved to combat recession by increasing state investment (which jumped 36 percent in real terms in 1980 and increased its share of GDCF from 39.4 percent to 48.5 percent).

These policies had almost immediate effects. Inflation almost completely disappeared by 1982; large and rapidly increasing trade balances re-emerged in 1981; and energy consumption increased only slightly between 1979 and 1981. Consequently the deflationary fiscal and monetary policies were phased out fairly quickly during 1980–1981. Unlike with the first crisis, however, taming inflation and running a trade surplus did not reinvigorate the economy. In fact, economic performance continued to deteriorate during 1981–1982. The growth rate of real GNP continued to decelerate to 5.7 percent in 1981 and 3.3 percent in 1982; the decline was even more marked in real industrial growth, which actually declined by 0.6 percent in 1982; and unemployment began to increase from 1.2 percent in 1980 to 2.1 percent in 1982 to 2.7 percent in 1983. The investment rate also fell significantly from 30 percent of GDCF in 1982 to 25 percent in 1983.

The cause for this continued slowdown clearly rested in the foreign trade sector. Unlike the recovery of the mid–1970s, exports continued to stagnate even after inflation was brought under control. The growth of exports in real terms continued to decline from 6 percent in 1980 to 4 percent in 1981 to 1 percent in 1982 (trade surpluses grew because the value of imports actually fell in real terms over these two years). The global recession and stagflation of the early 1980s, in contrast with the first and more severe oil crisis, therefore, produced greater contractions of world markets, which more strongly limited Taiwan's ability to use its rapid taming of inflation as a mechanism for boosting exports through enhanced international competitiveness. Moreover, economic expansion in Taiwan had become increasingly dependent on growing export markets (see Table 6.11), so that poor export performance stifled economic recovery.

Just as the economic scene appeared to be turning bleak, however, the sustained economic recovery that began in the United States in mid–1983 opened the way for another period of rapid growth based on expanding export production. Real exports leaped by 14 percent in 1983 and 19 percent in 1984, stagnated in 1985, and then jumped again by 25 percent a year during 1986–1987. The centrality of the American market to this new export surge is demonstrated by the fact that the United States' share of Taiwan's exports rose quickly from 34 percent in 1980 to 39 percent in 1982 to 45 percent in 1983 to 48 percent during 1984–1986. The trade surplus burgeoned as well from $1.4 billion in 1981 to $4.8 billion in 1983 to $8.5 billion in 1984 to $15.6 billion in 1986 to $19.2 billion in 1987. Rapid trade expansion revved up the economy, which grew by 9 percent a year during 1983–1984, 5 percent in the minirecession of 1985, and 11 percent during 1986–1987 (real GNP growth was projected to be in the 7 percent to 7.5 percent range for 1988 and 1989). GNP per capita rose rapidly, too, from $1,895 in 1979 to $3,048 in 1984 to $3,748 in 1986 to $4,991 in 1987 to $6,000 at the end of 1988 (although much of the jump in 1986–1988 results from a 40 percent appreciation of the NT$ against the US$). Real industrial product grew somewhat faster than GNP except for 1985, when it was 1.4 percent, as it averaged 13 percent annually for 1983–1984 and 1986–1987, indicating the increasingly industrial nature of the island's economy.[68]

The economic cycles of the 1970s and 1980s occurred against the backdrop of a basic change in economic strategy that was taken in response to Taiwan's declining competitiveness in labor-intensive production. Thus the government began to guide the economy toward a new transformation to such capital-intensive industries as machinery, steel, petrochemicals, and nonferrous metallurgy and to various types of high-technology industry, especially in the electronics and information-processing fields. Thus Taiwan hoped to establish a new international comparative advantage in more technology, skill, and capital-intensive products. During the 1970s the Ten Major Development Projects—which included steel, petrochemicals, shipbuilding, nuclear energy, and infrastructure projects—became the highly visible central component and symbol of this strategy. In the 1980s two new sets of government programs (with twelve and fourteen projects, respectively) have been started. In particular, the Science-Based Industrial Park that opened in Hsin-chu in 1980 was designed to become the R.O.C.'s Silicon Valley, which would bring together both domestic and foreign firms in high-technology industries.[69]

In a structural sense the new industries were rather diverse. For example, the steel industry was based on a state corporation; petrochemicals involved a complex "triple alliance" between state enterprises, MNCs, and the domestic private sector; and much of the high-tech industry was centered on relatively small, innovative firms.[70] As a result, the state's role in the economy fluctuated somewhat, being pushed upward by state investment in heavy industry and infrastructure projects and downward by the dynamic expansion of the high-technology sector. Thus the state's share of industrial production stabilized at 19 percent to 20 percent during the 1970s and then dropped gradually to 15 percent in 1986. In contrast, state investment, while swinging much more widely because of the government's countercyclical policies, was considerably higher in the 1980s than during the export-surge period (e.g., it averaged 45 percent of total GDCF for 1983–1986, compared with 35 percent for 1963–1968).

The success of this economic strategy was directly reflected in the R.O.C.'s production and trade statistics. During 1977–1986, for example, heavy industry grew at an annual rate of 12.2 percent, compared with 7.8 percent for light industry (see Table 6.18); the fastest annual growth rates for individual products over this period were generally recorded by sophisticated manufactures (along with a few simpler consumer products)—telephone sets (48 percent), electric fans (39 percent), electronic calculators (26 percent), machine tools (20 percent), motor vehicles (20 percent), sound recorders (18 percent), and integrated circuits (17 percent).[71] Consequently, although import substitution had little effect on the overall economy after the mid–1960s, significant import-substitution gains were made in such specific industries as machinery, iron and steel, electronics products, artificial fibers and fabrics, heavy chemicals, and rubber.[72] Taiwan's

Table 6.19
R.O.C.'s Export Mix

	1970	1975	1980	1986
Food Processing Products	12.8%	10.8%	5.6%	5.1%
Textiles	31.7%	27.8%	22.6%	18.3%
Wood Products	8.6%	4.4%	6.0%	4.4%
Rubber & Plastics	1.0%	7.4%	8.9%	9.4%
Chemicals	2.4%	2.0%	2.3%	2.7%
Electronics	12.3%	14.7%	18.2%	22.3%
Metal Manufactures	1.9%	2.5%	4.3%	5.9%
Machinery	3.2%	3.6%	3.8%	4.0%

Source: *Taiwan Statistical Data Book, 1987* (Taipei: Council for Economic Planning and Development, 1987), pp. 213, 228–229.

export mix reflected this industrial upgrading too, as shown by the data in Table 6.19. As late as 1970, food, textile, and wood manufactures composed 53 percent of all exports. Over the next two decades, these light industries consistently lost ground to more sophisticated products, falling to 28 percent of all exports in 1986. The principal export source became electronics, combining both high technology and labor-intensive assembly, which rose from 12 percent to 22 percent of all exports during this period. Heavier industries, such as rubber and plastics, metal manufactures, and machinery, also became more important as their combined share of the R.O.C.'s export mix tripled from 6 percent in 1970 to 19.5 percent in 1986. Thus Taiwan has clearly established its international competitiveness in these products and proved that it could move beyond assembly work by low-cost labor.

The new economic strategy also changed Taiwan's policy toward foreign capital. As discussed in the description of the export surge, foreign capital played a significant role in Taiwan's rapid growth during the 1960s and early 1970s by providing some technology and especially by integrating Taiwan into international marketing structures. With the R.O.C.'s dynamic growth, these contributions became less important. Foreign capital's share of total investment slipped to the 2 percent to 3 percent range after 1973. Foreign capital had been channeled into the export sector, which, as has been seen, became increasingly central in the R.O.C.'s economic dynamism. However, even here local businesses accounted for over 75 percent of exports during the 1970s; in the electronics industry, where foreign capital had been especially important, domestic firms' share of exports shot up from 29 percent in 1974 to 49.5 percent in 1980.[73]

The strategy of industrial upgrading created a stronger need for technological development. To some extent, this was pursued by encouraging local research and development activities, but the government also moved to attract foreign capital in the hope of promoting technology transfer. Thus many of the regulations governing foreign investment were loosened and liberalized during the 1980s with the result that foreign capital increased substantially from $164 million in 1977 to $466 million in 1980 to $770 million in 1986 to $1,223 million in 1987, which was equivalent to about 6.5 percent of total investment during 1985–1986, although foreign investment dropped sharply in the first half of 1988.[74] Foreign capital continued to be concentrated in high technology and heavy industries, particularly machinery, electronics, and nonmetallic minerals.[75] In general, Denis Simon concluded that the R.O.C. has been fairly successful in promoting technology transfers to help upgrade its industrial structure, although limited government leverage and domestic technological sophistication put definite constraints on this effort.[76] Thus the R.O.C. appeared to continue its successful record of attracting foreign capital and being able to control it in the sense of directing it into priority sectors and preventing it from dominating or denationalizing the domestic economy.

Taiwan's success so far in managing a basic economic transformation to more sophisticated production is not without significant problems and challenges, however. First, the R.O.C.'s industrial structure has been marked by a much greater role for small and medium enterprises than that of its Asian competitors, such as Japan and Korea. Rather than integrated factories under single ownership and management, complex subcontracting relations exist among small-scale entrepreneurs who own single pieces of equipment and capital that are put to multiple uses. This organizational form possessed important advantages for Taiwan's export-led growth. Problems of excess capacity were reduced; more important, producers could respond quickly to demand:

Taiwanese firms are noted by foreign buyers for their willingness to change, adapt and meet their customer's requirements even if it involves costly, small runs of special orders. Thus, they were able to rapidly respond to changes in fashion or trends as expressed by buyers in the developed economies.[77]

The emphasis on small-scale business also helped to promote technological diffusion from foreign capital to the domestic economy, since Chinese managers would work for several years for MNCs and then start their own firms. Thus the strong role of small businesses in Taiwan's economy promoted internal competitiveness and external flexibility—two interdependent factors that lie at the heart of the R.O.C.'s "economic miracle."[78]

Several central elements in the traditional Confucian culture, furthermore, appear to stimulate the small-scale enterprise and successful entrepreneurship that mark Taiwan's economic development. First, the Confucian value system provided, at least in theory and often in practice, a flexible social hierarchy with considerable upward mobility opportunities that were determined by a person's ability. Although education and civil service examination scores (rather than entrepreneurial skills) were most important for this mobility until the twentieth century, the absence of a rigid inherited class system certainly was important in

stimulating widespread business activities. Second, the strong emphasis on family
provides an incentive for savings and entrepreneurship to help build family
fortunes, analogously to the individualism that has been viewed as underlying
Western capitalist development.[79] Consequently Taiwan's economy has been
dominated by family-owned enterprises (extended families are necessary for
large-scale firms). According to Susan Greenhalgh, such firms are marked by
strong personal loyalty, rapid informal communications, and diversification and
decentralization—all of which promote economic flexibility and risk-spreading.[80]

However, such firms are undercapitalized and do not possess the resources to
undertake large-scale (or even more modest) research and development efforts.
Moreover, their short-term perspectives lead to excessive speculation and illegal
activities, such as counterfeiting, which distort the economy and embarrass the
government. Thus their former advantages are increasingly seen as hindrances
to the upgrading and transformation of Taiwan's economy to more technology-
and capital-intensive industries. The extent of this problem is not easy to determine, though. For example, small and medium-sized firms have assumed a
leading role in Taiwan's successful high-tech industries, pursuing strategies of
what Danny Lam has called ''guerrilla capitalism''[81]; Yin-min Ho has demonstrated that during the rapid export surge of the 1960s and 1970s, small firms
were just as economically efficient as large ones in the R.O.C.[82] Moreover, in
Japan small-scale flexible production continues to provide a major dynamic for
the sophisticated machine tool industry.[83] Thus the government faces a dilemma
in that its current efforts to make the private sector better structured for industrial
upgrading may, in fact, undercut one of the country's prime comparative advantages—the ability for ''flexible production.''

This dilemma is also reflected in the decreased willingness of Taiwan businessmen to invest in the economy. Up through the early 1980s the savings and
investment rates were relatively equal. Beginning in 1982, however, investment
began to fall steadily to 17 percent of GDP in 1986, while the savings rate
remained well above 30 percent. This resulted from a 2 percent-a-year decline
in real private investment (despite the inflows of foreign capital noted above);
unlike earlier private investment declines, this one did not produce a countervailing upswing in state investment, which actually fell by 7.5 percent annually
in real terms between 1982 and 1986. Thus, although the investment rate is still
healthy by international standards, its continued decline bespeaks a growing
threat to Taiwan's economic vitality.

△ The business community has clearly decided to invest abroad both because
of uncertainty about the R.O.C.'s international status and, much more important,
because of the country's declining ability to compete in the industries with which
it is most familiar. Thus outflow of capital from Taiwan skyrocketed from less
than $1 billion in 1981 to $15.6 billion in 1986. About 70 percent of the R.O.C.'s
outward investment has been directed toward the United States, about half of it
in the electronics field, as Taiwan businessmen seemingly hope to avoid protectionist pressures.[84] In the late 1980s, though, more foreign investment has

Table 6.20
Improved Standard of Living

	1946-1952*	1983
Health		
Crude Death Rate (per 1000 pop)	9.9	4.9
Life Expectancy (years)	58.6	72.4
Daily Energy Intake p.c. (calories)	2078	2720
Daily Protein Intake p.c. (grams)	49	77
Housing		
Living Space p.c. (sq meters)	4.6	17.5
Households with Electric Lighting (%)	33.0%	99.7%
Households with Piped Water (%)	14.4%	77.6%
Housing Invst % GNP	1.0%	3.4%
Education		
Literacy rate (%)	45.0%	90.0%
Children 6-11 in Primary School (%)	78.6%	99.8%
Children 12-14 in Junior HS (%)	48.3%**	90.1%
Youth 15-17 in Senior HS (%)	28.3%**	63.8%
Youth 18-21 in Jr. Col or College (%)	11.3%**	25.9%
Transportation and Communications		
Automobiles (per 1000 pop)	1	57
Motorcycles (per 1000 pop)	0.2	298
Telephones (per 1000 pop)	4	259
Mail per capita	7	62

*1946, 1949, or 1952.
**1966.

Source: Shirley W. Y. Kuo, "The Taiwan Economy in Transition," Paper presented at the Conference on Prospects for the Economy of Taiwan, Republic of China, in 1980s, National Central University, R.O.C., June 17–18, 1985, p. 23.

been directed toward Third World countries, where Taiwanese entrepreneurs can take advantage of low-cost labor to replicate their successful ventures at home. In particular, increasing flows of foreign investment to the mainland have become a central component of the "China fever" described in chapter 5.

Second, economic changes during the 1980s have at least the potential for eroding one of Taiwan's brightest accomplishments—the achievement of "growth with equity." Rapid growth in the R.O.C. has brought sustained improvements in the popular standard of living, as summarized by the data on health, housing, education, and transportation in Table 6.20. During the three decades between the 1950s and 1980s, for example, the crude death rate was more than cut in half; life expectancy increased from age fifty-eight to age seventy-two; the quantity and quality of diets increased considerably; the living space available per person quadrupled; the percentage of houses with electricity rose threefold (33 percent to 99 percent); the literacy rate doubled from 45 percent to 90 percent; education through junior high school became nearly universal; and the number of automobiles, motorcycles, and telephones skyrocketed. In addition, as displayed in the aggregate data in Table 6.18, the decade between 1977 and 1986 witnessed a continuing expansion in disposable income (i.e., the proportion of household budgets spent on food dropped from 41 percent to 32 percent), a doubling in supply of health personnel from thirty-five to seventy per 1,000 population, a continued low communicable disease rate, and a doubling in the real amount of educational funding per primary school student. Also relevant for the quality of life, Taiwan has undergone the "demographic transition" normally associated with industrialization and urbanization; by the late 1980s its population growth rate had fallen to about 1 percent. In comparative terms, moveover, Taiwan ranked much closer to the developed than the developing worlds in terms of an index of "physical quality of life," based on literacy rate, infant mortality, and life expectancy, as early as 1970 and had one of the fastest growth rates in the world on this index over the 1950s and 1960s.[85] Thus the R.O.C. has seemingly made considerable progress along the transition to becoming a middle-class society. For example, at the end of 1987, 100 households each possessed 107 motorcycles, 103 color televisions, 99 refrigerators, 89 telephones, 82 washing machines, 37 air conditioners, and 16 automobiles.[86]

Beyond such indicators of a radically improving standard of living, Taiwan has been quite proud of its record for increasing income equality, which approached the level found in advanced industrial nations during early the 1980s, in contrast to the normal pattern in developing countries where growth initially produces increased inequality. Over the first half of the 1980s, however, income inequality has begun to increase significantly. For example, the ratio of the total income of the richest fifth of the population to the poorest fifth rose from a low of 4.17 in 1980 to 4.50 in 1985, approximately the level that existed in the early 1970s, although this is still one of the lowest levels of inequality in the world[87]; it has almost certainly grown since then. The reason for this trend can easily be found in the transformation away from labor-intensive production, which has decreased the demand for unskilled and semiskilled workers. For example, in contrast to annual increases in real manufacturing wages of 10 percent per year between 1975 and 1979, these wages increased only 5 percent annually between 1980 and 1986. Additionally, the decline of the agricultural sector over the past two decades, which was discussed in the first section of this chapter, has evoked fears of growing urban-rural inequality (see the data on relative farm and nonfarm incomes in Table 6.5).[88]

Thus Taiwan's new economic strategy is now evidently increasing income differences, which partially explains the growing political assertiveness of labor and farmers in the late 1980s, noted in chapter 5. In addition, social change is breaking down the strong family solidarity (e.g., rising divorce rates and numbers of the elderly not living with their children) that has in the past supported many people with low personal incomes.[89] This suggests a need for a change in the regime's outlook toward social programs. In the past the government supported such programs as education that promote an "equality of opportunity" for citizens, while generally abjuring most social services that mitigate "inequalities in outcome.'' Rapid economic growth and family obligation were normally sufficient to provide a minimal standard of living for most of the population. With a growing number of ''losers'' from economic change and declining family support, however, the maintenance of ''growth with equity'' may well depend on a greatly increased welfare program.

More broadly, the challenge of the R.O.C.'s new economic transformation to small and medium-sized enterprises threatens a key factor behind Taiwan's good record for income equality and popular standard of living. In most developing countries, small-scale production (which has been termed the ''informal sector'') is based on exploitative wages, miserable working conditions, and many entrepreneurs who slip over the edge of financial ruin.[90] In Taiwan such conditions certainly exist; the lot of the ''part-time proletariat'' is one of ''bitter labor.''[91] However, there were a number of important mitigating conditions. Full employment exerted upward pressure on wages; most of the participants (e.g., unmarried young women) did not seem themselves as entering lifetime careers; and substantial upward mobility opportunities existed for both small businessmen and workers.[92] However, growing pressure on the small businesses in Taiwan could well drive it toward the less salubrious conditions that exist in the informal sector elsewhere.

Third, the government's attitudes toward social policy may be coming under stress as well. Sustained growth has permitted the R.O.C. to maintain fiscal conservatism in its budgetary policies and avoid the trap of ''indebted industrialization.'' Except for a small deficit in 1982, healthy budget surpluses were recorded throughout the 1980s; the ratio of government spending to GNP has remained fairly constant—23 percent in the 1970s and 25 percent in the 1980s. Thus Taiwan's foreign borrowing has been fairly limited; it used its huge accumulation of foreign reserves to pay back loans in the late 1980s; and in 1987 its debt service ratio stood at a low 4.5 percent of annual exports.[93]

While the R.O.C. has been conservative in its balanced budget and comparatively low spending levels, its budget priorities have moved in at least a slightly more liberal direction. For example, the share of administration and defense in the national budget fell from 60 percent in the 1950s to 50 percent in the late 1960s to 35 percent in the mid–1980s, while there have been corresponding increases in the budget allocations for education and culture and especially for social relief (whose share of the national budget doubled from 8 percent to 16 percent between 1968 and 1988). Most spectacularly, the proposed 1989 budget of $25.5 billion represented a major break from the past. It contained a major 25 percent increase over the year before and a deficit equal to 22 percent of government spending (two-thirds of which will be paid for by government bonds and one-third by drawing down on previous surpluses). There are several goals for this dramatic break with past fiscal conservatism: soaking up excess capital to combat inflation (in a far from conventional approach), providing investment funds to replace deteriorating private investment, giving added support for education and for social services and welfare, and increasing defense spending.[94] Furthermore, the proportion of the workforce receiving limited social protection through "labor insurance"[95] doubled from 31 percent to 62 percent between 1977 and 1986 (see Table 6.18). As in many other countries, therefore, economic development has stimulated a more liberal social role for the government in the R.O.C. Still, the government continues to place much more emphasis on economic expansion than on welfare policies to promote popular living standards[96]; in view of what may be a trend toward growing inequality, this may not be enough.

Fourth, the R.O.C. is now suffering from the fallout of the very success in international markets that has produced huge trade surpluses and the second largest accumulation of foreign reserves in the world of $73.5 billion at the end of 1988 (behind Japan's $92.5 billion).[97] The United States has accounted for at least three-quarters of the trade surplus recently ($10 billion of $10.6 billion in 1985, $13.6 billion of $15.6 billion in 1986, and $16.1 billion of $19.2 billion in 1987). This, in turn, has led to growing trade conflicts and American pressure on Taiwan. Because the United States remains the R.O.C.'s dominant export market (although trade diversification efforts reduced the United States' share of total exports from 48 percent in 1986 to about 35 percent in late–1988), such conflicts certainly have the potential to undercut Taiwan's economic position. For example, the 40-percent appreciation of the NT$ against the US$ between late 1986 and mid–1988 that the United States forced on the R.O.C. will almost certiainly dampen exports in the near future.[98] There is also the potential problem that the huge trade surpluses and accumulation of foreign reserves will set off an inflationary spiral as their smaller counterparts did in the early and late 1970s, despite the government's efforts since the late 1970s to stabilize exchange rates and money supply in response to the huge trade and price shifts that occurred.[99] For example, money supply jumped by a whopping 51 percent in 1986. Moreover, although the official rate of price increases has only been 1 percent or so since 1985, the tremendous explosion in land and stock prices that has occurred is a good indication of substantial hidden inflation (although there was a considerable stock market crash in October 1988). For example, land prices in some parts of Taipei have surpassed those in Manhattan.[100]

Finally, although Taiwan's macroeconomic strategies have proved phenomenally successful, rapid development and the creation of an increasingly sophisticated industrial economy have spotlighted several important microeconomic problems that need to be treated. For example, the financial system is antiquated and not adequate for a rapidly expanding economy (for example, its rigidities have been partially blamed for the decreasing investment in the late 1980s)[101]; the Cathay Group scandal of 1985 showed that business and political corruption represent a significant challenge; the efficiency of many state corporations is coming under question; there is a clear need for taxing and regulatory reform; and growing foreign pressures for the opening up of the domestic economy have generated strong internal resistance.[102] Thus, despite its past successes (or, in a few cases, because of them) Taiwan is now facing a series of complex and controversial decisions about the domestic economy.

The Dynamics of Rapid Growth in the Republic of China

In sum, the R.O.C. has been able to achieve rapid economic growth, major structural transformation, a rising popular standard of living, and a relatively equal distribution of income over the past forty years, despite its inauspicious political and economic circumstances in the early 1950s. This record of ''growth with equity'' represents one of the most spectacular Third World success stories in the postwar era. However, the nation is now confronting a series of economic dilemmas that, while probably not overly serious in the short term, raise significant questions about long-term strategies.

The state has clearly guided Taiwan's economic development. It has not done this through direct planning or the institution of a command economy. Rather, it has led the country through several key structural transformations that have allowed it to establish and benefit from a niche of ''comparative advantage'' in the international economic system while maintaining a market-based domestic economy. Thus both ''state'' and ''market'' play integral roles in a successful political economy.[103] For Taiwan, state policy created a broad economic environment in which entrepreneurial activity could flourish and transformed that environment periodically as the island's comparative advantage in the global economy changed. The dynamics of the R.O.C.'s growth, though, include not just the institutions and incentives created by the state, but also just as important, if not more so, the social norms and values that underlie private economic activities in the country (see the discussion of the impact of Confucian culture on economic development in chapter 7). The combination of state and market in the R.O.C., therefore, has created an extremely flexible economy that has undergone continuous restructuring to remain highly competitive in international markets.[104]

The question of external dependency is also relevant for understanding the dynamics of growth in Taiwan. The R.O.C.'s economic miracle indicates to an even greater extent than its diplomatic record, discussed in chapter 4, that small and dependent nations can prosper in the contemporary international system if they are adept enough at ''statecraft.''[105] In fact, Taiwan's success flows from being able to manipulate dependency conditions (i.e., reliance on a single capitalist patron, substantial entrance of foreign capital, and full integration into the global economy) that have been associated with economic distortions and stagnation in other developing countries. But, just as surely, Taiwan also illustrates the continuing reality of external dependency, for its current dilemmas generally stem from external changes (i.e., increasing U.S. economic pressure and the emergence of new labor-intensive producers). Thus, it might be ventured, external challenge and dependency have played key roles in forcing the continuing economic changes on which the R.O.C.'s success has rested up to now.

Notes

1. Bernard Gallin, *Hsin Hsing, Taiwan: A Chinese Village in Change* (Berkeley: University of California Press, 1966), ch. 2; A. James Gregor with Maria Hsia Chang

and Andrew B. Zimmerman, *Ideology and Development: Sun Yat-sen and the Econmic History of Taiwan* (Berkeley: Institute of East Asian Studies, University of Callifornia, 1981), ch. 2; Samuel P. S. Ho, *Economic Development of Taiwan, 1860–1970* (New Haven, Conn.: Yale University Press, 1978), pp. 159–174; Anthony Y. C. Koo, *The Role of Land Reform in Economic Development: A Case Study of Taiwan* (New York: Praeger, 1968) ch. 3; and Joseph A. Yager, *Transforming Agriculture in Taiwan: The Experience of the Joint Commission on Rural Reconstruction* (Ithaca, N.Y.: Cornell University Press, 1988), ch. 7.

2. *Taiwan Statistical Data Book, 1987* (Taipei: Council for Economic Planning and Development, 1987), p. 65.

3. For broader treatments of the income and standard of living gains that land reform brought to the countryside see Koo, *Case Study of Taiwan*, chs. 4–8; and Martin M. C. Yang, *Socio-economic Results of Land Reform in Taiwan* (Honolulu, Hawaii: East-West Center Press, 1970), chs. 4–8. In addition to strictly economic gains, major improvements in the rural health program were implemented, for example. See Yager, *Transforming Agriculture in Taiwan*, ch. 12.

4. T. H. Shen, *The Sino-American Joint Commission on Rural Reconstruction: Twenty Years of Cooperation for Agricultural Development* (Ithaca, N.Y.: Cornell University Press, 1970); and Yager, *Transforming Agriculture in Taiwan*, especially chs. 8 and 9. Gallin, *Hsin Hsing*, pp. 69–79 presents a case study of the operation of the Farmers' Association in one village.

5. Rong-I Wu, "The Distinctive Features of Taiwan's Development," in Peter L. Berger and Hsin-Huang Michael Hsaio, eds., *In Search of an East Asian Development Model* (New Brunswick, N.J.: Transaction Books, 1988), pp. 186–190. K. T. Li, *Economic Transformation of Taiwan, ROC* (London: Shepheard-Walwyn, 1988), ch. 29 presents a good case study of increasing rice production and productivity.

6. Erik Thorbecke, "Agricultural Development," in Walter Galenson, ed., *Economic Growth and Structural Change in Taiwan: The Postwar Experience of the Republic of China* (Ithaca, N.Y.: Cornell University Press, 1979), especially pp. 159, 182–183.

7. *Taiwan Statistical Data Book, 1987*, pp. 48, 50, 74.

8. Ho, *Economic Development of Taiwan*, p. 155.

9. Thorbecke, "Agricultural Development," p. 135. Yager, *Transforming Agriculture in Taiwan*, ch. 5 provides an excellent summary of agricultural development during these "good" years.

10. *Taiwan Statistical Data Book, 1987*, p. 302.

11. Walter Galenson, "The Labor Force, Wages, and Living Standards," in Walter Galenson, ed., *Economic Growth and Structural Change in Taiwan: The Postwar Experience of the Republic of China* (Ithaca, N.Y.: Cornell University Press, 1979), pp. 436–437.

12. Yager, *Transforming Agriculture in Taiwan*, pp. 247–253.

13. Shirley W. Y. Kuo, *The Taiwan Economy in Transition*, (Boulder, Colo.: Westview Press, 1983), p. 32.

14. Teng-hui Lee, *Intersectoral Capital Flows in the Economic Development of Taiwan, 1895–1960* (Ithaca, N.Y.: Cornell University Press, 1971), pp. 20–21. Kuo, *Taiwan Economy in Transition*, pp. 30–38 provides another detailed and sophisticated discussion of the hidden rice tax and its consequences for Taiwan's agriculture.

15. Eldon L. Johnson, Frederick C. Fliegel, John L. Woods, and Mel C. Chu, *The Agricultural Technology System of Taiwan* (Urbana: Office of International Agriculture, University of Illinois, 1987), p. A2.

16. Shu-min Huang, *Agricultural Degradation: Changing Community Systems in Rural Taiwan* (Lanham, Md.: University Press of America, 1981); and Yager, *Transforming Agriculture in Taiwan*, ch. 6 & pp. 257–263 discuss agricultural problems and the government's policy responses over the last decade in much broader perspective.

17. Ibid., p. 14.

18. Ibid., especially chs. 4–6; and *Taiwan Statistical Book, 1987*, pp. 69–73.

19. Simon Kuznets, "Growth and Structural Shifts," in Walter Galenson, ed., *Economic Growth and Structural Change in Taiwan: The Postwar Experience of the Republic of China* (Ithaca, N.Y.: Cornell University Press, 1979), pp. 52–53.

20. Kuo, *Taiwan Economy in Transition*, ch. 3; and K. T. Li, *The Evolution of Policy Behind Taiwan's Development Success* (New Haven: Yale University Press, 1988), pp. 119–132.

21. Tibor Scitovsky, "Economic Development in Taiwan and South Korea, 1965–1981," in Lawrence J. Lau, ed., *Models of Development: A Comparative Study of Economic Growth in South Korea and Taiwan* (San Francisco: Institute for Contemporary Studies, 1986), pp. 145–151.

22. Kuo, *Taiwan Economy in Transition*, ch. 13; Ching-yuan Lin, *Industrialization in Taiwan, 1946–72: Trade and Import-Substitution Policies for Developing Countries* (New York: Praeger, 1973), pp. 33–38; and Erik Lundberg, "Fiscal and Monetary Policies," in Walter Galenson, ed., *Economic Growth and Structural Change in Taiwan: The Postwar Experience of the Republic of China* (Ithaca, N.Y.: Cornell University Press, 1979), pp. 369–378.

23. Ho, *Economic Development of Taiwan*, pp. 190–193; and Lin, *Industrialization in Taiwan*, pp. 39–50.

24. Lin, *Industrialization in Taiwan*, p. 66.

25. Ibid., p. 68.

26. Ho, *Economic Development of Taiwan*, pp. 187–189.

27. Shirley W. Y. Kuo, Gustav Ranis, and John C. H. Fei, *The Taiwan Success Story: Rapid Growth with Improved Distribution in the Republic of China* (Boulder, Colo.: Westview Press, 1981), pp. 70–71.

28. David W. Chang, "U.S. Aid and Economic Progress in Taiwan," *Asian Survey* 5:3 (March 1965), pp. 152–160; Neil H. Jacoby, *U.S. Aid to Taiwan: A Study of Foreign Aid, Self-Help, and Development* (New York: Praeger, 1966); and Lundberg, "Fiscal and Monetary Policies," pp. 369–378.

29. Lin, *Industrialization in Taiwan*, p. 68.

30. Ibid., pp. 70–74.

31. Thomas B. Gold, *State and Society in the Taiwan Miracle* (Armonk, N.Y.: M. E. Sharpe, 1986), pp. 74–78.

32. Li, *Taiwan's Development Success*, ch. 4. Roy Hofheinz, Jr. and Kent E. Calder, *The Eastasia Edge* (New York: Basic Books, 1982), pp. 188–191, describe the Kaohsiung EPZ in detail.

33. Li, *Taiwan's Development Success*, pp. 133–141; Lin, *Industrialization in Taiwan*, ch. 5; Maurice Scott, "Foreign Trade," in Walter Galenson, ed., *Economic Growth and Structural Change in Taiwan: The Postwar Experience of the Republic of China* (Ithaca, N.Y.: Cornell University Press, 1979), pp. 321–345; and Rong-I Wu, "Trade Liberalization and Economic Development in Taiwan," *Journal of Chinese Studies* 4:1 (April 1987), pp. 81–98.

34. Shirley W. Y. Kuo and John C. H. Fei, "Causes and Roles of Export Expansion

in the Republic of China," in Walter Galenson, ed., *Foreign Trade and Investment: Economic Development in the Newly Industrializing Asian Countries* (Madison: University of Wisconsin Press, 1985), pp. 51–52. T. H. Lee and Kuo-shu Liang, "Taiwan," in Bela Balassa and Associates, eds., *Development Strategies in Semi-Industrial Economies* (Baltimore: Johns Hopkins University Press, 1982), pp. 318–332, provide a much more detailed discussion of nominal and effective protection during this period.

35. Scott, "Foreign Trade," p. 334.

36. Ho, *Economic Development of Taiwan*, pp. 221–223.

37. See Kuo, *Taiwan Economy in Transition*, pp. 54–57, for the data on "broad" unemployment.

38. Ho, *Economic Development of Taiwan*, pp. 216–220. For example, between 1954 and 1966 the share of "early" industries (food and textiles) in manufacturing value added fell from 61 percent to 33 percent, while the shares of "middle" industries (for example, wood, rubber, and chemicals) and "late" industries (for example, basic metals, machinery, and electronics) rose from 24 percent and 32 percent and from 13 percent to 33 percent respectively.

39. Gustav Ranis, "Industrial Development," in Walter Galenson, ed., *Economic Growth and Structural Change in Taiwan: The Postwar Experience of the Republic of China* (Ithaca, N.Y.: Cornell University Press, 1979), p. 223.

40. Ibid., pp. 222–232; Samuel P. S. Ho, "Decentralized Industrialization and Rural Development: Evidence from Taiwan," *Economic Development and Cultural Change* 28:1 (October 1979), pp. 77–96; and Yin-min Ho, "The Production Structure of the Manufacturing Sector and Its Distribution Implications: The Case of Taiwan," *Economic Development and Culture Change* 28:2 (June 1980), pp. 321–343.

41. Lundberg, "Fiscal and Monetary Policies," pp. 276–280, 287–294.

42. Gold, *State and Society*, ch. 6.

43. Chi Shive, "Trade Patterns and Trends of Taiwan," in Colin I. Bradford, Jr., and William H. Branson, eds., *Trade and Structural Change in Pacific Asia* (Chicago: University of Chicago Press, 1985), pp. 309–312.

44. Ranis, "Industrial Development," p. 252.

45. For a more detailed discussion of the impact of export growth on production and employment, see Ho, *Economic Development of Taiwan*, pp. 198–205; Kuo et al., *Taiwan Success Story*, ch. 6; and Kuo and Fei, "Causes and Roles of Export Expansion," pp. 66–76.

46. Ho, "Manufacturing Sector," pp. 321–343; and Ramon H. Meyers, "The Economic Development of the Republic of China on Taiwan, 1965–1981," in Lawrence J. Lau, ed., *Models of Development: A Comparative Study of Economic Growth in South Korea and Taiwan* (San Francisco, Calif.: Institute for Contemporary Studies, 1986), pp. 28–29.

47. Hsin-Huang Michael Hsiao, "An East Asian Development Model: Empirical Explorations," in Peter L. Berger and Hsin-Huang Michael Hsiao, eds., *In Search of an East Asian Development Model* (New Brunswick, N.J.: Transaction Books, 1988), pp. 34–35, 47–49.

48. Kuo and Fei, "Causes and Roles of Export Expansion," pp. 62–66; Lee and Liang, "Taiwan," pp. 341–346; Lin, *Industrialization in Taiwan*, pp. 131–137; Ranis, "Industrial Development," pp. 235–241; Scott, "Foreign Trade," pp. 353–369; and Shive, "Trade Patterns and Trends," pp. 316–320.

49. Gustav Ranis and Chi Shive, "Direct Foreign Investment in Taiwan's Development," in Walter Galenson, ed., *Foreign Trade and Investment: Economic Devel-*

opment and the Newly Industrializing Asian Countries (Madison: University of Wisconsin Press, 1985), p. 131.

50. Ho, *Economic Development of Taiwan*, pp. 215–220.

51. Kuo and Fei, "Causes and Roles of Export Expansion," pp. 56–57.

52. Lundberg, "Fiscal and Monetary Policies," pp. 298–300; and Myers, "Economic Development," pp. 16–19.

53. Myers, "Economic Development," pp. 31–34, 47–49; and Scitovsky, "Taiwan and South Korea," pp. 170–178.

54. Ho, *Economic Development of Taiwan*, pp. 240–246; and Lin, *Industrialization in Taiwan*, pp. 128–131.

55. Thomas J. Biersteker, *Distortion or Development? Contending Perspectives on the Multinational Corporation* (Cambridge, Mass.: MIT Press, 1981), chs. 1–3, presents an excellent summary of the contrasting developmentalist and dependency hypotheses about MNCs. Gregor with Chang and Zimmerman, *Ideology and Development*, pp. 97–106, summarize the role of foreign capital in Taiwan's development.

56. Ranis and Shive, "Direct Foreign Investment in Taiwan's Development," pp. 85–137. Also, see Lin, *Industrialization in Taiwan*, pp. 137–143.

57. Stephan Haggard and Tun-jen Cheng, "State and Foreign Capital in the East Asian NICs," in Frederic C. Deyo, ed., *The Political Economy of the New Asian Industrialism* (Ithaca, N.Y.: Cornell University Press, 1987), pp. 115–116. For example, over time new foreign-invested firms became much more export-oriented, indicating the success of the government's strategy of using foreign capital to stimulate exports. Thus MNCs established before 1960 exported only 18 percent of their output; this share of exports in total output escalated rapidly to 37 percent for those established during 1961–1966, 75 percent for those established during 1967–1971, and 93 percent for those established in 1973.

58. Thomas B. Gold, "Entrepreneurs, Multinationals, and the State," in Edwin A. Winckler and Susan Greenhalgh, eds., *Contending Approaches to the Political Economy of Taiwan* (Armonk, N.Y.: M. E. Sharpe, 1988), pp. 175–205; Gold, *State and Society*, pp. 83–87; Haggard and Cheng, "State and Foreign Capital," pp. 86–101; Ranis and Shive, "Direct Foreign Investment in Taiwan's Development," pp. 85–137; and Scitovsky, "South Korea and Taiwan," pp. 163–164.

59. Galenson, "Labor Force, Wages, and Living Standards," pp. 395–401; Lin, *Industrialization in Taiwan*, pp. 149–154; Andrew Mason, Sung-Yeal Koo, and Wi-sup Song, "Labor Force and Industrial Development in the Pacific Basin," in Roger Benjamin and Robert T. Kudrle, eds., *The Industrial Future of the Pacific Basin* (Boulder, Colo.: Westview Press, 1984), pp. 172–178; and Charlotte Shiang-yun Wang, "Social Mobility in Taiwan," in James C. Hsiung, ed., *Contemporary Republic of China: The Taiwan Experience, 1950–1980* (New York: Praeger, 1981), pp. 246–257.

60. John C. H. Fei, Gustav Ranis, and Shirley W. Y. Kuo, *Growth with Equity: The Taiwan Case* (New York: Oxford University Press, 1979), provide the most detailed and sophisticated analysis of income inequality in Taiwan. Also see Susan Greenhalgh, "Supranational Processes of Income Distribution," in Edwin A. Winckler and Susan Greenhalgh, eds., *Contending Approaches to the Political Economy of Taiwan* (Armonk, N.Y.: M. E. Sharpe, 1988), pp. 67–100.

61. Kuo, *Taiwan Economy in Transition*, chs. 9, 10; and Shive, "Trade Patterns and Trends," pp. 320–325.

62. Kuo, *Taiwan Economy in Transition*, ch. 10.

63. Ibid.

64. Ranis, "Industrial Development," pp. 255–260; and Li, *Economic Transformation of Taiwan*, ch. 28.

65. Kuo, *Taiwan Economy in Transition*, pp. 206–208.

66. Shirley W. Y. Kuo, "The Taiwan Economy in Transition." Paper presented at the Conference on Prospects for the Economy of Taiwan, Republic of China, in the 1980s, National Central University, R.O.C., June 17–18, 1985, p. 6.

67. Unlike most of the other deflationary policies that were milder than those imposed during the mid–1970s, the increases in interest rates were similar, if not greater. For example, the rediscount rate rose from 8.5 percent to 10.75 percent in 1973 and from 8.25 percent to 11 percent in 1979. See *Taiwan Statistical Data Book, 1987* (Taipei: Council for Economic Planning and Development, 1987), p. 145.

68. For 1987 data see U.S. Department of Commerce, International Trade Administration, *Foreign Economic Trends and Their Implications for the United States: Taiwan* (Washington, D.C.: U.S. Government Printing Office, 1988), p. 2.

69. Yuan-li Wu, *Becoming an Industrialized Nation: ROC's Development on Taiwan* (New York: Praeger, 1985), presents the most detailed discussion of this strategic reorientation. Also, see Gold, *State and Society*, ch. 7; Li, *Economic Transformation of Taiwan*, ch. 24; and Denis Fred Simon, "Taiwan's Political Economy and the Evolving Links Between the PRC, Hong Kong, and Taiwan," *AEI Foreign Policy and Defense Review* 6:3 (No. 3, 1986), pp. 42–51.

70. Gold, *State and Society*, pp. 100–106.

71. *Taiwan Statistical Data Book, 1987*, pp. 92–96.

72. Shive, "Trade Patterns and Trends," pp. 326–328.

73. Ranis and Shive, "Direct Foreign Investment in Taiwan's Development," p. 109.

74. U.S. Department of Commerce, International Trade Administration, *Investment Climate Statement: Taiwan* (Washington, D.C.: U.S. Government Printing Office, 1988).

75. Kuo, "Taiwan Economy in Transition," pp. 15–17.

76. Denis Fred Simon, "Technology Transfer and National Autonomy," in Edwin A. Winckler and Susan Greenhalgh, eds., *Contending Approaches to the Political Economy of Taiwan* (Armonk, N.Y.: M. E. Sharpe, 1988), pp. 206–223.

77. Danny Kin-Kong Lam, "Guerrilla Capitalism: Export Oriented Firms and the Economic Miracle in Taiwan (1973–1987)." Paper presented at the Annual Meeting of the America Association for Chinese Studies, Stanford University, October 21–23, 1988.

78. Ibid.; and Myers, "Economic Development," pp. 54–58.

79. John C. H. Fei, "Economic Development and Traditional Chinese Cultural Values," *Journal of Chinese Studies* 3:1 (April 1986), pp. 109–124; Susan Greenhalgh, "Networks and Their Nodes: Urban Society in Taiwan," *China Quarterly* 99 (September 1984), pp. 529–552; Stevan Harrell, "Why Do the Chinese Work So Hard? Reflections on an Entrepreneurial Ethic," *Modern China* 11:2 (April 1985), pp. 203–226; Herman Kahn, *World Economic Development 1979 and Beyond* (Boulder, Colo.: Westview Press, 1979), pp. 118–123; Wen Lang Li, "Entrepreneurial Roles and Societal Development in Taiwan," *Journal of Chinese Studies* 3:1 (April 1986), pp. 77–96; Robert G. Sutter, *Taiwan: Entering the 21st Century* (Lanham, Md.: University Press of America, 1988), ch. 3; Edwin A. Winckler, "Statism and Familism on Taiwan," in George C. Lodge and Ezra F. Vogel, eds., *Ideology and National Competitiveness: An Analysis of Nine Countries* (Boston, Mass.: Harvard Business School Press, 1987), pp. 173–206; Siu-lun Wong, "The Applicability of Asian Family Values to Other Sociocultural Settings," in

Peter L. Berger and Hsin-Huang Michael Hsiao, eds., *In Search of an East Asian Development Model* (New Brunswick, N.J.: Transaction Books, 1988), pp. 134–152; Siu-lun Wong, "Modernization and Chinese Culture in Hong Kong," *China Quarterly* 106 (June 1986), pp. 306–325; and Wu, *Becoming an Industrialized Nation*, ch. 7.

80. Susan Greenhalgh, "Families and Networks in Taiwan's Economic Development," in Edwin A. Winckler and Susan Greenhalgh, eds., *Contending Approaches to the Political Economy of Taiwan* (Armonk, N.Y.: M. E. Sharpe, 1988), pp. 224–245.

81. Lam, "Guerrilla Capitalism."

82. Ho, "Manufacturing Sector," pp. 321–343.

83. David Friedman, *The Misunderstood Miracle: Industrial Development and Political Change in Japan* (Ithaca, N.Y.: Cornell University Press, 1988).

84. Evelyn Richards, "Taiwan's Latest Export: Money," *Washington Post* 112:125 (April 9, 1989), pp. 141, 148, and 149; and U.S. Department of Commerce, *Investment Climate*, pp. 14–16.

85. Morris David Morris, *Measuring the Condition of the World's Poor: The Physical Quality of Life Index* (New York: Pergamon, 1979), pp. 68–69, 75.

86. Fei et al., *Growth with Equity*, present the most sophisticated analysis of income inequality. The data on household amenities come from *Free China Journal* 6:11 (February 20 1989), p. 7. For broader treatments of social development see Li, *Economic Transformation of Taiwan*, ch. 34; Wen Lang Li, "Social Development in the Republic of China, 1949–1981," in Hungdah Chiu and Shao-Chuan Leng, eds., *China: Seventy Years After the Hsin Hai Revolution* (Charlottesville, Va.: University of Virginia Press, 1984), pp. 478–499; Wen-hui Tsai, "Taiwan's Social Developments," in Hungdah Chiu, ed., *Survey of Recent Developments in China (Mainland and Taiwan), 1985–1986* (Baltimore, Md.: School of Law, University of Maryland, 1987), pp. 125–138; Yung Wei, "Modernization Process in Taiwan: An Allocative Analysis," *Asian Survey* 16:3 (March 1976), pp. 249–269; and Yung Wei, "Taiwan: A Modernizing Chinese Society," in Paul K. T. Sih, ed., *Taiwan in Modern Times* (New York: St. John's University Press, 1973), pp. 435–505. In addition, Li, *Taiwan's Development Success*, ch. 2 discusses the regime's population policy and the political limits on it.

87. Greenhalgh, "Income Distribution," p. 73.

88. Yun-peng Chu and Tien-wang Tsaur, "Growth, Stability, and Income Distribution in Taiwan." Paper presented at the Annual Meeting of the Western Social Science Association, San Diego, April 25–28, 1984.

89. Osman Tseng, "Industrialization Jolts the Family," *Free China Review* 38:12 (December 1988), pp. 12–15.

90. Alejandro Portes and John Walton, *Labor, Class and the International System* (New York: Academic Press, 1981).

91. Hill Gates, "Dependency and the Part-time Proletariat in Taiwan," *Modern China* 5:3 (July 1979), pp. 381–407.

92. Robert W. Stites, "Industrial Work as an Entrepreneurial Strategy," *Modern China* 11:2 (April 1985), pp. 227–246.

93. U.S. Department of Commerce, *Foreign Economic Trends: Taiwan*, p. 2; and Jeff Frieden, "Third World Indebted Industrialization: International Finance and State Capital in Mexico, Brazil, Algeria, and South Korea," *International Organization* 35:3 (Summer 1981), pp. 407–431 discusses the problem of "Indebted Industrialization."

94. I-hsin Chen and Wen-cheng Wu, "Record NT$699.77 Billion ROC Budget Proposed," *Free China Journal* 6:23 (April 3 1989), p. 5.

95. Galenson, "The Labor Force, Wages, and Living Standards," pp. 444–445, describes the system of labor insurance.

96. For example, income distribution in Taiwan is almost completely unaffected by taxes and government transfers. See Kuo et al., *Taiwan Success Story*, ch. 7.

97. "President Lee Indicates ROC Seeks Opportunities to Rejoin International Organizations," *Pacific Cultural Foundation Newsletter* 138 (December 1988), p. 2.

98. Susan Chira, "Taiwan Shift Jolts U.S. on Trade," *New York Times* 137: 47,505 (May 14, 1988), pp. 37–38; Li, *Taiwan's Development Success*, pp. 130–131; and U.S. Department of Commerce, *Foreign Economic Trends: Taiwan*, pp. 5–8.

99. Myers, "Economic Development," pp. 51–52.

100. John F. Copper, "Taiwan: A Nation in Transition," *Current History* 88:537 (April 1989), p. 174; and James D. Seymour, "Taiwan in 1988: No More Bandits," *Asian Survey* 29:1 (January 1989), p. 55.

101. For descriptions of the financial system and some of the major issues surrounding it see J. Alexander Caldwell, "The Financial System in Taiwan: Structure, Functions and Issues for the Future," *Asian Survey* 16:8 (August 1976), pp. 729–751; Gold, *State and Society*, pp. 108–110; Li, *Taiwan's Development Success*, pp. 109–110; Robert Wade, "East Asian Financial Systems as a Challenge to Economics: Lessons from Taiwan," *California Management Review* 27:4 (Summer 1985), pp. 106–127; Wu, *Becoming an Industrialized Nation*, ch. 4; Norman Yin, "Rejuvenating the Financial System," *Free China Review* 39:1 (January 1989), pp. 4–7; and Peter C. Y. Chow, "Money Market Segmentation and Financial Liberalization: A Revised Financial Repression Thesis in Taiwan," *Journal of Chinese Studies* 4:1 (April 1987), pp. 99–116. Wade, however, argues that the rigidities in the financial system have had some value for the state's industrial policy and have been much more market-conforming than state regulations in many other countries.

102. Kuo, "Taiwan Economy in Transition," provides a good summary of these issues.

103. Robert Gilpin, *The Political Economy of International Relations* (Princeton, N.J.: Princeton University Press, 1987), ch. 1, 3, 5.

104. Myers, "Economic Development," pp. 13–64; and Ramon H. Myers, "The Economic Transformation of the Republic of China on Taiwan," *China Quarterly* 99 (September 1984), pp. 500–528.

105. Davis B. Bobrow and Steve Chan, "Assets, Liabilities, and Strategic Conduct: Status Management by Japan, Taiwan, and South Korea," *Pacfiic Focus* 1:1 (Spring 1986), pp. 23–55; Davis B. Bobrow and Steve Chan, "Understanding Anomalous Successes: Japan, Taiwan, and South Korea," in Charles F. Hermann, Charles W. Kegley, Jr., and James N. Rosenau, eds., *New Directions in the Comparative Study of Foreign Policy* (Boston: Allen & Unwin, 1987), pp. 111–130; and Steve Chan, "Developing Strength from Weakness: The State in Taiwan," *Journal of Developing Societies* 4:1 (Spring 1988), pp. 38–51.

PART III

IMPLICATIONS

CHAPTER 7

The Taiwan Experience and Political Economy Paradigms

The Republic of China (R.O.C.) would seemingly present an important "critical case study" for assessing the three competing paradigms in the study of political economy. Taiwan has had one of the highest and most sustained growth rates in the world over the past four decades; its developmental experience does not appear unique in that it follows a broad East Asian pattern exhibited by Japan and the other "little dragons" (Hong Kong, Singapore, and South Korea). Thus the reasons for the R.O.C.'s dynamism should be of strong interest for students of development. This case is also valuable from a theoretical perspective because all three paradigms claim to explain the "Taiwan miracle." Developmentalists cite Taiwan as an example of laissez-faire, export-oriented capitalism[1]; statists view the R.O.C. as a prime case of successful state-led development.[2]; and dependency theorists argue that Taiwan represents upward mobility in the world system and attribute its success to being less dependent on foreign cpaital than most other developing countries.[3]

Comparing Taiwan's developmental history with the postulates of the three theoretical traditions, hence, should prove quite instructive. The first section of this conclusion lays a foundation for such an analysis by presenting a conceptual model of Taiwan's political economy and comparing this model with other patterns of growth in the postwar world. The second then draws specific implications from Taiwan for several central postulates of the three paradigms. Finally, the insights and limitations of these approaches are briefly contrasted.

A Model of the Republic of China's Political Economy

The R.O.C. has performed quite well on all the dimensions of development sketched in chapter 1. Growth has been rapid and continuous over the past four

Figure 7.1
Model of a Political Economy

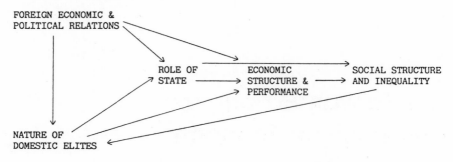

decades; a sophisticated industrial economy has been attained; a middle-class society is emerging; income inequality is quite low by international standards; the state has led development with a highly effective economic strategy; and, especially since the mid–1980s, major progress has been made toward democratization. The keystone of Taiwan's success story appears to be the flexibility and continuing restructuring that occurred in both the economy and the polity. Economically, the state's macroeconomic policy has meshed well with the entrepreneurial efforts of the private sector to take advantage of changing market conditions. Politically, a previous failed regime learned from its mistakes to reform itself and, in particular, permitted important changes in government institutions and elite composition. Thus political and economic change have been mutually reinforcing and have stimulated continuing readjustments in both spheres.

This section seeks to summarize the R.O.C.'s developmental history by presenting a model of the nation's political economy. The discussion of the contending perspectives on political economy in chapter 2 suggests that there are five principal elements in a political economy (see Figures 2.1 through 2.4): (1) the social structure and distribution of wealth and resources, (2) the structure and performance of the economy, (3) the role of the state in directing the economy and the society, (4) the nature of the political and economic elites, and (5) external economic and political relations. Figure 7.1 sketches the putative causal connections among these factors. Social structure and inequality are affected by both economic development and government policies. The structure and performance of the economy can be influenced by government policies that either facilitate or hinder the utilization of domestic resources and human capital, by the entrepreneurial skills and social demands of economic and business elites, and by foreign economic relations (e.g., trade, investment, and aid). The role of the state and its policies, in turn, derive from the nature of the domestic elites and from external political or economic pressures. Finally, the composition of the political and economic leaderships stems from some combination of indigenous social structure and external influences—the former, incidentally, constitutes the basic feedback loop in this model.

The social structure of the R.O.C. appears quite "modern" in form. The country has made the transition from an agricultural to an industrial society; the level of popular consumption has risen to a medium level that is quite high by the standards of developing countries; and income equality is quite low, approximating the levels found in advanced industrial societies. In short, a middle-class society is emerging. Furthermore, advances in all these areas have been quite rapid over the past several decades (with the exception of the recent upturn in income inequality). The major reason for this socioeconomic transformation and progress has been the R.O.C.'s rapid economic growth, which provided widespread mobility opportunities and created the full employment necessary to stimulate wage increases. The only government policy that has directly affected the social structure and inequality is the land reform of the 1950s. Since then there have been no major redistributive policies, although the regime has certainly had an indirect impact on social change through its strong support of education, which is vital for attaining individual social mobility.

In strong contrast to the "distortions" and "disarticulations" that mark the economies of many less developed countries, Taiwan has undergone a coherent and well-structured development, moving from land reform and modernization in the agricultural sphere to import-substitution industrialization to export-led, labor-intensive industrialization, and now to more capital-intensive, heavy, and high-technology industry. With the exception of the leveling off of agricultural production and productivity, it is hard to find much distortion here. The result has been a remarkable record of economic growth and (at least in retrospect) seemingly easy structural transformation.

All three possible influences on economic performance included in the model shown in Figure 7.1 appear to have been at work in the Taiwan case. First, the private sector clearly made a considerable contribution through both the entrepreneurial efforts of businessmen and the hard work and skills of workers and farmers. Second, state policies created the environment in which these domestic talents could be applied. Third, external factors were important—U.S. aid during the 1950s and early 1960s, foreign technology and marketing networks, and international markets proved highly profitable after the mid–1960s. Furthermore, government policy and external economic relations meshed together in an interactive manner. That is, government policies utilized and depended on external economic factors, whereas foreign economic relations almost certainly would not have had such a salutary impact had they not occurred within the framework of the regime's developmental strategy. For example, the U.S. aid was used in a productive manner rather than for "white elephant" projects or the padding of Swiss bank accounts; foreign capital was channeled into priority sectors and prevented from dominating and distorting the domestic economy; and the government encouraged industrial development that took advantage of the R.O.C.'s changing comparative advantage in the international division of labor. State policies also helped development by preventing business elites from holding back change or monopolizing the fruits of growth (e.g., land reform in the 1950s, economic liberalization in the 1960s, and labor legislation in the 1980s).

The state's role in Taiwan's economy, in turn, has been a subtle one that breaks with both capitalist and socialist stereotypes. The government has clearly played a leading role in directing the R.O.C.'s development. The several structural transformations, without which sustained growth would have been impossible, were the direct result of government decisions and policies. Moreover, substantial government investments in infrastructure and human capital (which occurred during the colonial period as well) provided a vital prerequisite for development. However, the government eschewed direct economic management and control, even though public corporations initially played a large role in the industrial sector. Rather, the decision was made to rely on private entrepreneurial initiative, and the business sector responded most strongly to these opportunities.

The state's role, in turn, can be explained, for the most part, by the interests and values of domestic elites. American influence, which was certainly considerable, given Taiwan's client-state position, was exerted in favor of the land reform in the 1950s and the export-oriented liberalization of the economy in the 1960s. However, these reforms and structural changes were pushed by top leaders within the country as well, so that the foreign influence was probably only marginal at best. The nature of the domestic elites as well appears to have been almost entirely a function of domestic, rather than external, forces. In fact, in direct contrast to many other Third World countries that have formed the focus of dependency analysis, foreign influences (particularly American advisors) were much more aligned with forces for change (i.e., economic technocrats) than with reactionary forces for stasis (i.e., landlords, business opponents of liberalization, and even military leaders).

What is perhaps most striking about the nature of domestic elites in the R.O.C. was their expansion over time as significant new groups or segments were added that generally had positive contributions to make to economic and political development. The first addition of economic technocrats was clearly a "revolution from above" decreed by Chiang Kai-shek and the top Kuomintang (KMT) leadership. The subsequent emergence of Taiwanese businessmen and electoral politicians into important leadership roles represents a "feedback" from changes in Taiwan's basic social structure as modeled in Figure 7.1. The state, thus, has become much more responsive to society over time. A question that still remains open is whether this will result in the business class using its growing power to dictate the evolving nature of Taiwan's political economy, or whether democratization will enhance the power of previously "quiescent" groups, such as labor and farmers.

The experience of the R.O.C., hence, proves that sustained rapid development is possible in the Third World. The Taiwanese political economy sketched above, though, differs considerably from two other developmental patterns that can be observed in the post–World War II world—the "dependent development" of Latin America and a few African countries, and what might be called the "socialist dependent development" that took place in Eastern Europe under the aegis of the Soviet Union. Both these other strategies produced spectacular growth over significant periods of time but then faltered in the long term. Comparing the R.O.C.'s developmental history and strategy with them should be instructive about some of the central elements in development.

Dependent development in Latin America was essentially based on import substitution, first for light industry and then for heavy industry, and a leading role of foreign capital in providing technology and organizing production. This stratgegy produced substantial growth and structural transformation in several countries, such as Brazil's "economic miracle" of the 1960s and early 1970s. However, such "secondary" import-substitution strategies necessitated increased imports of industrial inputs and capital equipment, which almost inevitably produced balance-of-payments and inflation problems that were exacerbated by the oil price explosion during the 1970s. Thus, although countries like Brazil and Mexico became much more competitive in international trade by the mid–1980s (witness their trade conflicts with the United States), their huge accumulated debts made sustained growth almost impossible. Just as important (if not more so) in terms of social development, even during the expansion period increases in real wages, social mobility opportunities, and the standard of living were limited to the small proportion of businessmen, managers, government officials, and workers in the "modern" sector.[4]

The development strategy in the Soviet bloc produced a longer period of rapid growth that involved much broader segments of the population than "dependent development," but is also clearly ran out of steam during the 1970s. Under the direction of the Soviet Union, rapid forced-draft industrialization emphasizing heavy industry was implemented in the late 1940s and early 1950s; two decades of rapid growth and industrial transformation ensued. After the initial suppression of popular living standards to provide investment capital associated with Stalinism, rapid growth led to greatly increased social mobility opportunities and a consumer revolution for most of the populations that lasted from the late 1950s to the early 1970s. The USSR also moved from the open exploitation of its satellites under Stalin to accepting an intrabloc trade system of exchanging Soviet raw materials for Eastern European manufactures that was clearly advantageous to the dependent economies. However, once the gains from the "extensive" growth of creating a heavy industrial base were exhausted, the Soviet bloc had extreme difficulty in making the transformation to more "intensive" development based on more sophisticated and consumer-oriented light industrial production. As a result, growth rates fell; the popular standard of living stagnated; and intrabloc economic conflict increased, setting the stage for Gorbachev's calls for "perestroika" or "restructuring."[5]

Taiwan's strategy (which can be at least partially generalized to other East

Asian countries) evidently produced better results than either capitalist-dependent development in Latin America or socialist-dependent development in Eastern Europe. Growth was sustained over a much longer period; despite the current economic dilemmas facing the R.O.C. that were discussed in the last section of chapter 6, a dead end has not been reached in terms of ongoing structural transformation. Unlike dependent development in Latin America, most of the population have benefited considerably from Taiwan's "economic miracle"; the rise in popular consumption and standard of living has been much more pronounced than in the Soviet bloc. Comparing these three development patterns, then, suggests several conclusions about the nature of development in the contemporary world.

First, rapid development does not require the long-term suppression of living standards and the perpetuation of gross socioeconomic inequality. This clearly did not happen in either "capitalist" Taiwan or "socialist" Eastern Europe, strongly implying that the lack of social progress in Latin American dependent development has been the result of policy choice, not economic necessity. Such social development, in addition, has occurred almost exclusively because of economic growth rather than because of redistributive social policies by the government. This was certainly the case in the R.O.C. and (perhaps surprisingly from an ideological perspective) was generally true in Eastern Europe as well.[6] On the other hand both Taiwan and the socialist countries provided considerable social investment in education, creating a foundation for individual social mobility. The question remains, however, of what happens when the broad mobility opportunities resulting from the initial industrialization growth spurt are choked off by declining growth and solidifying class structures. In Eastern Europe this has produced the irony of labor's becoming a "counterrevolutionary" force in the "land of the proletariat" (e.g., Solidarity in Poland). Taiwan may soon be facing a similarly ironic situation (g., current labor protests against moving offshore production to the People's Republic of China [P.R.C.]), although its continued dynamic growth has not made the problem acute yet.

Second, the comparative success of the R.O.C. in economic performance and the social outcomes that rapid growth produce seemingly results from its integrated and coherent development strategy that avoided the "distortions" associated with the other two patterns—command economic structures and an overemphasis on heavy industry in the Soviet bloc, and "enclave development" and the limited spread of "modernization" in Latin American dependent development. Thus economic structures and strategies certainly matter, which focuses attention on the internal and external determinants of economic performance.

Third, the role of the state was crucial in all three development patterns. This is obviously so in Eastern Europe, where Communist governments control almost all economic activity. This is also the case for Taiwan, both because explicit policy decisions guided each of the country's structural transformations and because government efforts were vital in managing the contributions that external economic relations made to domestic development. In dependent development in such countries as Brazil and Mexico the growing role of government in providing infrastructure, expanding state corporations, channeling the investment opportunities of "local capital," and managing the relations with foreign MNCs indicates a key role for the state as well, although not as extensive or dominant as in Eastern Europe or even Taiwan.

In strictly economic terms, what seems to be the key difference among these three state-led strategies is the degree of flexibility that they permit or entail. Taiwan has based its development on the creation of structures that encourage the maximum flexibility first to internal and subsequently to external demand. In contrast, Eastern Europe created an industrial pattern that proved highly resistant to change, and Latin American dependent development can be criticized for its stasis from several perspectives. Developmentalists decry "secondary" import substitution, which provides a costly escape from the forces of the international market. *Dependencistas*, for their part, point to the exclusion of the peasantry and labor from the ruling coalition as factors that prevent social progress. Thus, although the state must evidently play a central role in promoting development contrary to a purely capitalist logic, Taiwan's "capitalist variant" of such a strategy seems far superior to heavy-handed government control and direction of the economy or to government attempts to "freeze" the evolution of social structure and classes.

Fourth, external contributions or hindrances to indigenous development can vary greatly. In Taiwan the measures that Japan took to stimulate agricultural production provided a base for further development; during the 1950s and 1960s the government made excellent use of U.S. foreign aid; because of late entrance and government-designed incentives, foreign investment has generally contributed to growth rather than skewing economic structures; and the "export platform" stage of the R.O.C.'s development certainly fared well. The first of these contributions was entirely fortuitous, since Japan was concerned with its own well-being, not that of its colony. The others, though, were the result of specific state actions to harness external resources to the pursuit of domestic development.

The impact of external economic relations has been more ambiguous in the other two patterns. For Eastern Europe initial Stalinist policies both established the industrial structures that later produced high growth rates and grossly exploited the satellites in bilateral economic relations. Later the terms of intrabloc relations became much more favorable to the client-states as the USSR seemed willing to subsidize its political empire. However, the basic economic structures created obstacles to further development, and Soviet ideology and political interests became barriers to devising new policies to get Eastern Europe out of its economic malaise.[7] In Latin American dependent development the initial exploitation and distorting influences of external economic penetration evolved toward more positive contributions under pressure from developmentalist states, but foreign capital was still a central component of the "triple alliance" that produced the economic and social distortions discussed in more detail in chapter 2. External economic relations, therefore, are probably needed in most developmental situations. However, there is no guarantee that foreign economic penetration will produce positive results; in many instances it has certainly brought exploitation and underdevelopment. Consequently the role of the domestic management of foreign economic ties appears a key factor in whether a development strategy will be successful.

Fifth, this perspective turns attention to the nature of the links between external forces and the domestic elites. It is probably not coincidental that the leadership in the R.O.C. was by far the most autonomous among these three cases and faced the least constraints in manipulating foreign countries and companies in the interest of Taiwan's development project. The Eastern European elites were clearly the most dominated and constrained, which, as argued above, had countervailing implications for economic growth in the Soviet bloc. Third World leaders in such countries as Brazil occupied an intermediate position. While they faced significant constraints from the power of foreign capital and finance (e.g., International Monetary Fund [IMF]-imposed austerity programs), most developing countries have become quite independent in the political realm[8]; several of the nations undergoing dependent development have demonstrated an increasing ability to manage multinational corporation (MNC) penetration as well.

This raises the question of how much of the normally imputed ill effects of dependency stem from external pressures and how much is really the result of the nature and values of domestic socioeconomic and political elites. Taiwan's developmental success, for example, derived from the willingness of several key elite groups to forego the maximization of their political and economic positions, thereby allowing the creation of new sectors of the leadership that subsequently made important contributions to furthering economic modernization and transformation. The economic distortions associated with the other two patterns, in contrast, seemingly stemmed from the entrenched interests of current elites— the fears of Communist leaders that significant economic reform would grievously curtail their power, privileges, and status and the unwillingness of the businessmen and "state bourgeoisie" in most less developed countries to allow the fruits of industrialization to spread very widely in their societies. In short, the feedback loop from the social structure to the composition of domestic elites was much more operative in Taiwan than in the other two models. Additionally, this situation in Eastern Europe suggests, ironically, that the Marxist theory that capitalist society will ultimately disintegrate because of the growing contradiction between the "means" and "relations" of production is quite appropriate for "state socialism."

Long-term economic performance and social outcomes, to sum, were much better in Taiwan (as a representative of the East Asian development model) than in the pattern associated with socialist development in Eastern Europe or dependent development in Latin America. The state assumed a key role in directing all three strategies. The state in the R.O.C. was distinctive in that it promoted a strategy of economic flexibility and change in contrast to the attempts of the other two types of state to use their power to hold back economic and social change. The differences in strategy, in turn, can be explained both by the relative autonomy of elites in Taiwan from external forces and by their much greater willingness to tolerate and even stimulate change in the composition of the political and economic leadership.

Theoretical Implications

The three contending paradigms that explain the political economy of development in the contemporary world differ fundamentally in their basic assumptions and perspectives. The developmentalist approach argues that economic growth and industrial transformation result from a combination of laissez-faire economics, cultural modernization, and political modernization. Dependency theory assumes that a state's incorporation into the international capitalist division of labor determines its developmental potential and whether its economy and society will be distorted and disarticulated, so that the nature of a nation's dependency determines its economic outcomes. Statists, for their part, contend that state policy is the key factor determining developmental success and that national development strategies are strongly affected by the ties (or absence of them) between the state and various socioeconomic classes and groups. Thus *dependencistas* focus on long-term structural features of the global political economy; developmentalists view more short-term behavioral phenomena within countries as key; and statists occupy an intermediate position.

This section compares Taiwan's developmental experience with the expectations of the three paradigms. Taiwan's developmental history is more complex than would be predicted by any of the three approaches, but it also suggests that all three possess important explanatory insights. Thus, rather than "testing" each theory in turn, this chapter is organized thematically. It begins with a consideration of the structural legacy of Taiwan's incorporation into world markets and then turns to the operation of economic markets and the role of the state as potential explanations for why structural factors did not operate in accordance with the postulates of dependency theory. Next, the impact of class relations and Confucian culture on both state and market are considered. Finally, the role of external dependency and political development in the Taiwan model are discussed.

Taiwan's incorporation into the international political economy. A fundamental postulate of dependency theory is that the manner in which a country or colony is integrated into the international division of labor channels its future development potential, directly by placing it in a permanent structural economic niche and indirectly by creating reactionary domestic elites with a vested interest in maintaining the economic and political status quo. Taiwan's entrance into international trade as a large-scale exporter of agricultural goods, resulting from Japan's colonial decision to develop the island into a rice and sugar basket for the metropole, clearly conditioned the R.O.C.'s subsequent development. However, instead of producing the underdevelopment and distortion that dependency theory would predict for such a structural legacy, it created an integrated rather than an enclave economy, equalitarian rather than inequalitarian economic and social relationships, the expansion rather than the enforced contraction of human capital and mobility opportunities, and the periodic emergence of elites who pushed forward rather than held back development.

Dependency theory might still be consistent with Taiwan's development, though, if the R.O.C. could be conceptualized as a successful graduation from the periphery to the semiperiphery that is viewed as providing some dynamism to the global economic system without changing its essential structures.[9] Immanuel Wallerstein's world systems theory, thus, argues that a semiperiphery connects the core and periphery, acting as a periphery to the core and as a core for the periphery. In addition to this set of structural economic linkages, the semiperiphery is marked by an economy that falls between the industrialized core and agricultural periphery and by a strong state necessary to defend its small economic gains against the core.[10] In several important regards Taiwan fits this model: it has a strong state and medium level of development (although its industrial sophistication and socioeconomic equality probably surpass the levels normally assumed to exist in the semiperiphery); it exports more labor-intensive goods to developed countries and capital-intensive ones to developing nations; and significant investment is beginning to flow from Taiwan to the Third World (including the P.R.C.). However, Taiwan's economic linkages have been concentrated on markets in advanced industrial societies, which it has penetrated with goodly success. Thus, rather than acting as an economic and political bridgehead linking the core and periphery (as, for example, the Ivory Coast evidently does, despite having a much less developed economy than Taiwan's[11]), Taiwan has simply outcompeted the core on its own terms.

These are two rather contradictory ways to interpret this success and deviation from the normal assumptions about the nature of the semiperiphery. One is simply the conventional developmentalist argument that all countries can benefit from the free market and the operation of the product cycle. The other, much different perspective is represented by David Becker's neo-Marxist critique of dependency theory. Becker contends that the era of neocolonial dependency has been replaced by a new global system of production in which the ''international bourgeoisie'' are no longer necessarily tied to any particular national base or home country.[12] What is surprising perhaps is that entrepreneurs from Taiwan have been able to enter the international bourgeoisie as independent actors so quickly.

These developments have several implications for the assumptions of the various paradigms about the essential nature of international political economy. First, the structural perspective of dependency theory is supported, since the economic structures created by Taiwan's incorporation into the global division of labor clearly conditioned its subsequent development (in ways, incidentally, that were unanticipated by the Japanese colonialists). Second and in contrast, the actual *dependencia* postulates about these structural relations clearly are not universally true. In Taiwan's case an initial position as an exporter of agricultural and primary products was not necessarily inimical for development, as dependency theory usually asserts, since it served as the foundation for the R.O.C.'s rapid growth. Third, the effects of specific economic structures can change drastically over time. For example, small-scale production, which helped to spur both agricultural and industrial growth earlier, is now generally seen as a problem in both sectors.

This implies that structural conditions and effects, even those imposed by a grossly exploitative colonialism, can vary much more radically than the deterministic strands of dependency theory suggest. It is rather ironic, for example, that several critics of the R.O.C.'s "capitalist development" gainsay its undeniable growth performance by citing the legacy of Japanese policy.[13] Several reasons may be adduced for such structural "variation." Within the structural perspective Hirschman's less deterministic formulations certainly suggest themselves.[14] However, the failure of dependency theory's structural postulates to hold implies the need for recourse to the other two paradigms—in particular the developmentalists' emphasis on the operations of the international marketplace and the statists' concern with government-led development strategies.

Taiwan's development and "the magic of the marketplace." Another important question concerns the relevance of the Taiwan case for the fundamental debate between the developmentalist and dependency paradigms over whether free-market capitalism brings development or underdevelopment. Many have argued that the R.O.C. presents a model of capitalist industrialization that validates the developmentalist approach. Rapid growth resulted in an essentially free-market economy that came to be highly integrated with world markets. The sequence of development from agriculture to light industry to more sophisticated industrial production also followed the conventional model. Moreover, such growth lessened socioeconomic inequality rather than exacerbating it, and did not result in the fruits of development being limited to a small enclave. This export-driven strategy also demonstrates that a developing country can derive decided benefits from international trade and that its dominant export mix can change quite quickly (in Taiwan's case from agricultural goods to low-cost–labor light industry to more sophisticated capital, skill, and technology-intensive production in less than thirty years). Taiwan, in fact, became amazingly competitive in international markets. Stephen Krasner, for example, concluded that Taiwan and the other Asian newly industrializing countries (NICs) depart from the normal Third World opposition to liberal, laissez-faire international economic regimes because of their ability to adjust to world market conditions.[15]

Thus the developmental history of the R.O.C. conforms well to some of the basic assumptions of neoclassic economics in the developmentalist approach. Taiwan has prospered because it has followed the logic of the international market. It has upgraded its position in terms of "comparative advantage" from primary and low-value–added goods to increasingly sophisticated industrial and high-value–added products, demonstrating that the product cycle can work to the advantage of developing countries. Finally, the theory of hegemonic stability is also relevant for explaining the R.O.C.'s success because Taiwan benefited both from the liberal global economic order maintained during America's period of dominance and from the United States' willingness not to utilize its economic and political leverage in dealing with its client in Taipei.

It would be extremely hard to argue, however, that this pattern of development occurred simply because of the "magic of the marketplace." First, Taiwan's development was based on a series of structural transformations that almost certainly would have been forestalled if pure laissez-faire economics had operated. For example, the successful land reform clearly violated the sanctity of the market and property rights; without import-substitution policies, Taiwan doubtlessly would have continued as a primarily agricultural producer; and in the 1970s conventional economists warned the R.O.C. against trying to move away from low-cost, labor-intensive production.[16]

Second, dependency theorists could argue with much justification that Taiwan succeeded precisely because it deviated from normal patterns of capitalist development in the Third World. In particular, the R.O.C. government took an aggressive regulatory stance toward foreign capital (which certainly violated laissez-faire principles). Furthermore, the fact that the standard of living for most of the population rose along with industrial growth meant that a mass market was created that served to stimulate further growth (which is closer to the theory, if not the practice, of neoclassic economics about the stimulants for growth). Thus Taiwan's experience raises the question of what exactly qualifies as "capitalist development."

For example, all three paradigms could claim to explain the role of foreign capital in promoting the R.O.C.'s development with some degree of reasonableness. Developmentalists could point to the existence of considerable foreign investment, especially in the dynamic export sector; *dependencistas* could argue that the multinationals were far less intrusive and dominant and, thus, distorting and exploitative than in Latin American dependent development[17]; and statists could conclude that MNCs contributed to development in Taiwan because of state regulation and incentives. Even the "market" success of the island, therefore, does not support developmentalism unambiguously.

Third, and perhaps most centrally, Taiwan's developmental history directly challenges the developmentalist assumption that there is a universal pattern of economic growth that must be followed if the development project is to succeed. Michael Piore and Charles Sable have advanced a provocative thesis that challenges the conventional assumption that the advancement of industrialization is based increasingly, over time, on the mass production of standardized goods at the cheapest cost. Rather, they argue, "flexible production" strategies based on the skilled production of goods for specialized market segments are just as viable.[18] David Friedman, in particular, has applied this model in his interpretation of Japan's "misunderstood miracle" of rapid development as resting on the development of flexible production, in contrast to the United States' continuing commitment to mass production.[19] The conventional image of Taiwan is that it had relied on low-cost–labor mass production. However, Susan Greenhalgn, Danny Lam, and Edwin Winckler have convincingly argued that much of the R.O.C.'s success has stemmed from its flexible production based on small-scale entrepreneurship.[20] Thus the "Taiwan miracle" represents a direct challenge to the normal assumptions of developmentalism about the course of industrialization (which, incidentally, are generally shared by Marxists).

The contribution of the market to Taiwan's growth, hence, appears more complex than either the pro-market developmentalist approach or anti-market dependency perspective is wont to concede. First, Taiwan's export-led growth has depended on a subtle strategy of finding a niche in the international division of labor (in particular following Japan up the product cycle over time from simple labor-intensive goods to much more sophisticated production).[21] Beyond simply the magic of the marketplace, Taiwan's success has been affected both by structural factors in the international and domestic political economy and by the behavioral choices of its political leadership. Second, previous positive effects of the market are certainly not guaranteed for the future. Externally, the R.O.C. has become vulnerable to growing protectionism in the industrial world (especially from the United States) and is being squeezed in the international product cycle between Japan and the United States from above and industrializing states with cheaper labor from below. Internally, the market's ability to promote income equality through a strong demand for unskilled labor is being vitiated by the current structural transformation. This also suggests a third point, that the success of Taiwan's export-oriented strategy depended to a significant extent on favorable conditions in the world economy during the 1960s and 1970s (e.g., dynamic global demand, the beginning of offshore production by American and Japanese corporations, and American enforcement of a liberal trading order) that were not necessarily the results of international laissez-faire per se.

The state's role in the Taiwan's development. The state has obviously been a central element in the Taiwan success story. The role of the government in the R.O.C.'s economic strategy, in addition, conformed to both the developmentalist and dependency strands of statist thinking. The former views state actions as a supplement to the normal workings of capitalism, whereas the latter interprets them as a nationalist response to foreign penetration that is necessary to protect the domestic society.

State policy has supplemented the market to lead the R.O.C. through the series of structural transformations that created and maintained its international competitiveness. The government's orientations have worked well in a variety of areas. For example, the agricultural strategy proved fantastically successful in the short term in increasing production, promoting social equality and an increased standard of living, extracting resources to finance industrialization, and creating political support for the regime; government reforms and economic liberalization made possible the export-led surge; and the strong responses to the two oil crises of the 1970s simultaneously controlled inflation and restimulated the economy. The basic aim of these state policies, though, has been to promote Taiwan's ability to benefit from "comparative advantage" in the international economy rather than to protect the country from its competitors or to direct the economy away from the signals and incentives of the marketplace. Moreover, the state's surprising success, at least until recently, in economic negotiations has also made a major contribution to export-led growth.[22] Thus Taiwan clearly qualifies as an excellent illustration of the state acting to successfully supplement the market. In Richard Rosecrance's terminology, the R.O.C. is a "trading" state par excellence that has succeeded despite a high defense budget, which constitutes one of the disadvantages of a "territorial" state.[23]

The R.O.C. also qualifies as a nationalist state attempting to regulate foreign influences, in particular the presence of foreign capital. The government's successful management of MNCs in the pursuit of the domestic development project was discussed in detail in chapter 6. In addition, the state has also followed the prescriptions of dependency theory by suppressing the interests of "dominant classes" to permit the continuing structural transformation of the economy (e.g., landlords in the agricultural reform and the business class in export-oriented liberalization).[24] Finally, the state will almost inevitably have to assume a leading role in protecting the fruits of the "Taiwan miracle" from escalating American pressures on the R.O.C. as a consequence of the economic dislocations accompanying the United States' "declining hegemony."

Thus the regime evidently learned several lessons from China's past history of dependency and its own failures on the mainland, and acted in a manner far at variance from *dependencia* stereotypes of dependent capitalist states. Perhaps less obviously Taiwan's experience also confounds the expectations of developmentalist theory. First, the history of the R.O.C. clearly demonstrates that state and market can interact effectively to promote development. Second, the much different results of "state-building" on Taiwan as opposed to the mainland indicate that state intrusion is not necessarily disruptive, and can actually promote modernization and adjustment in local societies if it is not accompanied by rapacious revenue raising.

The state, hence, has clearly played a central role in Taiwan's development. However, the developmental history of the R.O.C. also shows the limitations of the statist approach. At the macro theoretical level the nascent statist paradigm has been criticized for assuming that state strength, autonomy, and developmental success are almost synonymous. Taiwan certainly confirms the critique that this is much too simplistic. First, even the almost definitional relation between state autonomy and strength can, at second glance, be complex and ambiguous. For example, Steve Chan forcefully argues that although the R.O.C. state may have been extremely strong and autonomous vis-a-vis the Taiwanese population, it was clearly weak and dependent internationally on a variety of dimensions.[25] Second, while Taiwan certainly conforms to predictions about strong developmentalist states, its very success contrasts with examples of strong states that cared little about development (e.g., the "crony capitalism" of the Philippines under Marcos) or declaredly developmentalist states whose strategies proved counterproductive (e.g., Burma or Chile). Finally, Taiwan's experience also is consistent with the proposition that economic growth creates social forces that undermine the autonomy of developmentalist states.[26]

The R.O.C.'s specific economic strategy also demonstrates that there is more to the political economy of growth that just state action. First, as K. T. Li (one of the principal architects of the Taiwan mircale) argues, the state's basic strategy over time has moved continually toward market liberalization and depoliticalization of the economy. That is, the state has pushed the country toward comparative advantage.[27] Thus, private economic activity (for example, the flexibility of small entrepreneurs) and social forces (for example, education's impact on entrepreneurship and labor productivity) must obviously be incorporated into explanations of Taiwan's success. Second, neoclassic advocates laud the R.O.C. for pursuing an export-led stragegy rather than secondary import substitution that allegedly subverts market forces. Yet countries such as Brazil that implemented secondary import substitution are now becoming competitive in world trade. What this suggests is that the path to industrialization is less important than whether the industrial structures that are created are rigid (as in the Eastern European case) or flexible enough to respond rapidly to economic change (as in Taiwan). Third, the state has felt that its investments in economic development and education to provide "equality of opportunity" will produce equitable social outcomes in the population, but this assumption is open to growing challenge.

More broadly, therefore, Taiwan's current strategy of structural transformation to more sophisticated production is raising problems in a number of areas. Attacks on small entrepreneurs may undercut the flexibility that has been a large part of the country's comparative advantage; concessions to foreign capital may rekindle dependency problems; and low priority for welfare and redistribution policies may generate social and political alienation. These dangers certainly suggest that one cannot simply conclude that a strong developmentalist state inevitably brings sustained growth.

Social forces and the R.O.C. state. To say that the state may assume a leading role in development is really not an explanation. What is needed is to ask why a specific state becomes committed to promoting economic development (instead of simply "milking" society as the Marcos regime did), and why it chooses specific strategies and policies. From this perspective Taiwan fits almost perfectly the three conditions postulated by Reuschemeyer and Evans to motivate a successful developmental state: (1) a developmentalist ideology, (2) a capable bureaucracy, and (3) autonomy from dominant domestic social classes.[28]

Taiwan also demonstrates, however, that these factors are far from static. The Japanese implemented a developmentalist ideology (albeit designed in the interests of the metropole) with a capable bureaucracy that was almost completely independent from the subject population. Yet, although substantial agricultural and light industrial growth occurred and although a base was laid for the postwar developmental explosion, Japan's exploitative colonialism meant that further development was probably precluded. After the forcible expulsion of the Japanese and the untoward interlude of the late 1940s, the chastened KMT "reformed" from a militaristic to a developmentalist ideology, brought a sophisticated bureaucracy with it to Taiwan, and used its autonomy from society to implement radical land reform and economic liberalization policies. Yet, as argued in chapters 5 and 6, a key component of this success was the evolution and broadening of the leadership as elite status was progressively opened up to new groups with requisite skills for Taiwan's ongoing development.

This pattern has two general implications about the impact of socal forces on the state's developmental role. First, and quite ironically, despite the "capitalist" nature of Taiwan's political economy, its success can be directly explained in terms of the Marxist concept of the contradiction that development brings between the expanding "means of production" and the tendency of the social and political "relations of production" to retard potential development by protecting elite monopolies. As discussed in the last section, this process clearly operated in both Latin America and Eastern Euorpe and goes a long way toward explaining the "distortions" in these two development models. For Taiwan, in contrast, elite change has produced much more of an evolving balance between the relations and means of production. Second, the structural factors central to dependency theory are clearly important here, since Taiwan's developmental process was clearly affected by the structure of elite coalitions. Again, however, these structural factors do not operate in the deterministic manner assumed by the dependency paradigm. Rather, Taiwan's elite coalitions were shaped by such idiosyncratic events as the imposition and ending of colonialism, the basic change in the KMT regime's goals after the Chinese civil war, and regime willingness to gradually move toward a policy of ethnic inclusiveness.

The role of the autonomous state in Taiwan's development has several implications about Mancur Olson's provocative theory that "the rise and decline of nations" can be explained by the power of "distributional coalitions" to use their power to distort the functioning of free markets, thereby causing economic inefficiency and retarding growth.[29] While Olson's work implies that state intervention generally disrupts market operations, Taiwan and several other East Asian developmental successes apparently used state power to protect the economy from distributional coalitions—which certainly adds a new dimension to this perspective.[30] Political stability and increasing democratization in Taiwan should, according to Olson's theory, promote the growing power of distributional coalitions; as previously discussed, this conclusion is widely accepted in terms of the diminishing power and autonomy of the state in the R.O.C.

This idea that the fundamental role of the state is shifting in Taiwan, though, does suggest at least the possibility for alternative outcomes. Very crudely, political regimes may be placed into a threefold classifications, depending on the role of the state: (1) statist ones in which the state dominates society (e.g., Taiwan or Eastern Europe), (2) corporatist ones in which the state mediates between several coalitions of social groups (e.g., Latin America),[31] and (3) pluralist systems in which the state basically responds to independent interest groups.[32] If Taiwan is evolving toward a pluralist system or a corporatist one like Latin America, Olson's thesis will probably apply, since the likely result would be increasing power of "dominant" social groups (e.g., businessmen), who could be expected to use political power to extract "monopoly rents." Another type of corporatism exists in the states with "small open" economies in Western Europe, however. As described by Peter Katzenstein, these corporatist states realize that they must remain open to changes emanating from the international economy (unlike nations with large markets like the United States) but use a corporatist consensus to "compensate" the socioeconomic groups that lose out in such changes.[33] If Taiwan were to move toward such a system, the state would have to become more responsive to society and assume broader redistributive and welfare policies, but it could also seek to forge a general social consensus in favor of continuing the economic flexibility underlying its current prosperity.

The role of Confucian culture in Taiwan's development. In addition to the state's structural linkages to society, the nation's political culture offers an important potential explanation for the role of the state and developmental outcomes. In fact, regime-society relations are normally assumed to reflect the dominant political culture. Developmentalist theory asserts that the replacement of traditional cultures with more modernizing value systems is a prerequisite for economic change. Taiwan provides an interesting test of this line of thought in that the Confucian culture of East Asia has recently been seen as one that promotes development.[34] For the R.O.C., as discussed in chapters 5 and 6, the traditional Confucian culture was supportive of developmental activities in several key respects. First, the entrepreneurial spirit of the culture has clearly been allowed to flourish. Second, the Confucian culture, with its stress on respect for authority and social harmony, seems a primary explanation for the political stability on Taiwan in the face of predictions from both developmentalist and dependency theory that rapid socioeconomic change should create instability. This contrasts sharply, incidentally, with nineteenth-century China, where a conservative Confucian bureaucracy stifled political and economic change, giving rise to the "received wisdom" until lately that Confucian culture inhibits development.[35]

A consideration of the central elements in Confucian culture indicates why it bears this ambiguous relation to development, because its implications for developmental activities are clearly contradictory. Its secularism, advocacy of a merit-based bureaucracy committed to national betterment, emphasis on individual contributions to collective (especially family) accumulation, and commitment to merit-based achievement are all seen as conducive for development. On the other hand, the low status of entrepreneurs, Confucian emphasis on ritual and order, and distrust of specialized expertise all create pressures for reactionary politics and stagnant economies. Moreover, other important aspects of Confucianism, such as familism, respect for hierarchy and authority, and contemplation of the past to determine and justify social values, are certainly central tenets of traditionalism.[36]

From a historical perspective, the very processes of economic development changed the emphasis that these various strands of Confucian culture received. Thus the challenge presented by Western imperialism certainly created an impetus for applying Confucian values to economic activity in new ways that promoted development, as occurred most dramatically in Japan after the Meiji restoration.[37] In more broadly philosophical terms, the neo-Confucian movement in China in the nineteenth and twentieth centuries represented an attempt to change China's political culture within the traditional value structure to effect what Thomas Metzger has called an "escape from predicament" in terms of both economic and psychological well-being.[38] At a more micro behavioral level, for example, the importance and complexity of the market economy in late-nineteenth-century China meant that government bureaucrats could no longer determine the "national interest" in splendid isolation, but had to concede that merchants and businessmen possessed technical expertise of vital importance for the country.[39] Finally, Siu-lun Wong goes beyond cultural factors per se in his interesting thesis that structural factors in an economy and polity (e.g., colonial administration and the refugee situation in Hong Kong) determine what cultural mores will dominate and whether a multifaceted culture, like Confucianism, will promote or inhibit developmental activities.[40]

The relation between Confucian culture and development in Taiwan has several important dimensions. First, Sunist doctrine stressed the need for both government direction and private initiative and capital in fostering economic development. Second, the subordination of the anti-development strands of Confucianism can be attributed to the ability of the KMT to reform itself and create an autonomous regime strong enough to overcome traditional elites opposed to economic change, although the success of rapid change now may be engendering significant problems of social stress and alienation. Third, the willingness of elites to forego maximizing their own material benefits might be tied to the Confucian value system, which gives the highest status to public-regarding bureaucrats, in contrast to money-grubbing businessmen. Fourth, most of the factors cited by Wong for Hong Kong apply to the R.O.C. as well—a "refugee" ethic disrupting the traditional institutions of social and political control, a government independent of dominant social classes, and a small and urbanized nation. Finally, the special role of the family and social networks in Chinese society has shaped the nature of business and entrepreneurship, as well as that of the polity, to a considerable extent in Taiwan, which, in turn, has influenced the specific links between the R.O.C.'s economy and the world economy.[41]

Thus, while cultural values can be directly related to the R.O.C.'s record of rapid growth, the relation is much more complex and multifaceted than pictured by the three paradigms—developmentalists who call for cultural modernization, *dependencistas* who view culture as part of the "superstructure," and statists who are not that directly concerned with culture per se. Rather, the characteristics of the indigenous culture appear integral to the island's developmental history, which is quite significant because traditional cultures have proved much more resistant to change than developmentalists originally assumed.[42] The Taiwan case, however, also indicates that more is involved than simply the basic norms in a cultural tradition, since Confucianism has facets that both promote and inhibit progress. Thus a (if not the) central element in elucidating the relation between culture and development is the specification of the structural and policy factors that encourage varying strands of complex cultural traditions.

Dependency and growth in Taiwan. Taiwan has certainly been subjected to serious dependency ties, both as a colony and as a participant in the postwar international economy. In view of its strong growth record, this would imply that external dependency is not always harmful. Why it has not been so for the R.O.C., though, involves the very specific nature of the island's external ties, which can be conceptualized as the unique combination of three dimensions of dependency linkages. First, McGowan and Smith make the valuable distinction between "market dependence" on foreign markets and "power dependence" on the decisions of specific external actors (e.g., MNCs, governments, or classes).[43] Second, situations of political clientelism on First World governments should be separated from foreign economic relations, since in the postcolonial age political and economic penetration of the developing world may follow quite different logics.[44] Finally, the converse of dependence can be either independence or interdependence (i.e., mutual dependence). Thus a dependent society can attempt to better its lot either by withdrawing from the international system or by developing power resources vis-à-vis external dominators.

The R.O.C. experienced substantial amounts of both power and market dependence. Power dependence might be considered the more deleterious a priori because it involves a foreign actor's explicit control over domestic outcomes. In Taiwan's case, however, power dependence was primarily part of a political relationship with the United States, which viewed the island as a valuable client in the cold war struggle. As a result, America was willing to "subsidize" the R.O.C. to a considerable extent through foreign aid, willingness (at least until the mid–1980s) not to drive particularly hard bargains in economic negotiations, and use of its influence to promote, not retard, liberalization. Power dependence on foreign capital is usually considered to be quite strong in most developing countries, but Taiwan is generally credited with limiting the power of MNCs and channeling them into activities supportive of the indigenous developmental project both because of state regulatory policies and because of the specific timing of foreign capital's large-scale introduction in the industrialization sequence.[45] The former factor represents the low incidence of another commonly assumed type of power dependence—that of domestic elites on foreign patrons.

Export-led growth quite consciously made Taiwan extremely dependent on international markets. Thus far, market dependence has been managed well and is seen as central to Taiwan's growth with equity. However, the potential danger of market dependency is clear on several fronts: growing protectionism in the United States, an increasing squeeze on Taiwan's place in the international product cycle, and the threat of a global recession. Much of this vulnerability stems from the fundamental change in the global economy resulting from America's declining fortunes, which are driving it toward the role of a "predatory" hegemon to protect its domestic economy.

The particular configuration of Taiwan's dependency syndrome, therefore, is an integral part of its successful political economy. Power dependence was not harmful (and was probably profitable) because it was part of a clientelistic relationship with a sponsor willing to subsidize the R.O.C. in pursuit of its own political goals. Power dependence was minimized in the economic realm and especially in terms of the selection of domestic elites. Finally, market dependency has thus far contributed to growth because a strong state with a successful managerial strategy preserved the nation's competitiveness in the global economy.

This indicates that Taiwan created a significant amount of interdependence with external actors through a paradoxical combination of strength (a strong state and attractive economic environment) and weakness (vulnerability to military threats from the P.R.C.). This shows that it is possible for an ostensibly weak Third World state to manipulate major economic and political powers.[46] On the other hand, Taiwan also demonstrates the ever present dangers of dependency. Thus Taiwan's successful management of its dependency relations with the United States has been challenged by changes in America's global economic position and view of the strategic triangle—factors over which the R.O.C. has no control.

All three paradigms, then, have something to say about the relation between dependency and development in the R.O.C. Dependency theory provides the basic concepts for analyzing Taiwan's relation to the broader international political economy; the island's current political and economic situations certainly demonstrate that weakness and dependency bring danger. Its assumption that dependency breeds underdevelopment does not hold because the complex nature of the country's dependency syndrome differed from the structures normally posited by *dependencistas*. The statist perspective certainly highlights one reason why this is so—government economic and international negotiating strategies. Developmentalism's emphasis on the burgeoning "interdependence" in the global political economy is certainly relevant[47]; the theory of "hegemonic stability" even provides an explanation for growing American economic pressure on its client in the late 1980s.[48]

Political development in the R.O.C. Despite its reputation as an authoritarian government, the R.O.C. also provides some grist for the debate about what constitutes political development. Taiwan's political history, for example, implies that the shift in emphasis in the developmentalist paradigm from democratization to institutionalization was probably a mistake for several reasons. First, closer scrutiny of the R.O.C. appears consistent with critiques of the developmentalist approach's stress on political institutionalization for ignoring the tendency of such authoritarian governments to be dominated by military regimes and/or by patrimonial bureaucracies whose values are antithetical to economic transformation, as, for instance, evidently occurred during the Republican period on the mainland.[49] In Taiwan, in direct contrast, the state's formulation and implementation of successful development strategies were associated with the evident decline of the relative power of the military within the regime and the limitation of the power of the lower, more traditional bureaucracy. More broadly, Taiwan's experience gives case study support to recent attacks based on comparative statistical analysis on the "institutionalist" assumption that authoritarian governments promote economic development more effectively than democratic ones.[50]

Second, as argued in the conclusion of chapter 5, rather than being antithetical, institutionalization and democratization in Taiwan have been intertwined and reciprocal. The initial authoritarian and institutionalized regime used its power to promote economic transformations that created strong forces for subsequent democratization. Political liberalization and democratization, in turn, strengthened the ties between the regime and society, which was probably essential for the preservation of political stability (i.e., institutionalization), rather than leading to an overloading of governmental structures and "political decay," although the raucous nature of contemporary politics in the R.O.C. suggests that some danger may exist in this direction. In the R.O.C., therefore, the developmental processes have created almost irresistible pressure for significant liberalization. This follows an early strand of developmentalist thought, incidentally, that economic development, particularly industrialization, almost inevitably creates social mobilization and increased participation in politics.[51] Thus economic transformation in the R.O.C. led to political liberalization rather than to the bureaucratic repression posited by dependency theory.[52]

Taiwan's experience in fact conforms well to the recent theoretical treatment of the transition from authoritarian to democratic rule that has occurred in a significant number of Third World societies. Some of the principal conclusions from such studies are that socioeconomic structural factors, while setting broad parameters, are much less important than situational and personal contingencies for determining the course of political change; that political liberalization has almost always been primarily a function of internal events and variables; that democratization is usually the result of an interaction between pressures from both above (i.e., within the regime) and below (in other words, from the domestic opposition); that institutionalized dictatorships generally leave organizational legacies constraining the nature of liberalization; and that the bourgeoisie and military leadership play key roles in political change.[53]

The R.O.C.'s political history certainly lends support to these propositions. First, the idiosyncratic nature of political development is clear, since it depended on such factors as the reformist tranformation of KMT ideology after its "loss of face" on the mainland, the personality and political skills of Chiang Ching-kuo, and the reverberations of drastic changes in America's diplomatic stance. Second, Taiwan's political evolution has been almost entirely driven by internal decisions, although at times (e.g., during the land reform and after Chiang Ching-kuo's death) America has exerted significant pressure for liberalization. Third, the interaction between elite debates and opposition pressure was pronounced in the "democratic revolution" of the late 1980s, when reformers within the regime were able to force more dramatic change than almost certainly would have occurred otherwise because of escalating popular discontent and expectations. Fourth, such factors as the regime's uncertain international status, the provisions of the R.O.C. Constitution, and the strength of the dominant KMT have created institutional legacies that inhibit democratization by making certain central issues "undebatable," holding back the direct democratic selection of such key bodies as the Legislative Yuan and National Assembly (and, indirectly, the president and executive organization that he chooses), and making it extremely difficult for an opposition party to compete for power effectively. Fifth, the ability of a "military" regime to check the power of the military establishment (while using the threat of the P.R.C. to mobilize the population in the traditional model of state-building) and the fact that the bourgeoisie has been dominated by an ethnic group that feels somewhat of an "outsider" vis-a-vis the regime undoubtedly have had a considerable impact on the success of political liberalization thus far.

This is not to say that democratization in Taiwan is without its problems or is necessarily irreversible. Significant conservative elements in the military and party clearly feel that the KMT is going "too far and too fast"; the working out of the new "rules of the game" between the government and opposition is a contentious process, especially for a Chinese society that values peace and ritual; and popular pressures may undermine effective economic strategy. Yet, if this chapter's central argument is true, that the key to Taiwan's success has been economic flexibility and periodic regime change promoting such flexibility, democratization appears central to the nation's continued well-being. From this perspective, growing popular participation and pressure are necessary to ensure both that elite change continues and that the R.O.C.'s economic strategy is devised to serve the interests of the bulk of the population (i.e., the growing need for redistributive policies).

Taiwan and the Contending Paradigms

This book has related a case study of the political and economic development in the R.O.C. to three principal political economy paradigms for analyzing development and dependency in the contemporary world. It sought to use the detailed description of a particular case to evaluate the general relations incorporated into these bodies of theory. In particular this comparative case study approach applied the complex historical experience of Taiwan to fashion suggestions for broadening the three research traditions, both by incorporating additional factors into their explanatory paradigms and by treating many of their variables in a more sophisticated and less deterministic manner, thus fulfilling the functions of a theoretical case study by inductively generating new hypotheses and by using a deviant case to suggest broader generalizations.

In particular the R.O.C.'s rapid growth and political development derive from a complex combination of the island's structural niche of multidimensional dependency in the world political economy, the operation of economic markets, and the role of the state, while the latter two, in turn, were affected by the nature of regime-society relations and Taiwan's Confucian culture. Thus the developmental history of Taiwan demonstrates that "growth with equity" is possible within an externally oriented, market-based economy. However, it also strongly implies that the eradication of colonial institutions, effective land reform, government-directed structural transformation, national management and regulation of foreign capital, and a fairly equalitarian distribution of wealth all play a central role in stimulating development. On the other hand, this set of relations also indicates that Taiwan's experience does not form a "developmental model" that can be mechanically transplanted elsewhere because its successful strategy was based on the confluence of a complex set of domestic and international conditions that are probably impossible to replicate.

The R.O.C. on Taiwan has been able to achieve an impressive record of development over the past four decades despite its small, resource-poor economy and externally threatened polity. The reasons for Taiwan's success include a possibly unique combination of long-term structural and more short-term and idiosyncratic behavioral factors. Important structural conditions include (a) the colonial legacy of an integrated economic base; (b) the special nature of Taiwan's dependency syndrome, especially its political clientelism to the United States; (c) the availability of a profitable niche in the global economy for a nation with the R.O.C.'s resource endowment; and (d) the operation of the labor market from the mid–1960s to the early 1980s under conditions of full employment and a strong demand for unskilled and semiskilled labor. Some of the imporant behavioral contributions to development are (a) heavy government investment in such human capital programs as education, (b) the radical land reform program, and (c) the entrepreneurial and working skills of the island's population.

The key factor of periodic regime change represents a combination of both structural elements (e.g., the imposition and ending of colonialism) and behavioral ones (for example, deliberate KMT decisions to broaden the representation of elite sectors). Growth and industrialization occurred because of a series of explicit policy decisions aimed at transforming the island's economy. Different political regimes pursued different goals. Thus it was the somewhat fortuitous sequence of regimes and policies that made successful development possible. This implies that regime change may well be a prerequisite for economic, social, and political transformation, since only a new regime would be willing to upset the status quo and risk alienating the powerful constituencies or classes whose power and status are tied to it. This also turns analytic attention back to the role of domestic elites, as has been advocated by some representatives of all three paradigms.[54]

More theoretically, the case of the R.O.C. implies that "normal science" within these paradigms is much too narrow for fully comprehending the political economy of the contemporary international system. Developmentalist theory believed that development would almost inevitably occur with the "passing of traditional society." Yet, in terms of its three central postulates, the Taiwan case certainly shows that even market-based growth involves far more than neoclassic economics and the spirit of enterprise, that traditional cultural values are just as important (if not more so) than "modernization," and that political development is far more complex than assumed by this approach.

Dependency theory, in contrast, argued that the capitalist world economy perpetuates the underdevelopment of the Third World because of the operation of a variety of factors connected with the international economic positions and internal class structures of the developing countries. The Taiwan experience implies that *dependencistas* are correct in citing many of these additional conditions of domestic and external political economy as essential for determining developmental success because they appear central to the R.O.C.'s development pattern. However, rather than forming a holistic and unalterable dependency syndrome, as this paradigm presupposes, these factors were clearly "variables," not "constants," since Taiwan's economic growth and transformation resulted from the country's deviation from the normal dependency situation on most of these conditions.

Finally, both the developmentalist and dependency perspectives can be criticized for their economic determinism; that is, the normal functioning of capitalist economies either makes development almost automatic (the former) or almost impossible (the latter). The crude statist paradigm, therefore, deserves praise for bringing the "political" back into "political economy"; Taiwan's developmental history certainly shows this tack to be justified. Thus it is not surprising that some scholars working within both of the other two strongly contending traditions have been drawn toward statist models. However, it is also obvious that the role of the state is just one of a number of central variables that affect a nation's political economy, so that by itself statism represents just one piece of the puzzle, not the entire jigsaw.

The case of the R.O.C., to sum, suggests that each of the three paradigms is too narrow, in the senses that it ignores important conditions and makes generalizations that are not universally valid. This certainly suggests the need for a more eclectic approach by scholars working within each tradition. Unfortunately a single case study does not directly point the way toward the broader generalizations of "grand theory" or paradigm construction. The importance of regime change and economic flexibility in the "Taiwan model," though, strongly suggests that even structural theories need to be rather "indeterminate." This also implies that each of the contending paradigms will continue to be pursued with vigor, since at least some of its insights are clearly valid. Hopefully, examining how individual cases fit (or perhaps, more accurately, do not fully fit) the basic assumptions of these paradigms will make such pursuit more sensitive and sophisticated.

Notes

1. Bela Balassa, *The Newly Industrializing Countries in the World Economy* (New York: Pergamon, 1981); Marion Levy, Jr., "Modernization Exhumed," *Journal of Developing Societies* 2:1 (Spring 1986), pp. 1–11; and Staffan Burenstam Linder, *The Pacific Century: Economic and Political Consequences of Asian Pacific Dynamism* (Stanford, Calif.: Stanford University Press, 1986).

2. Alice H. Amsden, "The State and Taiwan's Economic Development," in Peter B. Evans, Dietrich Rueschemeyer, and Theda Skocpol, eds., *Bringing the State Back In* (New York: Cambridge University Press, 1985), pp. 78–104; Bruce Cumings, "The Origins and Development of the Northeast Asian Political Economy: Industrial Sector, Product Cycle, and Political Consequences," *International Organization* 38:1 (Winter 1984), pp. 1–40; Thomas B. Gold, *State and Society in the Taiwan Miracle* (Armonk, N.Y.: M. E. Sharpe, 1986); and Stephan Haggard, "The Newly Industrializing Countries in the International System," *World Politics* 38:2 (January 1986), pp. 343–370.

3. George T. Crane, "The Taiwanese Ascent: System, State, and Movement in the World Economy," in Edward Friedman, ed., *Ascent and Decline in the World System* (Beverly Hills, Calif.: Sage, 1982), pp. 91–113; Peter Evans, "Class, State, and Dependence in East Asia: Lessons for Latin Americanists," in Frederic C. Deyo, ed., *The Political Economy of the New Asian Industrialism* (Ithaca, N.Y.: Cornell University Press, 1987), pp. 203–226; and Clive Hamilton, "Capitalist Industrialization in East Asia's Four Little Tigers," *Journal of Contemporary Asia* 13:1 (No. 1, 1983), pp. 35–73.

4. Fernando Henrique Cardoso, "Associated Dependent Development: Theoretical and Practical Implications," in Alfred Stepan, ed., *Authoritarian Brazil: Origins, Policy, and Future* (New Haven, Conn.: Yale University Press, 1973), pp. 149–172; Peter B. Evans, *Dependent Development: The Alliance of Multinational, State, and Local Capital in Brazil* (Princeton, N.J.: Princeton University Press, 1979); and Gary Gereffi, *The Pharmaceutical Industry and Dependency in the Third World* (Princeton, N.J.: Princeton University Press, 1983).

5. This model is more fully developed in Cal Clark and Donna Bahry, "Dependent Development: A Socialist Variant," *International Studies Quarterly* 27:3 (September 1983), pp. 271–293. For more detailed analyses see Walter D. Connor, *Socialism, Politics, and Equality: Hierarchy and Change in Eastern Europe and the USSR* (New York: Columbia University Press, 1979); David Lane, *The Socialist Industrial State: Toward a Political Sociology of State Socialism* (London: Allen & Unwin, 1976); and Paul Marer, "The Political Economy of Soviet Relations with Eastern Europe," in Sarah Meiklejohn Terry, ed., *Soviet Policy in Eastern Europe* (New Haven, Conn.: Yale University Press, 1984), pp. 155–188.

6. Frederic L. Pryor, *Public Expenditures in Communist and Capitalist Nations* (Homewood, Ill.: Richard D. Irwin, 1968), ch. 4.

7. Clark and Bahry, "Dependent Development: A Socialist Variant," pp. 271–293; and Marer, "Political Economy," pp. 155–188.

8. Neil R. Richardson, *Foreign Policy and Economic Dependence* (Austin: University of Texas Press, 1978).

9. Christopher Chase-Dunn, "Inequality, Structural Mobility, and Dependency Reversal in the Capitalist World Economy," in Charles F. Doran, George Modelski, and Cal Clark, eds., *North/South Relations: Studies of Dependency Reversal* (New York: Praeger, 1983), pp. 73–95.

10. Immanuel Wallerstein, *The Capitalist World Economy* (Cambridge: Cambridge University Press, 1979), ch. 5; and Immanuel Wallerstein, *The Modern World-System II: Mercantilism and the Consolidation of the European World Economy, 1600–1750* (New York: Academic Press, 1980), ch. 5.

11. Karen A. Mingst, "The Ivory Coast at the Semi-Periphery of the World-Economy," *International Studies Quarterly* 32:3 (September 1988), pp. 259–274.

12. David G. Becker, *The New Bourgeoisie and the Limits of Dependency: Mining, Class, and Power in "Revolutionary" Peru* (Princeton, N.J.: Princeton University Press, 1983).

13. Amsden, "State and Taiwan's Economic Development," pp. 78–106; Hill Gates, *Chinese Working-Class Lives: Getting By in Taiwan* (Ithaca, N.Y.: Cornell University Press, 1987), chs. 3 and 4; and Hamilton, "Capitalist Industrialization in East Asia's Four Little Tigers," pp. 35–73.

14. Albert O. Hirschman, *National Power and the Structure of Foreign Trade* (Berkeley: University of California Press, 1945).

15. Stephen D. Krasner, *Structural Conflict: The Third World Against Global Liberalism* (Berkeley: University of California Press, 1985), pp. 49–51.

16. Ian M. D. Little, "An Economic Reconnaissance," in Walter Galenson, ed., *Economic Growth and Structural Change in Taiwan: The Postwar Experience of the Republic of China* (Ithaca, N.Y.: Cornell University Press, 1979), pp. 501–507.

17. For example, from the mid–1960s on, the ratio of foreign investment to GNP on Taiwan has been about half that for all developing countries. See Susan Greenhalgh, "Supranational Processes of Income Distribution," in Edwin A. Winckler and Susan Greenhalgh, eds., *Contending Approaches to the Political Economy of Taiwan* (Armonk, N.Y.: M. E. Sharpe, 1988), pp. 80–86.

18. Michael J. Piore and Charles F. Sabel, *The Second Industrial Divide: Possibilities for Prosperity* (New York: Basic Books, 1984).

19. David Friedman, *The Misunderstood Miracle: Industrial Development and Political Change in Japan* (Ithaca, N.Y.: Cornell University Press, 1988).

20. Susan Greenhalgh, "Families and Networks in Taiwan's Economic Development," in Edwin A. Winckler and Susan Greenhalgh, eds., *Contending Approaches to the Political Economy of Taiwan* (Armonk, N.Y.: M. E. Sharpe, 1988), pp. 224–245; Danny Kin-Kong Lam, "Guerrilla Capitalism: Export Oriented Firms and the Economic Miracle in Taiwan (1973–1987)." Paper presented at the Annual Meeting of the American Association for Chinese Studies, Stanford University, October 21–23, 1988; and Edwin A. Winckler, "Statism and Familism on Taiwan," in George C. Lodge and Ezra F. Vogel, eds., *Ideology and National Competition: An Analysis of Nine Countries* (Boston: Harvard Business School Press, 1987), pp. 173–206. David Morawetz, *Why the Emperor's New Clothes Are Not Made in Columbia: A Case Study of Latin American and East Asian Manufactured Exports* (New York: Oxford University Press, 1981), also places great emphasis on the importance of flexibility for competition in international markets.

21. Cumings, "Origins and Development of the Northeast Asian Political Economy," pp. 1–40.

22. Davis B. Bobrow and Steve Chan, "Assets, Liabilities, and Strategic Conduct: Status Management by Japan, Taiwan, and South Korea," *Pacific Focus* 1:1 (Spring 1986), pp. 23–55; Davis B. Bobrow and Steve Chan, "Understanding Anomalous Successes: Japan, Taiwan, and South Korea," in Charles F. Hermann, Charles W. Kegley, Jr., and James N. Rosenau, eds., *New Directions in the Comparative Study of Foreign Policy* (Boston: Allen & Unwin, 1987), pp. 111–130; Steve Chan, "The Mouse That Roared: Taiwan's Management of Trade Relations with the U.S.," *Comparative Political Studies* 20:2 (July 1987), pp. 251–292; Haggard, "Newly Industrializing Countries in the International System," pp. 360–363; and David B. Yoffie, *Power and Protectionism: Strategies of the Newly Industrializing Countries* (New York: Columbia University Press, 1983).

23. Richard Rosecrance, *The Rise of the Trading State: Commerce and Conquest in the Modern World* (New York: Basic Books, 1986).

24. Haggard, "Newly Industrializing Countries in the International System," pp. 344–345; and Dietrich Rueschemeyer and Peter B. Evans, "The State and Economic Transformation: Toward an Analysis of the Conditions Underlying Effective Intervention," in Peter B. Evans, Dietrich Rueschemeyer, and Theda Skocpol, eds., *Bringing the State Back In* (Cambridge: Cambridge University Press, 1985), pp. 60–65.

25. Steve Chan, "Developing Strength from Weakness: The State in Taiwan," *Journal of Developing Societies* 4:1 (Spring 1988), pp. 38–51.

26. Chung-In Moon, "The Demise of a Developmentalist State? Neoconservative Reforms and Political Consequences in South Korea," *Journal of Developing Societies* 4:1 (Spring 1988), pp. 67–84; and Rueschemeyer and Evans, "State and Economic Transformation," pp. 44–77.

27. K. T. Li, *The Evolution of Policy Behind Taiwan's Development Success* (New Haven, Conn.: Yale University Press, 1988) especially ch. 5; and K. T. Li, *Economic Transformation of Taiwan ROC* (London: Shepheard-Walwyn, 1988), ch. 4.

28. Rueschemeyer and Evans, "The State and Economic Transformation," pp. 44–77.

29. Mancur Olson, *The Rise and Decline of Nations: Economic Growth, Stagflation, and Social Rigidities* (New Haven, Conn.: Yale University Press, 1982).

30. Steve Chan, "Growth with Equity: A Test of Olson's Theory for the Asian-Pacific Rim Countries," *Journal of Peace Research* 24:2 (June 1987), pp. 135–149, applies Olson's theory to the East Asian nations, where statism is quite prevalent.

31. James M. Malloy, ed., *Authoritarianism and Corporatism in Latin America* (Pittsburgh: University of Pittsburgh Press, 1987); Adam Przeworski and Michael Wallerstein, "The Structure of Class Conflict in Democratic Capitalist Societies," *American Poitical Science Review* 76:2 (June 1982), pp. 215–238; Phillippe Schmitter, "Still the Century of Corporatism," *Review of Politics* 36:1 (January 1974), pp. 85–131; and Howard J. Wiarda, *Corporatism and National Development in Latin America* (Boulder, Colo.: Westview Press, 1981).

32. Theodore J. Lowi, *The End of Liberalism*, 2nd ed. (New York: W. W. Norton, 1979).

33. Peter J. Katzenstein, *Small States in World Markets: Industrial Policy in Europe* (Ithaca, N.Y.: Cornell University Press, 1985).

34. Roy Hofheinz, Jr., and Kent E. Calder, *The Eastasia Edge* (New York: Basic Books, 1982), ch. 4; Herman Kahn, *World Economic Development 1979 and Beyond*

(Boulder, Colo.: Westview Press, 1979), pp. 118–123; and Lucian W. Pye, *Asian Power and Politics: The Cultural Dimensions of Authority* (Cambridge, Mass.: Harvard University Press, 1985), especially chs. 2 and 3.

35. Max Weber, *The Religion of China, Confucianism and Taoism* (Glencoe, Ill.: Free Press, 1951).

36. John C. H. Fei, "Economic Development and Traditional Chinese Cultural Values," *Journal of Chinese Studies* 3:1 (April 1986), pp. 109–124; Wen Lang Li, "Entrepreneurial Roles and Societal Development in Taiwan," *Journal of Chinese Studies* 3:1 (April 1986), pp. 77–96; and Pye, *Asian Power and Politics*, chs. 2 and 3.

37. Pye, *Asian Power and Politics*, ch. 6.

38. Thomas A. Metzger, *Escape from Predicament: Neo-Confucianism and China's Evolving Political Culture* (New York: Columbia University Press, 1977).

39. Joseph Fewsmith, *Party, State, and Local Elites in Republican China: Merchant Organizations and Politics in Shanghai, 1890–1930* (Honolulu: University of Hawaii Press, 1985), ch. 1.

40. Siu-lin Wong, "Modernization and Chinese Culture in Hong Kong," *China Quarterly* 106 (June 1986), pp. 306–325.

41. Greenhalgh, "Families and Networks," pp. 324–345; Edwin A. Winckler, "Elite Political Struggle, 1945–1985," in Edwin A. Winckler and Susan Greenhalgh, eds., *Contending Approaches to the Political Economy of Taiwan* (Armonk, N.Y.: M. E. Sharpe, 1988), pp. 151–171; and Edwin A. Winckler, "Roles Linking State and Society," in Emily Martin Ahern and Hill Gates, eds., *The Anthropology of Taiwanese Society* (Stanford, Calif.: Stanford University Press, 1981), pp. 50–86. Samuel K. C. Chang, "American and Chinese Managers in U.S. Companies in Taiwan: A Comparison," *California Management Review* 27:4 (Summer 1985), pp. 144–156, and Robert H. Silin, *Leadership and Values: The Organization of Large-Scale Taiwanese Enterprises* (Cambridge, Mass.: Harvard University Press, 1976), discuss business values and roles in more detail. For anthropological case studies of the role of the family and its relation to economic activities see Myron L. Cohen, *House United, House Divided: The Chinese Family in Taiwan* (New York: Columbia University Press, 1976); Norma Diamond, *K'un Shen: A Taiwan Village* (New York: Holt, Rinehart & Winston, 1969); Stevan Harrell, *Ploughshare Village: Culture and Context in Taiwan* (Seattle: University of Washington Press, 1982), ch. 5; and Margery Wolf, *The House of Lim: A Study of a Chinese Farm Family* (New York: Appleton-Century-Crofts, 1968). Finally, Metzger, *Escape from Predicament*, ch. 1, provides a more philosophical and humanistic treatment of familism and its relation to the "work ethic" in Chinese culture.

42. Pye, *Asian Power and Politics*, pp. 341–344.

43. Patrick J. McGowan and Dale L. Smith, "Economic Dependency in Black Africa: An Analysis of Competing Theories," *International Organization* 32:1 (Winter 1978), pp. 179–235.

44. Peter B. Evans, "Transnational Linkages and the Economic Role of the State: An Analysis of Developing and Industrialized Nations in the Post-World War II Period," in Peter B. Evans, Dietrich Rueschemeyer, and Theda Skocpol, eds., *Bringing the State Back In* (Cambridge: Cambridge University Press, 1985), pp. 192–226.

45. Tun-jen Cheng, "The Rise and Limits of the East Asian NICs," *Pacific Focus* 2:2 (Fall 1987), pp. 55–60.

46. Bobrow and Chan, "Assets, Liabilities, and Strategic Conduct," pp. 23–55; and Chan, "The Mouse That Roared," pp. 251–292, discuss the Taiwan case. For broader

considerations of the bargaining power of "weak" states see Richard L. Rothstein, *The Weak in the World of the Strong: The Developing Countries in the International System* (New York: Columbia University Press, 1977); and Yoffie, *Power and Protectionism*.

47. Robert O. Keohane and Joseph S. Nye, *Power and Interdependence: World Politics in Transition* (Boston: Little, Brown, 1977).

48. Robert Gilpin, *The Political Economy of International Relations* (Princeton, N.J.: Princeton University Press, 1987), pp. 72–92.

49. Vicky Randall and Robin Theobald, *Political Change and Underdevelopment: A Critical Introduction to Third World Politics* (Durham, N.C.: Duke University Press, 1985), ch. 3.

50. Erich Weede, "Price Distortion, Democracy or Regime Repressiveness, and Economic Growth Rates Among LDCs, 1973–1983." *Pacific Focus* 3:2 (Fall 1988), pp. 23–39.

51. Phillips Cutright, "National Political Development: Measurement and Analysis," *American Sociological Review* 28:2 (April 1963), pp. 253–264; Karl W. Deutsch, "Social Mobilization and Political Development," *American Political Science Review* 55:3 (September 1961), pp. 493–514; and Seymour Martin Lipset, "Some Social Requisites of Democracy: Economic Development and Political Legitimacy," *American Political Science Review* 53:1 (March 1959), pp. 69–105.

52. Edwin A. Winckler and Susan Greenhalgh, "Analytical Issues and Historical Episodes," in Edwin A. Winckler and Susan Greenhalgh, eds., *Contending Approaches to the Political Economy of Taiwan* (Armonk, N.Y.: M. E. Sharpe, 1988), pp. 10–11.

53. Guillermo A. O'Donnell, Philippe C. Schmitter, and Laurence Whitehead, eds., *Transitions from Authoritarian Rule: Prospects for Democracy* (Baltimore: Johns Hopkins University Press, 1986).

54. Samuel P. Huntington, *Political Order in Changing Societies* (New Haven, Conn.: Yale University Press, 1968), represents developmentalism; and Becker, *New Bourgeoisie*, a modified dependency approach. As might be expected, this emphasis is most pronounced in the statist literature. See Chan, "Developing Strength from Weakness," pp. 38–51; Haggard, "Newly Industrializing Countries in the International System," pp. 343–370; and John Gerard Ruggie, "Introduction: International Interdependence and the National Welfare," in John Gerard Ruggie, ed., *The Antinomies of Interdependence: National Welfare and the International Division of Labor* (New York: Columbia University Press, 1983), pp. 1–39.

Bibliographic Essay on Taiwan's Development

The scholarly literature in English concerning the Republic of China (R.O.C.) is surprisingly large but rather uneven in its coverage. The most extensive and sophisticated treatments come from the rather "odd couple" fields of neoclassic economics and anthropological field research. Studies of the political system have recently expanded considerably, and several books have applied broader sociological perspectives on development to the Taiwan case. Good histories of the island are available, but they are scattered in book chapters and periodical articles. Finally, the highly controversial topic of the pre–World War II Kuomintang (KMT) regime, which came to Taiwan in 1949, has received considerable historical study but remains subject to diametrically opposing interpretations.

Taiwan's record of rapid growth and industrial transformation over the past four decades has quite understandably attracted the attention of economists. Consequently economic phenomena, policies, and trends have been subjected to highly sophisticated analyses by a number of scholars. Shirley W. Y. Kuo, Gustav Ranis, and John C. H. Fei, *The Taiwan Success Story* (Westview Press, 1981), provide probably the best introductory overview of the R.O.C.'s postwar development that is highly accessible even to noneconomists. Samuel P. S. Ho, *Economic Development of Taiwan, 1860–1970* (Yale, 1978), represents a longer-range economic history of the island that links prewar and postwar economic factors. Excellent more detailed and/or more technical treatments include Walter Galenson, ed., *Economic Growth and Structural Change in Taiwan* (Cornell, 1979); Shirley W. Y. Kuo, *The Taiwan Economy in Transition* (Westview Press, 1983); Lawrence J. Lau, ed., *Models of Development: A Comparative Study of Economic Growth in South Korea and Taiwan* (Institute for Contemporary Studies, 1986); Teng-hui Lee, *Intersectoral Capital Flows in the Economic Devel-*

opment of Taiwan, 1895–1960 (Cornell, 1971); K. T. Li, *Economic Transfor-mation of Taiwan* (Shepheard-Welwyn, 1988); K. T. Li, *The Evolution of Policy Behind Taiwan's Development Success* (Yale, 1988); Ching-yuan Lin, *Industrialization in Taiwan, 1946–72* (Praeger, 1973); Yuan-li Wu, *Becoming an Industrialized Nation* (Praeger, 1985); Joseph A. Yager, *Transforming Agriculture in Taiwan* (Cornell, 1988); book chapters by Shirley W. Y. Kuo and John C. H. Fei and by Gustav Ranis and Chi Shive in Walter Galenson, ed., *Foreign Trade and Investment* (University of Wisconsin, 1985); and journal articles by Yin-min Ho in *Economic Development and Cultural Change* 28:2 (1980) and Ramon H. Myers in *China Quarterly* 99 (1984). Specialized studies of Taiwan's low level of income inequality and of the impact of foreign aid are provided, respectively, by John C. H. Fei, Gustav Ranis, and Shirley W. Y. Kuo, *Growth with Equity: The Taiwan Case* (Oxford, 1979); and by Neil S. Jacoby, *U.S. Aid to Taiwan* (Praeger, 1966). Several of these books can now be read with especial interest because Dr. Lee Teng-hui is the new president and Shirley Kuo the new minister of Finance of the R.O.C.; and K. T. Li was one of the leading architects of Taiwan's developmental strategy.

Most of these works have analyzed Taiwan's development primarily in terms of economic relations and phenomena. There have been several attempts to apply broader perspectives to Taiwan's developmental experience. The most notable and highly insightful are Thomas B. Gold, *State and Society in the Taiwan Miracle* (M. E. Sharpe, 1986); Edwin A. Winckler and Susan Greenhalgh, eds., *Contending Approaches to the Political Economy of Taiwan* (M. E. Sharpe, 1988); and book chapters by Alice H. Amsden in Peter Evans et al., eds., *Bringing the State Back In* (Cambridge, 1985), and Steve Chan in Cal Clark and Jonathan Lemco, eds., *State and Development* (Brill, 1988). Also see broader treatments of the "East Asian development model" in Frederic C. Deyo, ed., *The Political Economy of the New Asian Industrialism* (Cornell, 1987); Roy Hofheinz, Jr., and Kent E. Calder, *The Eastasia Edge* (Basic Books, 1982); and journal articles by Bruce Cumings in *International Organization* 38:1 (1984) and Stephan Haggard in *World Politics* 38:2 (1986).

Politics on Taiwan have received much less attention than economics, but still have been analyzed in ample detail. Ralph Clough, *Island China* (Harvard, 1978); and Robert G. Sutter, *Taiwan: Entering the 21st Century* (University Press of America, 1988) give comprehensive descriptions of domestic and foreign policies and their relationship to economic strategy. Lucian W. Pye, *Asian Power and Politics* (Harvard, 1985), provides a masterful overview of the relations among basic Confucian values, political institutions, and economic strategies for the East Asian nations, including Taiwan. Other important works that discuss the R.O.C.'s politics from a variety of perspectives include John F. Copper, *A Quiet Revolution* (Ethics and Public Policy Center, 1988); John F. Copper with George P. Chen, *Taiwan's Elections* (University of Maryland, 1984); James C. Hsiung, ed., *Contemporary Republic of China* (Praeger, 1981); Arthur J. Lerman, *Taiwan's Politics* (University Press of America, 1977); Mark Mancall, ed., *Formosa*

Today (Praeger, 1963); Douglas Mendal, *The Politics of Formosan Nationalism* (University of California, 1970); Fred W. Riggs, *Formosa Under Chinese Nationalist Rule* (Octagon, 1972); and journal articles by Tillman Durden in *Orbis* 18:4 (1975), Ramon H. Myers in *Asian Survey* 27:9 (1987), Thomas A. Metzger in *Issues and Studies* 23:2 (1987), and Edwin A. Winckler in *China Quarterly* 99 (1984).

U.S. relations with the R.O.C. during the critical period of the late 1940s and early 1950s have received extensive treatment. Some of the best works include Hertbert Feis, *The China Tangle* (Princeton, 1953); June M. Grasso, *Truman's Two-China Policy* (M. E. Sharpe, 1987); Tang Tsou, *America's Failure in China* (Chicago, 1973); and Nancy Bernkopf Tucker, *Patterns in the Dust* (Columbia, 1983). The evolution of Taiwan's foreign policy since then is well treated in Hungdah Chiu, ed., *China and the Taiwan Issues* (Praeger, 1979); Martin L. Lasater, *The Taiwan Issue in Sino-American Strategic Relations* (Westview, 1984); Edwin K. Snyder, A. James Gregor, and Maria Hsia Chang, *The Taiwan Relations Act and the Defense of the Republic of China* (University of California, 1980); Robert G. Sutter, *The China Quandary* (Westview, 1983); a book chapter by Thomas J. Bellows in Hungdah Chiu, ed., *Survey of Recent Events in China* (University of Maryland, 1987); and journal articles by Steve Chan in *Comparative Political Studies* 20:2 (1987), Thomas B. Gold in *Asian Survey* 27:3 (1987), Dennis Van Vranken Hickey in *Asian Survey* 28:8 (1988), and Yu-ming Shaw in *Foreign Affairs* 63:5 (1985).

Anthropological and sociological field studies form one of the best developed areas in the study of Taiwan. They have illuminated such topics as basic cultural values, family patterns, the impact of socioeconomic modernization, and local politics. Some of the best representatives of this scholarship include Emily Martin Ahern and Hill Gates, eds., *The Anthropology of Taiwanese Society* (Stanford, 1981); Myron L. Cohen, *House United, House Divided: The Chinese Family in Taiwan* (Columbia, 1976); Norma Diamond, *K'un Shen: A Taiwan Village* (Holt, Rinehart & Winston, 1969); Bernard Gallin, *Hsin Hsing, Taiwan: A Chinese Village in Change* (University of California, 1966); Hill Gates, *Chinese Working-Class Lives* (Cornell, 1987); Stevan Harrell, *Ploughshare Village: Culture and Context in Taiwan* (University of Washington, 1982); P. Steven Sangren, *History and Magical Power in a Chinese Community* (Stanford, 1987); Robert H. Silin, *Leadership and Values: The Organization of Large-Scale Taiwanese Enterprises* (Harvard, 1976); Margery Wolf, *The House of Lim* (Appleton-Century-Crofts, 1968); and Martin M. C. Yang, *Socioeconomic Results of Land Reform in Taiwan* (East-West Center Press, 1970).

Good historical treatments of Taiwan are contained in George W. Barclay, *Colonial Development and Population in Taiwan* (Princeton, 1954); Chiao-min Hsieh, *Taiwan—Ilha Formosa* (Butterworth's, 1964); George H. Kerr, *Formosa: Licensed Revolution and the Home Rule Movement* (University of Hawaii, 1974); Ronald G. Knapp, ed., *China's Island Frontier* (University of Hawaii, 1980); Paul K. T. Sih., ed., *Taiwan in Modern Times* (St. John's University, 1973);

and the two articles by Ramon H. Myers in *Journal of the Institute of Chinese Studies of the Chinese University of Hong Kong* 5:2 (1972).

Dr. Sun Yat-sen, founder of the Kuomintang, and his ideology are well treated in A. James Gregor with Maria Hsia Chang and Andrew B. Zimmerman, *Ideology and Development: Sun Yat-sen and the Economic History of Taiwan* (University of California, 1981); Harold Z. Schiffrin, *Sun Yat-sen and the Origins of the 1911 Revolution* (University of California, 1968); and C. Martin Wilbur, *Sun Yat-sen, Frustrated Patriot* (Columbia, 1976).

For good general political histories of the Kuomintang period reflecting a variety of interpretations see Robert E. Bedeski, *State-Building in Modern China* (University of California, 1981); George F. Botjer, *A Short History of Nationalist China* (G. P. Putnam, 1979); Brian Crozier, *The Man Who Lost China* (Charles Scribner's Sons, 1976); Lloyd E. Eastman, *The Abortive Revolution* (Harvard, 1974); Lloyd E. Eastman, *Seeds of Destruction* (Harvard, 1984); Suzanne Pepper, *Civil War in China* (University of California, 1978); Sterling Seagrave, *The Soong Dynasty* (Harper & Row, 1985); James E. Sheridan, *China in Disintegration* (Free Press, 1975); Paul K. T. Sih, ed., *The Strenuous Decade* (St. John's University, 1970); Hung-mao Tien, *Government and Politics in Kuomintang China* (Stanford, 1972); C. Martin Wilbur, *The Nationalist Revolution in China* (Cambridge, 1983); and George T. Yu, *Party Politics in Republican China* (University of California, 1966).

Parks M. Coble, *The Shanghai Capitalists and the Nationalist Government* (Harvard, 1980); Prasenjit Duara, *Culture, Power, and the State: Rural North China* (Stanford, 1988); Joseph Fewsmith, *Party, State, and Local Elites in Republican China* (University of Hawaii, 1985); Chalmers Johnson, *Peasant Nationalism and Communist Power* (Stanford, 1962); and Arthur N. Young, *China's Nation-Building Effort* (Stanford, 1971), present excellent case studies of economic issues.

Index

About the Author

CAL CLARK is Professor of Political Science at the University of Wyoming, Laramie. He coauthored *The Communist Balkans in International Politics* and coedited *North/South Relations*: *Studies in Dependency Reversal* (Praeger Publishers, 1983) and *State and Development*. His essays have appeared in *American Political Science Review*, *Comparative Political Studies*, *East Central Europe*, *International Studies Quarterly*, *Journal of Conflict Resolution*, *Journal of Political and Military Sociology*, *Policy Studies Journal*, *Political Methodology*, *Politics*, *Publius*, *Social Science Journal*, *Southeastern Europe*, and *Western Political Quarterly*.